T0092381

VMware vSphere Essentials

A Practical Approach to vSphere Deployment and Management

Luciano Patrão

Apress®

VMware vSphere Essentials: A Practical Approach to vSphere Deployment and Management

Luciano Patrão
Selfkant, Nordrhein-Westfalen, Germany

ISBN-13 (pbk): 979-8-8688-0207-2   ISBN-13 (electronic): 979-8-8688-0208-9
https://doi.org/10.1007/979-8-8688-0208-9

Managing Director, Apress Media LLC: Welmoed Spahr
Acquisitions Editor: Aditee Mirashi
Development Editor: James Markham
Editorial Assistant: Jessica Vakili
Copy Editor: Bill McManus

Cover designed by eStudioCalamar

Cover image designed by Freepik (www.freepik.com)

Distributed to the book trade worldwide by Springer Science+Business Media New York, 1 New York Plaza, Suite 4600, New York, NY 10004-1562, USA. Phone 1-800-SPRINGER, fax (201) 348-4505, e-mail orders-ny@springer-sbm.com, or visit www.springeronline.com. Apress Media, LLC is a California LLC and the sole member (owner) is Springer Science + Business Media Finance Inc (SSBM Finance Inc). SSBM Finance Inc is a **Delaware** corporation.

For information on translations, please e-mail booktranslations@springernature.com; for reprint, paperback, or audio rights, please e-mail bookpermissions@springernature.com.

Apress titles may be purchased in bulk for academic, corporate, or promotional use. eBook versions and licenses are also available for most titles. For more information, reference our Print and eBook Bulk Sales web page at https://www.apress.com/bulk-sales.

Any source code or other supplementary material referenced by the author in this book is available to readers on GitHub. For more detailed information, please visit https://www.apress.com/gp/services/source-code.

Paper in this product is recyclable

Dedication.

To my wonderful son, whose autism has made me a better parent and a better person. This book is dedicated to you in the hope that one day you will understand and be able to read its contents.

Your strength, resilience, and unwavering spirit have taught me the true meaning of determination and perseverance. Through your challenges and triumphs, you have shown me the beauty of embracing differences and the limitless possibilities that exist within each individual.

As I wrote these words, I kept hoping that one day you would be able to read them and learn from them. I believe in your ability to get past your challenges and do amazing things in the future.

No matter where your journey takes you, know that I am here to cheer you on and celebrate every milestone along the way. You are my beloved son, and I am forever grateful to have you in my life. This dedication is a testament to the depth of my love and belief in you.

May this dedication serve as a poignant reminder of my endless love and unwavering support, not only for you, my dear child, but for all parents who courageously face the unique challenges of raising a child with autism. May it stand as a symbol of solidarity and empathy for all those who navigate the intricate path of parenting in the context of autism.

*Your unwavering dedication, resilience,
and unconditional love in the face of these challenges
deserve the utmost admiration. Together, let us find
strength, solace, and unity as we embrace the extraordinary
journey of parenthood, hand in hand with autism.*

*Autism should not be seen as a tragedy; rather,
the lack of understanding and awareness truly holds
tragedy. It is high time that we strive to comprehend,
embrace, and offer unwavering support to individuals
on the autism spectrum, witnessing their incredible
journey of overcoming challenges and unleashing
their exceptional potential.*

Special dedication to my father:
*You should be here watching and living this.
Your memory and your impact on my life
will forever be cherished. I miss you…*

*With all my love and dedication,
a beloved father and a son.*

Table of Contents

About the Author

Luciano Patrão is a Portuguese professional who has established himself in Germany. With extensive experience in the field, he currently serves as a senior consultant and solution architect at ITQ, offering top-tier VMware infrastructure solutions and working as a PSO consultant for VMware.

Luciano has previously held notable positions as a technical project manager and technical lead in various consulting companies as a freelancer. Throughout his career, he has provided exceptional guidance and solutions to teams and clients in the areas of VMware infrastructures, backup, and data recovery.

Luciano is a VCAP-DCV Design 2023, VCP-Cloud 2023, VCP-DCV 2022, and VMware vSAN Specialist. He is also a vExpert vSAN, vExpert NSX, vExpert Cloud Provider for the last two years, vExpert Multi-Cloud 2023, vExpert for the last 8 years, and a Veeam Vanguard for the last 6 years.

As a firm believer in the power of knowledge sharing, Luciano actively writes technical content for multiple companies and owns the provirtualzone.com blog. Dedicated to virtualization, multi-cloud, storage, and backups, the blog is a platform to share insights and expertise with a broader audience.

About the Technical Reviewers

Frank Escaros-Buechsel is working as a global telco architect assisting major telecommunication providers globally to design, build, and manage consolidated IT/ICT platforms, on-board virtual network functions, and evolve existing platforms for 5G readiness.

Iwan Hoogendoorn started his IT career in 1999 as a helpdesk agent.

Soon after, Iwan started to learn Microsoft products and eventually achieved his MCP, MCSA, MCDBA, and MCSE certifications. While working as a Microsoft systems engineer, Iwan gained an excellent basis to develop additional skills and knowledge in computer networking. Networking became a passion in his life. This passion resulted in learning networking with Cisco products.

Iwan got the opportunity to work for VMware in 2016 as a senior NSX PSO consultant. In his time at VMware, he gained more knowledge on private and public clouds and the related products that VMware developed to build the Software-Defined Data Center (SDDC). After working for four years as a senior NSX PSO consultant (primarily with VMware NSX-v and

NSX-T), Iwan got promoted to a staff SDDC consultant focusing on the full SDDC stack, including hyperscaler offerings on the main public clouds like AWS (VMC on AWS), Microsoft (Azure VMware Solution), and Google (Google Cloud VMware Engine).

Iwan is certified on multiple VMware products, including NSX, and he is actively working together with the VMware certification program to develop network-related exams for VMware. In addition to his VMware certifications, Iwan is also AWS and TOGAF certified.

Acknowledgments

I would like to express my deepest gratitude to the readers and enthusiasts following my "VMware for Beginners" series on the BDRSuite blog. BDRSuite is the comprehensive backup and disaster recovery software from Vembu Technologies.

Over the years, the team at Vembu have given me the remarkable opportunity to write VMware content for their esteemed readers and customers. My first book may never have come out without their collaborative efforts. The unwavering support and encouragement from the team at Vembu have been instrumental in my journey as an author. Please visit https://www.bdrsuite.com/ for more information about BDRSuite Backup & Replication.

I want to thank the technical reviewers for reviewing this book and all the professionals involved in the publication process.

I want to express my heartfelt gratitude to my fantastic wife, whose solid support and belief in me have driven my pursuit of this long-overdue dream. Through her constant encouragement to pursue my dreams, I have been able to embark on this writing journey. Many times needs to take over things I am genuinely thankful for her love and unconditional support.

To my lovely daughters and my son, you are my world. Your understanding and patience when I was immersed in writing are deeply appreciated. Thank you for being the greatest joy in my life.

A special thanks go to my sister, brother-in-law, and nephews. Their love and support have been, and continue to be, vital in my entire life.

Finally, to all my friends, thank you for your support and motivation.

ACKNOWLEDGMENTS

I want to express my heartfelt gratitude to all those who have contributed to creating *VMware vSphere Essentials: A Practical Approach to vSphere Deployment and Management*. Thank you all for being part of my first journey to write a book.

Introduction

Welcome to *VMware vSphere Essentials: A Practical Approach to vSphere Deployment and Management.* After writing a successful "VMware for Beginners" series of blog posts for Vembu Technologies, a leading vendor of backup and disaster recovery solutions, I decided to write this book. This book fills a vacuum in the market for high-quality information on this subject and offers readers a thorough introduction to VMware virtualization.

This book is written for novices and those seeking more advanced notions about vSphere. It walks you through vSphere concepts and technology. It covers vSphere infrastructure creation, maintenance, and performance for beginners and advanced users.

Presentation Approach

I take a step-by-step approach in this book to guarantee that you grasp the fundamental concepts and practical procedures required to construct and manage virtual machines in a VMware vSphere system. Together, we will explore the key components of vSphere, with details and explanations for each feature, including the hypervisor, networking, Storage, and High Availability, unraveling their intricacies and highlighting best practices.

This book provides you with the full VMware knowledge to develop, set up, and maintain vSphere environments that meet modern computing needs.

We will also focus on advanced topics, such as resource optimization, performance monitoring, advanced settings, and automation, empowering you to take your virtualization skills to the next level.

The step-by-step instructions are designed to provide a high-level understanding and are accompanied by many screenshots illustrating the available options and recommended selections essential for accomplishing each task.

Whether you are an IT professional seeking to enhance your career prospects or an administrator looking to streamline your infrastructure, this book is your comprehensive guide to unlocking the immense potential of VMware technology.

Target Audience

This book is designed to offer to diverse individuals interested in virtualization technology, specifically VMware vSphere.

The book is tailored to meet the needs of the following diverse target audience:

- **Aspiring IT professionals:** This book is ideal for individuals looking to enter the IT field who want to understand virtualization technology, particularly VMware vSphere. It thoroughly introduces vSphere, beginning with the fundamentals and gradually progressing to more advanced concepts, making it a helpful resource for individuals new to virtualization.

- **System administrators:** System administrators seeking to enhance their knowledge and skills in virtualization and VMware vSphere will find this book valuable. It offers practical insights into deploying, managing, and optimizing virtualized environments, equipping system administrators with the tools needed to excel in their roles.

- **Advanced vSphere administrators:** This book serves as a valuable resource for experienced vSphere administrators looking to enhance their knowledge and delve into advanced concepts. It goes beyond the basics, providing administrators with the knowledge to optimize, troubleshoot, and fine-tune their vSphere settings.

- **IT professionals pursuing VMware certifications:** This book caters to IT professionals who are preparing for VMware certifications, such as the VMware Certified Professional - Data Center Virtualization (VCP-DCV) exams. It offers a structured approach to understanding vSphere and its advanced concepts, providing the necessary knowledge and insights to succeed in certification exams.

- **Virtualization consultants and trainers:** Virtualization consultants and trainers who provide guidance and education on VMware vSphere can utilize this book as a valuable reference. It covers various topics, from foundational knowledge to advanced techniques, serving as a comprehensive guide to support their consulting and training endeavors.

- **IT professionals transitioning to VMware:** Professionals with experience in other virtualization technologies who wish to transition to VMware vSphere will find this book invaluable. It provides a clear and structured pathway to acquire the necessary knowledge and skills to work with vSphere effectively.

- **Technology enthusiasts and self-learners:** This book caters to individuals who have a passion for technology and a keen interest in learning about virtualization. Whether you are a self-learner or simply curious about VMware vSphere, the book's gradual learning curve and practical approach make it accessible and engaging for technology enthusiasts of various backgrounds.

No matter your expertise or familiarity with virtualization, this book offers a comprehensive guide that empowers you to understand and utilize VMware vSphere effectively. So, let's dive in and embark on this exciting virtualization adventure together!

CHAPTER 1

Understanding Virtualization

Virtualization is a revolutionary concept, abstracting away the differences between actual hardware and its digital counterparts. It allows multiple virtual machines to exist on one physical computer, using hardware abstraction and a hypervisor. This boosts efficiency, scalability, and adaptability in managing applications and environments. With various kinds of virtualization available, this technology has many advantages, such as reduced expenses, optimized resource use, and simplified administration. Consequently, virtualization has become a commonplace asset for today's IT networks.

In this chapter we will cover the basics of virtualization and look at the various types of virtualization, their benefits, and how they relate to some of the more popular hypervisors on the market.

1.1 Benefits of Virtualization

Virtualization brings many advantages. For example, organizations can reduce energy expenses and optimize existing resources by virtualizing their physical infrastructure. The simple and swift process allows flexible and agile operations to keep up with changing requirements. Furthermore, virtualization increases system protection by enabling better division

© Luciano Patrão 2024
L. Patrão, *VMware vSphere Essentials*, https://doi.org/10.1007/979-8-8688-0208-9_1

among different environments and simplifying disaster recovery processes. Generally speaking, virtualization streamlines IT deployments, data centers, and cloud computing while boosting efficiency, scalability, and administrative control.

The following are some of the more important benefits of virtualization:

- **Cost savings:** Virtualization allows one physical server to run multiple virtual machines (VMs), reducing the need for additional hardware and lowering energy costs. This translates into significant cost savings in terms of infrastructure and maintenance.

- **Improved resource utilization:** Virtualization enables better use of hardware resources by allocating them efficiently among virtual machines based on current needs. This reduces the risk of resource wastage and enhances system performance.

- **Enhanced flexibility:** With virtualization, businesses can quickly create or deploy new virtual machines as needed without worrying about physical hardware constraints. This improves IT agility, enabling organizations to respond faster to business needs.

- **Increased security:** Virtualization provides an additional layer of security by isolating virtual machines from each other and the underlying hardware, which helps prevent malware or other security threats from spreading.

- **Disaster recovery:** Virtualization makes disaster recovery more manageable by allowing virtual machines to be quickly migrated to another physical server in the case of a hardware failure. This ensures minimal downtime and faster recovery from critical failures.

Virtualization technologies cover a wide range of tasks and areas of IT infrastructure. In the next section we'll quickly review the different types of virtualization.

1.2 Types of Virtualization

Various types of virtualization technology are available, enabling organizations to combine types to better utilize resources, increase adaptability, boost scalability, and simplify management. By utilizing virtualization, businesses may meet their IT demands more quickly, affordably, and effectively.

The following are some of the more common types of virtualization:

- **Server virtualization:** Server virtualization involves partitioning a physical server into multiple virtual machines, each running its own operating system (OS) and applications. This allows for efficient utilization of hardware resources, consolidation of servers, and easier management of workloads.

- **Desktop virtualization:** Desktop virtualization is the process of creating a digital representation of a computer's desktop that end users may access from any location. It offers a consolidated method of handling desktops, which simplifies upkeep, boosts security, and gives you more leeway when it comes to distributing virtual desktops to different devices.

- **Network virtualization:** Network virtualization is a technology that allows for establishing virtual networks by abstracting the underlying physical network architecture. This method logically separates network resources and increases the network's scalability, adaptability, and security. Virtual local area networks (LANs), switches, and routers are all possible thanks to network virtualization.

- **Storage virtualization:** Storage virtualization is the process of treating several storage systems (both physical and digital) as though they were a single logical storage system. Storage can be managed centrally, streamlining provisioning, strengthening data security, and allowing for new features such as data deduplication and thin provisioning. A good example is VMware vSAN.

- **Application virtualization:** Applications can run in isolated virtual environments thanks to application virtualization, which isolates them from the underlying operating system. A good example is containers and Kubernetes, like VMware Tanzu. Application virtualization enables applications to be deployed and executed on different systems without conflicts, simplifying application management and reducing compatibility issues.

- **Operating system virtualization:** Creating many isolated instances (containers) within a single OS instance is possible using operating system virtualization, also known as *containerization*. Lightweight and efficient virtualization for deploying programs is provided by containers, which share the same underlying OS kernel but function independently.

- **Data virtualization:** By eliminating the need to know where data is physically stored, data virtualization creates a single view of data from various locations. Data administration is made easier, and real-time data analysis and reporting are made possible, all thanks to its support for data integration, abstraction, and access.

Now that we have examined forms of virtualization, let's dive into one of its elements to help you gain a deeper understanding of its significance in the world of technology. In the following section we closely examine types of hypervisors.

1.3 Hypervisors

Hypervisors are software or firmware components that act as a virtual layer between the physical hardware and the virtual machines. Hypervisors abstract the underlying hardware resources, such as CPU, memory, and storage, and present them to each VM as if they were dedicated resources. Names such as VMware, Citrix Xen, Hyper-V, KVM, and Oracle VM are the most well known in the hypervisor market.

VMware (ESXi) is the market leader by far, with Hyper-V and Citrix XenServer the next in the list with their market share. On the other hand, KVM also has a market share, particularly within the Linux community and enterprise companies.

As depicted in Figure 1-1, there are two distinct types of hypervisors: Type 1 and Type 2.

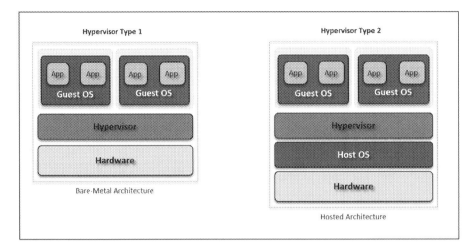

Figure 1-1. *Type 1 and Type 2 hypervisors*

Type 1 hypervisors leverage a bare-metal architecture (examples include VMware, Hyper-V, KVM, and Oracle VM).

In contrast, Type 2 hypervisors utilize a hosted architecture (examples include VMware Workstation/Fusion, Oracle VM VirtualBox, and Windows Virtual PC).

For instance, although Hyper-V and KVM operate in a server role, they are still considered bare-metal native hypervisors since they have direct access to the hardware and any VMs under their purview.

1.4 Summary

As we conclude our exploration of hypervisors, their functions, and their crucial role in abstracting hardware resources for cloud computing and server management, we have established a foundation for comprehending virtualization. As noted, VMware has a dominant presence in the hypervisor market, followed by Hyper V, Citrix Xen, and KVM. Moreover we discussed the distinctions between Type 1 and Type 2 hypervisors.

Moving forward from these concepts, our attention now shifts to a detailed examination of VMware, the most influential player in this field. In the next chapter we will discuss intricacies of VMware technology, specifically focusing on the vSphere platform. Our exploration will encompass what VMware entails the structure and functionalities of vSphere as its unique features and benefits within the virtualization landscape. By gaining an overview of VMware technology, you will deepen your understanding of its role and impact in the realm of virtualization while also fostering an appreciation for its innovative solutions.

CHAPTER 2

VMware and vSphere Overview

In the opening chapter, we embarked on a quick journey to explore the world of VMware and discover vSphere. In this chapter we will uncover the essence of VMware's innovative technology, which will enable you to understand its purpose and functionality. Additionally, we will delve into vSphere, VMWare's cloud computing virtualization platform, and the prominent features that make vSphere a powerful and indispensable tool for virtualization infrastructures. We'll also distinguish between a vSphere host and an ESXi host, shedding light on their unique characteristics and roles within the VMware ecosystem. Finally, we'll review some key VMware terminology.

2.1 What Is VMware

VMware, a notable software company in virtualization, provides a platform to create and supervise virtual machines (VMs). This platform can run several virtualized operating systems or applications on a single physical computer. This maximizes resource utilization while providing enhanced flexibility.

Among VMware's most prominent services is vSphere, which is considered the gold standard for server virtualization. vSphere enables organizations to consolidate their physical servers into a virtual

© Luciano Patrão 2024
L. Patrão, *VMware vSphere Essentials*, https://doi.org/10.1007/979-8-8688-0208-9_2

infrastructure, which simplifies management and helps reduce costs. vSphere offers a comprehensive suite of features and tools to optimize performance, boost security, and streamline virtual environment deployment and management. With vSphere, IT professionals can easily create virtual machines, allocate resources, and manage workloads, ensuring business continuity and minimizing downtime.

Aside from server virtualization, VMware extends its portfolio to include cloud computing solutions, desktop virtualization, and software-defined networking (SDN). This portfolio empowers organizations to embrace the benefits of a virtualized infrastructure across multiple domains. Now let's explore the wonders of vSphere and its transformative impact on the technological landscape.

2.2 What Is vSphere

vSphere, also known as Elastic Sky X Integrated (ESXi), runs independently of any operating system as it is a Type 1 hypervisor based on VMware's kernel. When working together with vCenter, vSphere has the capability of vSphere vMotion to move more than one virtual machine at a time from one host server to another.

People sometimes are confused about the difference between ESXi and vSphere. ESXi is included in vSphere, but the ESXi host is the core. In addition to VMware vSphere, there are other products and features that are part of the vSphere umbrella stack, such as vSphere Client, vMotion, vStorage, High Availability (HA), and (more recently added) vSphere with Tanzu, which are all part of vSphere umbrella stack, but needs a central management (vCenter) to use those features.

The VMware Hypervisor product is referred to as vSphere. The VMware Host is referred to as ESXi. In this book, I use the term *vSphere* to refer to the VMware Hypervisor.

With vSphere, you can create clusters, VMs, vApps, datastores, vSAN, Kubernetes, and containers when using vSphere Tanzu with vCenter.

Through vCenter, vSphere can create vSphere Clusters, or vSAN Clusters, with vSphere HA and vSphere DRS and provide Cluster services to your virtual machines.

As we explore the features and advantages of vSphere, it's crucial to acknowledge that these capabilities not only align with the benefits of virtualization we discussed earlier but also encompass unique attributes that position vSphere as a leader in the market. In the next chapter, we will discuss how utilizing vSphere with vCenter enhances these features' functionality, transforming vSphere into a flexible and robust virtualization platform.

2.3 Key Features and Benefits of vSphere

The key features and benefits of vSphere are similar to what we have described in the benefits of virtualization, but with vSphere, we can add the specific features that make vSphere the leader of the market.

As you will learn throughout this book, most vSphere features and benefits always depend on the use of vCenter and other tools.

2.3.1 Key Features

The key features of vSphere are as follows:

- **Server virtualization:** vSphere facilitates server virtualization, permitting multiple virtual machines to operate on a single physical server, which optimizes resource utilization and decreases hardware costs.

- **Dynamic resource allocation:** With features like Distributed Resource Scheduler (DRS), vSphere automatically balances workloads across hosts, ensuring efficient resource allocation and improved performance.

- **vSphere High Availability:** vSphere HA detects host failures and automatically restarts virtual machines on alternate hosts, minimizing downtime and enhancing application availability.

- **vSphere vMotion:** vMotion enables live migration of virtual machines from one host to another, allowing for workload balancing, hardware maintenance, and uninterrupted service.

- **vSphere Storage vMotion:** Storage vMotion enables the live migration of virtual machine disks between different storage arrays or datastores without disruption, simplifying storage maintenance, load balancing, and storage provisioning.

- **vSphere Distributed Switch (vDS):** vDS is a centralized network switch that spans multiple hosts, providing a consistent network configuration and simplifying network management in a virtual environment.

- **vSphere Replication:** vSphere Replication provides asynchronous replication of virtual machines at the hypervisor level, allowing for efficient disaster recovery and data protection across sites.

- **vSphere Fault Tolerance:** With Fault Tolerance (FT), vSphere provides continuous availability by creating a mirrored virtual machine that takes over seamlessly in case of a host failure.

- **Centralized management:** vSphere's vCenter Server offers a centralized management interface, simplifying the administration and monitoring of virtual environments.

To sum it up, vSphere has features that go beyond just technological advancements. These features, such as server virtualization, dynamic resource allocation, and high availability, provide a solution for resilient IT infrastructure management. With the flexibility of vMotion, the robustness of Fault Tolerance, and the centralized efficiency of vSphere Distributed Switch, each feature is designed to optimize, streamline, and secure the environment. VMware's commitment to innovation is evident in vSphere, as it offers a suite of tools that is essential for your virtualization needs.

2.3.2 Key Benefits

The following are the key benefits of vSphere, which overlap with those of virtualization in general:

- **Cost savings:** By consolidating servers and optimizing resource usage, vSphere reduces hardware and operational costs, leading to significant cost savings.

- **Increased efficiency:** vSphere improves efficiency by maximizing resource utilization, automating resource management tasks, and enabling faster provisioning and deployment of virtual machines.

- **Scalability:** With vSphere, businesses can adapt their virtual infrastructure to changing business requirements by adding or removing virtual machines, or any resource, as necessary.

- **Enhanced security:** vSphere provides advanced security features such as vSphere Encryption and Secure Boot, ensuring data protection and mitigating security risks.

- **Business continuity:** By leveraging features like HA, vSphere enhances business continuity by minimizing downtime and ensuring uninterrupted access to critical applications.

- **Disaster recovery:** vSphere's disaster recovery features, including Site Recovery Manager (SRM) and vSphere Replication, enable organizations to implement robust and efficient disaster recovery strategies.

- **Simplified IT management**: vSphere simplifies IT management through centralized administration, streamlined monitoring, and automated tasks, reducing the complexity of managing virtual environments.

The advantages of incorporating vSphere are remarkable and diverse. They go beyond cost savings, increased efficiency, and scalability. The advanced security features and improved business continuity capabilities that vSphere provides greatly contribute to protecting an organization's data and operations. vSphere's ability to adjust according to business requirements maintains availability. Delivery of reliable disaster recovery solutions makes it an invaluable asset for any organization. In essence, vSphere is not merely a virtual environment management tool; it serves as a catalyst for business expansion and technological resilience.

Now, as we move forward in our exploration of vSphere, let's delve into the VMware glossary. This will provide you with the essential definitions and terms necessary to navigate the world of vSphere with clarity and confidence.

2.4 VMware Glossary

As you explore the intricacies of VMware and its diverse ecosystem, it becomes essential to acquaint yourself with the terminology that defines and shapes this realm. The vocabulary used by VMware goes beyond jargon; it represents the fundamental concepts and innovative features that position VMware as a leader in virtualization technology.

Having an understanding of these terms is crucial for navigating through the layers of VMware solutions. Each term or naming convention captures a facet of VMware functionality and its practical application in real-world scenarios. Whether its grasping the concept of a hypervisor or delving into the intricacies of vMotion or DRS, this glossary will serve as your guide leading you through the landscape of VMware.

Therefore, this section holds more significance than being a glossary; it acts as an entryway to comprehension. As you familiarize yourself with these terms, you'll notice that the intricate world of VMware starts becoming more accessible and understandable. These terms will resurface throughout this book. Having a grasp of them will enhance your understanding of subsequent chapters.

The following list of VMware terminology, while not exhaustive, covers the most critical concepts that will recur throughout our exploration of VMware and vSphere.

- **VMware:** This is the company name. Cloud computing and virtualization technology are among the products offered by VMware.

- **VMware vSphere:** vSphere is VMware's Hypervisor, but it also includes vSphere Client, vMotion, vStorage, and HA, as well as vSphere with Tanzu, which vCenter provides.

- **VMware ESXi:** This is the bare-metal hypervisor server or host from vSphere.

- **VMware vSphere Web Client:** Manage the essential functions of vSphere remotely from any browser.

- **VMware vCenter Server:** VMware vCenter enables centralized management of vSphere virtual infrastructure. IT administrators can ensure security and availability, simplify daily tasks, and reduce the complexity of managing vSphere. vCenter manages virtual machines, multiple ESXi hosts, and all dependent components from a single centralized location.

- **VMware vCenter Web Client:** This is a web interface the enables you to connect to vCenter Server and its resources(ESXi hosts, VMs, etc.) remotely from any browser.

- **vSphere Standard Switch (vSS or vSwitch):** This is a local virtual switch that connects a VM or an ESXi service (such as iSCSI) to the ESXi physical network.

- **vSphere Distributed Switch (vDS):** This is the same as vSS but is shared and accessible through all ESXi hosts. It provides a centralized interface from which you can configure, monitor, and administer all networks in the vCenter. It also provides advanced VMware vSphere networking features.

- **vSphere Cluster:** This is a configuration that combines one or more ESXi hosts to provide CPU, memory, and storage resources to run VMs (or other virtual objects).

- **vSphere vMotion:** This allows live migrations of running virtual machines from one ESXi host to another with zero downtime, continuous service availability, and complete transaction integrity. With vMotion, IT administrators can migrate any VM power-on without downtime.

- **vSphere Storage vMotion (or vStorage):** Similar to vMotion, it allows VMs power-on live migrations from one storage system to another without downtime. It can be a VMFS datastore or an NFS/iSCSI.

- **vSphere High Availability (HA):** HA runs in vCenter at vSphere Cluster and provides high availability to VMs by automatically detecting failures on an ESXi host by migrating/restarting the VM to the next ESXi host available.

- **vSphere Distributed Resource Scheduler (DRS):** DRS offers resource management features including load balancing and VM deployment on a cluster of ESXi hosts. Suppose an ESXi host reaches a % resource used (set by the administrator or DRS default). In that case, DRS migrates the VM (or VMs) using vMotion to another host with more resources available to balance workloads.

- **VMware vSphere Fault Tolerance (FT):** This provides continuous availability for applications (with up to four virtual CPUs) by creating a live shadow instance of a virtual machine that mirrors the primary virtual machine.

- **vSphere Virtual Machine File System (VMFS):** VMFS is the file system proprietary to VMware. vSphere uses VMFS to create datastores, store VMs, and provide virtual disk resources to a virtual machine.

- **vmkernel:** This networking interface provides network connectivity services for the host and handles VMware vMotion, traffic management, and fault tolerance. vSAN, iSCSI, vMotion, and vStorage use the vmkernel network to work.

- **VMware Tools:** This is an optional set of drivers and utilities that increase both the VM Guest OS performance and the interaction between the VM Guest OS and ESXi.

2.5 Summary

Having delved into the intricacies of VMware and vSphere, including their roles and features in virtualization, you now possess an understanding of these technologies. With the explanation of the distinction between vSphere and ESXi hosts, supported by the VMware glossary, you have gained insights into the VMware ecosystem.

Moving on from this overview, our focus now shifts to aspects of implementing vSphere: system requirements and licensing. Chapter 3 provides significant details for those preparing to deploy vSphere, as it covers not only hardware and software requirements but also different licensing models. Mastering these elements is essential for implementing a compliant virtualization setup, ensuring that you are well prepared for deploying and operating VMware solutions effectively.

CHAPTER 3

System Requirements and Licensing

In this chapter, we will explore the details of VMware vSphere specifically related to the system requirements and licensing. This chapter is essential for preparing a vSphere deployment because it provides information regarding the hardware and software that you need along with a comprehensive guide to understanding the different licensing options available. It is crucial to grasp these components in order to optimize your environment and ensure compliance with VMware standards. Here we establish the foundation for setting up an effective infrastructure.

3.1 Hardware Requirements

Before we dive into the details of setting up ESXi 7.0, it's important that you understand the hardware requirements that support this virtualization platform. Having the right hardware configuration is crucial for unlocking the potential of ESXi 7.0, ensuring not only compatibility but also optimal performance and reliability. From processor capabilities and memory to networking and storage, each component plays a role in ensuring an efficient virtualized environment. So let's explore the hardware prerequisites for ESXi 7.0, which will lay the foundation for an effective setup.

© Luciano Patrão 2024
L. Patrão, *VMware vSphere Essentials*, https://doi.org/10.1007/979-8-8688-0208-9_3

- ESXi 7.0 requires at least two CPU processors per host.

- ESXi 7.0 requires 64-bit multicore x86 processors. For a comprehensive list of the wide variety of supported processors, visit the VMware Compatibility Guide at `https://www.vmware.com/resources/compatibility`.

- ESXi 7.0 requires that the NX/XD option be enabled in the BIOS for the CPU.

- ESXi 7.0 requires 8GB of physical RAM, minimum. To operate virtual machines in typical production environments, provide at least 8GB of RAM.

- On x64 CPUs, ESXi requires hardware virtualization (Intel VT-x or AMD RVI) to be enabled to support 64-bit virtual machines.

- ESXi 7.0 requires one or more Gigabit Ethernet controllers or quicker. View the VMware Compatibility Guide for a list of network adapter models supported by VMware.

- ESXi 7.0 requires a launch disk with persistent storage of at least 32GB, such as HDD, SSD, or NVMe. Use only USB, non-USB, and SD flash media devices for ESXi boot bank partitions. A launch device cannot be shared between hosts running ESXi.

- For Serial ATA (SATA), a disk is connected via SAS controllers or on-board SATA controllers that are supported. SATA devices are not considered local but remote. By default, these disks are not used as scratch partitions because they are considered remote.

3.2 Storage Requirements

The choice of storage in ESXi 7.0 plays a pivotal role in the overall performance and reliability of your virtual machines. Adequate storage not only allows for efficient management of data but also ensures smooth operation and scalability. The following are the essential storage prerequisites for ESXi 7.0:

- Use a persistent storage device that is at least 32GB in size for boot devices for the optimal performance of an ESXi 7.0 installation.

- A boot device with a minimum 8GB is required for upgrading to ESXi 7.0.

- At least a 32GB disk is needed when booting from a local drive, SAN, or iSCSI LUN to create system storage volumes, including a boot partition, boot banks, and a VMFS-L-based ESX-OSData volume. The old /scratch partition, the locker partition for VMware Tools, and the core dump destination are now part of the ESX-OSData volume.

- The following are additional settings for an ESXi 7.0 installation's optimal performance:

  - A local disk with a minimum capacity of 128GB for ESX-OSData. The disk store VMFS datastore, an ESX-OSData volume, and the boot partition.

  - A system that can handle at least 128 terabytes of written data (TBW).

21

- A piece of equipment with a sequential write speed of at least 100 MB/s.

- A RAID 1 mirrored device is advised to offer resilience in the event of device failure.

- Local disk or a NAS/SAN (iSCSI or FC) to install and store your virtual machines.

Note   You might read elsewhere that using a USB/SD card is no longer supported to install and run vSphere v7.0 or even v8. That is not 100% true. What is not supported is using a USB/SD card to store the ESX-OSData partition.

This particular partition's I/O read/writes should not be used in a USB/SD card because it cannot handle this amount of I/O. It would be best to move your vSphere installations to persistent storage. So if you are using a USB/SD card, you should have a persistent storage device to store this partition.

Starting with ESXi 7.0 Update 3, the VMware Tools partition is automatically formed on the RAM disk if the boot device is a USB or SD card without any local persistent storage, such as an HDD, SSD, or NVMe device. This could lead to poor performance and potential problems.

Note   In the next vSphere version (after vSphere 8), VMware plans to remove the use of USD/SD cards to install vSphere.

3.3 Software Requirements

To start your installation, you only need to download a vSphere 7.0 ISO to fulfill all the software requirements. You need a VMware account to download VMware products. If you don't have one, register and create an account https://customerconnect.vmware.com/home.

First, find vSphere in the VMware products and select the version you want to download (for purposes of following along in this book, select 7.0, as shown in Figure 3-1).

Figure 3-1. *Downloading vSphere (step 1 of 6)*

Next, select the product type (or license if you have one). For my own installation, I selected to use Enterprise Plus, as shown in Figure 3-2. Then click **Go To Downloads**.

Figure 3-2. *Downloading vSphere (step 2 of 6)*

After you click Go To Downloads, you should see the Download Product page shown in Figure 3-3 (if you don't have a registered or paid license). As indicated, the Select Version field enables you to download the latest version of vSphere 7 or a previous version.

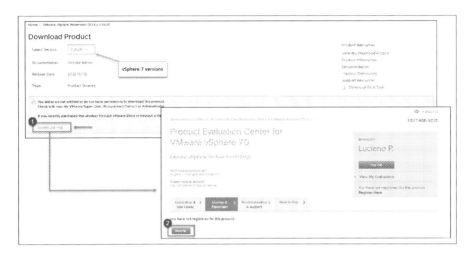

Figure 3-3. *Downloading vSphere (step 3 of 6)*

To register for a trial license, click **Download Trial** and then click **Register** in the pop-up window. On the registration page, fill out the remaining data and register (VMware will use your VMware account data to fill in most fields).

After registration, you can download vSphere 7 and have a complete evaluation license for 60 days, as shown in Figure 3-4. Click **Manually Download**.

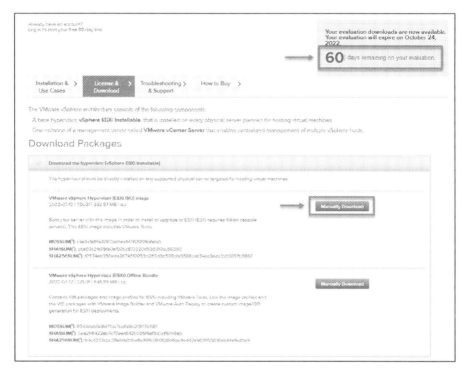

Figure 3-4. *Downloading vSphere (step 4 of 6)*

Note   Besides the two options shown in Figure 3-4 (full vSphere 7 and vSphere 7 Offline Bundle update), you can also download vCenter with this registration.

The previously described options apply if you have never registered or do not have a vSphere license. If you have a vSphere license or a company VMware account, after you select vSphere 7 Enterprise Plus (as shown in Figure 3-2 for this demonstration), you can access all vSphere suite products to download.

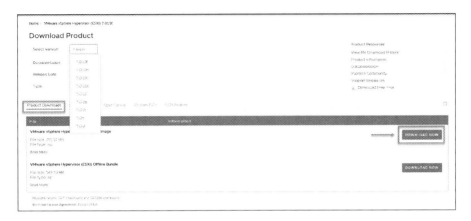

Figure 3-5. *Downloading vSphere (step 5 of 6)*

Note   Chapter 30 explains how to update to the latest version of vSphere. The vSphere 7 installation demonstrated in this chapter is version 7.0U3c, so Chapter 30 will demonstrate how to update to version 7.0U3f.

You might find that a vendor doesn't have a customized ISO for a particular version of vSphere. In that case, you need to use a lower or higher version. For example, HPE only has vSphere 7.0U3d and doesn't have 7.0U3c.

If you have an HPE, Dell, or Lenovo server, use the vendor-customized vSphere 7 version. Click the Custom ISOs tab and select your vSphere 7 hardware vendor ISO, as shown in Figure 3-6.

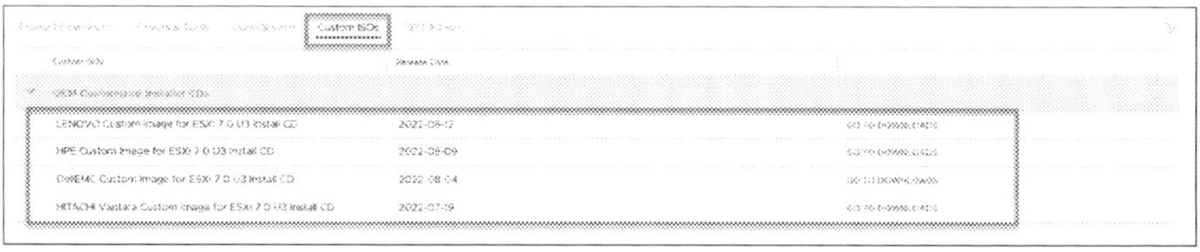

Figure 3-6. *Downloading vSphere (step 6 of 6)*

Note   The hardware and software requirements presented in this chapter are the minimum for installing vSphere 7.x. Check `https://docs.vmware.com/en/VMware-vSphere/7.0/com.vmware.vsphere.vcenterhost.doc/GUID-7AFCC64B-7D94-48A0-86CF-8E7EF55DF68F.html` for the complete requirements to install vSphere.

3.4 Licenses Requirements

Read the article at `https://news.vmware.com/company/cpu-pricing-model-update-feb-2020` for a full explanation of the new license model for vSphere 7.

The following is a quick overview of vSphere license features:

- **vSphere Standard:** Includes core virtualization features such as vMotion, High Availability (HA), Distributed Resource Scheduler (DRS), and vSphere Storage APIs.

27

It also supports up to 8 virtual CPUs per virtual machine and 64GB of virtual RAM per virtual machine; Fault Tolerance supports 2 virtual CPUs per virtual machine and 4TB of RAM per host.

vSphere Standard is more appropriate for small to medium-sized businesses that require fundamental virtualization capabilities.

- **vSphere Enterprise Plus:** Contains all the features of vSphere Standard and additional features such as vSphere Distributed Switch (dvSwitch), Host Profiles, Storage DRS, Virtual Machine Encryption, Distributed Power Management (DPM), and Network/Storage I/O Control.

  Additionally, Enterprise Plus supports up to 12TB of RAM per host and 128 vCPUs per virtual machine; Fault Tolerance supports 8 virtual CPUs per virtual machine and 6TB of vRAM per virtual machine.

  vSphere Enterprise Plus is better adapted for larger organizations that require advanced virtualization features such as network and storage administration, load balancing, and enhanced security.

The vSphere Enterprise license was a part of the vSphere licensing model prior to version 7.0. However, with the release of vSphere 7.0, VMware has simplified the vSphere licensing model and reduced the number of editions to two: vSphere Standard and vSphere Enterprise Plus.

Existing customers with active vSphere Enterprise licenses may still be able to use their licenses and receive support from VMware. However, new customers can no longer purchase vSphere Enterprise licenses directly from VMware.

It's important to note that the vSphere licensing model is subject to change, and it's recommended to check with VMware or a certified VMware partner to determine the most up-to-date licensing options and requirements for your environment. Consult the official VMware documentation or contact the VMware sales team for the most up-to-date and accurate details on specific features and licensing.

Visit `https://www.vmware.com/content/dam/digitalmarketing/vmware/en/pdf/products/vsphere/vmw-edition-comparison.pdf` to check the complete features included in each license.

- **Evaluation mode license:** This type of license is vSphere Enterprise Plus 60 days (meaning it has all vSphere features included), but if you add a Standard license after 20/30 days, vSphere will show only the features available on the Standard license. If you go back and reuse the evaluation mode license, you can use it for the remaining 60 days that were not used.

- **Upgraded licenses:** With the same license, it is possible to upgrade from 6.x to 6.5, 6.7, etc., but it is not possible to upgrade to a different version that starts with a different number, like vSphere 7. In this case, you need a new license.

Check `https://docs.vmware.com/en/VMware-vSphere/7.0/com.vmware.vsphere.vcenterhost.doc/GUID-7AFCC64B-7D94-48A0-86CF-8E7EF55DF68F.html` for more information about vSphere licensing.

Now that you have your license registered and have downloaded the vSphere 7 ISO, you can start installing vSphere 7.

3.5 Summary

This chapter thoroughly discussed the hardware and software requirements and licensing considerations for VMware vSphere. In Chapter 4 we'll focus on deploying a vSphere environment. This involves diving into hardware configuration, preparing and installing vSphere, and exploring nested environments, in detail. You'll receive practical guidance and step-by-step instructions for building a strong and efficient virtual infrastructure.

CHAPTER 4

Deploying a vSphere Environment

Diving into the deployment of a vSphere environment, we begin by focusing on the hardware configuration, ensuring that our physical setup meets the specific needs of vSphere.

4.1 Deployment Considerations

You need to consider various aspects related to deployment when planning to implement a vSphere environment.

Starting the process of setting up a vSphere environment can be quite intricate. It requires planning to ensure success, but the end results are worth it. The process is not simply a matter of completing tasks on a checklist; it involves comprehending how each component fits into your IT infrastructure. This section is designed to assist you in navigating these aspects, the goal being to guarantee that you have an understanding and informed approach when deploying your strategy.

Before we dive into the things to think about, let's first explore why each of these factors is so important for your deployment. Knowing the reasons behind each deployment consideration will not only help you with the implementation but also give you the ability to make flexible decisions as your IT needs change over time.

© Luciano Patrão 2024
L. Patrão, *VMware vSphere Essentials*, https://doi.org/10.1007/979-8-8688-0208-9_4

These are some of the deployment considerations:

- **Scalability:** Evaluate the system's scalability requirements and ensure that the hardware and software can handle the expected increase in load over time. Consider factors such as user growth, data volume, and transaction volume.

- **Security measures:** Implement robust security measures to protect the system from unauthorized access, data breaches, and other security threats. This may include encryption, access controls, firewalls, intrusion detection systems, and regular security audits.

- **Compatibility and integration:** Ensure seamless integration with existing infrastructure and systems. Consider compatibility with operating systems, databases, network protocols, and other relevant technologies. Conduct thorough compatibility testing to identify and address any potential issues. Make sure that the hardware used is compatible with the vSphere version you are deploying.

- **Performance optimization:** Optimize system performance to ensure efficient and responsive operation. This may involve optimizing virtual machine resources and storage, fine-tuning network configurations, and implementing caching mechanisms.

- **Disaster recovery and business continuity:** Develop and implement a robust disaster recovery plan to minimize downtime and data loss in the event of a system failure or disaster. Consider backup strategies, replication mechanisms, and failover procedures to ensure business continuity.

- **User acceptance and training:** Involve administrators in the deployment process by gathering feedback. Provide extensive training and support to ensure administrators' comfort and competence with vSphere and its devices and features. Address any usability issues or concerns raised by the users.

During the course of the book, we will discuss several of these factors, and you will learn how to improve and secure your vSphere deployment.

4.2 Hardware Configuration

vSphere installation is possible on various servers, including HP, Dell, Lenovo, and IBM. You can also install vSphere straight on your desktop machine or portable device. To ensure compatibility, it is mandatory to have a CPU with the NX/XD bit enabled in the BIOS and meet the remaining system requirements (as discussed in Chapter 3).

You can start the vSphere install process when the CPU requirements are set and virtualization support is enabled in the BIOS.

Figures 4-1 and 4-2 show two examples of BIOS configuration on a server, and Figure 4-3 shows an example of BIOS configuration on a computer.

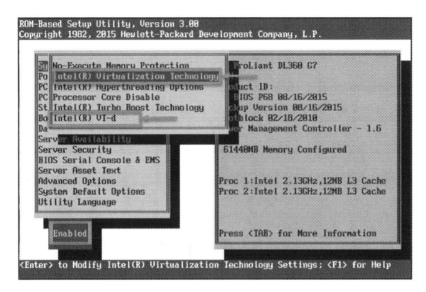

Figure 4-1. *HPE DL360-G7 example 1*

Figure 4-2. *HPE DL360-G9 example 2*

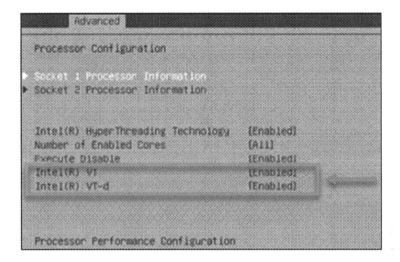

Figure 4-3. *Desktop/laptop example 1*

Depending on the server or computer and BIOS version or brand, the options may differ.

Ethernet controllers could be a problem when using unsupported VMware hardware. Some network cards won't be recognized when you install vSphere. It is best to visit the VMware Compatibility Guide (VCG) at HCL and check if the network card you plan to use is on the supported list.

4.3 Prepare and Install vSphere

To start installing vSphere, you need to mount the ISO in your remote console.

I am using an HPE server, so I will use a vendor-customized vSphere ISO, as explained in Chapter 4.

Note   Figure 4-4 is just an example of how to boot vSphere 7 (or another version) ISO in an HPE, so I use the iLO console to upload the ISO image to the virtual CD/DVD and start the installation.

- **IBM/Lenovo:** They use a system called Integrated Management Module (IMM) in some of their servers. For newer models, especially after Lenovo acquired IBM's x86 server line, they use XClarity Controller.

- **Cisco:** Cisco servers, part of the Cisco Unified Computing System (UCS) line, use Cisco Integrated Management Controller (CIMC).

- **Supermicro:** Supermicro servers have a feature called Intelligent Platform Management Interface (IPMI), which is quite common in the industry. It's similar to iLO and iDRAC and allows for remote management tasks.

- **Fujitsu:** Fujitsu servers use integrated Remote Management Controller (iRMC), which is their solution for server management and remote control.

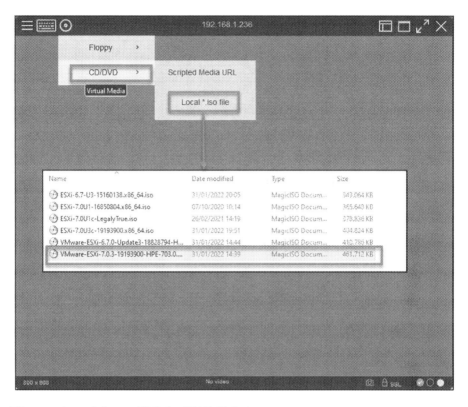

Figure 4-4. *Mount ISO in HPE iLO 1*

After your ISO is mounted on the server boot, you can boot the server and start the installation. This sequence is shown in Figures 4-5 through 4-19.

After booting with vSphere 7 ISO, vSphere starts loading the ESXi installer, as shown in Figure 4-5. You'll see a screen similar to Figure 4-6 after the installer is loaded successfully.

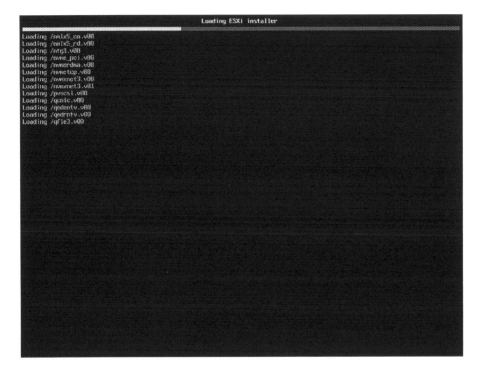

Figure 4-5. *(Installing vSphere 1 of 19)*

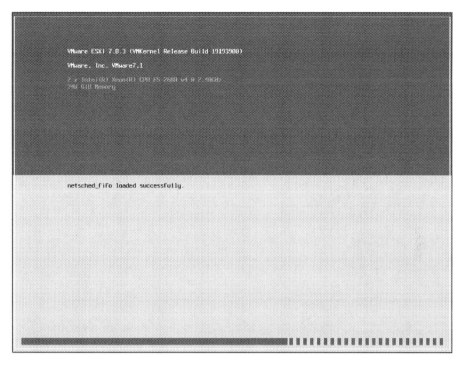

Figure 4-6. *(Installing vSphere 2 of 19)*

You can start selecting and configuring the installation when the loading is finished.

Note   To reduce the number of figures depicting this installation process, Figures 4-7 through 4-10 each include more than one screenshot, with numbers designating the order of steps.

Next, press **Enter** to start the installation (step 1 in Figure 4-7) and then press **F11** (step 2) to accept the EULA (mandatory) and continue the installation.

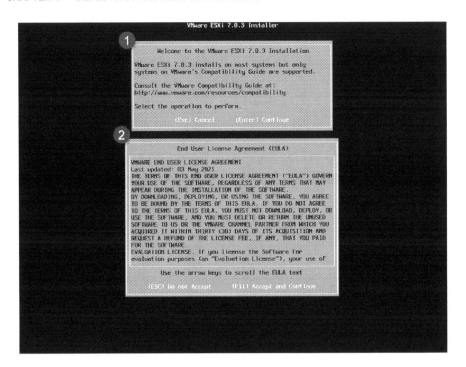

Figure 4-7. *(Installing vSphere 3 of 19)*

Next, the installation shows you how many local disk devices exist. In this case, it is a local disk with 16GiB, as shown in Figure 4-8 (step 3). Any RAID in your server, USB, or SD flash is displayed here.

You can also check what is inside that disk device (if there is an old vSphere installation or an SSD flash disk/card, the install informs you) by pressing **F1**. But as you can see Figure 4-8 (step 4), it is a new and clean disk, and vSphere is not installed. Press **Enter** to continue the installation.

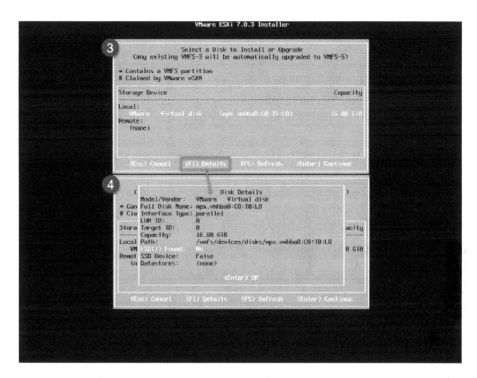

Figure 4-8. *(Installing vSphere 4 of 19)*

Next, select your country/language and press **Enter** (see Figure 4-9, step 5). On the next screen (step 6), enter the root password you will use to log in to your ESXi host. The following are the guidelines for ESXi passwords:

- For access via the Direct Console User Interface, the ESXi Shell, SSH, or the VMware Host Client, ESXi imposes password constraints.

- When you construct a password, you are required by default to use a combination of at least three characters from each of the following four character classes: lowercase letters, uppercase letters, digits, and special characters (e.g., underscore or dash).

41

- The length of the password is typically at least 7 characters and no more than 40 characters.

- Dictionary terms or parts of dictionary words are not permitted in passwords.

Caution   Take note of your password. Resetting the ESXi root password is difficult and often demands a new vSphere install.

You can check `https://docs.vmware.com/en/VMware-vSphere/7.0/com.vmware.vsphere.security.doc/GUID-DC96FFDB-F5F2-43EC-8C73-05ACDAE6BE43.html` for the complete ESXi host password policies and requirements.

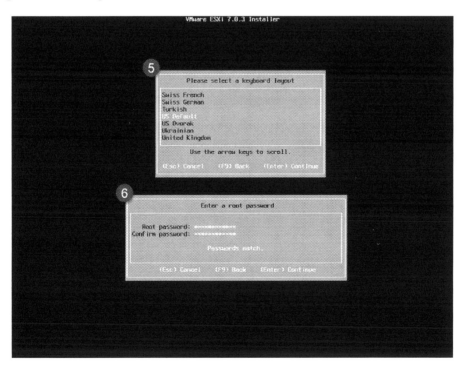

Figure 4-9. *(Installing vSphere 5 of 19)*

After the initial configurations, press **F11** to start the installation of
ESXi, as shown in step 7 of Figure 4-10. You will see a progress bar as the
installation takes place, as shown in step 8 (the time duration of the install
depends on your servers, which disk device you are using, and whether
your vSphere ISO takes longer to upload into the server). When the
installation is complete, as shown in step 9 of Figure 4-10, you can remove
the ISO from any virtual device or boot device and press **Enter** to reboot
the server. The screen shown in Figure 4-11 will display.

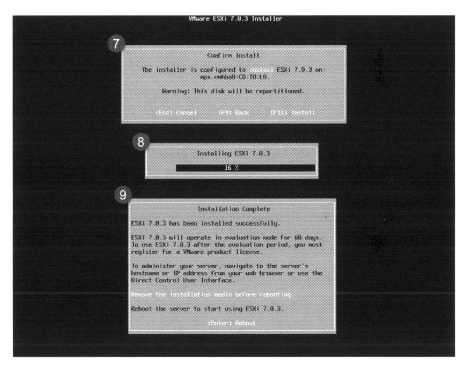

Figure 4-10. *(Installing vSphere 6 of 19)*

Figure 4-11. *(Installing vSphere 7 of 19)*

Now that you have installed your ESXi host, you must do
post-install tasks.

After your server reboots, to enter the ESXi host Direct Console User
Interface (DCUI), press **F2**, as shown in Figure 4-12.

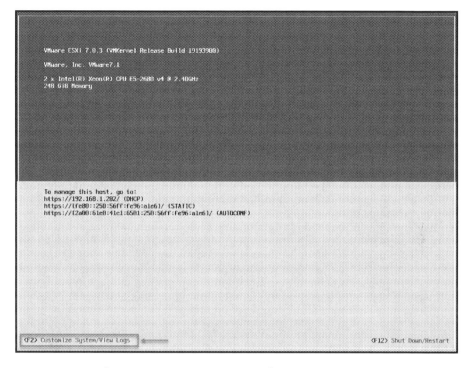

Figure 4-12. *(Installing vSphere 8 of 19)*

Note   If you have a DHCP server in your network, you already have an IP address for your ESXi host.

ESXi automatically picks up a DHCP IP address if you have connected your physical cables to your network cards.

Next, as shown in Figure 4-13, log in with the root user and the password you created in the earlier installation password step.

Figure 4-13. *(Installing vSphere 9 of 19)*

Now that you are inside the ESXi DCUI, you can manually configure your network and DNS settings. Select **Configure Management Network**, as shown in Figure 4-14

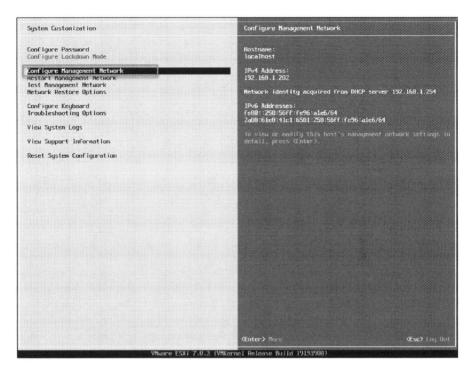

Figure 4-14. *(Installing vSphere 10 of 19)*

The first option on the Configure Management Network screen is to configure the network adapters. Select that option to see how many network adapter ports you have, as shown in Figure 4-15. By default, the ESXi host will enable your server's number one network port, which is vmnic0.

In this section, you will not change anything. In Chapter 15, you will add a second network port (in ESXi, this is vmnic1) to the management network for high availability. Press **Esc** to return the main menu.

The next option on the Configure Management Network screen is VLAN (optional). This option enables you to create and configure VLANs for your ESXi host network. But for now, we'll skip VLANs (you will learn about configuring VLANs in Chapter X, which covers ESXi networks).

47

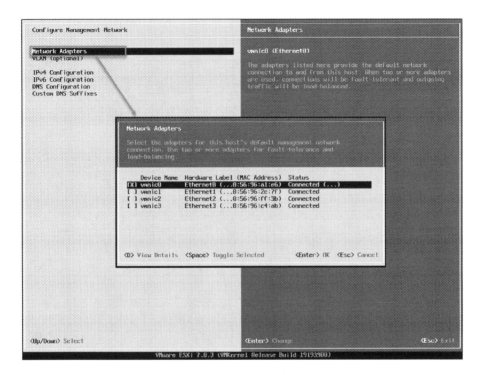

Figure 4-15. *(Installing vSphere 11 of 19)*

Next, you will configure a static IP address, DNS, and ESXi hostname, in that order.

Continuing in the Configure Management Network screen, select the option **IPv4 Configuration** and, as shown in Figure 4-16, select the option **Set static IPv4 address and network configuration**.

Add your IP address, subnet mask, and network gateway, and then press **Enter** to accept the values.

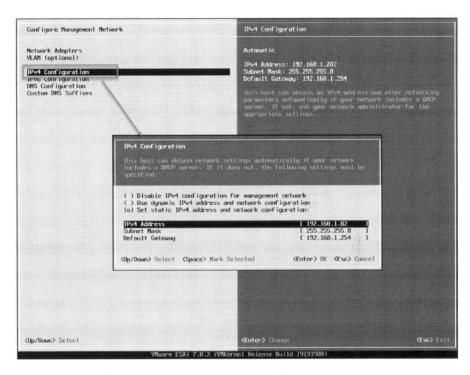

Figure 4-16. *(Installing vSphere 12 of 19)*

Note   You can also use static IPv6, but in this case, we leave the
IPv6 and use the default DHCP.

Next, select the **DNS Configuration** option. In the DNS Configuration
window that opens, add your DNS servers and ESXi hostname, as
demonstrated in Figure 4-17.

Note   Do not forget to create a DNS record for this IP/hostname
in your DNS server. Figure 4-17 shows an example created on a
Windows DNS Server.

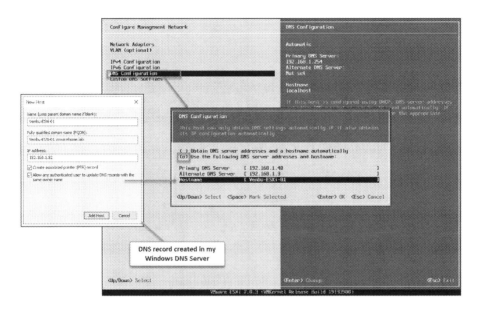

Figure 4-17. *(Installing vSphere 13 of 19)*

Although it is not mandatory, you should also add your DNS suffixes (network domain) for a better *query DNS for an IP address* service on your network. To do so, select **Custom DNS Suffixes** on the Configure Management Network screen, as shown in Figure 4-18.

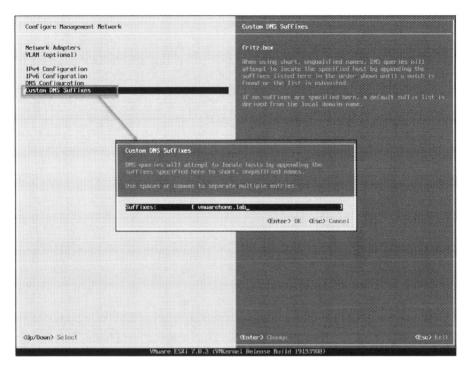

Figure 4-18. *(Installing vSphere 14 of 19)*

Now that you have all your network settings configured, press **Esc** to exit the Configure Management Network screen. The window shown in Figure 4-19 opens. To save the configuration, press **Y**.

Note   No configuration is saved if you do not save your changes.

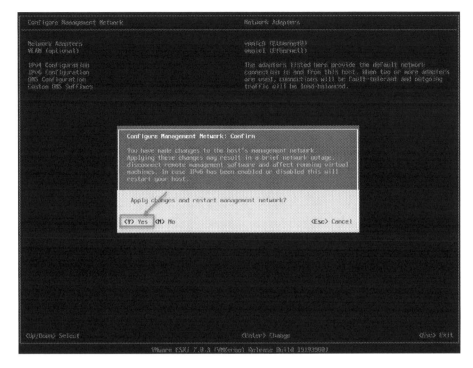

Figure 4-19. *(Installing vSphere 15 of 19)*

If all settings were added and saved correctly, you can see the new settings on the right side of the screen shown in Figure 4-20.

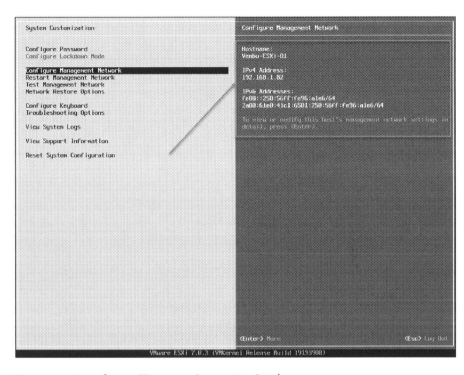

Figure 4-20. *(Installing vSphere 16 of 19)*

The final step is to run the **Test Management Network** option to see if the ESXi host is reachable in the network and if DNS can query your IP/DNS name, as shown in Figure 4-21, which confirms everything is working.

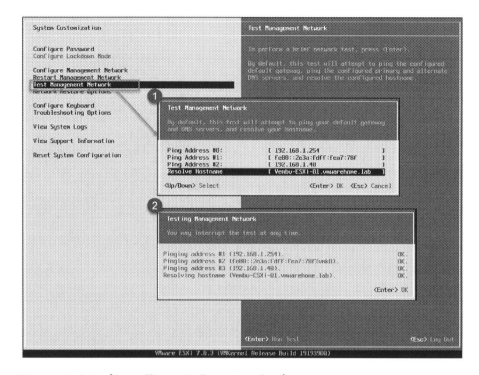

Figure 4-21. *(Installing vSphere 17 of 19)*

At this point, your ESXi installation is finished and you have completed the post-install tasks. You can now connect to the ESXi host using the vSphere Web Client host.

Press **Esc** a couple of times to leave the DCUI and log out.

4.3.1 Install vSphere 7 on an Unsupported CPU

Before you continue configuring your ESXi host using the vSphere Web Client host, let me explain what happens if you try installing vSphere 7 on an unsupported CPU.

Since vSphere 7, some legacy CPUs are no longer supported, but you can still install vSphere 7 on it (not recommended for production environments).

As explained previously, you can check whether any hardware is supported or unsupported in vSphere in the VMware Compatibility Guide (VCG). You can do this for a CPU or a server model. For example, my HP ProLiant DL360 G7 using Intel Xeon CPU E5620 is no longer supported (although I can still install vSphere 7 without any problem).

Search the VCG by CPU series, and you can find your CPU, in which vSphere versions are supported and which are not.

Figure 4-22 shows an example of the search results I received.

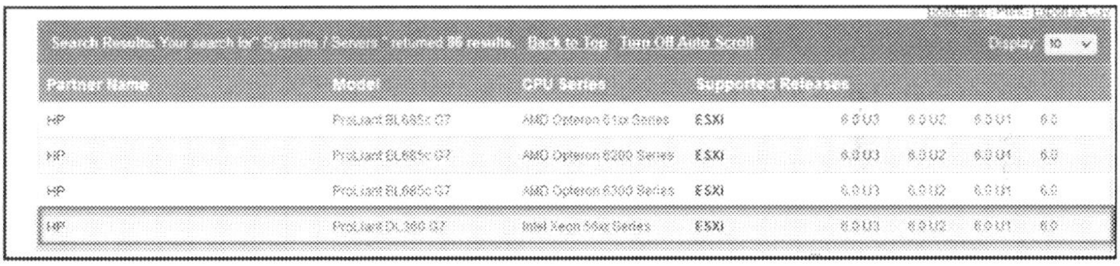

Figure 4-22. *(Installing vSphere 18 of 19)*

Note   VMware has a Knowledge Base article about changes in the CPU support. Check `https://kb.vmware.com/s/article/82794` for the list of all CPUs.

When installing vSphere in an unsupported CPU, you get the following error (see Figure 4-23): *CPU_SUPPORT_WARNING: The CPU in this host is not supported by ESXi 7.0.3. Please refer to the VMware Compatibility Guide (VCG) for the list of supported CPUs.*

You must add a parameter to the vSphere boot install to bypass this error. Boot the server with the ISO when the vSphere 7.0 boot starts (yellow screen), press **Shift-O** to open boot parameters, and add the parameter `AllowLegacyCPU=True`.

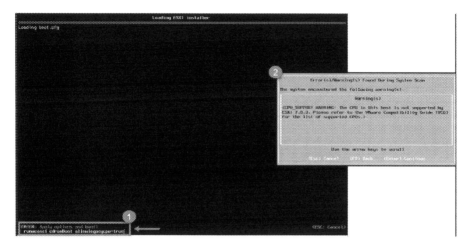

Figure 4-23. *(Installing vSphere 19 of 19)*

Note   This procedure will not work for all CPUs (if they are very old) and works for the most recent ones that are not supported anymore with vSphere 7.

Tip   I have written a detailed blog post about this subject, available at https://www.provirtualzone.com/install-vsphere-7-in-a-non-supported-hp-dl360-g7.

4.3.2 Connect to the vSphere Web Client Host

Now that you have installed and configured vSphere 7, open a browser and add ESXi host IP/FQDN.

Enter your username and root password and click **Log in**, as shown in Figure 4-24. You now should see a vSphere Web Client screen similar to 4-25, displaying all the resources and settings in your new ESXi host.

Figure 4-24. *(vSphere Web Client 1 of 2)*

Figure 4-25. *(vSphere Web Client 2 of 2)*

4.4 What Is a Virtual Nested Environment?

A Virtual VMware nested environment refers to the setup of running virtual machines within another virtual machine, which is hosted on a physical server or computer. This nested environment creates a virtualized infrastructure within an existing virtualized environment.

In the context of VMware, a nested environment typically involves running VMware hypervisors, such as ESXi, as VMs within another VMware hypervisor. This allows the installation of multiple virtual ESXi hosts, which can host additional VMs. Essentially, it's virtualization inception, where virtualization is nested within virtualization.

Nested environments are commonly used for testing, learning, and development purposes. They provide a way to simulate complex VMware setups, experiment with different configurations, and test software compatibility without needing multiple physical servers.

Enabling Virtualization within Virtualization:

The capacity to operate multiple virtualization layers is made possible by nested virtualization, which enables the development of virtual machines inside existing virtual machines. This is especially helpful when testing or running many hypervisors or virtualization platforms on a single host environment. It does away with the requirement for separate physical hardware and offers a practical method for conducting virtualization testing and research.

Nested virtualization can be use for several type of work, in development, testing, resource management and education. Lets explore each of these areas to understand why it is helpful to use such environments.

- **Development and testing environments:** Nested virtualization provides a reliable and efficient way to create isolated development and testing environments. Developers and testers can create VMs with different configurations, operating systems, and software stacks without needing dedicated physical machines. This accelerates software development cycles, promotes collaboration, and reduces infrastructure costs. Nested virtualization also enables the creation of complex network topologies and simulations, allowing thorough testing of network-based applications.

- **Resource utilization optimization:** By leveraging nested virtualization, organizations can maximize resource utilization on their existing infrastructure. Instead of dedicating separate physical servers for each workload or application, virtual machines can be nested within a single host, efficiently utilizing the available computing resources. This consolidation reduces hardware costs, simplifies management, and improves scalability. Nested virtualization also facilitates migrating legacy applications or environments into virtualized platforms, minimizing disruption and ensuring compatibility.

- **Training and education:** Nested virtualization is a valuable tool for training and educational purposes. It enables students and IT workers to create virtual lab settings to try different virtualization configurations, scenarios, and use cases. It provides a safe, isolated environment for learning, experimentation, and skill development.

Nested virtualization also supports the creation of training environments that simulate real-world production setups, enhancing the effectiveness of training programs.

4.5 Configure a Nested Environment

In this book, I show you how to set up and build a nested virtualization environment that you can use for testing or learning. A nested virtualization environment is a virtual machine that runs inside another virtual machine. This allows you to create a virtual lab with multiple ESXi hosts and vCenter servers, even if you only have one physical server or laptop.

There are several benefits to using nested virtualization for testing and learning. First, it is a cost-effective way to create a virtual lab. You can use the same physical server or laptop to create multiple virtual machines running a different operating system or application. Second, nested virtualization is easy to set up and manage. You can use the same tools and procedures that you would use to manage a physical environment. Third, nested virtualization allows you to test and learn the concepts of VMware vSphere without impacting a production environment. This is important because vSphere is a complex platform that can be difficult to learn without hands-on experience.

Here are some specific examples of what you can do with a nested virtualization environment:

- Create a cluster of ESXi hosts

- Deploy vCenter Server

- Configure vSAN

- Implement HA and DRS

- Test different operating systems and applications

Nested virtualization is a valuable tool for VMware professionals of all levels. It is a great way to learn the concepts of vSphere, test new features, and develop your skills.

Note   Nested virtualization environments are not designed for production use. They are intended for testing and learning only. If you need to create a production-ready environment, you should use physical servers.

4.5.1 Create the Nested Environment

For purposes of this demonstration, assume the VM "server" for our nested environment installation has the following resources:

- 4x vCPU

- 24GB memory

- 16GB local disk (for ESXi install)

Regarding the network, we will try to simulate the following physical implementations:

- Six virtual network adapter vNICs: VMXNET3 (since our physical host for this example has eight physical network cards, we can use six vNICs in this nested environment, but you can do this with only two vNICs).

  - Two vNICs for the management network (192.168.1.x)

  - Two vNICs for the NFS/iSCSI network (192.168.10.x) and vMotion network (192.168.0.x)

  - Two vNICs for the virtual machines network

Note   The IP subnets used here are just for this example. You can use different IP subnets. You can use subnets, and all can be routed, or you can use VLANs for each subnet. We only use routing for now. Later on, you will learn how to use VLANs.

4.5.2 Create a VM for Nested ESXi

Figure 4-26 identifies the steps to follow to begin creating a new VM. As the figure shows, the first step of the wizard is to select a creation type. Select **Create a new virtual machine** and then click **Next**.

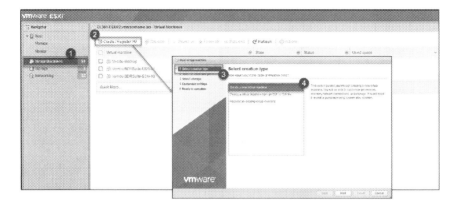

Figure 4-26. *Creating a new virtual machine*

When you are creating a VM for the nested vSphere 7, you need to expose the CPU virtualization to the vCPU VM guest OS (in this case, to vSphere). In the second step of the wizard, *Select a name and guest OS*, change the field *Guest OS family* to **Other** and the field *Guest OS version* to **VMware ESXi 7.0 or later**, as shown in the Figure 4-27. Click **Next**.

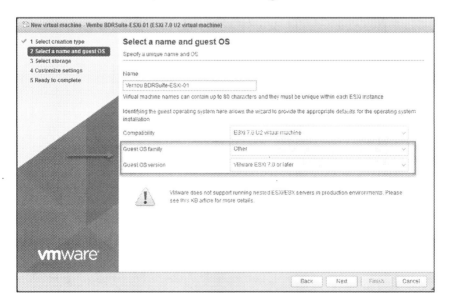

Figure 4-27. *(VM Settings 1 of 2)*

This *Figure VM Settings 1* is when you create a virtual machine.

Next, after the VM is created, click **Edit settings**, as shown on the left in Figure 4-28. On the *Edit settings* screen, click the **vCPU** drop-down arrow and check the options **Expose hardware assisted virtualization to the guest OS** and **Expose IOMMU to the guest OS**, as shown on the right in Figure 4-28.

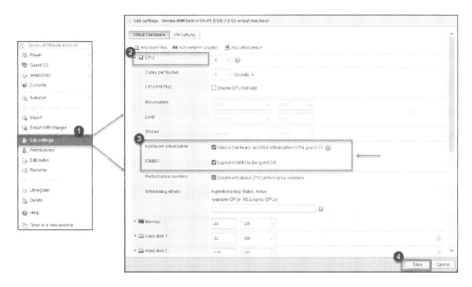

Figure 4-28. *(VM Settings 2 of 2)*

Although this book does not discuss VMware Workstation, I will quickly show you how to do this in VMware Workstation 16 for your nested vSphere 7.

When creating the VM for the nested vSphere, set the *Guest operating system* option to **Other** and the *Version* field to **VMware ESXi 7 and later**. See Figure 4-29.

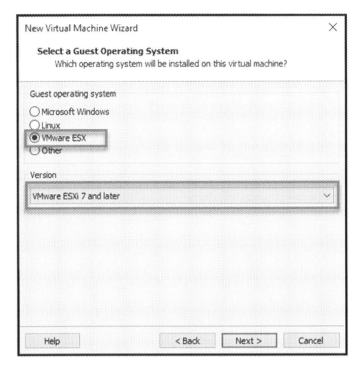

Figure 4-29. *(VM Settings - VMware Workstation 1 of 2)*

Next, after the VM is created, go to the VM, click **Edit virtual machine settings**, select **Processors**, and check the vCPU option **Virtualize Intel VT-x/EPT or AMD-V/RVI**. See Figure 4-30.

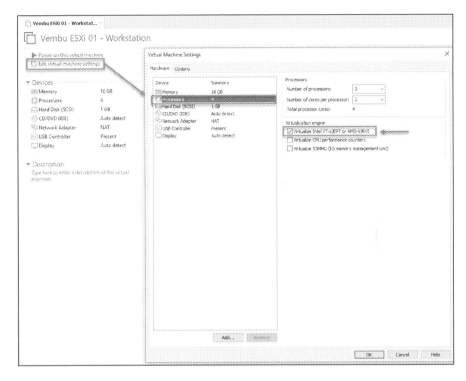

Figure 4-30. *(VM Settings - VMware Workstation 2 of 2)*

Note   My article at `https://www.provirtualzone.com/`
`nested-vmware-vsan-6-6-environment/` explains how to plan
and create nested vSphere step by step. The article is for the vSphere
6.5 version, but the process is the same for vSphere 7.0. The GUI
could be slightly different, but the options are the same.

After enabling virtualization in the VM (on a vSphere or VMware
Workstation), you need to mount your ISO in the VM to run the installation
in a nested environment. To learn how to mount the ISO in your VM for
nested ESXi, consult Chapter 7.

Note For our nested environment, after we create one nested VM for ESXi and install it, we will create two more VMs to have a complete vSphere cluster (to be discussed in the following chapters).

This book teaches you how to use VMware vSphere, a virtualization platform that allows you to run multiple operating systems on a single physical machine. However, not everyone has a home lab or a production/test environment to practice what they learn in the book. That's where nested vSphere comes in.

Nested vSphere is a way to run a vSphere environment inside another vSphere environment. This allows you to create a virtual lab to test and learn the concepts in the book without purchasing any additional hardware.

To build a nested vSphere environment, you will need a physical machine with enough resources to run a vSphere host and a few virtual machines. Once you have the necessary hardware, you can follow the instructions in the book to create your virtual lab.

With a nested vSphere environment, you can practice all the tasks you learn in the book, such as creating and managing virtual machines, configuring networks, and deploying applications. This will give you the skills and experience you need to use vSphere in a production environment.

Here are some specific benefits of using nested vSphere for learning:

- It is a cost-effective way to create a virtual lab.

- It is easy to set up and manage.

- It allows you to test and learn the concepts in the book without worrying about impacting a production environment.

- It gives you the flexibility to experiment with different configurations and settings.

If you want to learn how to use VMware vSphere, I recommend building a nested vSphere environment. It is a great way to get started with vSphere and learn the concepts in this book.

4.6 Summary

In this chapter you installed vSphere and now have an IP, DNS, hostname, etc. In the next chapter, you will learn how to configure the virtual networks.

CHAPTER 5

vSphere Networking

The initial network configurations covered in Chapter 4 were only to access the ESXi host. We now need a network for our virtual machines, storage, and so forth. This chapter discusses vSphere networking and demonstrates how it works in ESXi.

5.1 vSphere Virtual Network

In Figure 5-1 we see a physical and a virtual network Architecture and as you will learn in this book, they work differently.

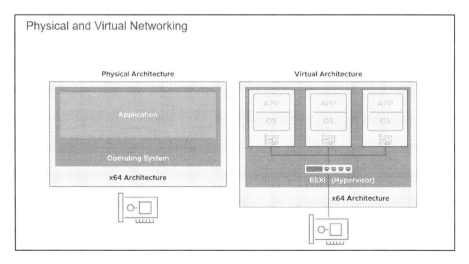

Figure 5-1. *This is a physical and virtual network architecture (Image source: @VMware)*

The following are the main components of vSphere networking:

- **Virtual switch (vSwitch):** A virtual switch is a software-based networking component that connects virtual machines (VMs) and the physical network. It acts as a bridge between VMs and the physical network, enabling communication.

- **Physical network adapters:** These are the physical network interface cards (NICs) installed in the ESXi host. These adapters provide connectivity between the ESXi host and the external physical network infrastructure.

- **Virtual network adapters:** These are virtual NICs (vNICs) associated with VMs. Each VM can have one or more vNICs connected to virtual switches. The vNICs emulate the behavior of physical NICs and provide network connectivity to VMs.

- **Port groups:** Port groups are logical groupings of ports on a virtual switch. They define the network configuration and policies for VMs connected to them. Port groups can have specific VLAN tagging, traffic shaping, security settings, and other network policies.

I will first show you how to view your virtual networks, port groups, and network interfaces and then explain how they work.

Open a browser, connect to the VMware Host Client using IP or a fully qualified domain name (FQDN), and enter the root and password in the installation. Figure 5-2 shows see the dashboard and an informational message about your trial license (we talk about changing licenses in Chapter 3).

Figure 5-2. *(Virtual Networking 1 of 10)*

The first step is to check your network configurations. As shown in Figure 5-2, click **Networking** in the Navigator panel. The first tab displayed by default is *Port groups*, which shows a list of your port groups.

5.2 What Are Port Groups?

A *port group* is a group of virtual ports on your virtual switch. Each port group has a specific network label, which must be unique to the host.

To better understand, we will call sub-networks (they are not, but to make it simple to understand) on a virtual switch.

Each of these port groups has an uplink (network interface) attached that belongs to the physical server. When installing an ESXi host, by default, it creates one Management port group and one VMs port group.

The Management port group is the network that manages the ESXi host network. For example, we used when we created the IP Address, Gateway, and DNS in the ESXi post-install.

The VMs port group is the network that was created to provide a network to VM Guest OS.

Figure 5-3 shows the networks that are created by default when you install vSphere.

Figure 5-3. *(Virtual Networking 2 of 10)*

Next, click the **Virtual switches** tab, shown in the Figure 5-4, to see the virtual switches in the ESXi host. By default, the ESXi installation creates one vSwitch called vSwitch0 (the name is created by default, but you can create any virtual switch with a different name). As you can see, two port groups exist in the virtual machine (the port groups listed in Figure 5-3). All port groups in the same virtual switch share the existing uplinks (network interfaces).

Figure 5-4. *(Virtual Networking 3 of 10)*

Next, click the **Physical NICs** tab, shown in Figure 5-5, to see the network interfaces that exist in this ESXi host. These are the actual physical network ports. It can be a physical card with four ports, or two network cards with two ports each. Each network port is called vmnic*x*, with *x* being the port number on your physical network card. This is similar to the numbering in Linux with eth0, eth1, eth2, etc.

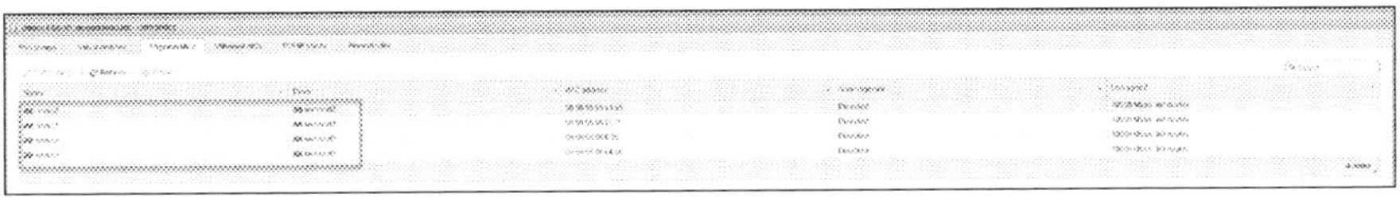

Figure 5-5. *(Virtual Networking 4 of 10)*

Figure 5-6 depicts an example of the initial network configuration.

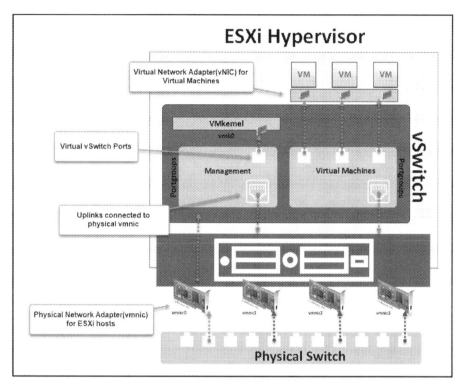

Figure 5-6. *(Virtual Networking 5 of 10)*

As shown in the figure, the ESXi host has four physical network cards, and only one (vmnic0, with the red arrow) was added to the virtual switch (vSwitch0). This means the virtual switch has only one uplink. Both port groups use the same physical connection, but in the virtual switch, traffic is separated by the port groups and uplink on each one. This is the standard default ESXi configuration after installation.

5.3 What Is a VMkernel?

As shown in Figure 5-6, the Management port group has VMkernel for the ESXi connection. VMkernel is where we have IP, subnet mask, and gateway. VMkernel is a POSIX (Portable Operating System Interface) that runs directly on the ESXi host and is used to connect the hypervisor (which could be a service) to the outside world. Simply put, VMkernel is a network point of contact from outside networks and works as a destination or source for the network.

The following are examples of services and network traffic that need a VMkernel:

- Management traffic

- vMotion traffic

- iSCSI Storage traffic

- NFS Storage traffic

- vSAN traffic

- vSphere Replication traffic

- vSphere Fault Tolerance traffic

All the above to be configured needs an IP address, subnet mask, and gateway. You should use the ESXi host default gateway for all VMkernel ports. Only in exceptional cases should you manually change the gateway.

From vCenter, we will configure more advanced networks and use Standard Switches and vSphere Distributed Switch (only available in vCenter).

Note   Before we start configuring the networking, we'll configure only the most basic settings to be able to make the ESXi host network and the Virtual Machines network available. I will show more advanced networking using separate virtual switches when we install vCenter in Chapter 8.

5.4 vSphere Network Redundancy

Since we are using only one network card for this demonstration, for redundancy purposes, let's add a second network card from the ESXi host to our vSwitch and port groups.

As shown in Figure 5-7, click **Networking**, then click the **Virtual switches** tab, and click the virtual switch you want to configure. In our case, it is **vSwitch0**.

Figure 5-7. *(Virtual Networking 6 of 10)*

As shown in Figure 5-8, we have only one vmnic and need to add another. Click **Add uplink** and select a new uplink. Since we have four network cards, select **vmnic1** and click **Save**.

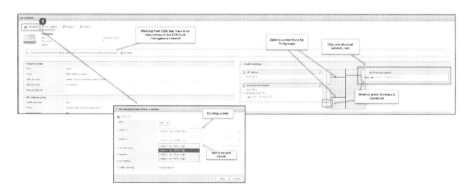

Figure 5-8. *(Virtual Networking 7 of 10)*

Now we have two uplinks in this virtual switch, and both are connected to the two port groups, as shown in Figure 5-9.

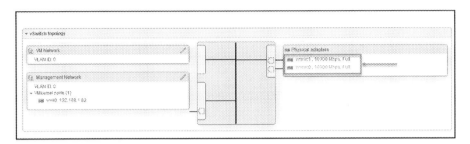

Figure 5-9. *(Virtual Networking 8 of 10)*

Why do we need two uplinks (don't forget that *uplinks* always refers to a physical network adapter) in our Management network? Because if one uplink is down (a cable problem, switch port issue, or a hardware problem with the network adapter), we will lose the connection to the ESXi host. Having two uplinks is not mandatory, but it is always good to use two for redundancy.

Because of redundancy, every VMkernel should have a minimum of two uplinks. As you will learn.

Now that we have our Management and VMs networks with two uplinks, we need to set the NIC teaming by setting the load balancing policy and failover order to work in case one uplink fails and the other uplink takes over. This can be done using the options shown in Figure 5-10.

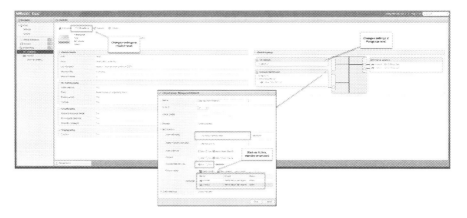

Figure 5-10. *(Virtual Networking 9 of 10)*

On a virtual switch, you may set several load-balancing algorithms to control how network traffic is split across a team's physical NICs. The following options are available in the *Load balancing* drop-down list shown in Figure 5-10:

- **Route Based on Originating Virtual Port:** Uplinks are selected by the virtual switch based on the virtual machine port IDs on the vSphere Standard Switch or vSphere Distributed Switch.

- **Route Based on Source MAC Hash:** The virtual switch chooses an uplink for a virtual machine depending on its MAC address. The virtual switch utilizes the virtual machine's MAC address and the number of uplinks in the NIC team to determine an uplink for a virtual machine.

- **Route Based on IP Hash:** The virtual switch selects uplinks for virtual machines based on each packet's source and destination IP address. It is similar to link aggregation and LACP on physical switches.

- **Route Based on Physical NIC Load:** This option
  is only available in vCenter. The routing process is
  determined based on the physical NIC. The load is
  determined by the Route Based on Originating Virtual
  Port mechanism, in which the virtual Switch assesses
  the current load on the uplinks and implements
  measures to alleviate excessive load on overloaded
  uplinks. This feature is only available with the vSphere
  Distributed Switch.

- **Use Explicit Failover Order:** This policy does not
  support genuine load balancing. The virtual switch
  always utilizes the uplink that is at the top of the list
  of Active adapters in the failover order and meets the
  failover detection criteria. If no uplinks are available in
  the Active list, the virtual switch utilizes uplinks from
  the Standby list.

Note   Check the VMware page `https://docs.vmware.com/en/`
`VMware-vSphere/7.0/com.vmware.vsphere.networking.`
`doc/GUID-959E1CFE-2AE4-4A67-B4D4-2D2E13765715.html`
for more information about load balancing algorithms.

Failover order is also set using the options shown in Figure 5-10.

- **Active, Active** (both are always active, and there is
  always one connected in case of a failure)

- **Active, Standby** (only one if connected while the
  second only takes over if the first one fails)

Virtual switch settings can be set at the vSwitch level or port group level. If set at the vSwitch level and not changed in the port group level, port groups inherit settings from the vSwitch. If you change settings in the port group, it ignores the settings from the vSwitch and assumes the port group settings.

For the VMs network, set the *Load balancing* drop-down list field to **Route Based on Physical NIC Load** and set the *Failover order* options to **Active, Active**.

For Virtual Machines, Storage, vMotion, etc., it is essential to set a good load balancing policy to balance traffic between the vmnics.

In the Management port group, we don't need to set a special policy, so set the *Load balancing* field to **Use Explicit Failover Order** and set the *Failover order* options to **Active, Active**, as shown in Figure 5-10. Leave the rest of the settings to inherit from the vSwitch.

We can add multiple vmnics and distribute them to the port groups but link specific vmnics to specific port groups. We can also set a vmnic as unused. Then the vmnic will not be used in this port group or vSwitch.

We will discuss these settings and policies in more detail when we have a vCenter.

After the changes discussed in this section, our design shown earlier in Figure 5-6 has been updated to the design shown in Figure 5-11.

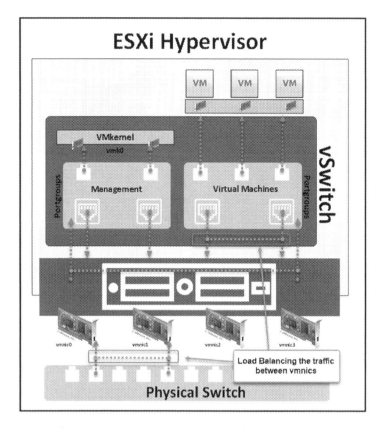

Figure 5-11. (*Virtual Networking 10 of 10*)

We have Management port group with Active/Active and the VM portgroup with load-balancing traffic.

When configuring the networking in your ESXi host, all traffic should be separated, which means a physical adapter for each traffic (like management network, VMs network, storage network).

The following is an example of an ideal configuration:

- Two network adapters for Management Network

- Two network adapters for Storage and vMotion

- 2x network adapter for Virtual Machines network

This configuration often is impossible in production because not all servers have six network ports or more. But, for example, we shouldn't mix the Storage with the Virtual Machines network, which means using the same physical network cards.

The VMs network uses considerable traffic and vMotion or Storage. Unless you have three or four network cards with 10GB set to load balance or 25GB connections, you could have traffic congestion in vMotion and Storage networks. With high latency and possible timeouts.

For vMotion and Storage, connections should always be a minimum of 10GB. So for your production, VMware Infrastructure, always take the time to create a proper network configuration.

5.5 Summary

In the previous sections we discus the basics of virtualization discussing its benefits, different types and the key role played by hypervisors. Our exploration then moved on to an examination of VMwares ecosystem emphasizing the features and advantages of vSphere. We also covered aspects, like system requirements licensing details and how to deploy vSphere effectively. Additionally we explored vSphere networking by looking at setting up networks, port groups VMkernel operations and the significance of network redundancy.

Looking ahead our attention now turns to vSphere Datastores. Here we will explore their function in VMware infrastructure management ways to handle storage resources effectively and strategies, for enhancing storage performance and capacity to meet the needs of virtualized environments.

CHAPTER 6

vSphere Datastores

In this chapter, we will discuss vSphere Datastore. As was the case in the discussion of vSphere networking in Chapter 5, we will discuss only the basics from an ESXi host perspective. We will discuss more advanced networking and Datastore after installing vCenter in Chapter 8.

6.1 vSphere System Boot Device Partitions

Between vSphere 6.x and 7.x, VMware changed the partitions layout, as shown in Figure 6-1. The partitions are stored in the device on which we install our ESXi host. As explained in Chapter 3, it can be on a SD/USB card (but as also discussed previously, it will be unsupported after vSphere 8x) or a local disk.

© Luciano Patrão 2024
L. Patrão, *VMware vSphere Essentials*, https://doi.org/10.1007/979-8-8688-0208-9_6

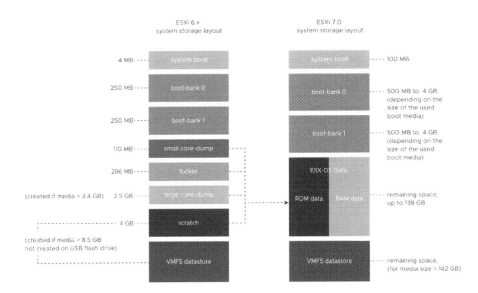

Figure 6-1. *(vSphere Datastores 1 of 9) (Image source: VMware)*

VMware changed the partition layout to be more flexible and to support other VMware and third-party solutions.

Boot bank partitions now are bigger, consolidate the system partitions, and are expandable. They provide more flexibility to manage our vSphere boot device partitions.

The following list provides a quick overview of each boot device partition in vSphere 7.x:

- **System boot:** Stores boot loader and EFI modules. File system type is FAT16.

- **Boot-bank 0:** System space to store ESXi boot modules. File system type is FAT16.

- **Boot-bank 1:** System space to store ESXi boot modules. File system type is FAT16.

- **ESX-OSData:** Acts as the unified location to store additional modules. File system type is VMFS-L.

VMS-L is a new partition created to consolidate the /scratch partition, locker partition for VMware Tools, and core dump destinations. The size of your ESX-OSData partition will always depend on your device size. It can be created up to 138GB in size.

Note   As discussed in Chapter 3, ESX-OSData has a lot of I/O requests (for example, logs, VMFS global traces, vSAN Entry Persistence Daemon [EPD] data, vSAN traces, and real-time databases). This is the only partition that you should not use on SD/USB cards.

You should always create ESX-OSData partitions on a persistent storage device (such as local disks) that are not shared between ESXi hosts.

System boot and Boot-bank partitions should be the ones that are created and running on the SD/USB cards.

During vSphere install, and after all partitions are created, the remaining space of your device (if it is local disks or another persistence device) can be used to create a Datastore to store virtual machines.

6.2 ESXi 7.0 System Storage Links

The subsystems that require access to the ESXi partitions obtain such access through the utilization of symbolic links as follows:

ESXi 7.0 system storage symbolic links.

- Boot-bank 0: /bootbank

- Boot-bank 1: /altbootbank

Persistent data

- /productLocker
- /locker
- /var/core
- /usr/lib/vmware/isoimages
- /usr/lib/vmware/floppies

Nonpersistent data

- /var/run
- /var/log
- /var/vmware
- /var/tmp
- /scratch

Note   All system storage inside *Persistent data* and *Nonpersistent data* belong to the ESX-OSData. And those are the ones that should not be running on your SD/USB card but instead on a persistent storage device.

Figure 6-2 provides a quick view of our vSphere installation.

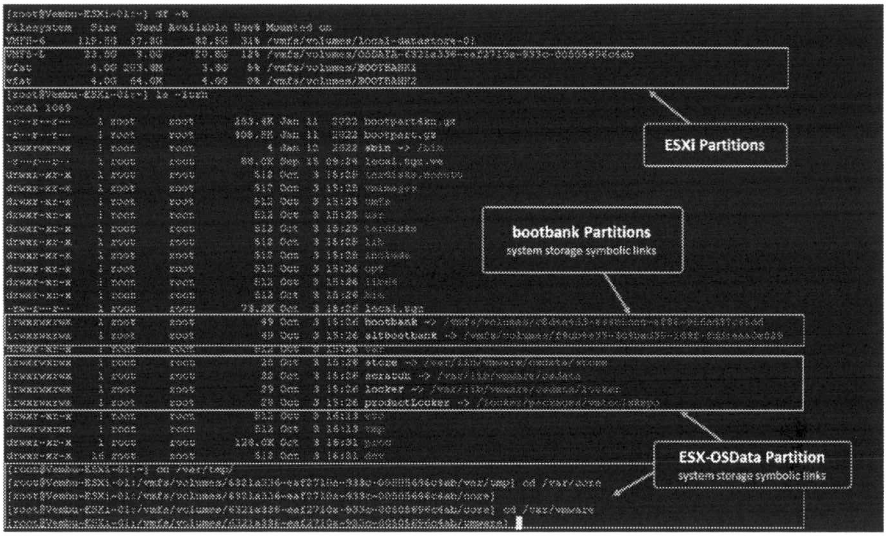

Figure 6-2. *(vSphere Datastores 2 of 9)*

After this quick review of ESXi partitions, we can create our first Datastore (to store virtual machines) in vSphere.

6.3 What Is a vSphere Datastore?

In vSphere, a Datastore storage container stores virtual machine files, templates, ISO images, and other data types. It is a centralized storage resource for the ESXi hosts within a vSphere environment. Datastores provide the necessary disk space to store virtual machine disks and files.

Here are some key points about vSphere Datastores:

- **Storage types:** Datastores can be created on various storage types, including local storage within the ESXi host (such as local disks or RAID arrays) or shared storage systems (such as SAN, NAS, or virtual SAN).

- **VMFS and NFS:** vSphere supports two primary types of
  Datastores: VMFS (Virtual Machine File System) and
  NFS (Network File System). VMFS is a clustered file
  system specifically designed for virtualization, while
  NFS is a standard file system protocol used for network-
  attached storage.

Note   We will discuss the type of Storage when we add Storage to
our ESXi host.

Datastores play a crucial role in vSphere environments by providing
a centralized storage location for virtual machine files, ensuring efficient
storage utilization, and enabling advanced features like vMotion and High
Availability. Administrators can effectively manage and allocate storage
resources by utilizing Datastores within their vSphere infrastructure.

6.4 How to Create a Datastore

First, we check the free storage devices in our vSphere to create a
Datastore.

Log in with your root account to the vSphere host web client, select
Storage in the Navigator panel, and then click the **Devices** tab, as shown
in Figure 6-3. Three devices are listed. The first is a CD-ROM device, the
second is a local disk with 120GB size, and the third is the 32GB local disk
on which ESXi is installed.

Figure 6-3. *(vSphere Datastores 3 of 9)*

Note   What you see in your vSphere always depends on the disk devices that you are using in your ESXi host. Figure 6-3 shows my nested VM in which I added an extra disk with 120GB.

To confirm that your 32GB storage device is the ESXi installation storage, click the device to see detailed information about the device. As shown in Figure 6-4, we have ESXi partitions here, so we should not touch this device.

Figure 6-4. *(vSphere Datastores 4 of 9)*

So we will use the local disk device with 120GB. Again, you can click and check if it is empty. After you are sure there are no partitions, you can continue.

Continuing on the Devices tab, click **New datastore** and give the datastore a name. See Figure 6-5. Click **Next**.

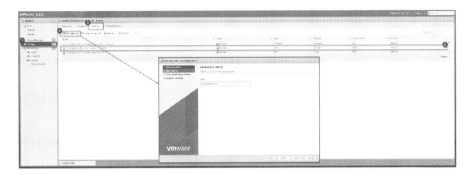

Figure 6-5. *(vSphere Datastores 5 of 9)*

Note   The name needs to be unique so that adding this host to a vCenter doesn't conflict with other ESXi hosts' Datastores names. For purpose of this demonstration, name it **local-datastore-01**.

Next, select the device on which you want to create this new Datastore. In our case it is the 120GB disk, as shown in Figure 6-6. Click **Next**.

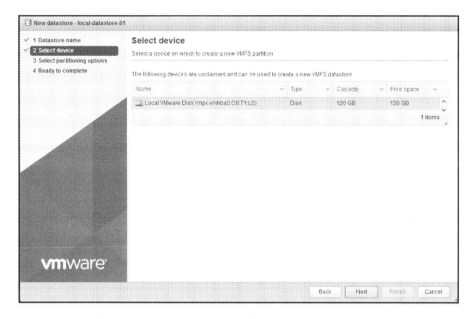

Figure 6-6. *(vSphere Datastores 6 of 9)*

Select **Use full disk**, as shown in Figure 6-7, and click **Next**.

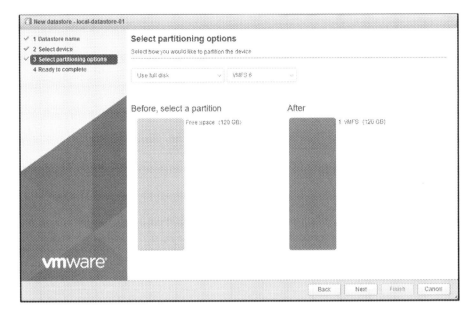

Figure 6-7. *(vSphere Datastores 7 of 7)*

On the *Ready to complete* screen, shown in Figure 6-8, double-check the information. If all is good, click **Finish**.

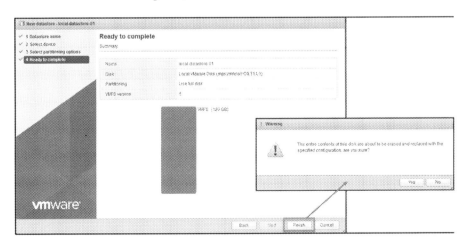

Figure 6-8. *(vSphere Datastores 8 of 9)*

Note   All data or partitions present in this disk will be deleted. So before clicking **Finish** to create a Datastore, always double-check that all the information is correct. When administrators select the wrong disk or storage device, many disasters happen.

Now you have your first Datastore in your vSphere. To view your newly created Datastore, select **Storage** in the Navigator panel and then click the **Datastores** tab. Click the Datastore name, and you see all the system information (size, free space, UUID, and location) about this Datastore, as shown in Figure 6-9.

Figure 6-9. *(vSphere Datastores 9 of 9)*

6.5 Summary

In this chapter we explore vSphere Datastores starting with a look, at system boot device partitions and the complexities of ESXi system storage connections. A significant part was focused on grasping the significance of vSphere Datastores and highlighting their role in the VMware infrastructure. We also guided you through the steps of creating a Datastore equipping you with the know how to handle storage resources in your environments.

With an understanding of managing Datastores you are now ready to move on to the stage; developing and overseeing virtual machines (VMs). This involves digging into VM files understanding hardware (vHW) utilizing VMware tools for improved performance and features and following a detailed process for setting up a VM. This knowledge is essential, for optimizing your setup ensuring deployment and management of VMs.

CHAPTER 7

Virtual Machines

In this chapter, you'll learn how to create virtual machines and store them on the Datastores that you created Chapter 6.

This is the last chapter in which the ESXi host is used and the screenshots are from a stand-alone ESXi. In the following chapters, we will move to VMware vCenter and start doing all the tasks through vCenter (Datastores, Storage, Virtual Machines, central networking, etc.).

Before I explain how to create a virtual machine, let's discuss some of the components and features of VMs and how a VM interacts with the ESXi host.

7.1 Virtual Machine Files

To understand the architecture and functionality of a VM in a VMware vSphere environment, it is crucial to recognize that a VM is essentially a collection of files. These files, stored in the VM's Datastore folder, are more than just data storage—they represent the structural and operational components of the VM itself.

Let's explore the types of files that constitute a VM and their respective roles:

- **Configuration files:** These are the backbone of a VM, containing settings and specifications that define the VM's hardware characteristics and operational behavior.

© Luciano Patrão 2024
L. Patrão, *VMware vSphere Essentials*, https://doi.org/10.1007/979-8-8688-0208-9_7

- **Hard disk files:** Central to a VM's data storage, these files act as the virtual equivalent of a physical hard disk, storing the operating system, applications, and user data.

- **Other essential files:** In addition to the preceding primary files, a VM consists of several other types of files, each serving a specific purpose, from logging activities to managing state and snapshot information. These files are as follows:

  - `.vmdk`: These are virtual disk characteristics files or configuration disk files. If a VM has more than one disk, the file for the second virtual disk is named `vmname_1.vmdk`, and so on.

  - `-flat.vmdk`: This is the second file for a virtual hard disk. Previous one `.vmdk` has the disk information, this `-flat.vmdk` is the data file.

Note   The file size depends on the type of virtual hard disk selected (thin or thick). For thick disks, the full size is stored in the Datastore, which in this case is 35GB. But if it was a thin virtual hard disk, the file size depends on what is already used.

It means only uses space that is really used on OS (but we will discuss the type of disks in the following chapters).

In the Datastore browser, you only see the `.vmdk` files, not the flat files.

- `.vmsd`: These files include information about the virtual machine snapshots. The database contains information about the snapshots of the virtual machine and serves as the primary source of data for the Snapshot Manager. The file contains line entries establishing the connections between snapshots and their respective child disks.

- `.vmsn`: This type of file contains the present setup and, if applicable, the operational condition of the virtual machine, assuming a nonmemory snapshot was taken. The system has the ability to return to a previous state of a virtual machine.

- `.vmx`: This file is the virtual machine configuration file. It has all the information about the VM resources and configurations.

- `.vswp`: This file is the virtual machine swap file. The `.vswp` file allows vSphere to swap out less active memory pages to disk, making room for more active processes in physical memory.

- `-delta.vmdk`: This file receives all the changes in a virtual hard disk after you create a snapshot. All changes are saved in this file until the snapshot is removed. The delta disk shows the difference between the virtual disk's current state and the state it was in when the last snapshot was taken.

- `.log`: This is the log file for the virtual machine.

You can learn more about each file type on the following VMware pages:

- Virtual machine files: `https://docs.vmware.com/en/VMware-vSphere/7.0/com.vmware.vsphere.vm_admin.doc/GUID-CEFF6D89-8C19-4143-8C26-4B6D6734D2CB.html`

- Snapshot files: `https://docs.vmware.com/en/VMware-vSphere/7.0/com.vmware.vsphere.vm_admin.doc/GUID-38F4D574-ADE7-4B80-AEAB-7EC502A379F4.html`

By familiarizing yourself with these files, you'll gain a deeper understanding of how VMs operate within the vSphere environment. This knowledge is key to managing and optimizing your virtual infrastructure, ensuring efficient and reliable operation of your VMs.

After this brief explanation about some of the tools and features that work together with a virtual machine and the type of files that create a VM, let's start creating our first VM.

7.2 What Is VM Virtual Hardware (vHW)?

In the context of vSphere, VM Virtual Hardware (vHW) refers to the virtual hardware version of a VM. It represents the virtual hardware configuration and capabilities presented to the VM by the virtualization platform.

Each release of vSphere introduces a new version of virtual hardware, denoted by a numerical value. For example, vSphere 6.7 introduced version 14, while vSphere 7.0 introduced version 17. These versions bring enhancements, new features, and improved performance to the virtual hardware platform.

The vHW represents the features and hardware functions available and supported by a virtual machine. For example, the maximum vCPU that is supported, how many and what type of virtual networks cards is supported, vHW also shows and applies what OS are supported on the virtual machine.

So, having the latest vHW in your virtual machines is always essential.
Check `https://docs.vmware.com/en/VMware-vSphere/7.0/com.`
`vmware.vsphere.vm_admin.doc/GUID-789C3913-1053-4850-A0F0-`
`E29C3D32B6DA.html` to get all the resources available on vHW versions.

7.3 What Is VMware Tools?

VMware Tools is a software (agent) installed automatically in the operating
system by the ESXi host (or manually by the administrator) as a tool.

It is a suite of services and utilities that enhances the virtual machine
guest operating system (guest OS) performance and improves virtual
machine management while interacting with the guest OS.

VMware Tools interacts with the guest OS to use the best resources and
drivers between the guest OS and the ESXi.

VMware Tools provides a lot of improvements and functionality in the
operating system by fixing the following:

- Low video resolution

- Inadequate color depth

- Incorrect display of network speed

- Restricted movement of the mouse

- Inability to copy and paste and drag and drop files

- Missing sound

- Provides the ability to take snapshots of the guest OS

- Synchronizes the time in the guest OS with the time on
  the host

VMware Tools also has the ability to do the following tasks:

- Pass messages from the host operating system to the guest operating system.

- Customize guest operating systems as a part of the vCenter Server and other VMware products.

- Run scripts that help automate guest operating system operations. The scripts run when the power state of the virtual machine changes.

- Synchronize the time in the guest operating system with the time on the host operating system

---

Note   Open VM Tools (`open-vm-tools`) is recommended in virtual machines with Guest OS Linux versions. Open VM Tools is open source (that is, not developed by VMware).

Check out `https://kb.vmware.com/s/article/340` for more information about VMware Tools.

7.4 How to Create a Virtual Machine

In vSphere, creating a virtual machine is very simple.

To start, select **Virtual Machines** in the Navigator panel and then click **Create/Register VM** (see Figure 7-1). On the first screen of the wizard that opens, select the option **Create a new virtual machine** (we will discuss the other option, to deploy a VM from an OVF or OVA file). Click **Next**.

Figure 7-1. *(Virtual Machines 1 of 12)*

Next, select which type of operating system to install in your virtual machine, so that vSphere knows what system is installed and prepares a VM. The options on the *Select a name and guest OS* screen are as follows (see Figure 7-2):

- **Compatibility:** This setting ensures the virtual machine will work. Since we have installed vSphere 7, we will use the latest update, in this case update 3. So, the virtual machine will be created with the Virtual Hardware v19, and the latest VMware Tools can be installed in the virtual machine.

- **Guest OS family:** This option is to select the OS family(like Windows, Linux or other). Inside the option "other" Guest OS we have other type of Apple OS, Linux, Oracle Solaris, ESXi, etc.

Note   For purposes of this test environment, do not check the Enable Windows Virtualization Based Security check box. VBS is a security feature provided by Microsoft for Windows 2016 and later. If you choose to enable VBS in the future, first make sure that you are aware of the requirements to enable this feature. For more details about VBS, see `https://learn.microsoft.com/en-us/windows-hardware/design/device-experiences/oem-vbs`.

- **Guest OS version:** Select your OS version (I selected Microsoft Windows Server 2019 for this VM) and click **Next**. See Figure 7-2. (Not that the rest of this demonstration assumes that you have selected a Windows version.)

Figure 7-2. *(Virtual Machines 2 of 12)*

Now you need to select where to store this virtual machine. Assuming you followed the steps in Chapter 6 and named your new Datastore local-datastore-01, select that, as shown in Figure 7-3. Click **Next**.

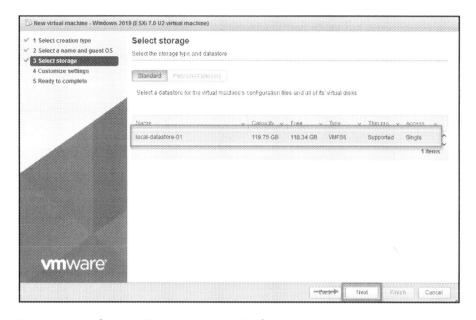

Figure 7-3. *(Virtual Machines 3 of 12)*

Next, on the Customize settings screen, select this virtual machine's resources (CPU, memory, etc.), as shown in Figure 7-4.

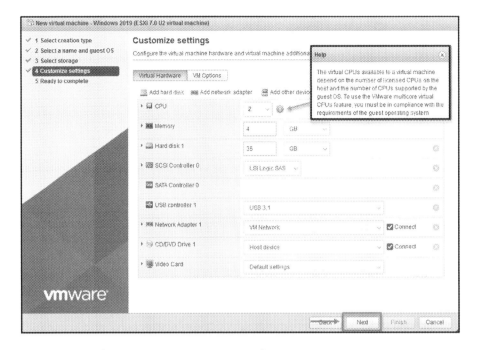

Figure 7-4. *(Virtual Machines 4 of 12)*

Note   When you select an operating system, vSphere automatically provides the minimum requirements for the virtual machine to run that OS.

For purpose of this demonstration, use the default for vCPU and vMemory and reduce the disk size to only 35GB. If you plan to change this size, be aware of your ESXi host limits. You should never use more memory than you have in your server. The number of vCPUs available for a virtual machine always equals the physical CPUs you have in your server (double if you are using Hyperthreading).

Regarding vMemory, you can set it to more than you have in your physical server, *but memory overcommitment can affect the performance on the virtual machine.*

Network:

You will use the network we created in the previous chapter, where we created a **VM Network** network for virtual machines.

Click **Next** to continue to the *Ready to complete* step, shown in Figure 7-5. Double-check the information you have selected in the previous steps and confirm by clicking **Finish**.

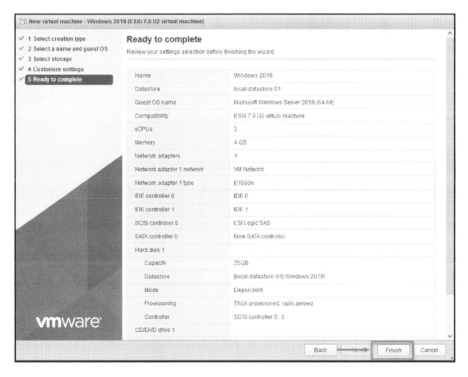

Figure 7-5. *(Virtual Machines 5 of 12)*

105

As shown in Figure 7-6, our new virtual machine was created in our vSphere.

Figure 7-6. *(Virtual Machines 6 of 12)*

We now have our first Datastore to store virtual machines and one virtual machine created on the same Datastore. Now we will install the OS on the virtual machine, and for that we need a Windows ISO.

To use a Windows ISO in our VM, vSphere needs to access that ISO file. And for virtual machines, vSphere can only access ISO files stored in Datastores. So, we need to upload a Windows ISO file to our Datastore. (This discussion assumes that you have the Windows ISO already on your computer.) Go to vSphere, and in ***Datastores***, select your Datastore(in our case in Figure 7-7 is local-datastore-01) and then click the ***Datastore browser*** tab.

Since we will add an ISO file, click the **Create directory** button and create a directory named **ISO Files** (see Figure 7-7) to upload this ISO and all the ISOs we will need in the future. This is not mandatory; it is just for better management.

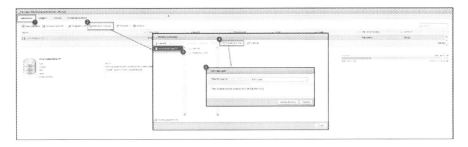

Figure 7-7. *(Virtual Machines 7 of 12)*

After creating the folder, click the **Upload** option and select the Windows ISO file stored on your computer, as shown in the top image in Figure 7-8. vSphere will start uploading the file; you can see it in the upload task vSphere tasks.

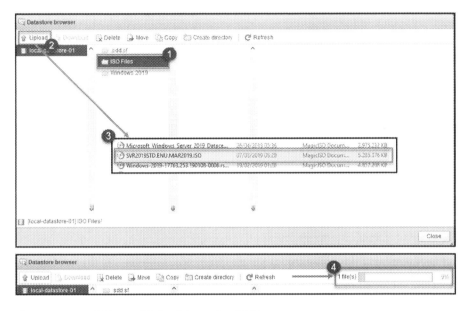

Figure 7-8. *(Virtual Machines 8 of 12)*

After the upload is finished, confirm that the file is uploaded, as shown in Figure 7-9.

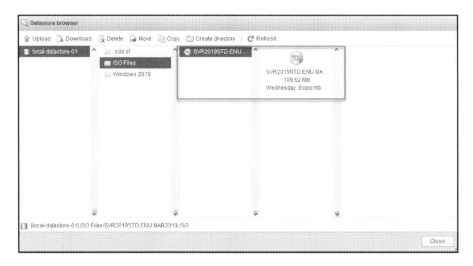

Figure 7-9. *(Virtual Machines 9 of 12)*

The next several steps are depicted in Figure 7-10. Go back to the **Virtual Machines** option and right-click your virtual machine (or select the **Actions** option) and select option **Edit settings**. In the *Edit settings* window, select **CD/DVD Drive**, select **Datastore ISO file** and click **Browse**. In the Datastore browser that opens, select your Datastore and the folder (if you have created it) and select the Windows ISO file.

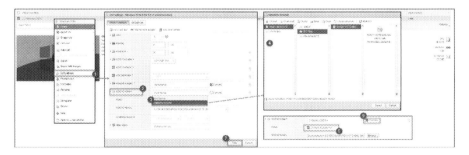

Figure 7-10. *(Virtual Machines 10 of 12)*

Check the **Connect** check box and the **Connect at power on** check box after the virtual machine is set with the Datastore ISO file. That way, when the virtual machine starts, it launches the ISO file on the boot.

After, power on your virtual machine and start installing the Windows OS. You should see the Virtual Machine Windows console, as shown in Figure 7-11. To interact with the Windows console, click inside the Windows console; the keyboard and mouse then work inside the Windows console.

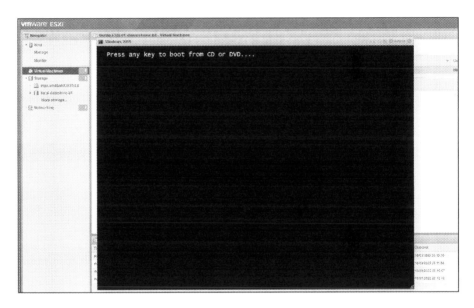

Figure 7-11. *(Virtual Machines 11 of 12)*

Note   To leave the console and return to your computer, press **Alt-Ctrl**.

Next, press any key to start installing your operating system. The installation of an OS is a standard install, like an install in a physical server, as Figure 7-12 shows. There is no difference.

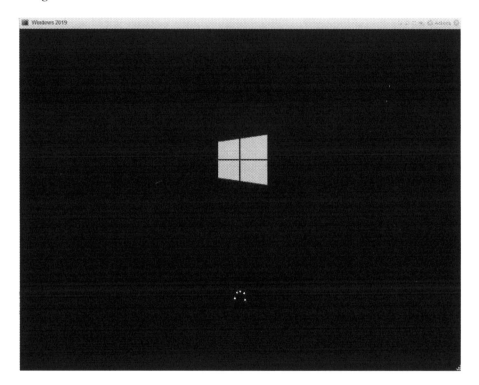

Figure 7-12. *(Virtual Machines 12 of 12)*

The preceding example is a Windows installation example, but the same process applies for any other OS (like Linux). Upload the ISO file, add it to the virtual machine, and start the installation.

7.5 Summary

During our exploration of machines (VMs) we have explorng the elements needed for their setup and maintenance. We began by examining the files that comprise a VM shedding light on how these components work in the VMware ecosystem. A closer look, at hardware (vHW) helped us grasp the resources accessible to VMs. The conversation around VMware tools emphasized their role in improving VM performance and user engagement bridging the gap, between physical hardware capabilities. Lastly we outlined the steps involved in creating a VM starting from the configuration to installing the guest operating system empowering you with the know how to effectively deploy VMs within your environment.

Now that we've covered the ins and outs of virtual machines, in Chapter 8 we'll explore VMware vCenter. Chapter 8 is important because it delves into the heart of vCenter, including its role, licensing options, installation procedures, and the intricacies of the vCenter Single Sign-On (SSO) Domain. Each of these elements plays a role in mastering the management and operational capabilities offered by the VMware platform. Moving from VM details to a focus on the vCenter management framework represents a significant stride toward comprehending the extensive VMware ecosystem.

CHAPTER 8

VMware vCenter

In Chapter 7, we discussed virtual machines, including what they are, their configurations, and how to create them. We are now ready to switch our configuration from ESXi host management to central management using VMware vCenter. In vCenter, we can manage multiple ESXi hosts and create ESXi Clusters, Datastore Clusters, Distributed Switches, etc. So, all the chapters from here forward will focus on creating a VMware environment through vCenter.

8.1 What Is VMware vCenter?

To fully understand the functionalities of VMware vCenter, it is important to recognize it as the central management platform within the VMware vSphere ecosystem. vCenter goes beyond being a tool; it serves as the hub for overseeing a virtualized data center. This section delves into the layers of complexity and capabilities that vCenter comprises.

vCenter acts as a control center for streamlining the management of ESXi hosts, virtual machines, and other crucial components of the VMware infrastructure. Its significance goes beyond administration tasks; it plays a role in efficiently and effectively managing virtual environments.

Here are some key points and features of VMware vCenter:

- **Centralized management:** vCenter provides a single point of control and management for multiple ESXi hosts and their virtual machines. It allows

© Luciano Patrão 2024
L. Patrão, *VMware vSphere Essentials*, https://doi.org/10.1007/979-8-8688-0208-9_8

administrators to manage and monitor the virtual infrastructure from a unified interface, simplifying administration tasks.

- **Resource pooling:** vCenter enables resource pooling by aggregating multiple ESXi hosts' computing, storage, and networking resources into logical resource pools. This allows for efficient allocation and management of resources across the virtual infrastructure.

- **High availability and fault tolerance:** vCenter facilitates advanced features like vSphere High Availability (HA) and vSphere Fault Tolerance (FT). HA provides automatic restart of virtual machines on alternate hosts in case of an ESXi host failure, ensuring minimal downtime. FT provides continuous availability by creating a live shadow instance of a VM on a separate host, allowing for seamless failover in case of host failure.

- **vSphere vMotion and Storage vMotion:** vCenter enables vMotion and Storage vMotion capabilities. vMotion allows live migration of virtual machines between different ESXi hosts without any disruption, providing flexibility for balancing workload, maintenance, and optimizing resource usage. Storage vMotion allows live virtual machine storage migration between different datastores while the VM runs without downtime.

- **vSphere Distributed Resource Scheduler (DRS):** DRS is a feature provided by vCenter that automatically balances workloads across multiple ESXi hosts based on resource utilization, ensuring optimal performance and resource allocation. DRS dynamically migrates virtual machines across hosts to maintain balanced resource usage.

- **Centralized monitoring and reporting:** vCenter provides the virtual infrastructure's comprehensive monitoring and reporting capabilities. It offers real-time performance monitoring, capacity planning, and reporting on resource utilization, allowing administrators to identify and troubleshoot issues efficiently.

- **Integration with Additional VMware solutions:** vCenter integrates with other VMware solutions and products such as vSAN (Virtual SAN), NSX (Network Virtualization), vRealize Suite, and more. This integration enables enhanced capabilities and extends the management and operational features of the virtual infrastructure.

Overall, VMware vCenter manages and administers VMware vSphere environments. It provides centralized control, advanced features for high availability and live migration, resource pooling, monitoring, and integration with other VMware solutions, contributing to efficient virtual infrastructure management and administration.

Note   We will discuss in detail each vCenter feature in the following chapters.

8.2 vCenter Licenses

There are three types of vCenter licensing: Standard, Foundation, and Essentials.

vCenter Server licenses for Standard or Foundation are sold separately from vSphere licensing, except vCenter Server Essentials licensing. The vCenter Essentials license is included with a vSphere Essentials Kit.

The "normal" license is the Standard licenses that includes all vCenter features, and when you install vCenter, the evaluation mode is the Standard license. See Figure 8-1

Features	Essentials	Foundation	Standard
Management service	X	X	X
Database server	X	X	X
VMware vCenter APIs	X	X	X
Inventory service	X	X	X
vCenter Single Sign-On	X	X	X
vCenter Server Appliance Migration Tool	X	X	X
vRealize Orchestrator			X
vCenter High Availability (VCHA)			X
vCenter Server Backup & Restore			X
Enhanced Linked Mode (ELM)			X
ESXi Host Management (max)	3 Hosts	4 Hosts	2500 Hosts

Figure 8-1. *(VMware vCenter 1 of 2)*

When you install a vCenter Server system, it is automatically in evaluation mode. There is no need to add a license; the vCenter Server system expires 60 days after the product is installed.

When the license or evaluation period of a vCenter Server system expires, all hosts disconnect from that vCenter Server system. The virtual machines running on the disconnected hosts remain intact.

To download the VMware vCenter ISO to install in your ESXi host, log in to your VMware account and download the latest vCenter 7 ISO. See Figure 8-2.

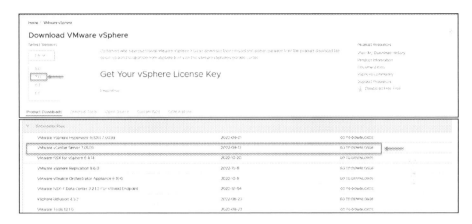

Figure 8-2. *(VMware vCenter 2 of 2)*

After you select your vCenter version and build, download the ISO, not the upgrade bundle (we will use that in later chapters when we upgrade our environment).

8.3 Install vCenter

After downloading your ISO file, you must run it from a Windows machine. You can mount the ISO (`VMware-VCSA-all-7.0.3-20395099.iso`) in your Windows machine or extract the whole ISO. For this case, I mount the ISO in my F: drive..

The file to run the installer, `installer.exe`, is located in `F:\vcsa-ui-installer\win32`. Run the file and start the installation of vCenter.

As shown in Figure 8-3, with the `installer.exe` file, you can install, upgrade, migrate, or restore a vCenter. Select the **Install** option.

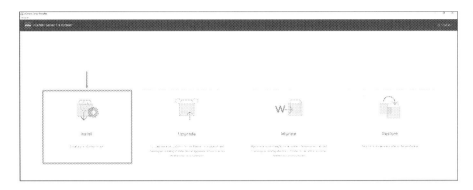

Figure 8-3. *(vCenter Install 1 of 18)*

When you install or upgrade vCenter, it deploys in two stages:

- **Stage 1, Deploy vCenter Server:** Creates the vCenter Appliance in your ESXi host and configures an IP address, gateway.

- **Stage 2, Set up vCenter Server:** Mainly creates the vCenter Single Sign-On Domain (covered later in this chapter)

To launch Stage 1, click **Next**, as shown in Figure 8-4.

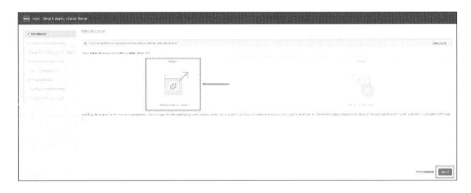

Figure 8-4. *(vCenter Install 2 of 18)*

In step 2, accept the end user license agreement and click **Next**.

In step 3, shown in Figure 8-5, set the ESXi host and the credentials for installing this vCenter Appliance. Add the ESXi host and credentials we built in the previous chapter and click **Next**. In the Certificate Warning pop-up window, click **Yes** to accept the certificate and continue.

Figure 8-5. *(vCenter Install 3 of 18)*

Since vCenter will be a virtual machine in your ESXi host, you need to set a name for your vCenter VM and set a root password for the vCenter Appliance, as shown in Figure 8-6.

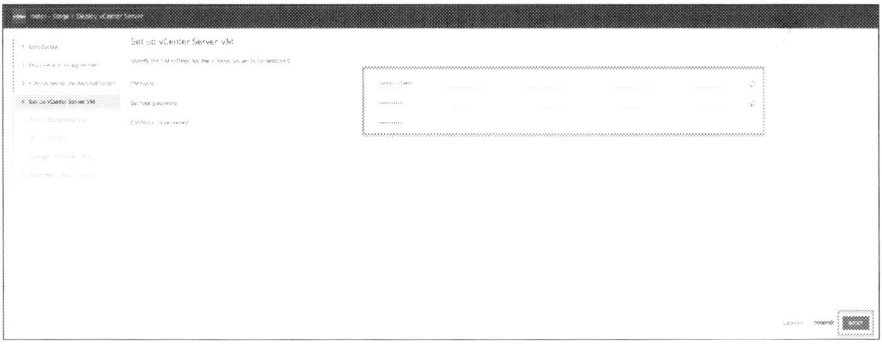

Figure 8-6. *(vCenter Install 4 of 18)*

Next, in step 5, select the deployment size of your vCenter, as shown in Figure 8-7. Which *Deployment size* option you should choose depends on your environment. If you are building for a test lab, as in this demonstration, then the Tiny option is more than enough at 579GB (it can manage up to 10 ESXi hosts and up to 100 VMs), but if you are building for a production environment, you need to select whatever size you will need for your future environment.

The *Storage size* setting is also essential. If you plan to have all full stats, alarms, tasks, etc., you need a bigger disk size to allocate all that information because it will have a bigger DB. In that case, you can select from Large to X-Large. The size in GB depends on the *Deployment size* setting.

For purposes of building the test lab demonstrated in this book, stick to the **Tiny** option for *Deployment size* and the **Default** option for *Storage size*. Click **Next**.

Caution   Don't forget that you need to have in your ESXi host a Datastore with the size that could allocate the vCenter size.

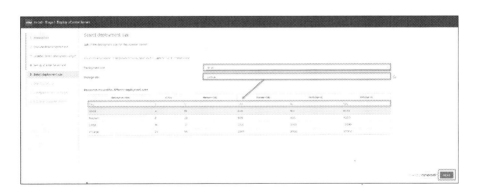

Figure 8-7. *(vCenter Install 5 of 18)*

In this section, we select Datastore to install our vCenter Appliance. As previously mentioned, we need enough space to deploy the 579GB Appliance. But since in our ESXi host, we only have 150GB; select the option **Enable Thin Disk Mode**.

Note   We will discuss disk type in further chapters, but Thin Disk means that we will only use the needed space. Although the disk is 579GB, it only uses/writes 20/30GB. So by using this option, we can install the Appliance and save storage space.

If you had more physical disks in your ESXi host, vCenter would create one host vSAN Datastore to deploy this vCenter Appliance (I will explain vSAN in a further Chapter 32). We will skip this option.

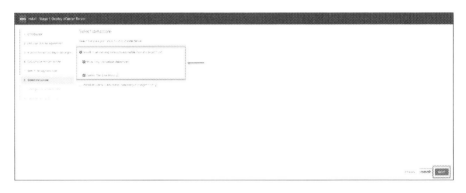

Figure 8-8. *(vCenter Install 6 of 18)*

In step 7, shown in Figure 8-9, add the VM network we created in the latest chapters regarding networks for virtual machines.

121

Figure 8-9. *(vCenter Install 7 of 18)*

You need to add an IP address, gateway, or DNS. Or you can use your DHCP server to set this (in that case, you need to change from static to DHCP). Only change ports if this is mandatory in your company environment. If not, leave the default. Click **Next**.

Caution   You need to create a DNS record for your vCenter. If not, installing it will fail.

In the final step of Stage 1, shown in Figure 8-10, confirm all the information; if everything is okay, click **Finish** to deploy the vCenter Appliance in your ESXi host.

Figure 8-10. *(vCenter Install 8 of 18)*

vCenter Appliance starts deploying Stage 1, displaying the progress bar shown in the top image in Figure 8-11. After it is finished and displays the message shown in the bottom image, click **Continue**.

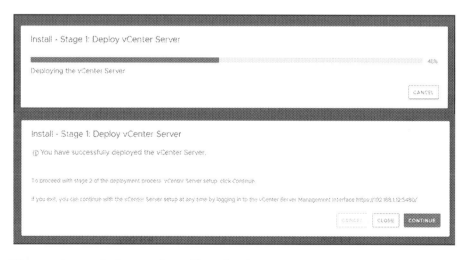

Figure 8-11. *(vCenter Install 9 of 18)*

Next, you are taken to the Setup Wizard shown in Figure 8-12, where you can start deploying vCenter Stage 2 by clicking **Next**.

123

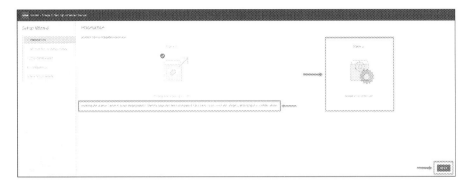

Figure 8-12. *(vCenter Install 10 of 18)*

In step 2 of the Setup Wizard, configure the *Time synchronization mode* and *NPT servers* fields. Figure 8-13 shows step 2 along with an embedded image of the expanded *Time synchronization mode* drop-down list. vCenter uses time synchronization between vCenter and ESXi hosts, so be sure you have vCenter and ESXi using the same NTP servers or select to synchronize time with ESXi hosts.

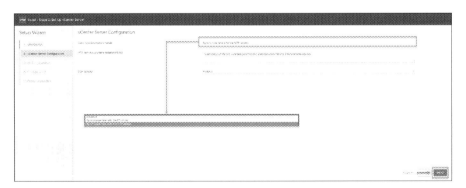

Figure 8-13. *(vCenter Install 11 of 18)*

In step 2, you can also enable SSH access to your vCenter. In homelab, we should always enabling to help in troubleshooting.

In an organization, the choice of whether to enable SSH depends on the organization's security policies in production; if permitted, you should enable SSH only if you use it. If not, leave it disabled.

Step 3 of the Setup Wizard is *SSO Configuration*, in which you configure the vCenter Single Sign-On Domain for your vCenter (the SSO Domain is described in detail in the next section). As shown in Figure 8-14, name your SSO Domain (for purposes of the example test lab, use the default vsphere.local) and set the username and password for the SSO administrator. Click **Next**.

Figure 8-14. *(vCenter Install 12 of 18)*

Step 4 of the Setup Wizard, shown in Figure 8-15, gives you the option to join the VMware Customer Experience Improvement Program (CEIP). Read the details provided and decide whether you want to join. If you don't want to participate in CEIP, clear the check box below the details.

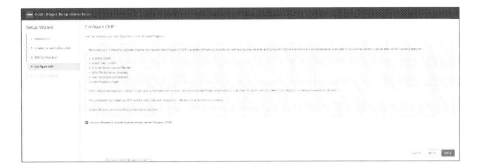

Figure 8-15. *(vCenter Install 13 of 18)*

Click **Next** to continue and finish your vCenter installation.

On the *Ready to complete* page, shown in Figure 8-16, double-check all the information and, if all is good, click **Finish**. Your vCenter installation will begin and you will see the progress bar shown in Figure 8-17.

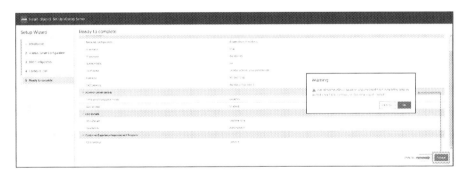

Figure 8-16. *(vCenter Install 14 of 18)*

Figure 8-17. *(vCenter Install 15 of 18)*

After the installation is finished, click **Close**. vCenter automatically opens the *vCenter Server Appliance Management Interface (VAMI)* page. We will not need it for now. Chapter 9 discuss VAMI in depth.

Tip   If for any reason you can't continue to Stage 2, or you need to pause or something, you can restart Stage 2 by opening the vCenter VAMI page, `https://IP-FQDN:5480`, and clicking **Setup**.

This will bring you to the beginning of the vCenter Server configuration, as shown in Figure 8-18. At this point, your new vCenter Server has been installed successfully, but you still need to make it available for use by configuring it.

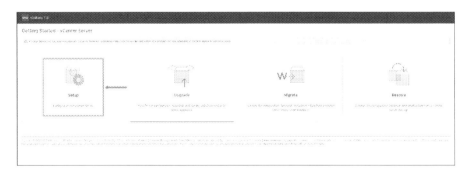

Figure 8-18. *(vCenter Install 16 of 18)*

We finish our vCenter installation, for this chapter at least, in the ESXi host. As shown in Figure 8-19, you can log in to your vCenter with the `https://IP-FQDN` and use the SSO Domain administrator user: `administrator@vsphere.local`.

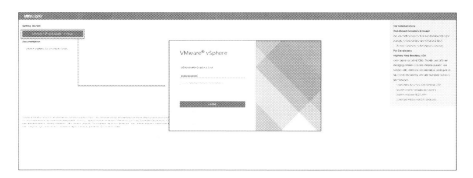

Figure 8-19. *(vCenter Install 17 of 18)*

For now vCenter is empty (see Figure 8-20), but in Chapter 10, we will start configuring and managing vCenter. We will start by creating a Datacenter and ESXi host Cluster and adding ESXi hosts to our vCenter.

Figure 8-20. *(vCenter Install 18 of 18)*

8.4 What Is the vCenter Server Single Sign-On Domain?

The domain that vSphere utilizes to link together vCenter Servers in a federation is known as an SSO Domain. Tags, Licenses, Categories, Global Permissions, Roles, and Privileges are all part of an SSO domain. Administrators can choose an alternative domain name when installing vCenter Server in place of the SSO Domain name, which by default is set to `vsphere.local`.

We can also use an SSO Domain to use an Active Directory or LDAP identity source to allow users and groups to authenticate in vCenter.

A management server, the vCenter Lookup Service, the Security Token Service (STS), and the VMware Directory Service (`vmdir`) are all components of vCenter Single Sign-On. Additionally, certificate management relies on the VMware Directory Service.

8.5 Summary

In this chapter we explored the role of vCenter Server in centralizing and overseeing infrastructure. We began by introducing vCenter highlighting its functions and the benefits it provides for handling environments. Following that we discussed vCenter licenses to clarify the licensing options. How they impact your virtual setup. The installation steps, for vCenter were then explained in detail to help you set up vCenter smoothly. Lastly we delved into the significance of the vCenter Server Single Sign On (SSO) Domain emphasizing its role in securing and simplifying access to the vSphere environment, for management and operational integrity of your virtual infrastructure.

Having introduced the integral role of vCenter SSO in unifying vCenter Servers, we turn our attention to the functionalities of VAMI for streamlined management and operational efficiency.

CHAPTER 9

vCenter Server Appliance Management Interface (VAMI)

The management interface of the vCenter Server Appliance (VCSA), known as the vCenter Server Appliance Management Interface (VAMI), plays a role in administering VMware VCSA. With its web-based user interface, it simplifies and streamlines the configuration and monitoring processes for the VCSA. Designed to cater to both newcomers and users, VAMI eliminates the need for command-line interactions.

In this chapter we will delve into the range of capabilities offered by VAMI. These include setups such as networking and time settings, as well as more advanced functions such as update management and access control. By leveraging VAMI, you not only can easily configure your VCSA initially, but also ensure its ongoing health and performance with minimal effort. Whether its monitoring system health, managing backups or troubleshooting issues, VAMI equips you with tools for efficient management of your virtual environment.

© Luciano Patrão 2024
L. Patrão, *VMware vSphere Essentials*, https://doi.org/10.1007/979-8-8688-0208-9_9

9.1 Tasks That Can Be Accomplished Using VAMI

With the VAMI administrators have a range of tools to effectively manage the vCenter Server Appliance. They can handle tasks such, as setting up monitoring system performance, managing updates, handling backups and restores controlling access, troubleshooting issues and configuring networking settings.

- Basic configuration
  - Set up networking configurations, such as IP addresses, DNS, and proxy settings.
  - Adjust time settings and configure NTP servers.
  - Manage the appliance password.
  - Handle SSL certificates.
- Monitoring
  - Keep an eye on the health of your VCSA, including system health, disk space availability, and database health.
  - Monitor the performance metrics of your VCSA.
- Update management
  - Check for updates and patches for your VCSA.
  - Stage and install updates and patches as needed.
- Backup and restore
  - Configure backup settings for your VCSA.
  - Schedule automatic backups.
  - Perform manual backups when necessary.
  - Restore from backups if required.

- Access control

  - Manage user access by creating new user accounts with roles assigned to them.

- Troubleshooting

  - Access system logs and other diagnostic information to identify and troubleshoot any issues that may arise.

- Networking

  - Configure firewall settings to manage various networking options.

These features provided by VAMI make it convenient for users to effectively manage their vCenter Server Appliance without complexity or technical expertise.

Essentially, VAMI is a component for managing the vCenter Server Appliance. It combines simplicity with functionality, making it an integral part of overcoming challenges in VCSA management. Its wide range of features greatly contributes to providing a solution. It ensures that your VCSA remains strong, responsive, and adaptable to evolving virtualization requirements.

VAMI provides a way to ensure that your VCSA is appropriately set up, regularly updated, and functioning smoothly without delving into command-line configurations.

9.2 How to Access VAMI

To access VAMI, you need to use port 5480 (this port can be customized). Open your browser and type `https://IP-FQDN:5480`. For purposes of this example, we will use `https://192.168.1.112:5480`.

133

Log in using the user root and password that you created when installing vCenter. You should see a window similar to Figure 9-1.

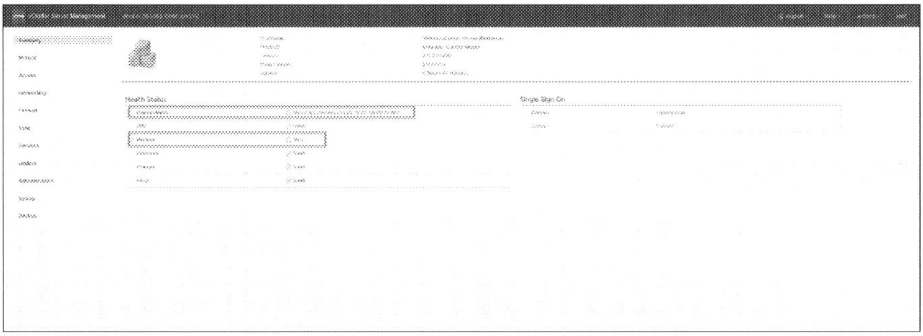

Figure 9-1. *(VAMI 1 of 9)*

Figure 9-1 shows a couple of warnings regarding memory reaching almost 100%. In VAMI, we can monitor any issues or warnings regarding the vCenter Appliance. There is nothing to worry about in this case, because this is a temporary spike in memory and goes back to normal after several minutes.

Let's check out some of the options in the navigation panel on the left in VAMI.

Note   You don't need to know about all the options in the VAMI at this point, so only the list covers only the more important ones.

- **Monitor:** This page has tabs to check CPU & Memory, Disks (whether they are full), Network (errors, package, etc.), and vCenter Database (space used, alarms, events, etc.). See Figure 9-2.

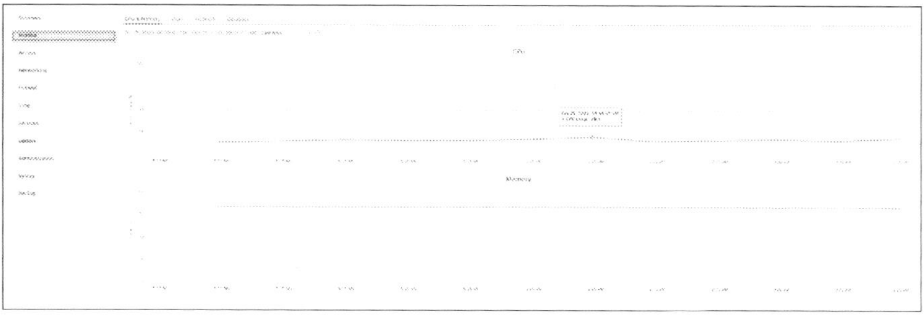

Figure 9-2. *(VAMI 2 of 9)*

- **Access:** This page is where you can enable or disable access to vCenter SSH, the Console, or even the Direct Console User Interface (DCUI). If you want to restrict access to SSH in vCenter, disable it here. Or, if you want to enable it, enable it here. See Figure 9-3.

Figure 9-3. *(VAMI 3 of 9)*

- **Networking:** This page displays everything related to networking in vCenter (IP address, gateway, DNS, proxy, etc.). See Figure 9-4. Be cautious about changing the configuration here, since you could lose access to your vCenter if you change the wrong settings.

Figure 9-4. *(VAMI 4 of 9)*

9.3 How to Change the vCenter IP Address

We can also use the Networking page (shown in Figure 9-4) to change the vCenter IP address or FQDN.

Note   Again, use this option carefully and ensure you are using the correct IPs and FQDN before applying your changes. If you change the IP or FQDN, ensure you have a DNS entry and a DNS forward for the new IP/FQDN.

Before you make any changes to the vCenter network, take a snapshot. See the "Creating and Managing Snapshots" section in Chapter 22 for simple instructions on how to do this.

To change DNS, IP address, or FQDN, click **Edit** on the right side of the *Networking* page, select your network adapter in step 1 of the Edit Network Settings wizard (see Figure 9-5), and then click **Next**.

Figure 9-5. *(VAMI 5 of 9)*

Note   To change the IP address of the vCenter Server Appliance, first confirm that its system name is set as an FQDN, which is the primary network identifier (PNID). If the system name was initially set as an IP address during deployment, it can be changed to an FQDN later.

You can quickly check your PNID by running the following command in your vCenter console:

```
/usr/lib/vmware-vmafd//bin/vmafd-cli get-pnid --server-name
localhost
```

In step 3 of the Edit Network Settings wizard, shown in Figure 9-6, make your changes, double-check them, and then click **Next**.

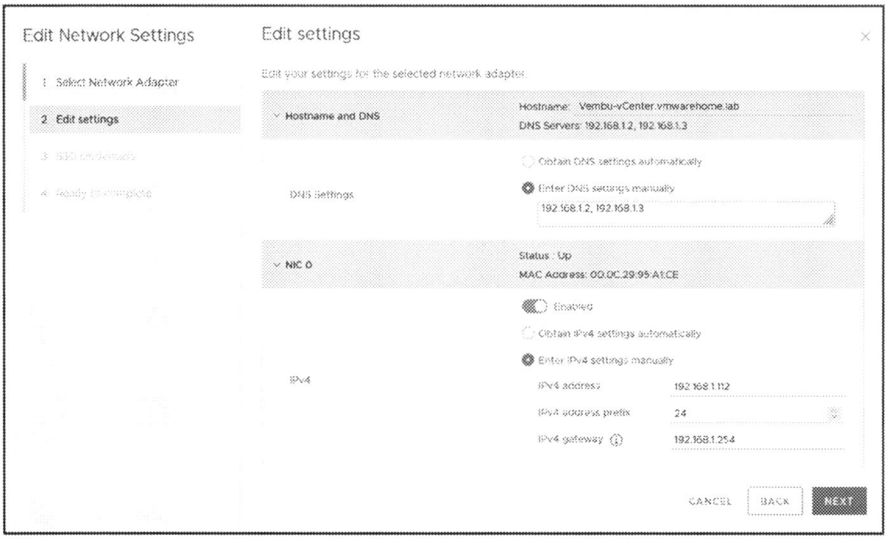

Figure 9-6. *(VAMI 6 of 9)*

In step 3, shown in Figure 9-7, enter your SSO domain username and password to confirm the changes, and click **Next**.

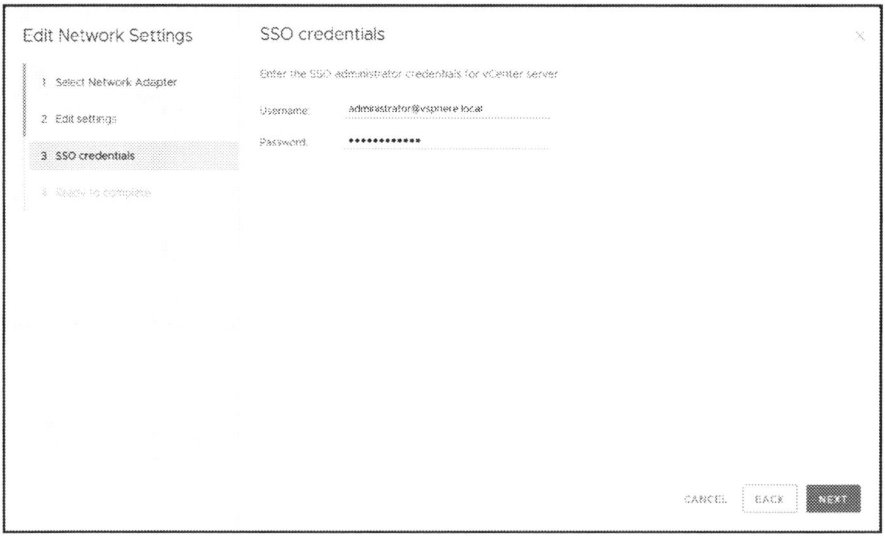

Figure 9-7. *(VAMI 7 of 9)*

Before you finish, you need to acknowledge the impact of changing the network (particularly the IP address) of your vCenter and that you have made a backup. You are also reminded of the following actions that will be required after your network settings have been reconfigured and your vCenter Server is running (see Figure 9-8):

- All deployed plug-ins will need to be reregistered.

- All custom certificates will need to be regenerated.

- vCenter HA will need to be reconfigured.

- Hybrid Link with Cloud vCenter server will need to be recreated.

- Active Directory will need to be rejoined.

After you check everything, acknowledge the option that you made a backup of your vCenter Server (in our example, a snapshot), then click **Finish**.

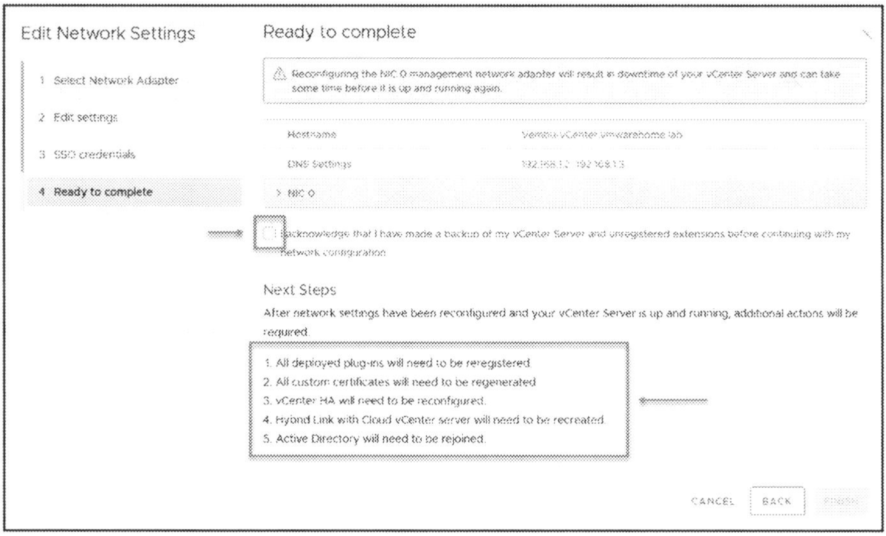

Figure 9-8. *(VAMI 8 of 9)*

After your changes take effect, you should reboot your vCenter.

To wrap up the chapter, we'll check the Services page, shown in Figure 9-9. Here, you can check all services from vCenter. It is an excellent place to start when troubleshooting any issues with vCenter (not starting the DCUI or other issues) and checking if services are all up. If not, you can start them manually.

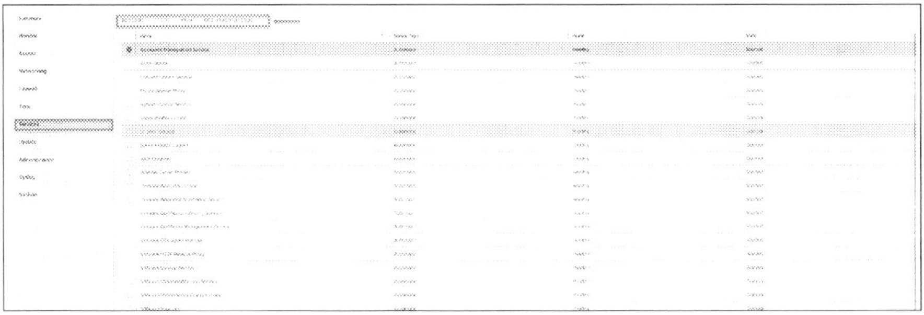

Figure 9-9. *(VAMI 9 of 9)*

You can and should also update your vCenter using VAMI, but that will be discuss in Chapter 29.

9.4 Summary

Now that you are familiar with managing vCenter through VAMI, next you'll learn how vCenter organizes its virtualized environment by structuring it into Datacenters. These Datacenters serve as the components for managing and organizing resources and vCenter virtual structure.

CHAPTER 10

Datacenters and Clusters

This chapter explores the elements of vSphere architecture with a focus, on Datacenters and Clusters within vCenter. It begins by detailing the importance of vCenter Datacenters in structuring infrastructure then progresses to discussing the establishment and oversight of vCenter Clusters to optimize resources and ensure uptime. The chapter also explains the process of integrating ESXi hosts with vCenter, for management and introduces vSphere Cluster Services (vCLS) for maintaining cluster well being. This chapter aims to provide a clear understanding of setting up and managing a robust and scalable virtual environment.

10.1 What Is a vCenter Datacenter?

In vSphere, a vCenter Datacenter is a logical container representing a virtual VMware vCenter infrastructure. It provides a hierarchical organization for the virtual resources and objects managed by vCenter.

A vCenter Datacenter acts as a container for clusters, hosts, virtual machines, networks, and datastores. For example, each Datacenter can contain different objects depending on the user's needs. You could create one Datacenter for each organizational unit in your company, some high-performance environments, and other less demanding ones.

© Luciano Patrão 2024
L. Patrão, *VMware vSphere Essentials*, https://doi.org/10.1007/979-8-8688-0208-9_10

With vCenter Datacenters, administrators can efficiently organize, manage, and control the virtual resources within their vSphere environments. Using Datacenters provides a flexible and scalable structure for resource pooling, resource management, security, and policy enforcement, helping streamline the virtual infrastructure's administration.

10.1.1 Create a vCenter Datacenter

On the main page of the vSphere Client, navigate to **Home** and then to **Hosts and Clusters**. Right-click the name of your vCenter, select **New Datacenter** in the context menu, and give a name to your new Datacenter, as shown in Figure 10-1. If you don't give your Datacenter a custom name, vCenter will use the default name Datacenter. Click **OK**.

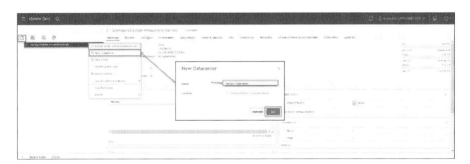

Figure 10-1. *(vCenter Datacenter 1 of 1)*

Now that you have a vCenter Datacenter, the next task is to create a vCenter ESXi host Cluster.

10.2 What Is a vCenter Cluster?

A cluster is made up of ESXi hosts. When a host is added to a cluster, host resources become part of that Cluster resource pool. So, as more hosts are added to the cluster, more resources are available.

Starting with vSphere 6.7, you can create and configure a hyper-converged cluster so that storage, networking, and compute are all running on industry-standard x86 servers in a single software layer.

You must create clusters if you want to enable vSphere High Availability or vSphere Distributed Resource Scheduler, as well as VMware vSAN. Starting with vSphere 7.0, you can now use a single image to create your cluster.

You can also easily update and upgrade the software on the hosts in your cluster with images from vSphere Lifecycle Manager. Additionally, starting with vSphere 7.0 Update 2, during cluster creation, you can choose a reference host and use its image for the newly created Cluster.

When you create a Cluster, you can enable the following:

- vSphere Distributed Resource Scheduler (DRS)

- vSphere High Availability (HA)

- Virtual Storage Area Network (vSAN)

You can also manage all hosts in the cluster with a single image. This option will allow you to assign one image to all hosts in a cluster, which removes variability between hosts.

It also provides more features like hardware compatibility checking, cluster-wide remediation, and easier upgrades. It requires hosts to be running ESXi 7.0 or newer and replaces baselines. Once enabled, baselines cannot be used in this cluster.

We will not discuss these features further in this chapter. Chapter 17 is dedicated to DRS and Chapter 19 is dedicated to HA.

10.2.1 Create a Cluster

In the vSphere Client, right-click the Datacenter name, select **New Cluster** in the context menu, and give a name to your new Cluster, as shown in Figure 10-2. If you don't give it a custom name, vCenter will use the default name New Cluster. Click **Next** and then click **Finish**.

Figure 10-2. *(vCenter Cluster 1 of 1)*

With your first vCenter Cluster in place, the next task is time to add your ESXi host to the Cluster.

Note   As you will learn in subsequent chapters, DRS, HA, vMotion, and other features require a Cluster with more than one ESXi host, so in this chapter you will add two or more additional ESXi hosts to this Cluster so that you will be able to enable this features.

You can create some extra ESXi hosts (at least one more) following the initial chapter on how to create a Nested VM. Following that process, create an extra ESXi for your vCenter Cluster.

10.3 Add Your ESXi Host to vCenter

To add your ESXi host to vCenter, in the vSphere Client, right-click the Cluster name and select **Add Hosts** in the context menu. In the *Add hosts* pop-up wizard, shown in Figure 10-3, add the ESXi host you previously created (name, user **root**, and your password). If the user and password are the same for all ESXi hosts, you can enable the option **Use the same credentials for all hosts** (no need to add to each one). Click **Next**.

Figure 10-3. *(Add ESXi host vCenter 1 of 13)*

Select all ESXi three hosts and import all certificates from the ESXi host to vCenter.

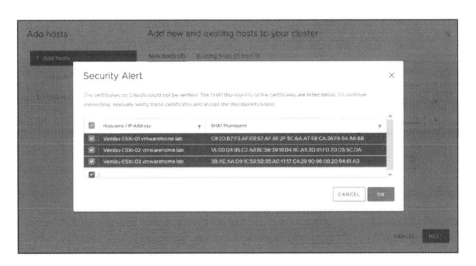

Figure 10-4. *(Add ESXi host vCenter 2 of 13)*

Step 2 of the *Add hosts* wizard, review the ESXi host summary and check if you have any warnings. Figure 10-5 shows one warning, indicating one VM already exists in one of the ESXi hosts and is powered on. Usually, this is not a problem. It is just to inform you about the ESXi host you are adding to the vCenter. This particular case is the vCenter you created in the previous chapter. Click **Next** to continue.

Figure 10-5. *(Add ESXi host vCenter 3 of 13)*

In the final wizard step, shown in Figure 10-6, double-check the ESXi host information. If all is okay, click **Finish** to add the ESXi hosts to your Cluster.

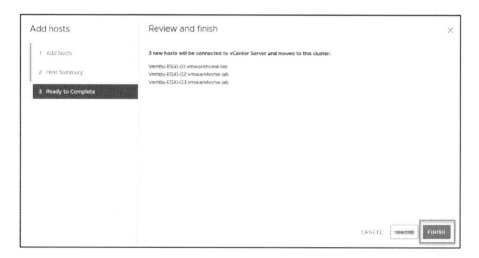

Figure 10-6. *(Add ESXi host vCenter 4 of 13)*

If there is no problem with the IP/FQDN or the network of your ESXi hosts, vCenter starts to import them to the Cluster.

Now you have created your vCenter Cluster. As shown in Figure 10-7, one of the hosts in this demonstration has a yellow warning icon.

Figure 10-7. *(Add ESXi host vCenter 6 of 13)*

Select the ESXi host, and the *Summary* tab displays the warning messages, as shown in Figure 10-8. The warnings are about the console ESXi Shell and SSH being enabled for this host.

Figure 10-8. *(Add ESXi host vCenter 7 of 13)*

Note   For security reasons, SSH in a production environment should always be disabled by default and enabled only when necessary. That is why the VMware warning is asking for confirmation that this is really necessary.

Since this is a test environment, click **Suppress Warning** and then click **Yes**, and vCenter will no longer warn you about this issue.

10.4 Quick Tips for Managing Hosts in vCenter Server

In your VMware environment, you currently have a vCenter installed, a Datacenter, and a Cluster created with three ESXi hosts added. Here are some quick tips for managing hosts in the vCenter Server.

10.4.1 Put a Host in Maintenance Mode

Maintenance mode is a state in which administrators can work on the ESXi host while still powered on, to perform tasks such as upgrading/updating ESXi host and everything is in it(vSphere, security patches, drivers everything), applying patches, drivers, troubleshooting, and so forth.

When putting an ESXi host in maintenance mode, if any VMs on it are currently powered on, vCenter will move (using vMotion) them to the next available host. You can also move powered off VMs if you want to. Or, for example, if you want to move the host to another Cluster or Datacenter.

To put a host in maintenance mode, right-click the host, select **Maintenance Mode** in the context menu, and then click **Enter Maintenance Mode**, as shown in Figure 10-9. Figure 10-10 shows the icon that is displayed for a host in maintenance mode.

Figure 10-9. *(Add ESXi host vCenter 8 of 13)*

Figure 10-10. *(Add ESXi host vCenter 9 of 13)*

10.4.2 Disconnect and Reconnect a Host

Disconnecting a host managed by a vCenter Server system leaves the host in place but temporarily suspends all activity. Disconnecting doesn't remove the host from your vCenter Server, but it stops every single monitoring activity that the vCenter Server performs.

To disconnect a host, right-click the host, select **Connection** in the context menu, and then click **Disconnect**, as shown in Figure 10-11. To reconnect, perform the same action but click **Connect** after selecting **Connection**.

Figure 10-11. *(Add ESXi host vCenter 10 of 13)*

10.4.3 Relocate a Host

You can move a host to another location by dragging it to the new location. You can put the host in a folder, in a cluster, or as a stand-alone object in the Datacenter.

To relocate a host to a cluster, right-click the host, select **Move To** in the context menu, select the cluster, and click **OK**, as shown in Figure 10-12.

Figure 10-12. *(Add ESXi host vCenter 11 of 13)*

10.4.4 Remove a Host from the vCenter Server

To discontinue monitoring and managing a managed server, it must be removed from the vCenter Server and it must be in maintenance mode.

To remove a host in maintenance mode, right-click the host, select **Remove from Inventory** in the context menu, and then click **Yes** in the confirmation dialog box shown in Figure 10-13.

Figure 10-13. *(Add ESXi host vCenter 12 of 13)*

Note   Removing a host from inventory is only possible if it is in maintenance mode and is not used by any vCenter Virtual Switches (Distributed Virtual Switches—vDS).

10.4.5 Reboot or Shut Down an ESXi Host

To reboot or power off ESXi hosts, use the vSphere Client rather than the vCenter Server. You can choose to disconnect a managed host from the vCenter Server if you want, but it won't be removed from the inventory.

To perform either action, right-click the host, select **Power** in the context menu, and then choose the action, as shown in Figure 10-14.

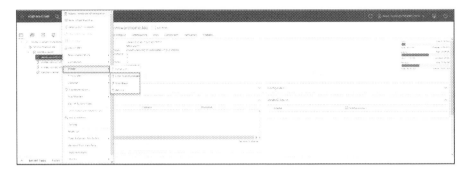

Figure 10-14. *(Add ESXi host vCenter 13 of 13)*

10.5 What Is vSphere Cluster Services?

After you create your Cluster, you will notice some VMs labeled vCLS
running in each host, as shown in Figure 10-15. vSphere Cluster Services
(vCLS) ensures that if the vCenter Server becomes unavailable, cluster
services remain available to maintain the resources and health of the
workloads that run in the clusters. vCentre Server is still required to run
DRS and HA.

Figure 10-15. *(vSphere vCLS 1 of 2)*

vCLS agents maintain the health of cluster services by running a virtual
machine on each host. The vCLS agents are created when you add hosts
to clusters. There should be three vCLS agents in every vSphere cluster,
spread out within the cluster.

Adding one or two more hosts doesn't incur an additional cost; if only one
or two hosts exist, there will be one or two vCLS agents per cluster, respectively.

When you upgrade your vSphere, your vCLS instance, it's upgraded with it. vCLS is only available in vSphere 7.0 Update 1 and newer.

If you upgrade to vSphere 7.0 Update 1 (or deploy a new one), activation of vCLS will happen automatically.

New anti-affinity rules are applied automatically every three minutes and will distribute vCLS VMs among different hosts if they are all located on the same host at that time.

If you click the VMs and Templates tab (the icon highlighted in Figure 10-16), you can expand the vCLS folder to see all the VMs inside.

Figure 10-16. *(vSphere vCLS 2 of 2)*

We will discuss vSphere Cluster Services in more detail in Chapter 30.

10.6 Summary

In this Chapter we discussed the structures for arranging and optimizing resources in a vSphere setup. We discussed the significance of the vCenter Datacenter acting as a hub, for all virtual assets in a location streamlining the management of intricate environments. Additionally we explored vCenter Clusters illustrating how they unite ESXi hosts to enhance resource allocation boost availability and support virtual machine scalability. The process of incorporating ESXi hosts into the vCenter was explained to highlight the advantages of administration. Lastly we introduced vSphere Cluster Services (vCLS) to emphasize its role in ensuring cluster services health and availability. Vital for upholding an effective virtual infrastructure.

CHAPTER 11

vCenter Datastores

In this chapter, before you learn how to create a vMotion network, you'll learn how to create iSCSI and NFS Datastores, since vMotion needs shared Storage.

In this chapter we will discuss the process of setting up iSCSI and NFS Datastores, which are crucial, for enabling shared storage needed for vMotion. You will discover how to set up an iSCSI, handle iSCSI connections and explore details about storage options, multipath setups well, as different devices and functionalities linked to them.

We have already created a vCenter Datacenter and a Cluster and added three ESXi hosts to the Cluster, so it is time to add shared storage for the ESXi hosts. In this chapter we will focus on those features and settings that we can use when we have central management for our ESXi hosts. We will start by discussing some types of Datastores and Storage in the ESXi and vCenter.

11.1 Datastore Types

We have already discussed Datastores a bit in Chapter 6, but now we will discuss them in more detail for vCenter.

You can create four types of Datastores in your ESXi hosts:

- VMFS Datastores
  - iSCSI Storage
  - Fibre Channel Storage

© Luciano Patrão 2024
L. Patrão, *VMware vSphere Essentials*, https://doi.org/10.1007/979-8-8688-0208-9_11

- NFS Datastores

  - NFS (v3 and v4.1)

- vSAN Datastores

  - When creating a vSAN Cluster

- VMware vSphere Virtual Volumes (vVols)

In this chapter, we discuss only iSCSI VMFS and NFS Datastores vSAN and vVols Datastores are not discussed in this book, possibly in the new book version.

11.1.1 VMFS Datastores

ESXi uses Datastores to store virtual disks. The datastores are logical containers that give virtual machines a standard paradigm for storing virtual machine files while concealing details of actual Storage from them.

The native vSphere Virtual Machine File System (VMFS) format is used by the Datastores that you deploy on block storage devices. It is an exclusive high-performance file system format explicitly designed for storing virtual computers.

The block-based storage device your ESXi host detects can be prepared in advance by setting up the VMFS datastore using the vSphere Client. The VMFS datastore can be expanded to cover many physical storage components, including local Storage and storage area network (SAN) logical unit numbers (LUNs). You can use this functionality to pool Storage and create the flexible Datastore you need for your virtual machines.

While the virtual machines are running on the datastore, you can increase its capacity. This feature allows you to add new space to your VMFS Datastores as needed for your virtual machines.

VMFS is designed for concurrent access from multiple physical machines and enforces access controls on virtual machine files.

vSphere VMFS Datastores can be used with SAN Storage by creating iSCSI LUNs and Fibre Channel Storage Volumes at the Storage level.

11.1.2 NFS Datastores

An NFS volume on a network-attached storage (NAS) server is accessed by an NFS client built into ESXi using the Network File System (NFS) protocol over TCP/IP.

The NFS volume can be mounted and used by the ESXi host as Storage. vSphere supports versions 3 and 4.1 of the NFS protocol.

A storage administrator typically creates the NFS volume or directory and exports it from the NFS server. The NFS volume does not require formatting using a local file system like VMFS.

NFS datastores can store ISO images, virtual machine templates, and other types of files in addition to virtual disks.

You can link the virtual machine's CD-ROM device to an ISO file using the Datastore for the ISO images. After that, you can install a guest operating system using the ISO file.

Instead, you mount the NFS volume directly on the ESXi hosts and utilize it like a VMFS datastore to store and boot virtual machines.

vSphere NFS Datastores can be used by NAS by creating shared folders at the Storage level.

Note   To understand better both types of Storage, check out my article in the Vembu blog at `https://www.bdrsuite.com/blog/nfs-vs-iscsi-which-is-best-for-you/`.

11.2 Configure iSCSI Datastores

First, you need to create an iSCSI LUN in your SAN Storage. The method of creation differs among storage vendors. It is not possible to explain all the vendors in this book, so check with your Storage vendor manual on how to create an iSCSI LUN in your SAN.

An iSCSI LUN needs a Target to be mounted and an Initiator to connect. An initiator can be a network card (HBA) or an iSCSI Software Adapter. Since we don't have HBA in our VMware test lab configuration, we will use an iSCSI Software Adapter. Also important in an iSCSI infrastructure is an iSCSI Qualified Name (IQN), discussed first.

11.2.1 IQN

Each iSCSI element on an iSCSI network has a unique iSCSI name and is assigned an address for access. Each iSCSI element, whether an Initiator or Target, has a unique IQN. The IQN is a logical name that is not associated with a specific IP address.

The IQN has the following characteristics:

- An IQN is always unique.

- There can be no two initiators or targets with the same name.

- An IQN can have up to 255 characters.

- Only numbers (0–9), letters (A–Z and a–z), colons (:), hyphens (-), and periods are permitted. The IQN format is as follows: *iqn.yyyy-mm.naming-authority:unique name*

The unique name on your IQN can be any name you want to use, such as the name of your host. To name your IQN, For instance, in my case, my Storage Target IQN is **iqn.2000-01.com.synology:HomeStorage.Target-1.75c007f110**. It has the year, month, storage vendor, and storage domain with an ID.

We created two iSCSI LUNs in our Storage and mapped them to the Target (with an IQN): **Vembu-iSCSI01** and **Vembu-iSCSI02**, with 250GB each.

Storage Target and IQN:

As you can see in Figure 11-1, you have the option to enable CHAP in your Storage Target, as described next.

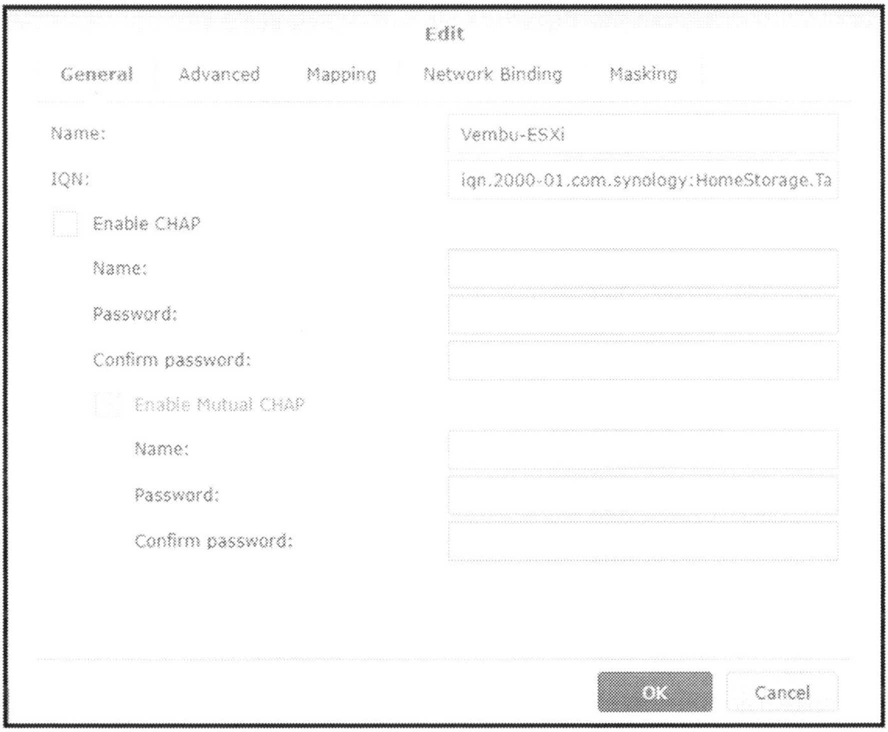

Figure 11-1. *(Install iSCSI Datastore 1 of 25)*

11.2.2 CHAP

The Challenge Handshake Authentication Protocol (CHAP) enables the exchange of authenticated data between iSCSI initiators and targets. CHAP usernames and passwords are defined on both the Initiator and the storage system when using CHAP authentication.

If you need extra security to connect your iSCSI LUNs to your ESXi hosts, you can use CHAP by adding a username and password know from.

159

Only Target and Initiator will know this username/password. With this extra security level, you can ensure that only hosts with authenticated CHAP can connect to this iSCSI LUN. But since this is a test environment, we will not enable CHAP.

11.2.3 iSCSI VMkernel

Now that you have your iSCSI LUN created, it is time to configure your ESXi hosts to connect to this iSCSI LUN and create a VMFS Datastore.

For purposes of the test lab, we need to create two VMkernel interfaces (see Chapter 5 for a refresher on what a VMkernel is) per ESXi host for our iSCSI network. We can create our iSCSI network using a Standard Switch or a vSphere Distributed Switch (vDS).

I will only show how to use a Standard Virtual Switch for the iSCSI in this example. Chapter 14 discusses vCenter vDS in more detail, and there you will also learn how to use it for iSCSI.

Creating a VMkernel for iSCSI requires two paths: active and passive (unused). If one of the paths goes down, the Initiator will automatically use the passive path (but from the other VMkernel while using port binding and iSCSI Multipath) to prevent Permanent Device Loss (PDL) and All-Paths-Down (APD); Not the action, but the result that we have is a *iSCSI Multipathing*.

Note   For more information about PDL and APD, refer to `https://kb.vmware.com/s/article/2004684`.

Next diagram (Install iSCSI Datastore 2) shows:

VMkernel vmk1 is connected to vmnic2 and has a passive connection to vmnc3, and VMkernel vmk2 is connected to vmnic3 and has a passive connection to vmnc2. Both physical cards (vmnics) will be binding with an ESXi feature called *network port binding*. Port binding ensures that the vmnics are aggregated to each other and connected to the target as one unit for high availability.

11.2.4 Network Port Binding

When numerous VMkernel ports for iSCSI are located in the same broadcast domain and IP subnet, port binding is utilized in iSCSI to enable multiple pathways to an iSCSI array that broadcasts a single IP address.

You should keep the following in mind when utilizing port binding:

- For iSCSI communication, all VMkernel ports must be located in the same broadcast domain and IP subnet.

- The same vSwitch must house each VMkernel port utilized for iSCSI communication.

The design shown in Figure 11-2 is an iSCSI Multipath example that has four VMkernel ports using port binding to connect to only one Target. The multiple VMkernel ports all reside in the same IP subnet and broadcast domain. In this type of design (the same one we will use in our test lab configuration), all VMkernel ports need to be in the same network. If not, multipathing will not work.

Note   Whereas the example in Figure 11-2 uses four VMkernel ports (and four vmnics), we'll only use two ports in our test lab configuration. But the configuration is the same, just fewer paths.

With this type of configuration, we have High Availability in our iSCSI network.

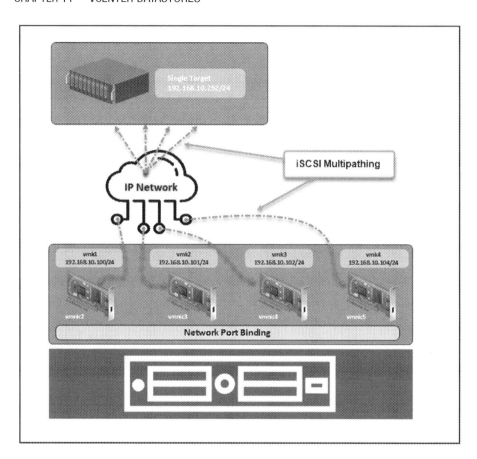

Figure 11-2. *(Install iSCSI Datastore 2 of 25)*

Figure 11-3 shows our test lab configuration.

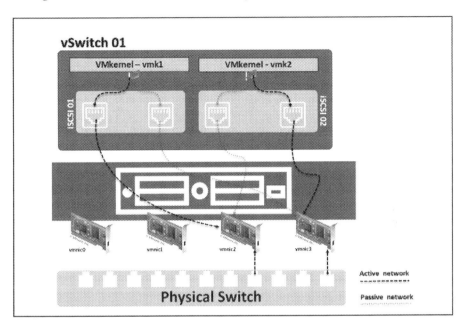

Figure 11-3. *(Install iSCSI Datastore 3 of 25)*

Let us explain how to implement the above design.

How to create an iSCSI Software Adapter?

As indicated in Figure 11-4, log in to the vCenter Client, select your ESXi host, click the **Configure** tab, select **Storage Adapters**, click the **Add Software Adapter** drop-down arrow, and select **Add iSCSI adapter**. Read the message and then click **OK** to confirm.

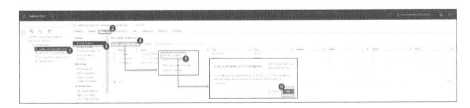

Figure 11-4. *(Install iSCSI Datastore 4 of 25)*

As shown at the top of Figure 11-5, you now have an iSCSI Software Adapter with its own IQN. The lower half of Figure 11-5 shows how you can edit the Software Adapter to change the IQN or add CHAP authentication.

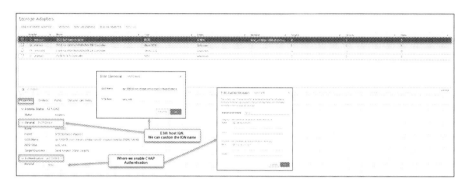

Figure 11-5. *(Install iSCSI Datastore 5 of 25)*

11.3 Create an iSCSI VMkernel

As previously discussed, since we do not have physical HBA cards for iSCSI (that would be a destination Initiator), we need to create an iSCSI software adapter and build our iSCSI network with that.

As shown in Figure 11-6, select your ESXi host, click the **Configure** tab, select **Virtual Switches**, and click **Add Networking**. In step 1 of the Add Networking wizard that opens, choose **VMware Network Adapter** and then click **Next**.

164

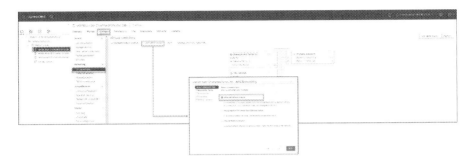

Figure 11-6. *(Install iSCSI Datastore 6 of 25)*

Next, as shown in Figure 11-7, select **New standard switch** and set
the Jumbo Frames *MTU (Bytes)* option to **9000** (only use MTU if all your
network devices and ports connected to this physical network interface are
set to MTU 9000). If you don't know, or it is not set to MTU 9000, leave the
default 1500. Click **Next**.

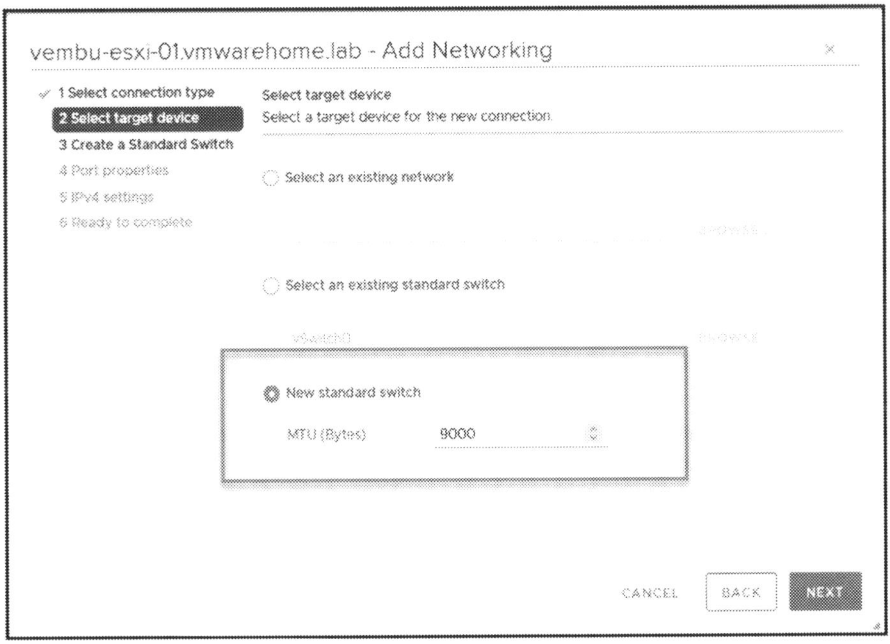

vembu-esxi-01.vmwarehome.lab - Add Networking   ×

✓ 1 Select connection type   Select target device
  2 Select target device   Select a target device for the new connection.
  3 Create a Standard Switch
  4 Port properties   ○ Select an existing network
  5 IPv4 settings
  6 Ready to complete

                                  ○ Select an existing standard switch

                                  ◉ New standard switch

                                     MTU (Bytes)   9000   ⌄

                                                    CANCEL   BACK   NEXT

Figure 11-7. *(Install iSCSI Datastore 7 of 25)*

165

Note   To allow an ESX host to send larger frames onto the physical network, the network must support jumbo frames end to end. An iSCSI network performs much better when using jumbo frames. Therefore, use jumbo frames if your iSCSI network has all software initiators and targets and the network switches can handle them.

Next, in step 3 of the wizard shown in Figure 11-8, click the + button to add the physical network cards (vmnics) to your new vSwitch.

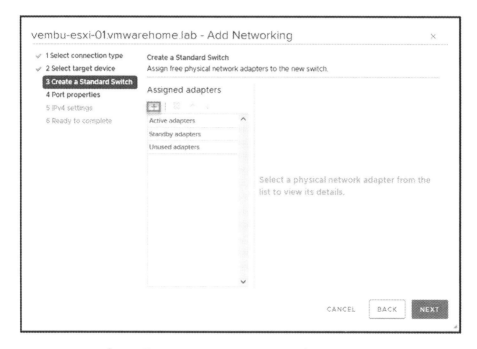

Figure 11-8. (*Install iSCSI Datastore 8 of 25*)

As discussed in previous chapters, if you have extra network cards, use them for Storage, in this case for iSCSI. And if you followed the initial chapters and created a nested ESXi environment, if you didn't initially add two new virtual networks to the nested ESXi VM.

For our test lab, as shown in the design (see Figure 11-3), we will use vmnic2 and vmnic3. Click **OK** to return to the wizard.

Note   Figure 11-9 shows that the vmnics broadcast the subnet 192.168.10.0/24. This is because I have created a VLAN 10 for the Storage network in my physical switch, and all ports of the physical Switch that are connect to the Storage are using the same VLAN/Subnet.

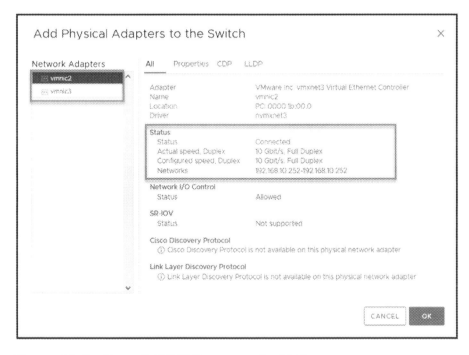

Figure 11-9. *(Install iSCSI Datastore 9 of 25)*

Click **Next** in step 3 to continue the configuration of the VMkernel and vSwitch. In step 4, shown in Figure 11-10, you can change the port group name (I always do this for better management and to recognize the different port groups). If you don't want to change it, leave the default. There's no need to change anything else in this step, so click **Next**.

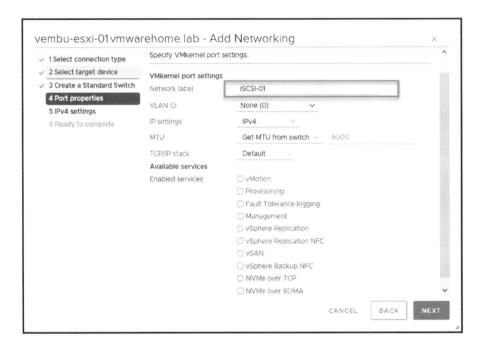

Figure 11-10. *(Install iSCSI Datastore 10 of 25)*

In step 5, shown in Figure 11-11, add an IP address for the iSCSI VMkernel. Don't forget that this subnet should be the same as your Storage IP Target, as shown in the first design (see Figure 11-2). Click **Next**.

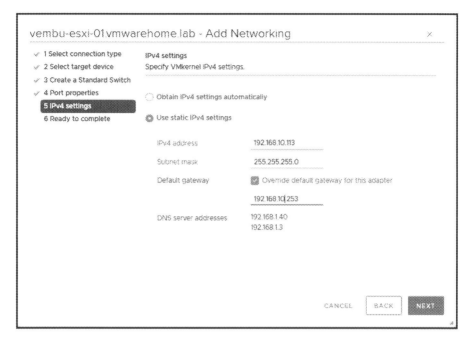

Figure 11-11. *(Install iSCSI Datastore 11 of 25)*

Note   iSCSI doesn't need a gateway and should never be routed. So leave the default gateway. Since we are routing Storage between networks, we have added a gateway in this example. But this is only for particular network configurations.

Next, in the final step of the wizard, shown in Figure 11-12, double-check the information and click **Finish**.

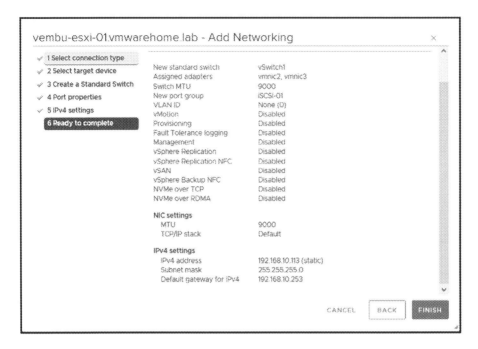

Figure 11-12. *(Install iSCSI Datastore 12 of 25)*

Figure 11-13 shows that we now have a new vSwitch called vSwitch1 and a port group called iSCSI-01. Figure 11-13 also shows a new VMkernel created with the IP address 192.168.10.113.

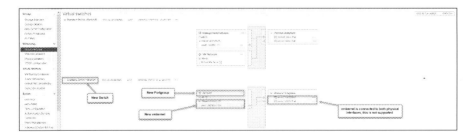

Figure 11-13. *(Install iSCSI Datastore 13 of 25)*

The first VMkernel was created, but the Teaming is wrong, so we need to fix it. By default, vSwitch will always set both vmnics to active. But this is not supported for iSCSI and port binding, so we need to change this after we create the VMkernel.

Let's set the configuration as active/passive (unused) so that we can create a port binding (if vmnics are both active, the configuration will not let you create a port binding).

On the port group named iSCSI-01, click the **...** icon and select **Edit Settings**, as shown in Figure 11-14. In the Edit Settings dialog box, select the **Teaming and failover** option, and set the *Load balancing* field to **Use explicit failover order** (meaning that in case of one vmnic fail, it will use the configured failover order).

Figure 11-14. *(Install iSCSI Datastore 15 of 25)*

Next, in the *Failover order* section of the Edit Settings dialog box, enable **Override** and move one of the vmnics to the *Unused adapters* list. For purposes of our test lab design, iSCSI-01, the NIC vmnic2 is in use and vmnic3 is not used for this port group, so move vmnic3 to the *Unused adapters* list. Click **OK** to exit the Edit Settings dialog box.

As you can see in Figure 11-15, the `iSCSI-01` VMkernel is now connected only to `vmnic2`. In the iSCSI Storage, there is only one path from `iSCSI-01`, and it is to `vmnic2`.

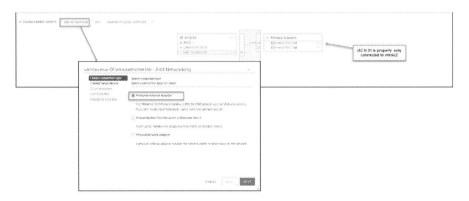

Figure 11-15. *(Install iSCSI Datastore 16 of 25)*

We now have our first iSCSI VMkernel created. But since the minimum is two, we need to create a second one. It's time to return to the Add Networking wizard. Click **Add Networking** in your `vSwitch1` and select the option **VMkernel Network Adapter**. Click **Next**.

The wizard procedure is the same as earlier, but this time we will not create a Standard Switch since it already exists. Instead, we will create a port group called `iSCSI-02` and a VMkernel in that port group.

In step 2 of the wizard, shown in Figure 11-16, choose **Select an existing standard switch**.

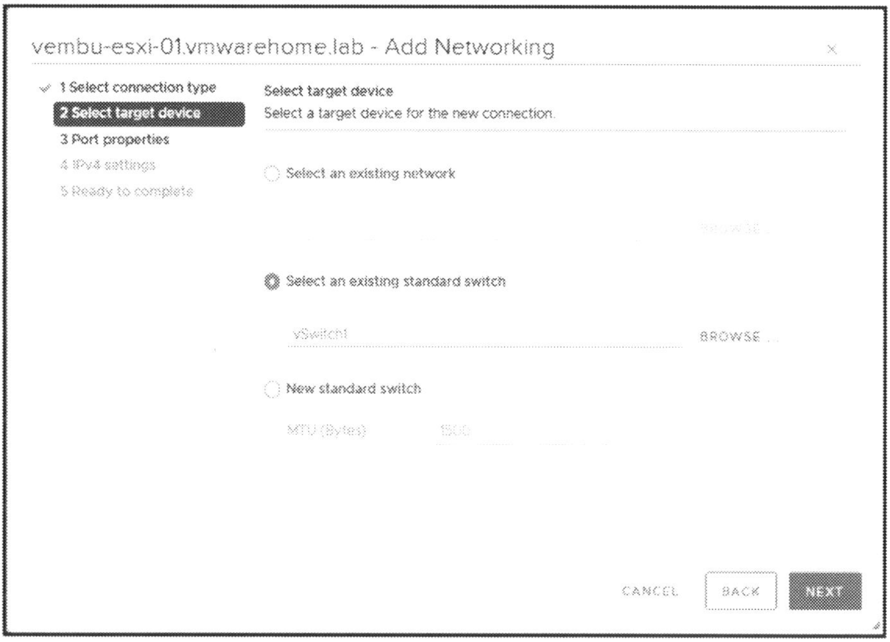

Figure 11-16. *(Install iSCSI Datastore 17 of 25)*

The rest of the options are the same as described earlier, so there is no need to display them again.

In step 3, *Port properties*, create a port group named (in this case) **iSCSI-02**) and click **Next**. In step 4, set an IP address for the VMkernel (in this case, **192.168.10.114**). Click **Next**, and then click **Finish** in step 5.

As shown in Figure 11-17, the test lab now has two port groups (iSCSI-01 and iSCSI-02) with a VMkernel in each one. The iSCSI-02 port group is connected to vmnic3 (don't forget to edit the iSCSI-02 port group to set vmnic2 as unused).

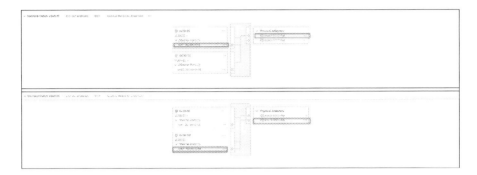

Figure 11-17. *(Install iSCSI Datastore 18 of 25)*

Since we are using a Standard Virtual Switch, we need to follow this process in all the ESXi hosts in the Cluster that are connected to our iSCSI Storage.

Note   If we were using vDS, it would set the configuration for all ESXi hosts (except creating the VMkernel, which we always need to create manually and set the IP addresses).

Figure 11-18 shows the final result for our iSCSI network in all ESXi hosts.

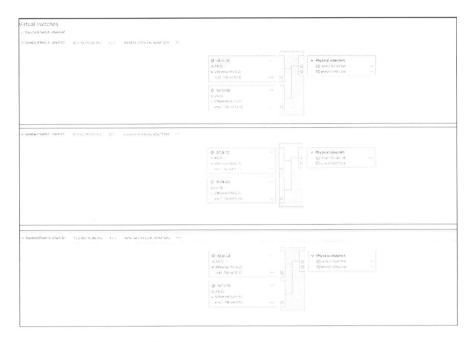

Figure 11-18. *(Install iSCSI Datastore 19 of 25)*

Having finished our iSCSI network and created all the VMkernels, it is time to go back to the iSCSI Software Adapter connect and bind the VMkernel adapters to create a Network port binding.

As shown in Figure 11-19, select the ESXi host, click the **Configure** tab, select **Storage Adapters**, select the **iSCSI Software Adapter**. In the iSCSI Software Adapter section, click the **Network Port Binding** tab, click **Add**, and then select the previously created VMkernel (in our case, vmk1 and vmk2). Click **OK**.

Figure 11-19. *(Install iSCSI Datastore 20 of 25)*

Note   As you can see in Figure 11-19, when you select just one
VMkernel, the Status indicates *Compliant.* It means that the port
group and VMkernel are correctly configured.

Now that we've created our network port binding, we must add our
Storage device to the iSCSI Software Adapter. As shown in Figure 11-20,
click **Dynamic Discovery** and add the IP address of your Storage device.
After you create network port binding and add your Storage device, click
Rescan Storage so that the ESXi host can connect to your Storage. Click
OK in the Rescan Storage dialog box to rescan.

Figure 11-20. *(Install iSCSI Datastore 21 of 25)*

After the rescan, and if all the configuration is correct, the ESXi host should now be connected to your Storage device.

Go to the **Paths** tab, shown in Figure 11-21, and you should see all the paths from your ESXi host to the Storage device. Since our test lab has two VMkernel, you should see two paths for each LUN, and you should see many LUNs and paths because we have several LUNS in the Storage.

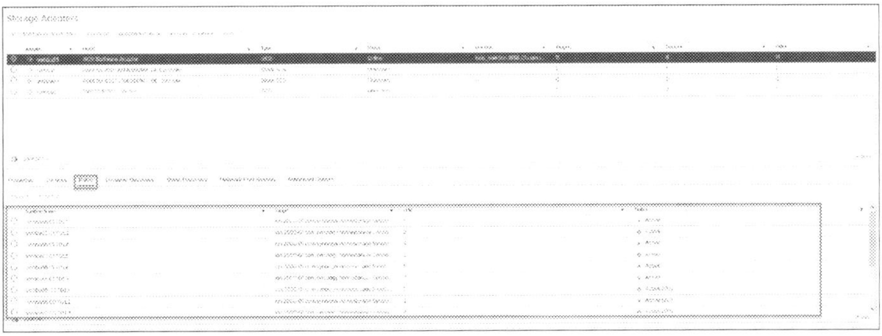

Figure 11-21. *(Install iSCSI Datastore 22 of 25)*

Figure 11-22. *(Install iSCSI Datastore 23 of 25)*

All the LUNs and Target are open (no CHAP), so any ESXi host connecting to the Storage will see all the LUNs. If we had added CHAP in our iSCSI Software adapter, you would only see the LUNS that has the same user and password CHAP on the source. Using CHAP is a way to control who can see what. Figure 11-21 is an example in which we configured that only these IPs can see these LUNs.

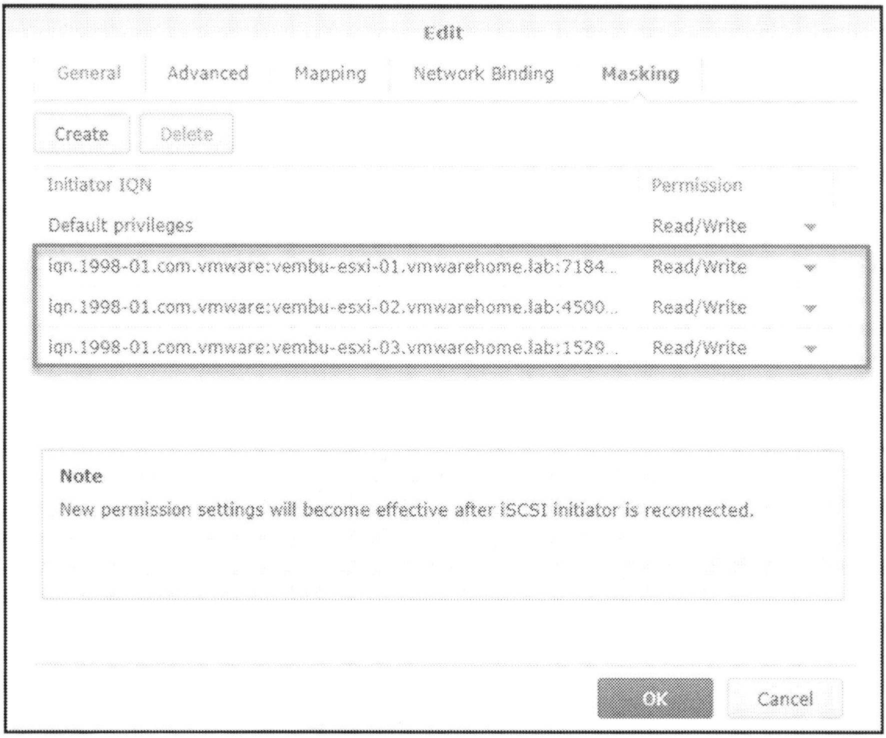

Figure 11-23. *(Install iSCSI Datastore 24 of 25)*

We can also restrict the connections to the LUNs from the Storage side by iSCSI Software Adapter IQN. By setting the IQN, only the added IQN can connect to this LUN. These settings are done in the Storage Target; for example, using our iSCSI Software Adapter IQNs. Check first each IQN in the iSCSI Software Adapter and then add to your Storage Target.

Adding IQN to the Storage Target. LUNs are masked only to these IQNs.

To finalize the iSCSI Datastores section, do not forget to enable the option **Allow multiple sessions** in the Storage Target, as shown in Figure 11-24. Since we have multiple paths, Storage needs to accept multiple sessions to the LUN. If this option is not enabled, you can corrupt the LUN, and only one ESXi host at a time can see the LUN (and consequently the Datastore).

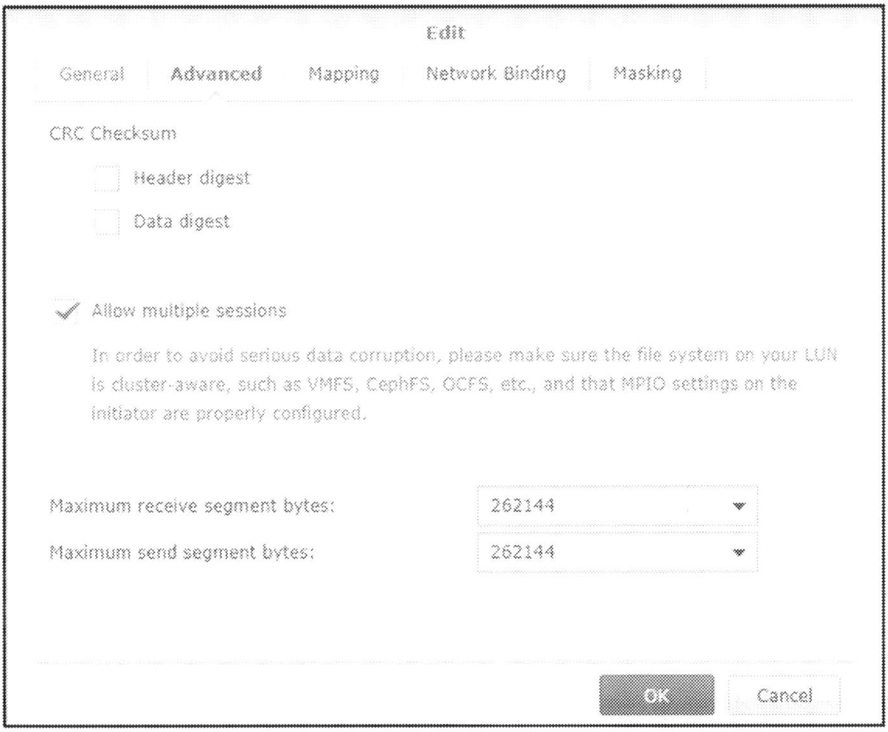

Figure 11-24. (*Install iSCSI Datastore 25 of 25*)

Since now we can see our Storage and all paths are green, we can create an iSCSI VMFS Datastore.

11.4 Configure NFS Datastores

I will provide an example from my Synology. The options differ for other NAS vendors, but the process is the same. Check your vendor manual to create an NFS on your NAS.

To create an NFS in your NAS Storage, you need to create a volume and then a shared folder bound to that volume.

Note   You could select a folder in your NAS and create a shared folder to share with your ESXi host. But to store virtual machines, this is not the best practice.

Create a volume from your free space in your NAS, or use an existing volume and create a shared folder with a quota. Figure 11-25 shows the Synology Shared Folder Creation Wizard that I used for this process.

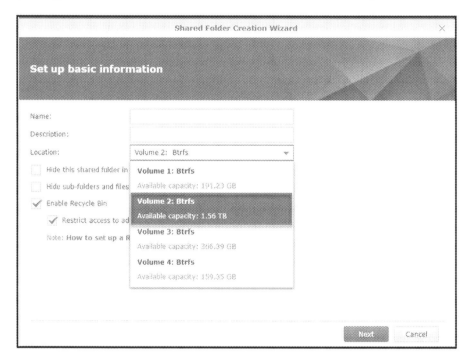

Figure 11-25.   *(Install NFS Datastore 1 of 14)*

Note   Since we already have a volume of 1.5TB, we don't need to create a volume.

After you have a volume (recently created or an existing one), create your shared folder. Figure 11-26 shows your NFS Share Folder to be create.

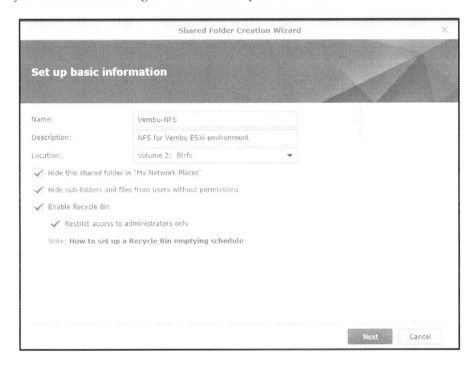

Figure 11-26. *(Install NFS Datastore 2 of 14)*

Since we are using a shared volume and it is used in other shared folders, we need to set a quota. If not, NFS could consume the full volume and have problems with the other shared folders. I set my quota in this NFS for 350GB, as shown in Figure 11-27.

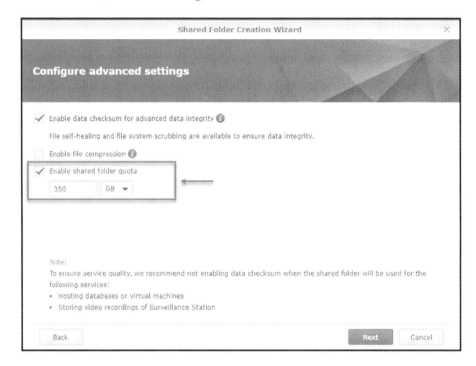

Figure 11-27. *(Install NFS Datastore 3 of 14)*

Provide the permissions and which ESXi hosts your NFS will or can connect to. Add the IP/CIDR of your ESXi host (NFS VMkernel created in the next section Create vSwitch and VMkernel for NFS).

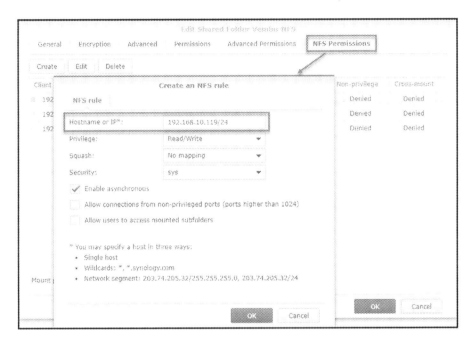

Figure 11-28. *(Install NFS Datastore 4 of 14)*

Then you have your ESXi hosts added and the mount path to use when adding the NFS shared folder in the ESXi hosts.

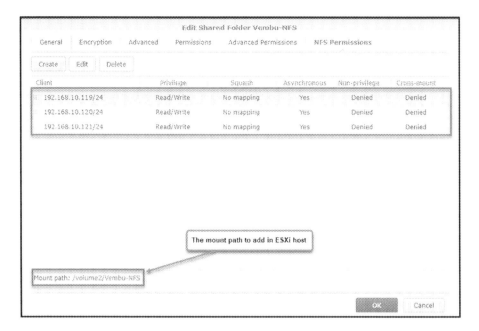

Figure 11-29. *(Install NFS Datastore 5 of 14)*

After this final step I have created a NFS Shared Folder in our NAS Storage.

Note   Again, the preceding example is just for Synology NAS. For other vendors, check your vendor manual.

11.5 Create vSwitch and VMkernel for NFS

We can apply different types of configuration networks to set our NFS network and add NFS Datastores.

The standard and simple one is when using a Single Target and setting one VMkernel path to your NAS shared folder. Figure 11-30 shows an example of how the network is set when using a Single Target using a NIC Teaming IP hash in our Storage Virtual Switch.

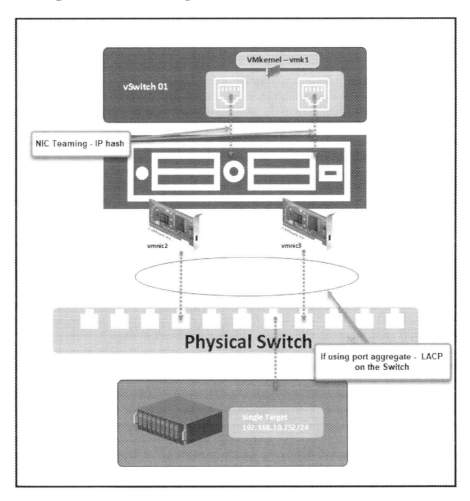

Figure 11-30. *(Install NFS Datastore 6 of 14)*

This won't do much to balance the load between NICs, but it will allow you to connect a new NIC when one of your old ones is down.

Note   The NIC Teaming failback option should be set to **No**. The reason for this is that if there are any intermittent issues on the network, you want to be able to replace the downed NIC before your network starts failing.

If you set the Link Aggregation Control Protocol (LACP) on your physical switch and a NIC Teaming IP hash, you provide load balance between vmnics (since NFS v3 doesn't support multipath, you can have these performance improvements only if you use NFS v4.1).

Note   We will implement this option in our Vembu VMware lab (without LACP).

In the next example, Multi-Target, the performance balance is distributed between vmnics and connections in your NAS Storage. As shown in Figure 11-31, one VMkernel will be connected to one Target (where you have some shared folders), and the other VMkernel will be connected to another shared folder (this must also be set in your NAS Storage).

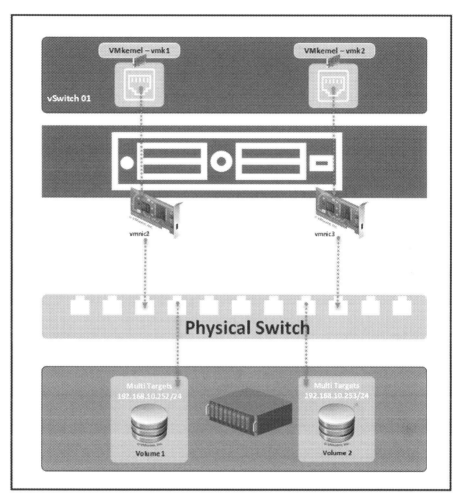

Figure 11-31. *(Install NFS Datastore 7 of 14)*

You can find more detailed information about network configurations and other NFS advanced options at `https://core.vmware.com/resource/best-practices-running-nfs-vmware-vsphere/`.

When using a Multi-Target configuration, you can use two or more VMkernels—it all depends on the number of Storage IP addresses you have.

11.6 Create an NFS VMkernel

Unlike the iSCSI network, creating the NFS networking in an ESXi host is much easier and requires fewer steps.

For the NFS VMkernel, we need to create one NFS VMkernel in the same subnet that has the NFS Storage network, and that is it. We will need two VMkernel (or more) if we use a multi-target network configuration, one for each subnet or VLAN. The process is similar to that already discussed for the iSCSI VMkernel.

As shown in Figure 11-32, select **Virtual switches**, select the ESXi host on which to create the VMkernel, and click **Add Networking**. In step 1 of the Add Networking wizard, select **VMkernel Network Adapter** and click **Next**.

Figure 11-32. *(Install NFS Datastore 8 of 14)*

Next, in the iSCSI, we select to create a new Standard Switch, but since we have already created one for iSCSI, we will use the same Virtual Switch (vSwitch1) to create our NFS VMkernel.

Note   If you only have NFS and it is the first VMkernel you create, follow the steps to create a new Standard Switch shown in the previous section How to create iSCSI VMkernel.

In step 2 (see Figure 11-33), choose **Select an existing standard switch**, click **Browse**, and choose the vSwitch you will use (which is **vSwitch1** for the test lab).

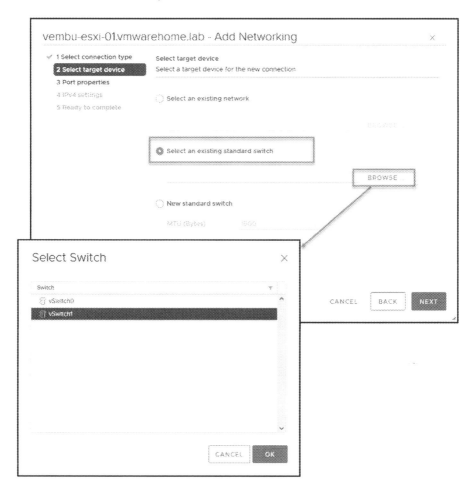

Figure 11-33. *(Install NFS Datastore 9 of 14)*

Next, in step 3 (see Figure 11-34), add all the information needed to create the VMkernel, including the name and VLAN (if using), and set the MTU to **9000** (if using on a new vSwitch; if using an existing vSwitch, it will use the MTU already set in the vSwitch). Click **Next**.

189

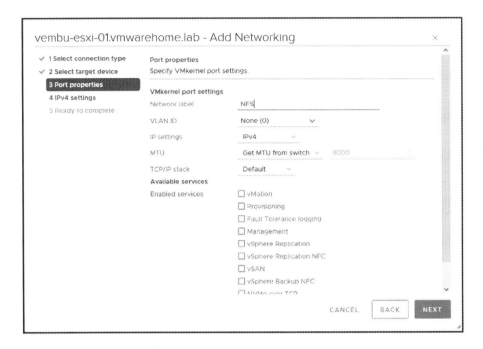

Figure 11-34. *(Install NFS Datastore 10 of 14)*

The next step is to add your IP, subnet mask, and so forth, as shown in Figure 11-35. Click **Next** when you are finished.

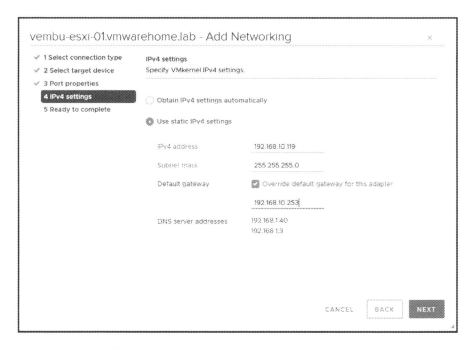

Figure 11-35. *(Install NFS Datastore 11 of 14)*

Note   Unless you have special routing, there is no need to change the gateway. As we did in the iSCSI VMkernel configuration, we have a particular gateway for Storage. But do not change the default if you don't have any special routing.

In the final wizard step, shown in Figure 11-36, double-check the information and finish creating the NFS VMkernel by clicking **Finish**.

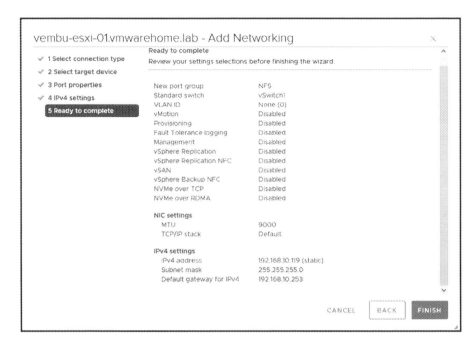

Figure 11-36. *(Install NFS Datastore 12 of 14)*

Figure 11-37 shows that now we have a new NFS VMkernel in our vSwitch1 and that both vmnics are connected to the VMkernel. Unlike with iSCSI, we can use both vmnics to connect to our NFS NAS, using a single target.

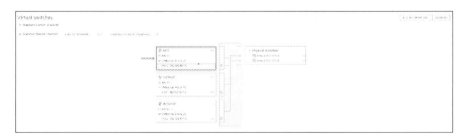

Figure 11-37. *(Install NFS Datastore 13 of 14)*

But, as a best practice, we should change the NIC Teaming to have a better balance and high availability in case one vmnic is not working. So change the *Load balancing* to "Route base on IP hash" and *Fallback* to "NO" as shown in Figure 11-38. There is little balance in the load between NICs if you are not using LACP (we are not using it here).

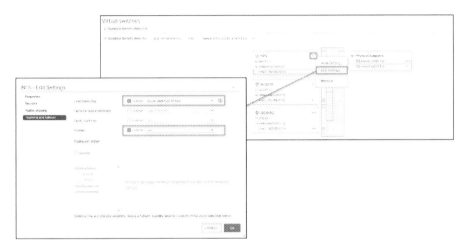

Figure 11-38. *(Install NFS Datastore 14 of 14)*

Note   Chapter 16 discusses LACP and shows examples.

So, now we have an NFS VMkernel network, and it is possible to connect our ESXi host to our NFS NAS and mount a shared folder to create a Datastore.

Do not forget to use the NFS Datastores in all the ESXi hosts. You need to do this in each ESXi host.

Note   If you are using NFS and iSCSI in your environment connected to the same SAN/NAS, as a best practice, run iSCSI and NFS in different subnets or VLANs.

In this case, we are using the same subnet because if a test environment, but in a production environment, you should follow the Best Practices and separate the traffic from iSCSI and NFS.

Note   Sometimes, you may have issues using IP Hash when not using LACP (you may notice some dropped packages). In that case, you should change the *Load balancing* option to **Use explicit failover order**.

11.7 Create VFMS Datastores (iSCSI)

You can either create VFMS Datastores at the ESXi host level or create it at the Cluster level to automatically set it in all ESXi hosts.

For purposes of the test lab, I will demonstrate how to create a VFMS Datastore in the Cluster. As shown in Figure 11-39, right-click the name of the Cluster, select **Storage** in the context menu, and click **New Datastore** (you already learned this in Chapter 6, but at the ESXi host level).

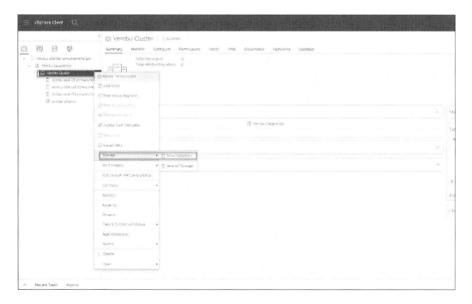

Figure 11-39. *(Create Datastore 1 of 9)*

In step 1 of the New Datastore wizard, shown in Figure 11-40, select
VMFS and click **Next**.

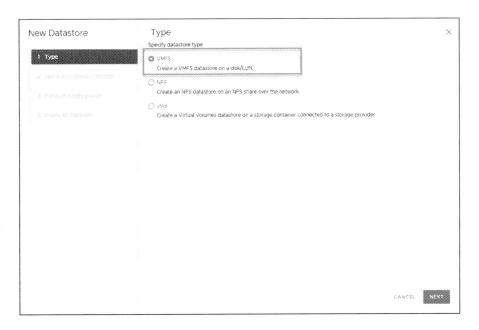

Figure 11-40. *(Create Datastore 2 of 9)*

In step 2 of the wizard, add a name for the Datastore (in this case,
iSCSI-01). Since we are setting this at the Cluster level, select one host first
from the *Select a host* drop-down list, as shown in Figure 11-41, and then
select two new LUNs of 250GB from my Synology. Click **Next**.

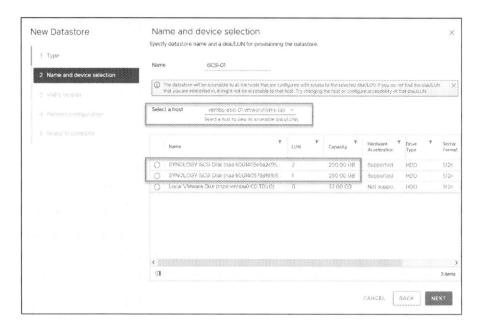

Figure 11-41. *(Create Datastore 3 of 9)*

Added a name for the Datastore (iSCSI-01), then selected one LUN and clicked **Next**.

In step 3 of the wizard, shown in Figure 11-42, select **VMFS 6** and click **Next**. You should always select the newest version. These days, VMFS 5 is used only for particular cases.

Figure 11-42. *(Create Datastore 4 of 9)*

Note   VMFS 5 is not upgradeable. If you select VMFS 5 and want
to upgrade to VMFS 6, you need to create a new VMFS 6 Datastore,
move all VMs to the new Datastore, and then delete the VMFS 5
Datastore.

In step 4 (see Figure 11-43), unless you want to use only a part of the size of this LUN and want to change the block size, leave all the default settings and click **Next** to continue.

Figure 11-43. *(Create Datastore 5 of 9)*

In the last wizard step (see Figure 11-44), double-check all the information and then click **Finish**.

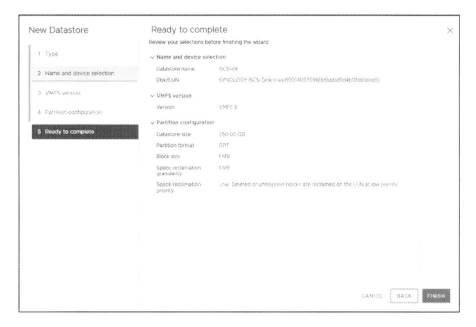

Figure 11-44. *(Create Datastore 6 of 9)*

As Figure 11-45 shows, we now have a new Datastore called iSCSI-01.

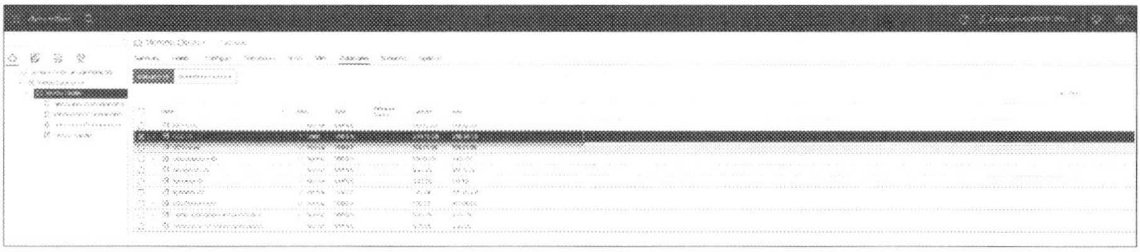

Figure 11-45. *(Create Datastore 7 of 9)*

If you click the Datastore and go to **Hosts** tab, you can see now which ESXi hosts are connected to this Datastore, as shown in Figure 11-46.

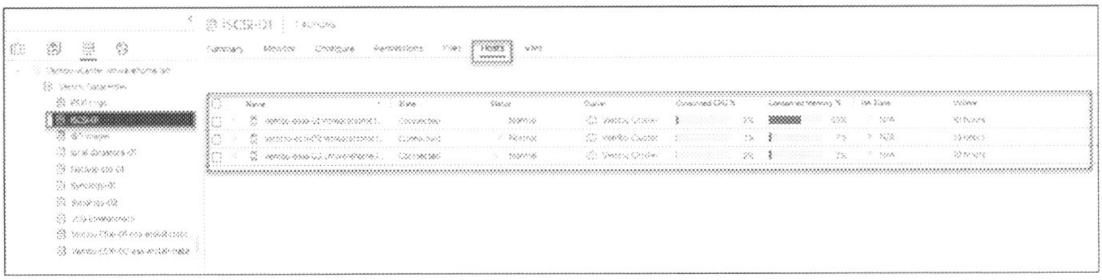

Figure 11-46. *(Create Datastore 8 of 9)*

If you make any changes on the Storage side (like resizing the Datastore, changing CHAP, adding IPs to the Target, etc.), you always need to rescan the Storage Adapter on the ESXi hosts. See Figure 11-47 for the steps to launch the rescan.

Figure 11-47. *(Create Datastore 9 of 9)*

Our iSCSI VMFS Datastore is created and available in all ESX hosts.

11.8 Create NFS Datastores

As explained in a previous chapter, we can use a Single Target or Multi-Target configuration, using one or more vmnics to the same Target. Here is where it is essential to select which NFS version to use. Since here we are only talking about Multipath, that only v4.1 supports, the rest of the features are not relevant for this section.

There are also some restrictions on NFS Datastore features when using NFSv4.1. Double-check if you plan to use any of those features before selecting v3 or v4.1.

Figure 11-48 provides a comparison of which vSphere features are supported and not supported when using NFSv3 or NFSv4.1, with the differences highlighted (Storage DRS is one example).

The following table lists major vSphere solutions that NFS versions support.

vSphere Features	NFS version 3	NFS version 4.1
vMotion and Storage vMotion	Yes	Yes
High Availability (HA)	Yes	Yes
Fault Tolerance (FT)	Yes	Yes
Distributed Resource Scheduler (DRS)	Yes	Yes
Host Profiles	Yes	Yes
Storage DRS	Yes	No
Storage I/O Control	Yes	No
Site Recovery Manager	Yes	No
Virtual Volumes	Yes	Yes
vSphere Replication	Yes	Yes
vRealize Operations Manager	Yes	Yes

Figure 11-48. *(Create NFS Datastores 1 of 8)*

Now that you know which vSphere features you can use with each NFS version, we can create our NFS Datastore.

Since we will mount this NFS Datastore to all ESXi hosts in a Cluster, we can mount the NFS using the Cluster option (and not by ESXi host).

As shown in Figure 11-49, right-click the Cluster name, select **Storage**, click **New Datastore**, and select **NFS**. Click **Next**.

Figure 11-49. *(Create NFS Datastores 2 of 8)*

In the case of our test lab, since we will not need to use any of the features that are not supported by NFSv4.1, select the **NFS 4.1** option in step 2, as shown in Figure 11-50. Click **Next**.

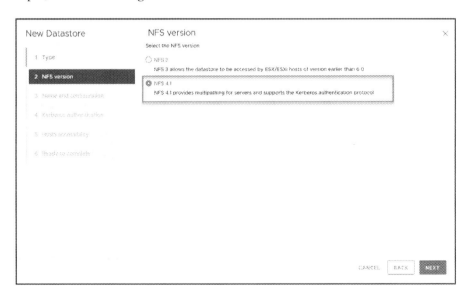

Figure 11-50. *(Create NFS Datastores 3 of 8)*

In step 3 of the wizard, shown in Figure 11-51, add the information about your NFS share. First, give the Datastore a name, add the folder (shown for my Synology NFS in the figure), and then add your NAS server. If you have more than one IP address (Multi-Target option for Multipath), you can click **Add** to add one by one all the the NAS IP Addresses and then click Next.

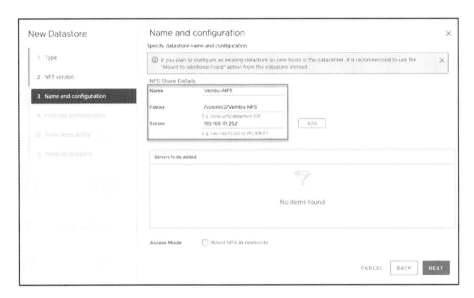

Figure 11-51. *(Create NFS Datastores 4 of 8)*

Step 4 is the Kerberos authentication option (see Figure 11-52). You can set it here if your NAS uses NFS shares with Active Directory users. Since we are not using Kerberos, leave the default **Don't use Kerberos authentication** and click **Next**.

Figure 11-52. *(Create NFS Datastores 5 of 8)*

Note   Kerberos is another feature that is used only in NFSv4.1.

In step 5, shown in Figure 11-53, set on which ESXi hosts to mount this NFS share. For the test lab, select to use all of them. Click **Next**.

205

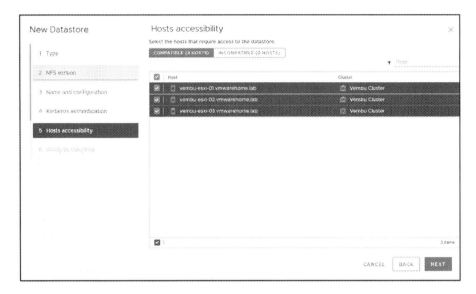

Figure 11-53. *(Create NFS Datastores 6 of 8)*

Before finalizing the Datastore creation, double-check the information (see Figure 11-54). If all is good, click **Finish**.

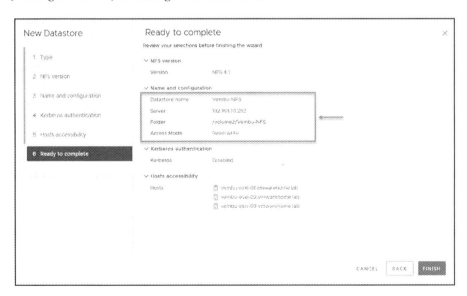

Figure 11-54. *(Create NFS Datastores 7 of 8)*

And now we have our NFS Datastore created, as shown in Figure 11-55.

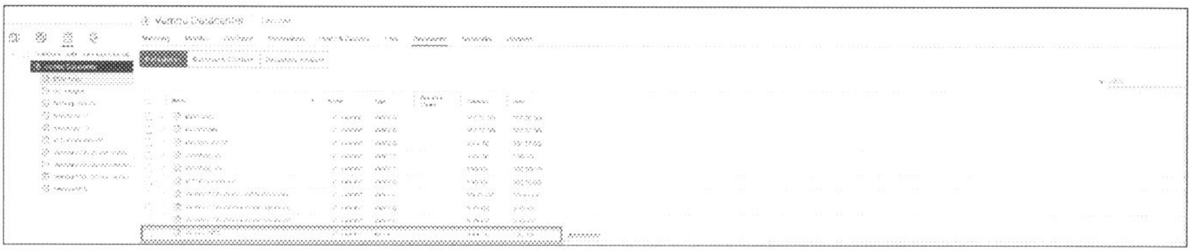

Figure 11-55. *(Create NFS Datastores 8 of 8)*

11.9 Summary

In this chapter we explored setting up types of datastores in vCenter, including iSCSI, NFS, and VMFS.

In Chapter 12, we shift our focus to the crucial aspects of effectively managing datastores. We will dive into tasks such as deleting and resizing VMFS datastores and troubleshooting NFS issues. Mastering these skills is essential for ensuring the health, performance, and adaptability of your data storage solutions.

CHAPTER 12

Managing Datastores

When dealing with virtual environments, managing datastores is important. This section takes a dive into the management techniques for VMFS datastores, which are vital foundations in VMware environments. We start by discussing the process of deleting a VMFS. While it may seem straightforward, it requires attention to avoid any data loss and to maintain system integrity.

Then we explore the intricacies of resizing a VMFS. As storage requirements change over time, having the ability to resize datastores efficiently without disrupting operations is crucial for maintaining a responsive infrastructure.

Furthermore, we address the challenging task of troubleshooting NFS issues. Given the complexity of network storage, being able to resolve NFS problems is an necessary skill in ensuring operation within your virtual environment. Through examples and step-by-step guidance, this chapter aims to provide you with the tools and knowledge to effectively manage and troubleshoot your datastores while ensuring they continue supporting your virtual infrastructure seamlessly.

12.1 Delete a VMFS Datastore

Before trying to delete the VMFS, check the prerequisites:

- Remove or migrate all virtual machines from the datastore.

L. Patrão, *VMware vSphere Essentials*, https://doi.org/10.1007/979-8-8688-0208-9_12

- Disable Storage DRS for the datastore.

- Disable Storage I/O Control for the datastore.

Make sure that the datastore is not used for vSphere HA heartbeating.

First, unmount the VMFS Datastore from all hosts. As shown in Figure 12-1, right-click the Datastore, select **Unmount Database**, and select the ESXi hosts you want to unmount (since it is to delete, select all of them). Click **OK**.

Figure 12-1. *(Managing Datastores 1 of 7)*

Note   The unmount task may take some seconds to finish.

The Datastore now is labeled *inaccessible*, and you can launch the delete by right-clicking the Datastore, choosing **Delete Datastore**, and confirming the deletion by clicking **Yes**, as shown in Figure 12-2.

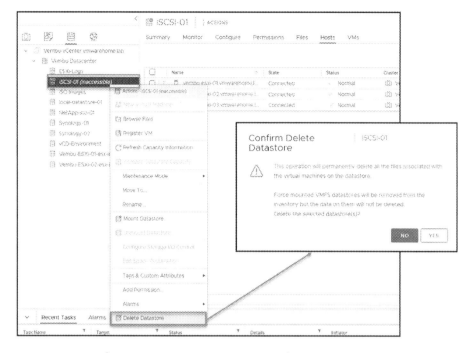

Figure 12-2. *(Managing Datastores 2 of 7)*

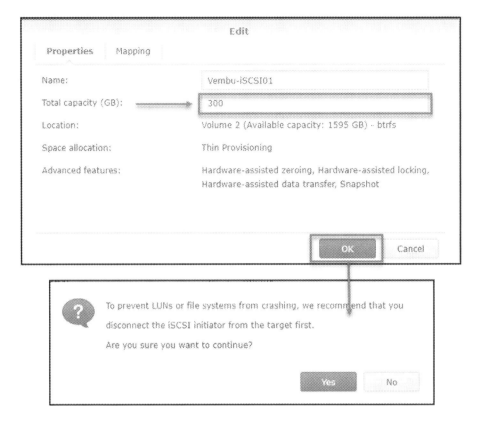

Figure 12-3. *(Managing Datastores 3 of 7)*

After this, the Datastore is deleted from vCenter and all ESXi hosts.

12.2 Resize a VMFS Datastore

The first step to resize a VMFS Datastore is to expand the LUN size in the Storage device. Always stop any VM running on this Datastore, and disconnect the iSCSI Initiator first for safety. On the Storage device, you can disable the Target temporarily while making these changes.

After the resizing is finished on the Storage size, go back to vCenter, click **Rescan Storage** and then **OK** to perform a storage rescan (described in Chapter 11 and shown in Figure 11-21), and then select the Datastore. Right-click the Datastore and select **Increase Datastore Capacity**.

Note   If you disable the Storage Target, enable it again before rescanning.

As you can see in Figure 12-4, our LUN 1 already has 300GB size. Select the Datastore and click **Next**.

Figure 12-4. *(Managing Datastores 4 of 7)*

Next, use the *Increase Size by* option (see Figure 12-5) to choose by how much you want to increase the size of the Datastore. By default, vCenter selects the full size. Then click **Next**.

Figure 12-5. *(Managing Datastores 5 of 7)*

In the last wizard step, shown in Figure 12-6, double-check the information and then click **Finish**.

Figure 12-6. *(Managing Datastores 6 of 7)*

The iSCSI-01 Datastore is now resized to 300GB, as shown in Figure 12-7.

Figure 12-7. *(Managing Datastores 7 of 7)*

Note   You may need to click the **Refresh** button to see the new size.

12.3 NFS Troubleshooting

After you configure your NFS vSphere networking (vSwitch, vmkernel, etc.), if you experience any issues mounting the NFS share, you can troubleshoot the network if it can reach the NAS Storage.

Log in to the ESXi host SSH console and ping using the vmkping command. Using vmkping, you can ping using the VMkernel you created as the source for the ping.

First, see what is the VMkernel vmk and IP by using the command esxcfg-vmknic -l. As shown in Figure 12-8, the NFS that we created before is the vmk3 with the IP address 192.168.10.119.

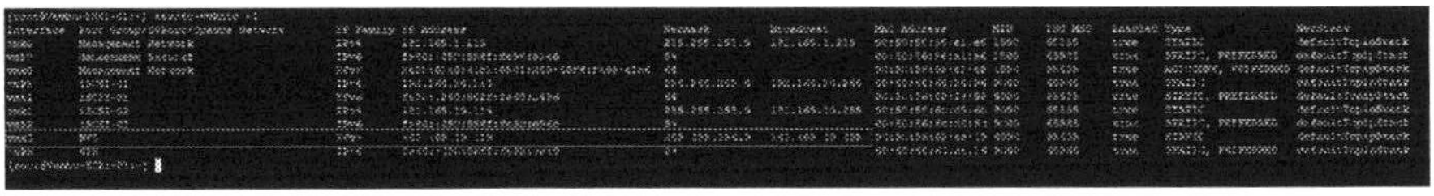

Figure 12-8. *(NFS Troubleshooting 1 of 6)*

Now ping the NAS Storage IP using vmkdping, as shown in Figure 12-9.

Figure 12-9. *(NFS Troubleshooting 2 of 6)*

Next, check whether the VMkernel and vSwitch are properly configured with MTU 9000 to use jumbo frames. Use this command, the output of which is shown in Figure 12-10:

```
vmkping -4 -c 6 -d -s 8972 -v 192.168.10.252 -I vmk3
```

Figure 12-10. *(NFS Troubleshooting 3 of 6)*

Figure 12-11 explains all the parameters in this vmkping command.

Figure 12-11. *(NFS Troubleshooting 4 of 6)*

If you can't mount the NFS share and receive the error *The NFS server denied the mount request* in your vCenter Tasks window, as shown in Figure 12-12, most of the time this error is regarding permissions on the NAS Storage side. Storage recognizes that the NFS share exists, but it is not allowed to mount it on this server.

Figure 12-12. *(NFS Troubleshooting 5 of 6)*

In this case, you can check the ESXi host vmkernel.log file for additional information about this or other errors. The log is located in the ESXi hosts in /var/log. Use the command grep Vembu-NFS-02 vmkernel.log.

We don't have much information for this example since the ESXi host cannot check NAS Storage permissions. Start by checking which IPs permissions are set in your NAS NFS shared folder.

Figure 12-13 shows an example. In this case, we don't have any ESXi host VMkernel IP added to the permissions section, so this ESXi host cannot connect to this NFS shared folder.

Figure 12-13. *(NFS Troubleshooting 6 of 6)*

So, we need to add the VMkernel IP address or add a subnet wildcard like 192.168.10.0/24. After adding the IP address, the issue was fixed in the previous example.

Suppose you receive a timeout error like this:

Mount failed: Unable to complete Sysinfo operation. Please see the VMkernel log file for more details.: Timeout

Then it is not possible to connect to the NAS Storage. Check the IP address you added for the server (if that is the correct Target NAS Storage IP) or check if the VMkernel is adequately configured and test the network (as previously shown using the `vmkping` command).

12.4 Summary

In this chapter we explored the management of datastores, in our environment, which is essential for overseeing and enhancing infrastructure. We kick off by discussing the steps involved in removing a VMFS datastore highlighting the significance of planning to avoid any loss of data. Following that we delve into the intricacies of adjusting the size of a VMFS datastore, an ability as storage requirements change, with a focus, on minimizing disruptions to operations.

Further, the chapter addresses troubleshooting NFS issues, a common challenge given the intricacies of network storage. Through detailed examples and guidance, you're equipped to tackle NFS-related problems, enhancing your ability to maintain seamless operation in your virtual environment.

Key actions such as ensuring all virtual machines are migrated or removed from the datastore before deletion, understanding how to safely expand datastore capacity, and effectively troubleshooting NFS configurations are covered. These steps are critical for managing storage resources efficiently and ensuring your datastores continue to support the virtual infrastructure effectively.

CHAPTER 13

vSphere Storage Policies and Encryption

Storage policies and encryption are components in maintaining performance and strong security for virtual machines (VMs). In this chapter we will explore vSphere Storage Policies, which can be customized to meet I/O requirements and improve VM performance. We will also delve into the importance of storage encryption, a feature that ensures data integrity and confidentiality in today's security environment.

Understanding and effectively implementing these policies and encryption techniques is vital. They not only establish a foundation for efficient storage management but also serve as the backbone of a secure and resilient virtual infrastructure. This chapter will guide you through the process of optimizing your storage environment, from creating Storage I/O Controls to configuring VM storage policies for host-based data services. Additionally, we will cover the application of these policies to VMs. To round out the chapter, we'll examine how to set up encryption key providers, providing a comprehensive understanding of both the practical aspects and security considerations in vSphere storage management.

© Luciano Patrão 2024
L. Patrão, *VMware vSphere Essentials*, https://doi.org/10.1007/979-8-8688-0208-9_13

A VM storage policy in VMware vSphere is a collection of rules that define the storage requirements for a VM. These rules can be used to control the following:

- The type of storage that is provided for the VM, such as block, NFS, vSAN, or vVols.

- How the VM is placed within the storage, such as on a specific datastore or RAID group.

- Which data services are offered for the VM, such as deduplication, compression, encryption, or replication.

VM storage policies can be used to improve the performance, availability, and security of your VMs. For example, you can create a policy that specifies that all VMs storing sensitive data must be placed on a datastore protected by replication. This will help to ensure that your data is protected in the event of a disaster.

13.1 Understanding vSphere Storage Policies

A set of regulations known as vSphere Storage Policies specify how VMs can store data. These policies may be used to guarantee that virtual machines are installed on datastores that satisfy their unique storage needs.

Storage policies can be used to define the following:

- **The type of storage on which VMs should be located:** You may, for instance, devise a policy that stipulates that VMs must be stored on a datastore that employs a certain storage protocol, such as iSCSI or Fibre Channel. In this case, the policy would specify the protocol.

The operational qualities of the storage medium that VMs should be located on: For instance, you may draft a policy that dictates VMs must be stored on a datastore that meets a certain threshold for the number of input/output operations per second (IOPS) or throughput. For example, you may have large application VMs with large databases that require a certain datastore because they have a lot of IOPS and you are looking for improved performance.

- **The accessibility of the storage medium in which VMs should be installed:** For instance, you may develop a policy that dictates that VMs must be stored on a datastore that replicates its data or is configured for high availability (HA).

Before we create our VM Storage Policy, we will create two Storage Policies, one for encryption and one for Storge I/O Control. This will enable you to understand how Storage Policies work and how they can be used in your VM Storage Policy.

13.2 Storage Policy - Storage I/O

Storage I/O Control (SPBM-SIOC) is a feature in VMware vSphere that allows you to control the I/O performance of your VMs. SIOC works by monitoring the I/O latency of datastores and throttling the I/O of VMs causing the latency. This can help to improve the performance of all VMs on the datastore by preventing a few VMs from hogging all the resources.

SIOC works by allocating shares and limits to VMs. *Shares* are a relative measure of importance, while *limits* are a hard cap on the amount of I/O a VM can consume. When SIOC detects that a datastore is experiencing I/O latency, it throttles the I/O of VMs with a lower share than the VMs that are causing the latency. This ensures that the VMs causing the latency do not get all the resources and that the other VMs on the datastore can still perform well.

SIOC can be configured on a per-datastore basis. You can specify the following settings for each datastore:

- **I/O throttling threshold:** The I/O latency threshold that SIOC will use to throttle I/O.

- **I/O throttling ratio:** The ratio by which SIOC will throttle I/O. For example, if the I/O throttling threshold is 50ms and the I/O throttling ratio is 2, then SIOC will throttle the I/O of VMs causing latency by 200%.

- **I/O throttling delay:** The delay before SIOC starts throttling I/O. This is useful to prevent SIOC from throttling I/O for transient spikes in latency.

SIOC can be a valuable tool for improving the performance of your VMs. However, it is vital to use it carefully. If you throttle the I/O of VMs too much, you may impact the performance of the VMs. You should also consider the I/O requirements of your VMs when configuring SIOC. For example, if you have a VM running a database, you may want to give it a higher share than a VM running a web server.

13.3 Create a Storage I/O Control

In your vCenter, select the main menu, select **Policies and Profiles**, select **Storage Policy Components**, and click **Create**, as shown in Figure 13-1. In the *Name* field of the New Storage Policy Component dialog box, name your Storage Policy. For purposes of the test lab, use the name **vSphere Essentials - Storage Policy SIOC**. Then, in the *Category* drop-down list, select **Storage I/O Control**. As you can see in Figure 13-1, the other option is to create an Encryption Storage Policy, discussed in the next section.

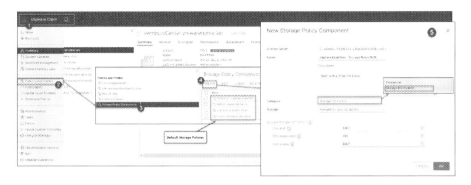

Figure 13-1. *(vSphere Storage Policies 1 of 14)*

In the VMware Storage I/O Control section, set the *IOPS shares* field to **2000**. This indicates that the datastore that we'll use for this Storage Policy will have reserved shares and won't be used in conjunction with any other datastores.

We also have an IOPS cap. The maximum IOPS for every VM kept in this datastore is 3000, so set the *IOPS limit* field to **3000**. With this cap, we ensure that the VMs kept in this datastore won't consume all of the storage's IOPS.

Caution   Use extreme caution when setting the *IOPS limit* option. Be sure the number corresponds to the kind of virtual machines you are keeping in this datastore.

Take into account that the I/O size for *IOPS limit* is normalized to 32KB. This means that if you set *IOPS limit* to 10,000 and the typical I/O size from the VM was 64KB, then you could do only 5000 IOPS. If your block size is 4KB/8KB/16KB or 32KB, you would be able to achieve the 10,000 IOPS limit.

Figure 13-2 shows that you have some default Storage Policies for SIOC, with High, Low, and Normal IOPS. You can use the default SIOC in your VM Storage Policy if it fits your needs.

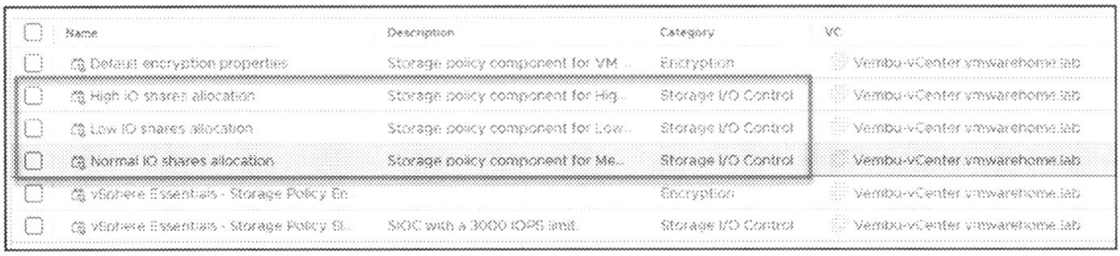

Figure 13-2. *(vSphere Storage Policies 2 of 14)*

13.4 Storage Policy - Encryption

Storage Policy - Encryption (SPBM-Encryption) is a feature in VMware vSphere that allows you to encrypt the data on your VMs. Encryption can help to protect your data from unauthorized access.

SPBM-Encryption encrypts the data on the VM's disks before it is written to the datastore. vCenter Server or a third-party key manager manages the encryption key. When the VM boots, it decrypts the data on its disks and uses it as usual.

SPBM-Encryption can be configured on a per-VM basis. You can specify the following settings for each VM:

- **Encryption algorithm:** The encryption algorithm that will be used to encrypt the data

- **Key provider:** The key provider that will be used to manage the encryption keys

- **Key rotation:** Whether or not the encryption keys will be rotated on a regular basis

- **Key management:** Whether you will manage the encryption keys yourself or have vCenter Server manage them for you

226

SPBM encryption can be a valuable tool for protecting your data from unauthorized access. However, using it carefully is essential. If you encrypt the data on your VMs, you cannot access the data without the encryption key. It would be best to consider the performance impact of encryption before enabling it for your VMs.

13.5 Create a Storage Policy - Encryption

Creating a custom Storage Policy Encryption is the same process as shown previously in Figure 13-1, but in the final step you select the *Category* setting **Encryption** instead of Storage I/O Control. You then see the option *Allow I/O filters before encryption*, as shown in Figure 13-3. This option in a VM storage policy in vSphere determines whether I/O filters can be applied to the VM before the data is encrypted. This can improve the performance of the VM, but it can also reduce the security of the data.

Figure 13-3. *(vSphere Storage Policies 3 of 14)*

I/O filters are software components that can be used to modify the data that is being transferred between a VM and its datastore. For example, I/O filters can be used to deduplicate, compress, or encrypt data.

When the *Allow I/O filters before the encryption* option is enabled (set to True), I/O filters will be applied to the VM before the data is encrypted.

This can improve the performance of the VM because the I/O filters will not have to process encrypted data. However, it can also reduce the security of the data because the I/O filters will be able to access the data in clear text before it is encrypted.

Whether or not to enable the *Allow I/O filters before the encryption* option depends on your specific requirements. If you are concerned about the performance of your VMs, you may want to enable this option. However, if you are concerned about the security of your data, you may want to disable this option. In our test lab configuration, will not allow I/O filters before the encryption, so make sure this option is set to **False**.

13.6 VM Storage Policy for Host-Based Data Services

Host-based services options in VMware vSphere allow you to enable and configure the ESXi host's data services. These services can improve the performance, availability, and security of your VMs. This is the default policy for your VM Storage Encryption, but you can create a custom policy.

The Create VM Storage Policy wizard in the vSphere Client enables you to define VM storage policy. This wizard creates data service rules for ESXi hosts. These VM storage policy rules activate virtual machine data services.

Caching, I/O control, and encryption are data services. VMware offers data encryption. Host-installed third-party I/O filters provide other services. Data services are general and independent of datastores. Datastore-specific storage policy rules are optional.

If your policy includes rules specific to datastores, it can enforce encryption through both the host and storage I/O filters, resulting in the virtual machine data being encrypted twice by the I/O filter and the storage system. vSphere Virtual Volumes (vVols) and I/O filter replication cannot coexist in a storage policy.

Once you have enabled host-based services for a VM, the services will be available to the VM when it is powered on. The services will be used to improve the performance, availability, and security of the VM.

It is important to note that not all host-based services are supported on all ESXi hosts. You should check the compatibility matrix for your ESXi host to see which services are supported.

Here are some additional things to keep in mind about host-based services:

- Host-based services can have a performance impact on your VMs. You should carefully evaluate the performance impact before enabling host-based services for your VMs.

- Host-based services can increase the complexity of your vSphere environment. You should carefully plan your host-based services configuration to ensure it is manageable.

- Host-based services can be a security risk. You should carefully configure your host-based services to protect your data from unauthorized access.

13.7 Create VM Storage Policy for Host-Based Data Services

In the vSphere Client, select **Policies and Profiles**, then **VM Storage Policies**, and click **Create** to open the Create VM Storage Policy wizard and start creating your VM storage policy for host-based data services.

In step 1, shown in Figure 13-4, name your Storage Policy. For purposes of the test lab, use the name **vSphere Essentials - VM Storage Policy Host-Based**. Then, if you prefer, add a description (it is not mandatory). Click **Next**.

Figure 13-4. *(vSphere Storage Policies 4 of 14)*

In step 2, *Policy structure* (see Figure 13-5), click **Enable host based rules** to enable host-based rules in this VM Storage Policy. Next in step 2, in the *Datastore specific rules* section, you can select datastore-specific rules, allowing you to create rules specific to a particular datastore type. For example, you could create a rule specifying that all VMs placed on a vSAN datastore must be encrypted. This will help to protect your data from unauthorized access. The options are as follows:

- **Enable rules for "vSAN" storage:** This option enables datastore-specific rules for vSAN datastores. This is useful to configure data services for vSAN datastores, such as deduplication, compression, or encryption.

- **Enable rules for "vSANDirect" storage:** This feature, introduced in version vSphere 7 Update 3, is specifically tailored for containerized applications. It works well in conjunction with VMware Tanzu Kubernetes Grid. By attaching datastores to ESXi hosts, vSANDirect offers optimized storage performance. It's important to note that vSANDirect is meant for containerized environments and is not suitable for VM workloads. Leveraging vSANDirect can greatly improve storage efficiency and performance for applications running in containers.

Note   The preceding two rules are used only if you use vSAN in your environment.

Figure 13-5. *(vSphere Storage Policies 5 of 14)*

Enable tag based placement rules: This option allows you to create rules based on tags. You can assign labels to datastores, VMs, and other objects in vSphere. For example, you could assign a "high performance" tag to all datastores dedicated to running high-performance VMs. You could then create a rule that specifies that all VMs tagged with "high performance" must be placed on a datastore tagged with "high performance." This will help ensure that your high-performance VMs are always on the best possible storage.

In the test lab environment, we won't be using tags or vSAN; therefore, leave these settings deactivated. Click **Next**.

In step 3 of the wizard, *Host based services*, you configure the Encryption and Storage I/O Control settings on their respective tabs, described here:

- **Encryption:** This tab, shown in Figure 13-6, includes the following options:

- **Disabled:** This option disables host-based services for the VM. This means that no data services will be provided to the VM by the ESXi host.

- **Use storage policy component:** This option uses the data services defined in the storage policy component associated with the VM. This is the default option.

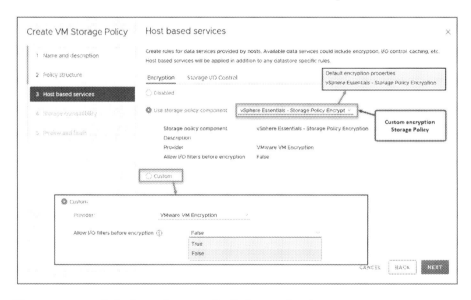

Figure 13-6. *(vSphere Storage Policies 6 of 14)*

Note   We previously created some custom Storage Policies (encryption or Storage I/O Control). We can now use this option in our host-based services. In our case, we previously created one Storage I/O Control.

- **Custom:** This option allows you to specify custom data services for the VM. You can choose from the following data services: Deduplication, Compression, Encryption, and Replication. Figure 13-6 shows that you can use the default VMware VM Encryption provider in the *Custom* option and turn the I/O filters on or off before encryption.

- **Storage I/O Control:** This tab, shown in Figure 13-7, includes options to configure SIOC (previously discussed). In VM Storage Policy SIOC we will disable or add our policy created before, or don't use any default/custom and create a custom SIOC just for this VM Storage Policy. This tab includes the following options:

- **Disabled:** This option disables host-based services for the VM. This means that no data services will be provided to the VM by the ESXi host. This option is useful if you do not want any data services to be provided to the VM. This may be useful for VMs that do not need any data services, such as small VMs or VMs that are not used often.

- **Use storage policy component:** This option uses the data services defined in the storage policy component associated with the VM. This is the default option. This is the most common option, as it ensures that the VM always uses the most appropriate data services for its needs. We will use the **vSphere Essentials - Storage Policy SIOC** Storage Policy SIOC created in the previous section.

- **Custom:** This option allows you to specify custom data services for the VM. You set limits for your environment. This option is useful if you have specific requirements for the data services that are provided to the VM. For example, you may want to specify that the VM should be encrypted, or that it should be replicated to a remote location. Figure 13-7 shows the VMware Storage IO Control provider selected. The remainder of this list describes the other fields in the *Custom* option.

- **IOPS limit:** Sets an upper boundary on the number of IOPS a VM or VMDK can perform. It ensures that the VM or its disks do not consume I/O beyond this limit, regardless of available I/O resources on the datastore.

- **IOPS reservation:** Defines a guaranteed minimum number of IOPS that will be reserved for the VM or its VMDKs. With this setting, you're ensuring that even under storage contention, the VM or disk will always have this minimum level of performance.

- **IOPS shares:** Represents the relative priority or weight of a VM's I/O allocation when there is contention. VMs with more shares will be allocated more I/O resources during contention than VMs with fewer shares.

It is essential to carefully consider your requirements before choosing the option for host-based services in a VM storage policy. You should also monitor the performance of your VMs to ensure that the provided data services are meeting your needs. Click **Next** to proceed to step 4 of the Create VM Storage Policy wizard.

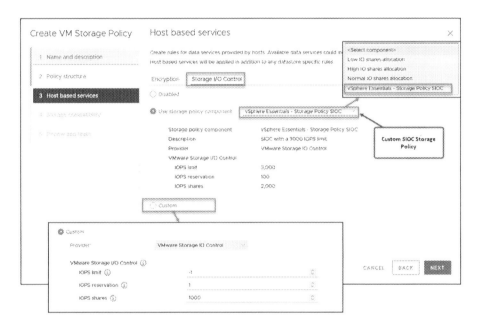

Figure 13-7. *(vSphere Storage Policies 7 of 14)*

Step 4, shown in Figure 13-8, lists all existing datastores compatible with the VM Storage Policy we created. You can also click the **Incompatible** tab to check the ones that are not compatible, shown in the lower-right image.

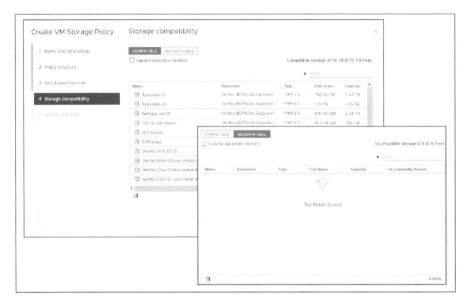

Figure 13-8. *(vSphere Storage Policies 8 of 14)*

The compatibility status of datastores is important to know so that you can create or move your VMs to the correct datastore and have your VM Storage Policy applied.

Figure 13-8 shows that all datastores are compatible with the VM Storage Policy created. The *Incompatible* tab is empty. Click **Next**.

Finally, review all the settings you have configured in the previous wizard steps (see Figure 13-9) and finish creating your VM Storage Policy by clicking **Finish**.

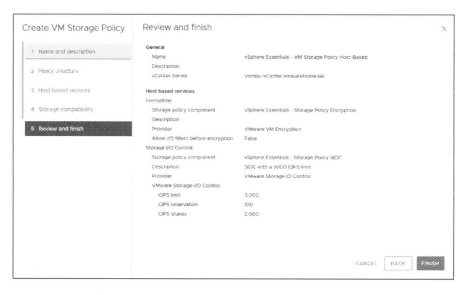

Figure 13-9. *(vSphere Storage Policies 9 of 14)*

After your VM Storage Policy is finished, you can edit or clone it (or any existing Storage Policy or VM Storage Policy in the list of existing Policies) by selecting it and clicking **Edit** or **Clone**. See Figure 13-10.

Figure 13-10. *(vSphere Storage Policies 10 of 14)*

You can change any settings in the VM Storage Policy and Storage Policy **Clone** option. However, as shown in Figure 13-11, you cannot change the Category and Provider settings with the **Edit** option in SIOC or and Encryption policy serve distinct purposes and operate differently.

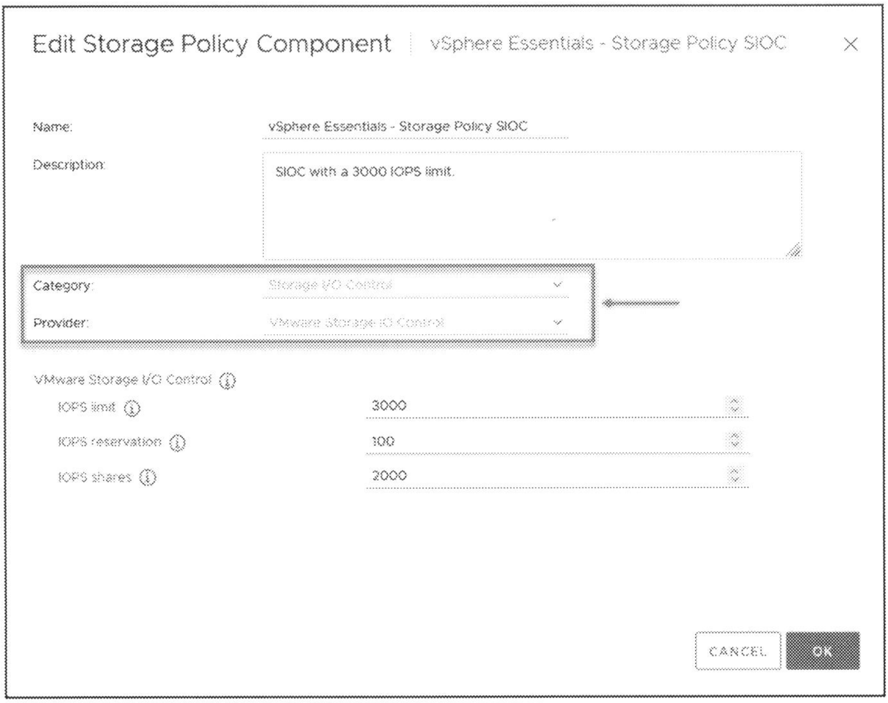

Figure 13-11. *(vSphere Storage Policies 11 of 14)*

13.8 Apply VM Storage Policy to VMs

After creating all our Storage Policies and VM Storage Policies, we need to apply them to the existing VMs or use them when creating a new VM.

You need to **Edit VM setting**s, select the Hard Disk, and change the *VM Storage policy* option for the existing VM. However, as shown in Figure 13-12, although this VM was created, it is incompatible with the VM Storage Policy we previously created.

238

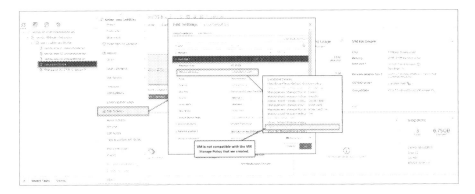

Figure 13-12. *(vSphere Storage Policies 12 of 14)*

If we try to create a VM with the new encrypted VM Storage Policy, we get the error shown in Figure 13-13: *A general runtime error occurred. Cannot apply encryption policy. You must set the default key provider.*

Figure 13-13. *(vSphere Storage Policies 13 of 14)*

This error occurs because we are trying to encrypt our datastore and VMs but haven't created a key provider. We select the ESXi host, configure tab and in Security and Key Providers option we that is empty. As shown in the Figure 13-14.

Figure 13-14. *(vSphere Storage Policies 14 of 14)*

So, we need to add a key provider in our vCenter. But before we add a key provider, let's examine what exactly is a key provider.

13.8.1 What Is a Key Provider?

A *security key provider* is a software component responsible for managing the encryption keys used to protect your data. Storage vendors typically implement security key providers.

When you create a VM storage policy specifying that encryption should be enabled, you can specify the security key provider you want to use. The security key provider will then manage the encryption keys used to encrypt the data on the VM's disks.

There are two types of security key providers:

- **Local security key providers:** Store the encryption keys on the ESXi host. This is the most common type of security key provider.

- **Remote security key providers:** Store the encryption keys on a remote server. This type of security key provider is more secure than local security key providers, but it is also more complex to configure.

The decision of whether to use a local or remote security key provider depends on your specific requirements. If you need a high level of security, you should use a remote security key provider. You should use a local security key provider for a more straightforward configuration.

Without a key provider, vCenter cannot handle the encryption.

13.9 Add an Encryption Key Provider

To add a key provider, go to vCenter, click the **Configure** tab, select **Key Providers** in the *Security* section, and select either of the following options (see Figure 13-15):

- **Add Native Key Provider:** This option adds the vCenter Server Native Key Provider to the VM storage policy. The vCenter Server Native Key Provider is a local security key provider that stores the encryption keys on the ESXi host. This is the most common option to use.

- **Add Standard Key Provider:** This option adds a third-party security key provider to the VM storage policy. Third-party security key providers can offer more features and security than the vCenter Server Native Key Provider. However, they are also more complex to configure.

Figure 13-15. *(Key Provider 1 of 4)*

The decision of whether to use the vCenter Server Native Key Provider or a third-party security key provider depends on your specific requirements. If you need a simple and secure solution, use the vCenter

Server Native Key Provider. If you need more features and security, you should use a third-party security key provider.

Here are some of the benefits of using the vCenter Server Native Key Provider:

- **Simple to configure:** The vCenter Server Native Key Provider is easy to configure and manage.

- **Secure:** The vCenter Server Native Key Provider uses strong encryption algorithms to protect your data.

- **Consistent:** The vCenter Server Native Key Provider is available on all supported ESXi hosts.

Here are some of the benefits of using a third-party security key provider:

- **More features:** Third-party security key providers can offer more features than the vCenter Server Native Key Provider, such as centralized key management and auditing.

- **More secure:** Third-party security key providers can offer more security than the vCenter Server Native Key Provider, such as hardware security modules and multifactor authentication.

- **Scalable:** Third-party security key providers can be scaled to meet the needs of your environment. For example, you can use multiple third-party security key providers to store the encryption keys for your VMs. This option adds the vCenter Server Native Key Provider to the VM storage policy.

For our test lab environment, add the default Native Key Provider managed by vCenter, which is free, by using the option **Add Native Key Provider** and then clicking **Add Key Provider** in the dialog box

242

(see Figure 13-15). If you use the option **Add Standard Key Provider**, this requires a third-party service that usually has a service cost. For production, you should always use the latter option.

Caution   Enable the option *Use key provider only with TPM protected ESXi hosts* (shown in Figure 13-15) only if you have hardware TPM.

Next, to finalize your key provider, you need to back it up. As shown in Figure 13-16, select **Key Providers**, click the **Back-Up** option, check the option **Protect Native Key Provider data with password**, and provide a password for your key provider. Click **Copy Password** to copy and save your password in a secure place. Check the check box to confirm your action. Finally, click **Back Up Key Provider**.

Figure 13-16. *(Key Provider 2 of 4)*

Caution   If you lose your password, you cannot unencrypt any data.

Note   Always select the option to protect the Native Key Provider data with a password. Backing up the Native Key Provider without password protection exposes its configuration data and the virtual machines encrypted with key providers to potential security threats.

After you click Back Up Key Provider, the Key Provider file is downloaded to your computer, as shown in Figure 13-17. Store the file in a secure place.

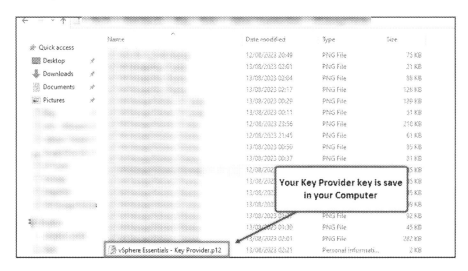

Figure 13-17. *(Key Provider 3 of 4)*

Now your key provider is active (see Figure 13-18), and you can use any of the Storage or VM Encryption policies you have previously created.

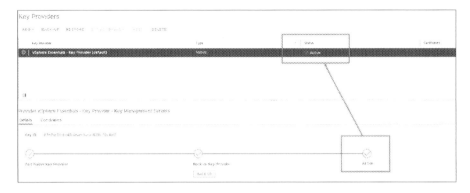

Figure 13-18. *(Key Provider 4 of 4)*

As Figure 13-19 shows, the VM and virtual disk are now encrypted when we create a new VM and select our VM Storage Policy.

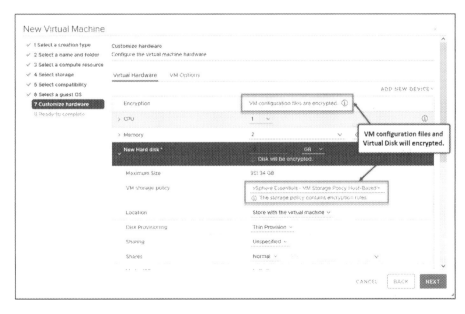

Figure 13-19. *(vSphere Storage Policies 14 of 15)*

To encrypt VMs that already exist, we need to encrypt the VM configuration files first and then the VM virtual disk.

The VM needs to be powered off to encrypt the VM configuration files. Go to **VM settings**, click the **VM Options** tab, expand the **Encryption** section, and then *VM Encryption* and use change to your VM Storage Policy.

By selecting the option **Disk**, it also encrypts the virtual disk. Then you don't need to return to the VM Settings and change the virtual disk VM Storage Policy.

The VM configuration files and virtual disk will both be encrypted.

Note   If the VM has any snapshots, it is not possible to encrypt the virtual disks. If you want to encrypt the virtual disks, delete all snapshots from the VM.

When you encrypt your VM, you can also choose to encrypt vMotion and vSphere Fault Tolerance (FT) for the VM. Check Figure 13-20 for the options you have to encrypt those two vSphere features.

Figure 13-20. *(vSphere Storage Policies 15 of 15)*

13.10 Summary

This chapterfocuses on enhancing performance and security for virtual machines (VMs). It covers how custom storage policies can meet specific I/O requirements to boost VM performance and details the significance of storage encryption for protecting data integrity and confidentiality.

The discussion includes optimizing storage through Storage I/O Controls (SIOC) and configuring VM policies for host-based data services, alongside their application to VMs. The setup of encryption providers is also addressed, providing a rounded understanding of the practicalities and security considerations in managing vSphere storage.

Key points include the importance of tailoring storage configurations to improve performance and offer essential data services like deduplication, compression, and encryption. The guidance offered helps establish efficient storage management and a secure virtual infrastructure, emphasizing encryption for data protection and the strategic use of SIOC for performance enhancement.

CHAPTER 14

vSphere Distributed Switch

Now that we have our vCenter installed and configured, we can discuss vSphere Distributed Switch (vDS) and how to create a vDS.

Figure 14-1 shows the design of our test lab vSphere environment using the vSphere Distributed Switches that we will work on in this chapter and subsequent chapters. The design has three ESXi hosts and four physical NICs distributed in the following two vDSs with two physical NICs each.

- **Storage vDS:**

  - Two uplinks (physical NICs) per ESXi host

  - Two port groups (Storage and vMotion)

  In this case, we use the Storage port group to connect our ESXi hosts to Storage and the second port group for the vMotion network.

- **Virtual Machines vDS:**

  - Two uplinks (physical NICs) per ESXi host

  - Four port groups (Management, Production VMs, Marketing VMs, and Development VMs)

© Luciano Patrão 2024
L. Patrão, *VMware vSphere Essentials*, https://doi.org/10.1007/979-8-8688-0208-9_14

Using this type of configuration in our vDS for virtual machines and ESXi hosts management, we can separate the traffic using the same vDS with different VLANs for each department and network.

Note In a standard production environment, it is best practice to physically separate management traffic from VM traffic. This separation ensures optimal performance and enhances security. However, in our scenario, we are working within a nested test environment. Given this context, it is acceptable to configure our setup with both management and VM traffic sharing the same physical network interfaces. This approach simplifies our test configuration without the typical concerns of combining these traffic types in a production environment.

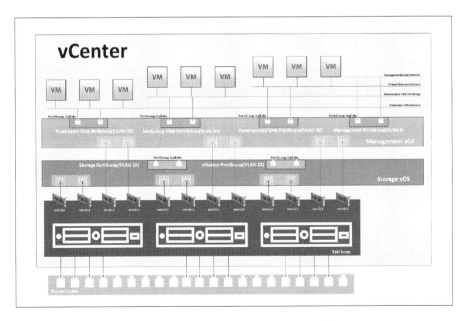

Figure 14-1. *(vSphere Distributed Switch 1 of 28)*

14.1 What Is vSphere Distributed Switch?

vSphere Distributed Switch (vDS) is a centralized and advanced virtual switch designed for VMware vSphere environments. Unlike standard virtual switches operating locally within a single ESXi host, vSphere Distributed Switches provide a consistent network configuration across multiple hosts, clusters.

vSphere Distributed Switches are managed by vCenter, which allows administrators to create, configure, monitor, and manage network settings across all ESXi hosts associated with the vDSs. vDSs can simplify network management tasks for large-scale VMware vSphere deployments using a centralized management interface.

Some of the key features of vSphere Distributed Switches include

- **Centralized network management:** vDS allows you to centrally manage network settings such as private vLANs, QoS, LACP, and security policies from a single location.

- **Advanced network traffic management**: vDS supports features such as vSphere Network I/O Control (NIOC), which allows you to prioritize traffic and allocate bandwidth based on specific requirements.

- **Network monitoring and troubleshooting:** vDS provides enhanced network visibility and monitoring capabilities, including NetFlow and port mirroring support.

- **Improved scalability:** vDS can support up to 30,000 virtual ports and 1024 ESXi hosts in a single switch, providing scalable networking for even the largest VMware vSphere environments.

14.2 vSphere Distributed Switch Main Features

The features described and shown in this section are available only on vSphere Distributed Switches, not Standard Switches. This section explains each feature and shows how to select it in vCenter. You will find all the main features in the vDS configuration section, but we will examine them individually.

The configuration and enabling (some are disabled by default) of the main features are done on the vDS level. It then can be enabled or configured in the port group.

Figure 14-2. *(vSphere Distributed Switch 2 of 28)*

14.2.1 Back Up and Restore vDS Network Configuration

Essentially, the backup and restore feature allows administrators to save a snapshot of their vDS configuration, which can be used to restore the network settings in case of accidental deletion or other unexpected events.

This backup and restore process ensures that the virtual network remains operational and minimizes downtime due to network failures.

The backup and restore process can be performed using the vSphere Client GUI by browsing for the vSphere Distributed Switch, right-clicking it, selecting **Settings**, and clicking the **Export Configuration** option, as shown in Figure 14-3. As also shown, you can restore the backed-up file by instead clicking **Restore Configuration**.

The backup and restore vDS network configuration feature can also be used if you want to migrate to a new vCenter and need a copy of the network from the old vCenter.

I have often used this feature in production when it is impossible to do a complete migration to migrate a legacy vCenter (version 6.5/6.7) to a new vCenter.

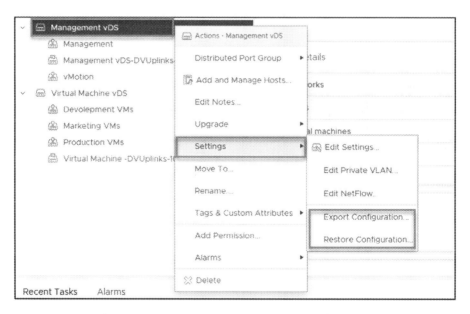

Figure 14-3. *(vSphere Distributed Switch 3 of 28)*

14.2.2 Link Aggregation Control Protocol Support

The Link Aggregation Control Protocol (LACP) in vSphere Distributed Switch is called LAG (Link Aggregation Group). In a vDS, LAG consolidates multiple network links into a single logical link. This process allows for higher bandwidth, improved redundancy, and load balancing across multiple physical network interfaces.

By configuring a LAG on a vDS, administrators can bundle two or more vmnics into a single logical interface. This interface appears as a single connection to connected VMs, providing multiple paths for traffic to flow between the physical hosts. This setup allows for improved performance and availability.

Note   Enabling LACP on a vDS is contingent upon the support for LACP on your physical switch. Always verify that your physical networking hardware is compatible with LACP before enabling it on a vDS.

LAG in a vDS can be configured using LACP or static LAG techniques. LACP provides dynamic negotiation between the physical switch and the vDS, while Static LAG requires manual configuration of the physical switch. To configure LAG in a vDS, you must first create a LAG group by selecting the vDS, then specifying the LAG parameters such as LAG mode (LACP or Static), number of uplinks, and load balancing algorithm. Once the LAG group is created, it can be assigned to a port group, enabling the virtual machines to use the consolidated link.

Enabling LACP can be done only at the vDS level, not on the vDS port group.

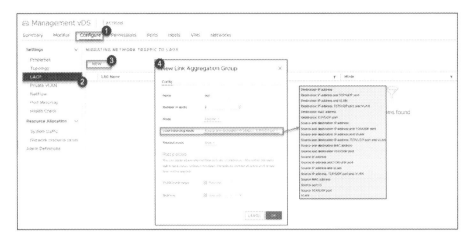

Figure 14-4. *(vSphere Distributed Switch 4 of 28)*

14.2.3 Inbound Traffic Shaping

Inbound Traffic Shaping in vSphere Distributed Switch is a technique used to control the amount of incoming traffic allowed to pass through a particular port or set of ports on the virtual switch.

With Inbound Traffic Shaping, administrators can limit the rate at which incoming traffic flows into a virtual machine or a group of virtual machines. Administrators can prevent network congestion by restricting the amount of inbound traffic and ensuring that the available bandwidth is utilized effectively.

In vDS, Inbound Traffic Shaping is implemented using a traffic shaper, which allows administrators to set an upper limit on the rate of incoming traffic. The traffic shaper buffers incoming traffic and then releases it in compliance with the allowed rate, thereby controlling traffic flow into the virtual machine or port group.

To configure Inbound Traffic Shaping in vDS, you must first select the port group or virtual machine for which you want to enable traffic shaping. You can then specify the desired traffic shaping policy by defining the maximum peak bandwidth, average bandwidth, and burst size. Once the policy is applied, the traffic shaper limits the rate of incoming traffic according to the specified parameters.

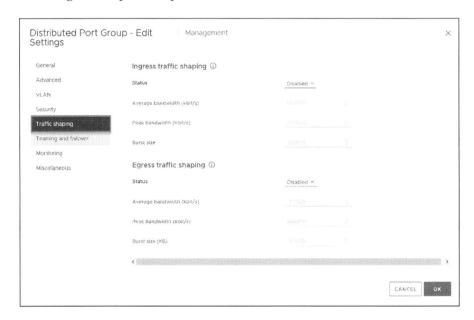

Figure 14-5. *(vSphere Distributed Switch 5 of 28)*

14.2.4 Port Binding and Port Allocation

Figure 14-6. *(vSphere Distributed Switch 6 of 28)*

Here is a quick explanation of port binding:

- **Static binding:** Connects a virtual machine to a distributed port group by assigning a distributed port.

- **Ephemeral binding:** The behavior is similar to a Standard Virtual Switch (VSS) when you choose this choice. In the port group, one port is allocated for each connected virtual machine up to the maximum number of ports available. The number of ports is automatically set to 0, and each port group is allocated one port.

257

Note   This option is very useful for connecting vCenter Appliance. If vCenter goes down, you still have a network since Ephemeral is not bout to vCenter, only to ESXI hosts.

14.2.5 Port Mirror

Port Mirror is mainly used for traffic analyses and troubleshooting. It could be to analyze package drops or security.

In a vSphere Distributed Switch, Port Mirroring is a feature used to copy network traffic from a source port or set of ports to a destination port, which can be monitored or analyzed for troubleshooting, security, or other purposes.

With Port Mirroring, administrators can create a copy of the network traffic passing through a virtual switch and direct it to a destination port or virtual machine, where it can be captured and analyzed using a network analyzer such as Wireshark. This allows them to gain insight into the network behavior, detect security threats, or troubleshoot issues.

To configure Port Mirroring in vDS, first create a port mirror session by defining a source port or set of ports and a destination port or virtual machine. Specify the direction of traffic to be copied, either ingress (incoming traffic) or egress (outgoing traffic), or both. You can also limit the amount of mirrored traffic by setting a filter based on protocols, VLANs, or MAC addresses.

Once the port mirror session is configured, the selected traffic will be copied to the destination port or virtual machine, which can then capture and analyze the data. It is important to note that Port Mirroring can consume significant network resources and may impact the performance of virtual machines, so it is recommended to use it selectively and with care.

Figure 14-7. *(vSphere Distributed Switch 7 of 28)*

14.2.6 VM Port Blocking

As the name identifies, VM Port blocking is a security feature to block traffic in a VM port. In a vDS, VM Port Blocking is a security feature that allows administrators to restrict the network traffic that is allowed to enter or exit a specific virtual machine.

With VM port blocking, administrators can control the network traffic flow between virtual machines or between a virtual machine and the external network. This feature can be used to enforce network security policies, prevent unauthorized access, or protect sensitive data.

Once the rules are applied, any traffic that matches them will be blocked at the virtual machine's port, preventing it from entering or exiting it. You can also choose to log the blocked traffic, which can help in troubleshooting or auditing.

It is important to note that VM Port Blocking is only effective within the virtual environment and does not provide protection against attacks from outside the virtual infrastructure, so it should be used as part of a comprehensive security strategy only from a virtual machines perspective.

Figure 14-8. *(vSphere Distributed Switch 8 of 28)*

14.2.7 Health Check

Health Check, which is disabled by default, includes the following features (see Figure 14-9):

- VLAN and MTU

- Teaming and failover

Both Health Check features check the vDS traffic and inform if any configurations are not correctly configured.

For example, if you set jumbo frames (MTU 9000), all the network devices connected to these ports must be enabled with jumbo frames. If jumbo frames are not enabled on all devices, it can lead to packet fragmentation. This means that when a device tries to transmit a packet that exceeds the network's maximum packet size, it has to divide the packet into smaller segments. These segments must then be reassembled at the receiving end, which can increase latency and reduce throughput.

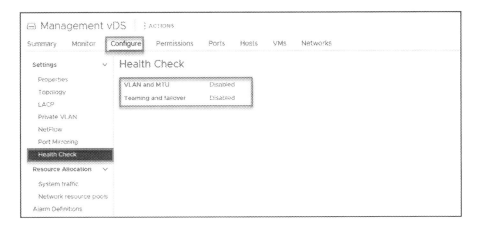

Figure 14-9. *(vSphere Distributed Switch 9 of 28)*

14.2.8 Network Resource Pools

Network resource pools allow administrators to allocate a portion of the available network resources to a specific group of virtual machines. See Figure 14-10. This can be useful in environments where some virtual machines require higher levels of network performance than others or where network resources must be reserved for critical applications.

When a virtual machine is powered on, it is assigned to a specific port group associated with a network resource pool. The virtual machine can then utilize the portion of the reserved network resources allocated to the pool it belongs to. This ensures that the virtual machine always has access to the bandwidth reserved for its pool, even during periods of high network congestion.

If we look at our infrastructure design in the next chapter, we see that we have Virtual Machines, for example, from Production and Development. Virtual Machines from Development should not have priority or use a big part of the bandwidth, so we create a Network Pool in which they can use only the bandwidth allocated to them, and provide to Production VMs more bandwidth.

In this case, we use a Network resource Pool to prevent development VMs from monopolizing network resources and degrading overall network performance.

Figure 14-10. *(vSphere Distributed Switch 10 of 28)*

14.2.9 Private VLANs

There are three types of private VLANs (PVLANs): Isolated, Community, and Promiscuous. Each type provides a different level of isolation and connectivity between virtual machines. To access the PVLAN options, right-click the vDS, select **Settings**, and click **Edit Private VLAN**, as shown in Figure 14-11.

- **Isolated PVLAN:** An isolated PVLAN allows a virtual machine to communicate only with its own virtual interface. It cannot communicate with other virtual machines, even within the same primary VLAN. You might choose to configure isolated PVLANs when VMs host sensitive applications, like financial systems, to ensure they are completely segregated from other network traffic for security purposes.

- **Community PVLAN:** A community PVLAN allows virtual machines to communicate with each other within the same primary VLAN. However, each virtual machine can only communicate with other virtual machines in the same community, not those in other communities or isolated PVLANs. Community PVLANs could be used in a departmental setup, such as allowing communication among VMs in the HR department while keeping them isolated from the IT and Marketing departments' VMs.

- **Promiscuous PVLAN:** A promiscuous PVLAN allows a virtual machine to communicate with all other devices on the primary VLAN, including other virtual machines and physical devices. Promiscuous PVLANs are often set up for VMs that act as servers or gateways, providing services like DHCP or routing to other VMs within the primary VLAN.

Figure 14-11. *(vSphere Distributed Switch 11 of 28)*

14.2.10 NetFlow

NetFlow collects information about each packet that enters or exits a
virtual machine's network interface, including the source and destination
IP addresses, protocols, ports, and other metadata. This information is
then aggregated and sent to a NetFlow collector, which can be used to
analyze the network traffic patterns and identify potential issues.

Once NetFlow is enabled, the vDS will start collecting information
about the network traffic flow and sending it to the designated NetFlow
collector. The collected data can be used to generate reports, troubleshoot
network issues, monitor network performance, and detect security threats.

By using NetFlow in vDS, you can gain visibility into the network traffic
flow, identify potential bottlenecks, and optimize network performance.
NetFlow can also help identify network security threats and provide
insights into virtual machines' network behavior.

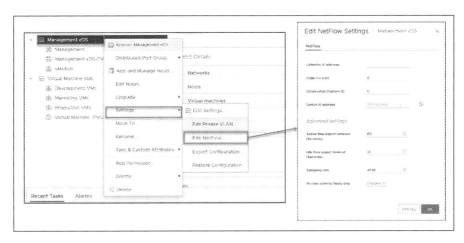

Figure 14-12. *(vSphere Distributed Switch 12 of 28)*

14.2.11 vDS Tags and Custom Attributes

Both Tags and Custom Attributes in vDS can perform bulk operations, such as filtering, sorting, searching, and reporting, which can help manage large-scale virtual environments.

For example, administrators can use Tags to apply security policies or configure Quality of Service (QoS) settings across groups of virtual machines.

Custom Attributes can be used to track compliance requirements, maintenance schedules, or licensing information for virtual machines.

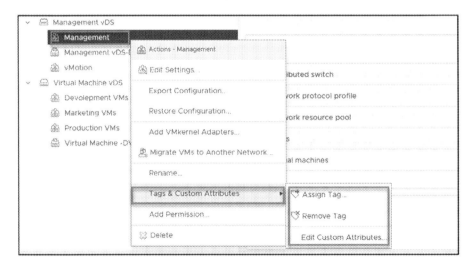

Figure 14-13. *(vSphere Distributed Switch 13 of 28)*

14.3 vSphere Distributed
Switch Requirements

It is crucial to understand the foundational requirements that underpin the successful deployment of vSwitches. The prerequisites for utilizing vDS are not overly complex, but there are specific conditions and configurations that must be met. This section outlines these essential requirements, providing a clear checklist to ensure your system is ready for the integration and optimal functioning of vDS.

Although the prerequisites for using vDS are not extensive, specific the following requirements must be fulfilled:

- **License:** vSphere Distributed Switch is only available if you have a vSphere Enterprise Plus license for your ESXi hosts. This license provides access to advanced vSphere features, including distributed switching.

  Additionally, it is worth mentioning that vDS can also be accessed through other licensing options. Specifically, if you have a vSAN or an NSX license, you will also have the capability to use vDS. This is particularly relevant for environments in which vSAN is used for storage virtualization or NSX is used for network virtualization, as these licenses extend the functionality to include vDS.

- **vCenter Server:** vSphere Distributed Switch is only available in vCenter, so you must be running vCenter Server to create a vDS. You cannot use vSphere Distributed Switch if you are running stand-alone hosts not connected to vCenter Server.

- **Hardware requirements:** There are not many hardware requirements to use vDS, but the ESXi host needs at least one physical Ethernet adapter per host to configure and use a vDS.

- **VLANs:** If you are using VLANs with vSphere Distributed Switch, you need to ensure that the VLAN IDs are consistent across all hosts that are connected to the vDS.

267

14.4 Create and Configure a vSphere Distributed Switch

To create a vSphere Distributed Switch, in the vCenter, click the **Networking** (shown as step 1 in Figure 14-14), right-click the Datacenter (Vembu in our test lab), select **Distributed Switch** in the context menu, and click **New Distributed Switch**.

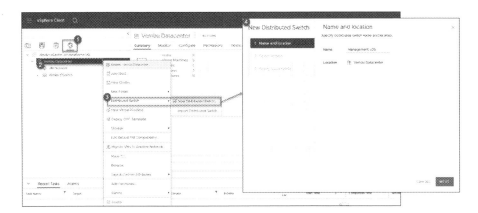

Figure 14-14. *(vSphere Distributed Switch 14 of 28)*

In the first step of the wizard, give your vDS a name (following the design in Figure 14-1, name it **Management vDS**). Click **Next**.

In step 2 of the wizard, shown in Figure 14-15, select the vDS version. Select the most recent version unless you have a particular reason not to. Click **Next**.

Note   In some scenarios you might not want to update to the latest version immediately. For example, if you are in the process of upgrading a mixed-host environment, it is prudent to hold off on updating the vDS until all the hosts are running on the latest version. Updating the vDS too early in such a scenario can lead to compatibility issues, as older ESXi hosts might not support the newer vDS version. This careful approach ensures a smooth transition and maintains a stable environment during the upgrade process.

Tip   You can check the new features per version by clicking the corresponding option, as shown in Figure 14-15.

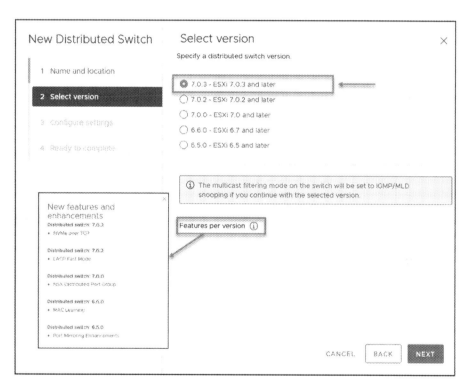

Figure 14-15. *(vSphere Distributed Switch 15 of 28)*

Next, select the number of uplinks (physical Ethernet cards) you will use in this vDS. Following the design in Figure 14-1, configure each vDS to have **2** vmnics. Since vDS does not work without a logical port group, create the first port group now and name it **Management**, as shown in Figure 14-16.

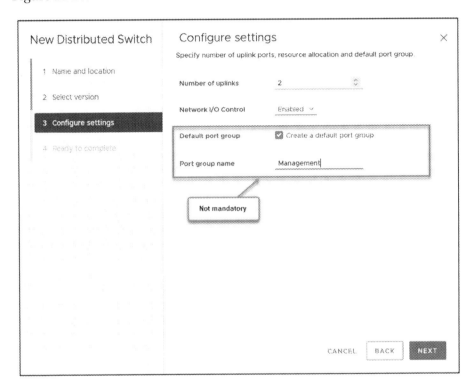

Figure 14-16. *(vSphere Distributed Switch 16 of 28)*

You can now finish creating vDS by clicking **Finish**, as shown in Figure 14-17.

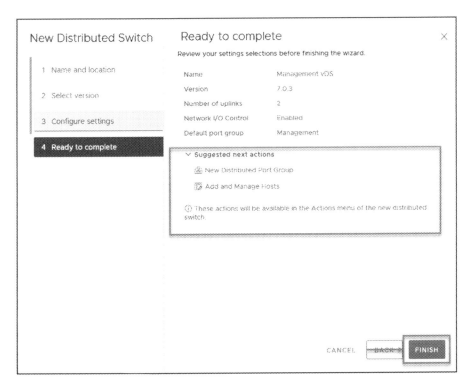

Figure 14-17. *(vSphere Distributed Switch 17 of 28)*

Figure 14-18 shows the newly created vSphere Distributed Switch.

Figure 14-18. *(vSphere Distributed Switch 18 of 28)*

Having created the vDS, we will add the ESXi hosts that will work with this vDS. We will use all three ESXi hosts in the Cluster. We can select all in the Cluster or use specific ones.

As shown in Figure 14-19, right-click the vDS just created, click **Add and Manage Hosts** in the context menu, and then choose the **Add hosts** option in step 1 of the wizard. Click **Next**.

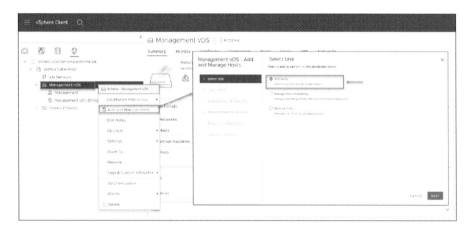

Figure 14-19. *(vSphere Distributed Switch 19 of 28)*

Next, select the ESXi hosts that will be added to this vDS. In our case, it is all three. See Figure 14-20. Click **Next**.

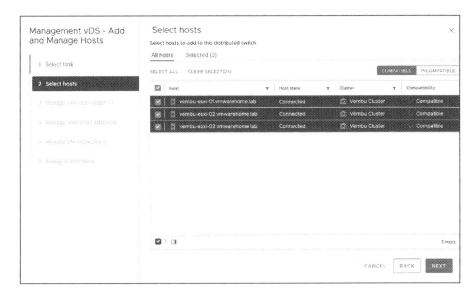

Figure 14-20. *(vSphere Distributed Switch 20 of 28)*

Step 3, shown in Figure 14-21, is the configuration of the essential part of the vDS network: select which network adapters (vmnics) this vDS will use. The options are *Adapters on all hosts* or *Adapters per host*. Since we will use the same vmnics in all ESXi hosts in our test lab environment, select **Adapters on all hosts**. Selecting this option, vDS automatically selects the same vmnic in all ESXi hosts.

If, for example, in ESXi host A, we will add vmnic1 and vmnic3, but in the ESXi host B vmnic2 and vmnic3, we need to select the option ***Adapters per host*** and select vmnics per host.

After you check which vmnics are available and not being used in another vDS or Standard Switch (vmnic5 and vmnic6 in Figure 14-21), assign an uplink number. In this case, select the **(Auto-assign)** option to better manage the uplink numbers.

Note   Recall that in the previous chapters we configured four vmnics (vmnic0 to vmnic4) and two Standard Switches (vSwitch0 for management and VMs network and vSwitch1 for Storage), which is why they are displayed as in use in Figure 14-21.

We added two vmnics (you can do this by adding two vmnics in your nested vSphere VMs) just to create this new vDS. After we finish all the vDS configuration, we will migrate all vmnics (1 to 4) to this new vDS and remove vmnic5 and vmnic6. Click **Next**.

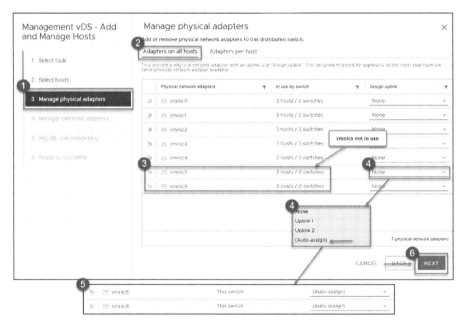

Figure 14-21. *(vSphere Distributed Switch 21 of 28)*

Step 4 of the wizard (see Figure 14-22) is applicable if we want to migrate any vmkernel (like ESXi host management, vMotion, or iSCSI vmkernel) to this new vDS and assign any port group that we have already created. We will not do this now. We will discuss that process in Chapter 15. So, click **Next** to skip this step.

Figure 14-22. *(vSphere Distributed Switch 22 of 28)*

Step 5 of the wizard is *Migrate VM networking*, as shown in Figure 14-23. Again, we will not migrate any network until Chapter 15, so click **Next** to skip this step.

275

Figure 14-23. *(vSphere Distributed Switch 23 of 28)*

For the final step of the wizard, review your settings as shown in Figure 14-24 and click **Finish**. Your vDS will be created using the three ESXi hosts in your Cluster and it will use vmnic5 and vmnic6.

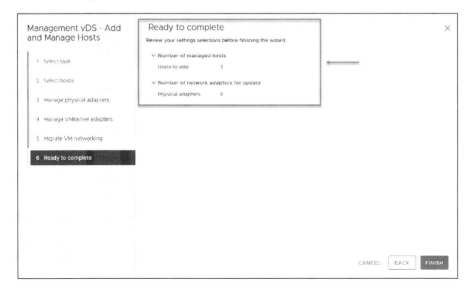

Figure 14-24. *(vSphere Distributed Switch 24 of 28)*

To finish this vDS section, we now create a vDS port group inside the vDS we created. As you remember, we created one port group (Management) automatically when we created the vDS. As depicted in our design in Figure 14-1, we now need to create all the Virtual Machines vDS port groups in this vDS.

As shown in Figure 14-25, right-click the vDS, select **Distributed Port Group** in the context menu, click **New Distributed Port Group**, and type the name of your vDS port group (in this case, **Production VMs**). Click **Next**.

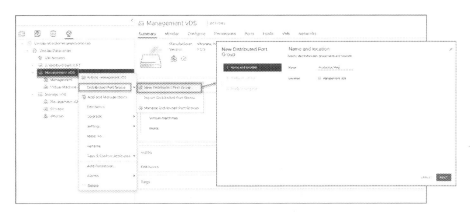

Figure 14-25. *(vSphere Distributed Switch 25 of 28)*

In the next step of the wizard, shown in Figure 14-26, we don't need to change anything. Just add the VLAN that we have in our design (if you were not using VLANs, you would leave it to the default setting, **none**).

Note   Customize default policies configuration only if you are using any of the above main features we have listed above that are disabled by default. That is not our case for this example.

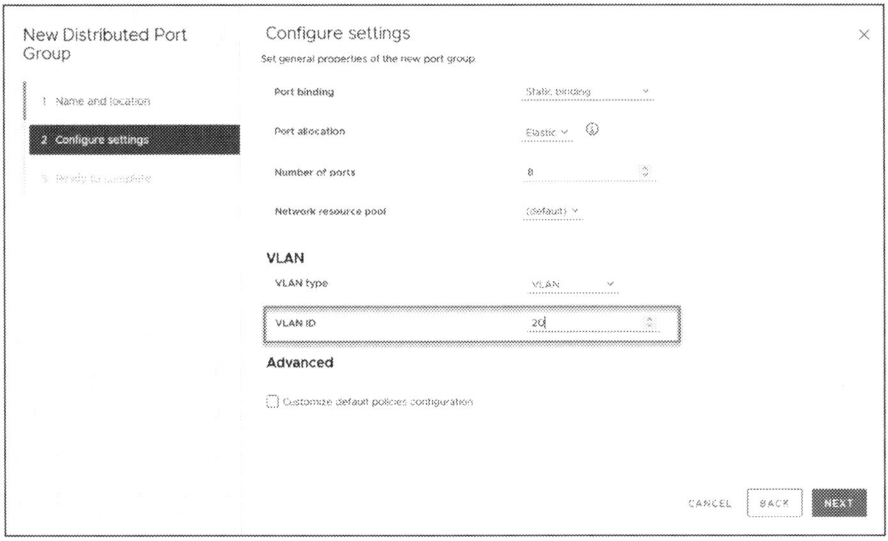

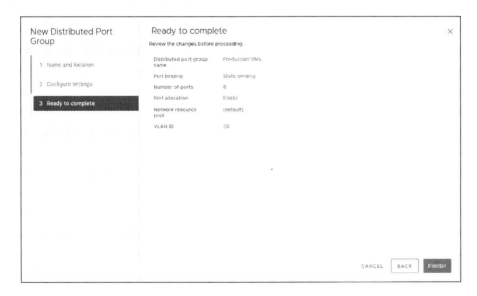

Figure 14-26. *(vSphere Distributed Switch 26 of 28)*

Double-check the information (see Figure 14-27) and click **Finish** to create the new vDS port group.

Figure 14-27. *(vSphere Distributed Switch 27 of 28)*

Repeat the preceding wizard steps to create the other two Virtual Machines network port groups in the design, Marketing VMs and Development VMs.

To complete the design shown in Figure 14-1, you also need to create the second vSphere Distributed Switch, Storage vDS, and its two port groups, Storage and vMotion. Follow the steps in this section to create the Storage vDS and port groups, substituting the correct names where applicable.

Figure 14-28 shows all the vDSs and port groups after they have been created.

Figure 14-28. *(vSphere Distributed Switch 28 of 28)*

14.5 Summary

This chapter introduces the vSphere Distributed Switch (vDS), an essential tool for network management in VMware environments. After establishing our vCenter, we focus on creating and configuring vDS, underscoring its importance in enabling advanced network management across ESXi hosts. vDS allows for the centralization of network configurations, providing a more streamlined management experience and enhanced capabilities compared to standard switches.

The chapter outlines the setup of two distinct vDS instances: one aimed at storage, with two uplinks per ESXi host and dedicated port groups for Storage and vMotion, and another for virtual machine traffic management, also equipped with two uplinks and various port groups designed for different operational or departmental needs.

We highlight key vDS features such as centralized network management, advanced traffic management options, network monitoring tools, and the ability to scale, demonstrating how vDS significantly improves network performance and reliability. Additionally, the chapter covers vDS-exclusive functionalities like Backup and Restore, LACP support, and Inbound Traffic Shaping, which collectively contribute to enhanced network performance and security.

Further, the discussion extends to practical configurations including Link Aggregation, Port Binding, Port Mirroring, and VM Port Blocking, providing valuable insights into optimizing and securing the network.

The chapter wraps up with the creation of vDS and port groups, laying the groundwork for advanced configurations and migration strategies in future discussions. This establishes a solid foundation for utilizing vDS to create a more efficient, secure, and manageable network infrastructure in your vSphere environments.

Having covered the basics of vSphere Distributed Switch, we now turn to its advanced configurations. Chapter 15 delves into utilizing VLANs within vDS for optimized network management and guides you through migrating from Standard vSwitch to vDS, enhancing network efficiency in VMware vSphere.

CHAPTER 15

Advanced Configuration with vSphere Distributed Switch

15.1 Use VLANs in vSphere Distributed Switch

Since we cannot migrate our networks before we add VLANs, we will first add VLANs to our new vDS and port groups.

Note Although this section applies only to environments that use VLANs, using VLANs is an important part of the vDS configuration, so I will discuss it here. You can skip this step if you are not using VLANs in your environment.

© Luciano Patrão 2024
L. Patrão, *VMware vSphere Essentials*, https://doi.org/10.1007/979-8-8688-0208-9_15

First, you need to add all VLANs at the vDS level. You do so on the Logical vDS port group (created automatically by the vDS). If you have only one VLAN to use, choose the **VLAN** option from the drop-down list. If you have several port groups and several VLANs (as in the case of our test lab design), then choose the option **VLAN trunking**.

To configure VLAN trunking, you can add VLANs in either of two different ways, as shown in Figure 15-1: add the whole VLAN trunk number range (0–4094) or just add the VLANs that will be used, separated by a comma. For security reasons (ensuring users do not use the wrong VLANs) and for better management of your networks, the second option is better.

Figure 15-1. *(Advanced vDS - VLANs 1 of 21)*

After you add the VLANs that your vDS will use, you can add a VLAN for each port group. In this example, add the Management port group VLAN, as shown in Figure 15-2. You can use this example to add to the rest of your port groups.

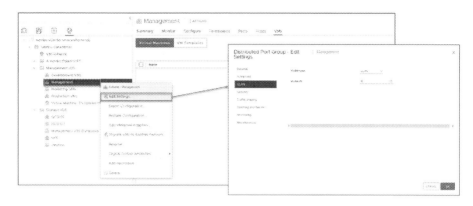

Figure 15-2. *(Advanced vDS - VLANs 2 of 21)*

And now all your port groups are using individual VLANs.

When you use VLANs in your VMs Networks, you need to consider that the Guest OS network adapter may also need to use the VLAN (if you are trunking the VLANs or using more than one VLAN in a port group).

Figure 15-3 shows a simple example of a Windows Server adding the VLAN to the VMXNET3 VMware network adapter.

Figure 15-3. *(Advanced vDS - VLANs 3 of 21)*

Now your vDS and port groups are ready for the network migration.

Note   In the configuration shown in Figure 15-3, I assume that
you understand VLANs and how to configure them in your physical
switch. Because any VLAN that is used in any vmnic is connected to a
physical port switch, that port needs to have VLANs configured.

15.2 Migrate from a Standard vSwitch to vSphere Distributed Switch

Since the VMware test lab environment that we have built since the
beginning of this book has some specific Storage networks (such as NFS
and iSCSI), Figure 15-4 is already updated with the same port groups we
have in the Standard Switch. We also updated the Storage vDS to consider
those port groups needing migration.

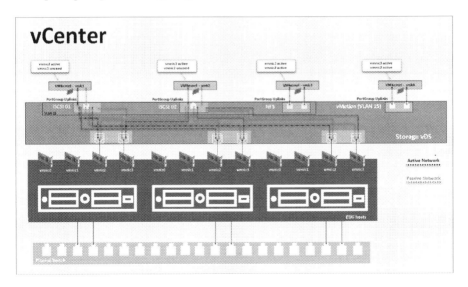

Figure 15-4. *(Advanced vDS - VLANs 4 of 21)*

The folowing list shows all the existing Standard Switches existing in our nested environment:

- **For the Management and Virtual Machines network:** In the Figure 15-5 we see the existing Standard Switches for Management and VM Network Port groups and the vDS Port groups to witch we will migrate.

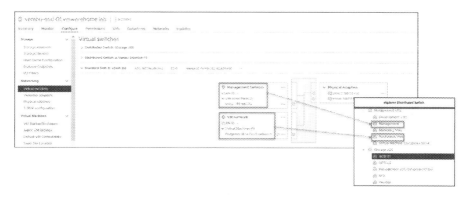

Figure 15-5. *(Advanced vDS - VLANs 5 of 21)*

- **For the Storage network:** Also in the Figure 15-6 we see the same, but for Storage network with the iSCSI and NFS Standard Port groups will be migrated to witch vDS Port groups.

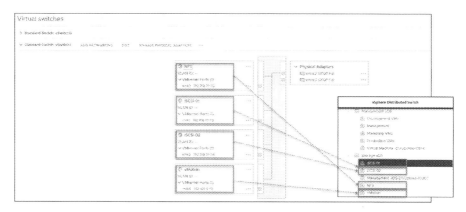

Figure 15-6. *(Advanced vDS - VLANs 6 of 21)*

Next, we will go through how to add the vmnics to the Management vDS and how to migrate the VMkernel and the port groups. We will also migrate the Virtual Machines network.

> **Note**   This chapter assumes that you have already created the Management and Storage vDSs, so we will only do the network migration. If you have not created the vDSs, follow the instructions in Chapter 14 to do so.

If you have already created your vDS and added the ESXi hosts but have not added vmnics and migrated the networks, right-click the **Management vDS**, click **Add and Manage Hosts** in the context menu, and select the **Manage host networking** in the first step of the wizard, shown in Figure 15-7. Select **Add hosts** instead if you have created the vDS or are creating it for the first time. Both options have the same steps (except when adding the hosts, since no hosts are added to the vDS). Click **Next**.

Figure 15-7. *(Advanced vDS - VLANs 7 of 21)*

Next, select the hosts you are migrating to the network. For purposes of the text lab, we are migrating the full Cluster, so select all three ESXi hosts and click **Next**. See Figure 15-8.

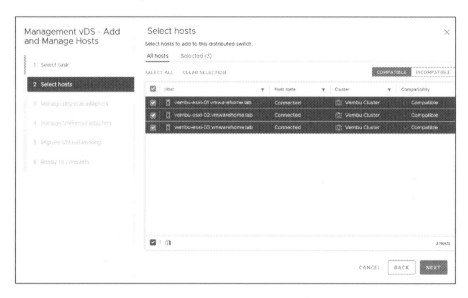

Figure 15-8. *(Advanced vDS - VLANs 8 of 21)*

In step 3 of the wizard, shown in Figure 15-9, select the vmnics that will be used on this vDS. Since we are migrating the Management network, as shown in our design, select **vmnic0** and **vmnic1**. In the *Assign uplink* column, select **(Auto-assign)** or select the uplink number. Click **Next**.

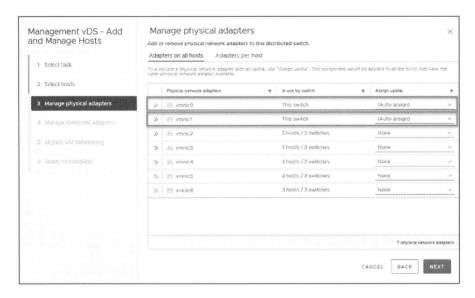

Figure 15-9. *(Advanced vDS - VLANs 9 of 21)*

In step 4 of the wizard, we will migrate the VMkernel network from the ESXi host managment, that has the vmnic0 (check Chapter 5 vSphere Networking on how to check management VMkernel and witch vmnics is using) and will assign a new Port group in the vDS by clicking the **Assign Port Group** option. Select the Port group, in this case is **Management**, and click **Assign**.

Note   Since all ESXi hosts use the vmnics for management, we can do this for all ESXi hosts in just one step. You must use the **Adapters per host** tab if your environment uses different vmnics on different ESXi hosts.

Figure 15-10. *(Advanced vDS - VLANs 10 of 21)*

Next, migrate the Virtual Machines network. Our environment has two VMs using the Standard Switch network. Since migrating VM networking is disabled by default, you need to enable it by checking the **Migrate virtual machine networking** check box (see Figure 15-11). The process is similar to when we migrate the VMkernel network and assign a port group by clicking **Assign Port Group** and selecting a port group to use on this VMs. For this case, select the **Production VMs** port group.

Note   In this example, VMs have only one network adapter, adapter 1. If VMs have more adapters, they will show here, and you would need to assign a port group for each adapter.

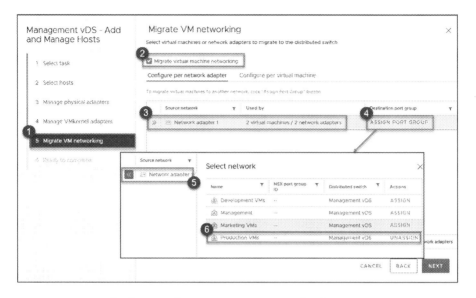

Figure 15-11. *(Advanced vDS - VLANs 11 of 21)*

But if you have several VMs and some belong to different departments, we need to use the **Configure per virtual machine** option. Figure 15-12 shows an example in which one VM is placed in the Production VMs network and the other is placed in the Marketing VMs network.

Figure 15-12. *(Advanced vDS - VLANs 12 of 21)*

After you select all VMkernel and Virtual Machines networks, the wizard shows all the information (how many networks or VMs will be migrated), as shown in Figure 15-13. Click **Finish** to start the migration from your Standard Switch to the new vDS.

Figure 15-13. *(Advanced vDS - VLANs 13 of 21)*

If all goes smoothly and there are no issues, you will see the tasks being executed, and vCenter will migrate all the networks.

While this process is designed to be seamless and generally does not cause significant downtime for the ESXi hosts and VMs, it's important to note that minimal downtime may occur during the network switchover. This could manifest as a brief interruption lasting for one or two missed pings. Such brief disruptions are normal and should be planned for, especially in environments where continuous connectivity is critical.

Note   If there is any issue with the ESXi hosts migration, misconfiguration in the new vDS, and ESXi hosts is not connected, vCenter will roll back the migration and give an error/warning. This is a protective measure so that you don't lose any ESXi host network.

In our case, in one port group, there was an added wrong VLAN (a typo), and the first attempt was not finished properly. We needed to double-check all vDSs to find the problem.

Now you can select an ESXi host, go to the Switches option, and select the new vDS, and you will see vmk0 now migrated to the new vDS created.

Figure 15-14. *(Advanced vDS - VLANs 14 of 21)*

In the vDS, in this case the Management vDS, you can click the **VMs** tab to see the VMs that were migrated, as shown in Figure 15-15.

Figure 15-15. *(Advanced vDS - VLANs 15 of 21)*

To check the migration (or for troubleshooting), you should ping one or two VMs during the migration to double-check that there is no problem with the VMs network. Figure 15-16 shows ping results indicating that all migrations were done successfully.

Figure 15-16. *(Advanced vDS - VLANs 16 of 21)*

To round out this chapter, we will review the other vDS, Storage. Since this Storage vDS will use iSCSI, it needs some particular configuration in the uplinks. Similar to what we have done in the chapter that we discuss iSCSI, but now in the vDS.

First, Figure 15-17 shows the output of our Storage vDS.

Figure 15-17. *(Advanced vDS - VLANs 17 of 21)*

In Chapter 11 when we create iSCSI Port binding. We need to do the same in the vDS.

As shown in Figure 15-18, our iSCIS 01 port group has Uplink 1 active and Uplink 2 unused. So, the iSCSI 02 port group needs to have Uplink 2 active and Uplink 1 unused so that we can use iSCSI port binding.

Figure 15-18. *(Advanced vDS - VLANs 18 of 21)*

We set Teaming and Failover both Uplinks to active for the vDS level, NFS, and vMotion port group.

Note   For the NFS, and vMotion Port group we set both Uplinks to active in the vDS on the *Teaming and Failover* option, since they need both active/active to have multipath created, like it was in the Standard Switch.

Then when we migrate all the Storage VMkernel it should be like shown in Figure 15-19, when migrating `vmnic2` and `vmnic3` (used for Storage, as shown in our design).

Figure 15-19. *(Advanced vDS - VLANs 19 of 21)*

And in each ESXi host, you will see the Storage vDS migrated from the Standard Switch.

Figure 15-20. *(Advanced vDS - VLANs 20 of 21*

For the final step, delete all the old Standard Switches from each ESXi host, using the steps shown in Figure 15-21.

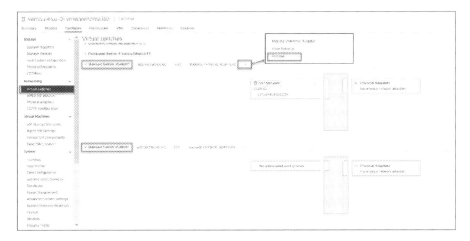

Figure 15-21. *(Advanced vDS - VLANs 21 of 21)*

15.3 Summary

In this chapter on Advanced Configuration with vSphere Distributed Switch, we explore the integration of VLANs into vDS and the process of migrating from Standard vSwitch to vDS. Initially, we emphasize the necessity of adding VLANs to the new vDS and Port groups, a step crucial for environments utilizing VLANs to segment network traffic effectively. This includes configuring VLAN trunking to manage multiple VLANs efficiently, ensuring secure and organized network setups.

The chapter then guides through the migration of VMkernel networks to vDS, highlighting the preparation of the same Port groups found in Standard Switch for a seamless transition. Detailed instructions are provided for adding ESXi hosts and vmnics to the vDS, migrating VMkernel networks for management, and reassigning virtual machines to new port groups on the vDS. This process is essential for leveraging the advanced features and centralized management capabilities of vDS over standard switches.

Special attention is given to configuring VLAN settings for each Port group and considering VLAN configurations within guest operating systems when necessary. The chapter concludes with the successful migration of network settings from Standard vSwitch to vDS, ensuring enhanced network management and performance in vSphere environments. Through this chapter, readers gain insights into effectively using VLANs within vDS and executing network migrations to optimize their vSphere infrastructure.

CHAPTER 16

Configuring LACP in vSphere Distributed Switch

In this chapter we will discuss the importance of Link Aggregation Control Protocol (LACP) in the vSphere Distributed Switch (vDS) environment. LACP plays a role in enhancing network performance and reliability by combining network connections. By understanding how to configure and utilize LACP within vDS, you will be well equipped to optimize your VMware infrastructure for increased throughput and redundancy.

16.1 What Is Link Aggregation Control Protocol (LACP)

Before diving into the usage of a feature, it's essential to understand its purpose and functionality. In this section, we explore LACP, also known as Ether-Channel, Ethernet trunk, port channel, LACP, vPC, and Multi-Link Trunking. It's important to note that the availability and configuration of LACP may vary depending on the specific switch vendor and model you are using.

© Luciano Patrão 2024
L. Patrão, *VMware vSphere Essentials*, https://doi.org/10.1007/979-8-8688-0208-9_16

Link aggregation combines multiple physical network links into a single logical link, providing higher bandwidth and redundancy in case of link failures. Two common link aggregation methods are used: EtherChannel and LACP (IEEE 802.3ad).

Link aggregation, which enables multiple physical links between network devices to function as a single logical link, can be achieved through both trunking and LACP. However, they differ in their approach:

- **Trunking**: In trunk mode, individual ports within a link aggregation group are statically configured to form a trunk. The Switch treats these ports as a logical interface, facilitating traffic exchange between switches or network devices. Trunking doesn't require negotiation between devices and operates independently of any specific protocol.

- **LACP**: LACP is a standard protocol that allows two devices to dynamically negotiate and form a link aggregation group. LACP utilizes control frames for negotiation and management, providing advanced load-balancing techniques beyond trunking. With LACP, switches can automatically detect and configure link aggregation with other LACP-enabled switches.

In summary, while both trunking and LACP achieve link aggregation, trunking relies on static configuration without protocol negotiation. On the other hand, LACP is a dynamic, protocol-based approach that enables the automatic formation and management of link aggregation groups between devices.

Understanding these concepts will help you to proceed with configuring and using LACP in the vSphere Distributed Switch.

Link aggregation concepts:

Link aggregation is the process of combining multiple physical network links into a single logical link, providing higher bandwidth and redundancy in case of link failures. There are two common methods used for link aggregation:

- **EtherChannel**: EtherChannel is a proprietary technology offered by Cisco that allows for up to eight physical Ethernet links to be combined into a single logical link, providing fast connectivity and failover protection between switches, routers, and servers.

- **LACP or IEEE 802.3ad**: LACP is an IEEE standard included in the 802.3ad specification that uses a Link Aggregation Control Protocol to bundle several physical ports into a single logical channel automatically. When two devices support LACP, they can negotiate the creation of a link aggregation group and the load-balancing method used to distribute traffic across the links.

While both technologies achieve the same goal of link aggregation, they have some differences. EtherChannel is a Cisco-proprietary technology that can be used only with Cisco equipment. In contrast, LACP is an open standard that can be used with any vendor's equipment that supports it. Additionally, EtherChannel provides greater flexibility in load balancing, while LACP mandates a specific load-balancing algorithm.

Figure 16-1 illustrates the design of a vDS with LACP using Link Aggregation Group (LAG) configuration and the connection to physical network interfaces and switch ports. In this scenario, we have three ESXi hosts connected to the Management vDS. Each vmnic (virtual machine network interface card) from the ESXi hosts is connected to corresponding physical switch ports and configured with LACP at the switch level.

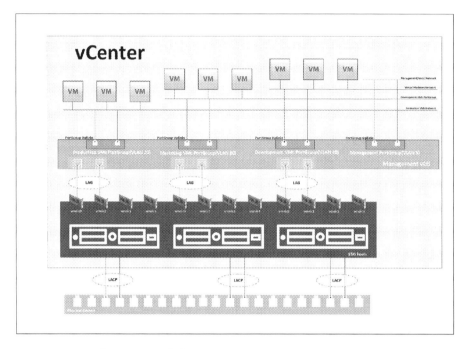

Figure 16-1. *(LACP 1 of 1)*

This configuration exemplifies implementing LACP in your environment, showcasing how the vDS, ESXi hosts, and physical switches are interconnected and configured to utilize LACP for improved network performance and redundancy.

A Link Aggregation Group (LAG) is a logical grouping of multiple physical network links or ports combined to form a single high-bandwidth connection. LAGs are commonly used to increase network capacity, enhance redundancy, and improve overall network performance.

The diagram in Figure 16-1 illustrates the concept of a LAG. The vDS has three ESXi hosts, each of which has multiple physical network interface cards (NICs) connected to the physical switch. Instead of treating these individual NICs as separate connections, you can create a LAG by combining them into a single logical link. For example, you can configure LACP on the physical switch and the vDS to enable dynamic negotiation and management of the LAG. LACP will establish a LAG between the physical switch and the vDS by bundling the multiple NICs together.

Once the LAG is formed, virtual machines and other network resources in your vSphere environment can utilize the combined bandwidth and redundancy provided by the LAG. This means traffic can be distributed across the individual NICs within the LAG, allowing for increased throughput and improved resilience.

By using LAGs, you can effectively utilize multiple physical links as a single logical link, providing higher bandwidth and fault tolerance for the VMs networks.

16.2 Requirements and Limitations of LACP in vSphere

In order to effectively manage your network, it is crucial to understand the requirements and limitations associated with implementing the Link Aggregation Control Protocol in vSphere vDS. It's important to consider how LACP will integrate with your existing network infrastructure, including hardware and software compatibility as the configuration of physical NICs. By being aware of these limitations, you can optimize your network planning to fully leverage LACP's benefits within your vSphere environment.

The following restrictions and limitations apply when using LACP in vSphere vDS:

- LACP requires a vSphere Enterprise Plus license for the vDS feature.

- An ESXi host supports NIC teaming only on a single physical switch or a stack of switches.

- Link aggregation is not supported when using different trunked switches. To enable link aggregation, the

Switch must be configured to perform 802.3ad link aggregation in static mode ON, while the virtual Switch should have its *Load balancing* method set to **Route based on IP hash** (demonstrated later in this chapter).

- Enabling either **Route based on IP hash** without 802.3ad aggregation or vice versa causes disruptions in networking. Therefore, it is recommended first to change the virtual Switch. This results in the service console being unavailable. Still, the physical switch management interface remains accessible, enabling aggregation on the involved switch ports and restoring networking.

- Do not use LACP for iSCSI software multipathing. iSCSI software multipathing requires just one uplink per VMkernel, and link aggregation gives it more than one.

- Do not use beacon probing with IP HASH load balancing.

- Do not configure standby or unused uplinks with IP HASH load balancing.

- VMware supports only one EtherChannel bond per Virtual Standard Switch (vSS).

- ESXi supports LACP on vDS only.

- In vSphere Distributed Switch 5.5 and later, all load-balancing algorithms of LACP are supported.

You need to ensure that the load-balancing algorithm used in ESXi matches the load-balancing algorithm implemented on the physical switch is essential. For inquiries regarding the specific load-balancing algorithm employed by the physical Switch, please consult the physical switch vendor's documentation.

Caution   Due to potential network disruption, changes to link aggregation should be done during a maintenance window.

As with any networking change, there is a chance for network disruption, so a maintenance period is recommended for changes. This is especially true on a vDS because vCenter owns the vDS, and the hosts alone cannot change the vDS if the connection to vCenter is lost.

Enabling LACP can complicate vCenter or host management recovery in production-down scenarios because the LACP connection may need to be broken to move back to a Standard Switch if necessary (since LACP is not supported on a Standard Switch).

Limitations:

- vSphere Distributed Switches are the only supported switch type for LACP configuration.

- LACP cannot be used for software iSCSI multipathing.

- Host Profiles do not include LACP configuration settings.

- LACP is not supported within guest operating systems, including nested ESXi hosts.

- LACP cannot be used together with the ESXi Dump Collector.

Note   The management port must be connected to a vSphere Standard Switch to use the ESXi Dump Collector.

- Port Mirroring cannot be used with LACP to mirror LACPDU packets used for negotiation and control.

- The teaming health check does not function for LAG ports, as the LACP protocol ensures the health of individual LAG ports. However, VLAN and MTU health checks can still be performed on LAG ports.

- Enhanced LACP support is limited to a single LAG per distributed port (dvPortGroup) or port group to handle the traffic.

- Up to 64 LAGs can be created on a distributed switch, with each host supporting up to 64 LAGs.

  - The actual number of usable LAGs depends on the capabilities of the physical environment and the virtual network topology.

  - For example, if the physical switch allows a maximum of four ports in an LACP port channel, you can connect up to four physical NICs per host to a LAG.

  - LACP is currently not supported with Single Root I/O Virtualization (SR-IOV, discussed in Chapter 26).

16.3 Configure LACP in vSphere Distributed Switch

Let's begin by configuring LACP in the vDS we created in the previous chapter about vDS. We will create a vDS named Vembu-LAG with a port group called LACP-LAG vDS.

Note   Means that user can see different names that we have already seen in previous chapters, since this part needs to be done in physical lab, not nested. As stated above LACP is not supported in nested environments.

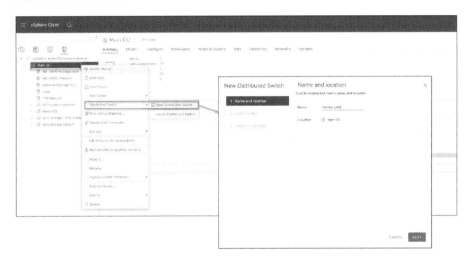

Figure 16-2.   *(LACP in vSphere vDS 1 of 13)*

Although I will demonstrate the steps using our nested environment (the same we have been using since the beginning of this book), it's important to note that the actual LACP and physical configurations are performed in our physical VMware environment, which has been expressly set up with LACP for the purpose of this chapter.

After the vDS and port group are created, select the vDS you just created, click the **Configure** tab, select the **LACP** option, and then click **NEW**, as shown in Figure 16-3. Create a LAG called **LAG-Vembu**.

Figure 16-3. *(LACP in vSphere vDS 2 of 13)*

Set the *Number of ports* option to **2** to match the number of uplinks in
your vDS.

Link Aggregation Group mode:

The vSphere Distributed Switch (vDS) LACP mode option is a
configuration setting that determines how the vDS handles LACP
negotiation with physical switches.

There are two LACP mode options available in vSphere vDS:

- **Active LACP mode**: In Active LACP mode, the vDS
  initiates the LACP negotiation with the physical switch.
  The vDS sends LACP packets to the switch and waits
  for a response. If the switch responds, the vDS forms a
  LAG with the switch.

- **Passive LACP mode**: In Passive LACP mode, the vDS
  does not initiate LACP negotiation with the physical
  switch. Instead, it listens for LACP packets from the
  switch. If it receives a packet, it will respond and form a
  LAG with the switch.

The choice of LACP mode depends on your network configuration
and requirements. Active LACP mode is recommended if you have control

over the physical switch and want to ensure that the vDS initiates the LACP negotiation. This allows you to configure specific settings, such as the LAG load-balancing algorithm, on both the vDS and the physical switch.

On the other hand, Passive LACP mode may be more appropriate if you connect the vDS to a third-party switch or an external service provider's network. In this scenario, you may not control the switch configuration, so Passive LACP mode allows the vDS to adapt to the switch's negotiation behavior.

Overall, the LACP mode option in vSphere vDS allows you to configure the LACP negotiation behavior to match your network environment, ensuring optimal performance and reliability.

In our example, Passive mode is used in the vDS LAG and Active mode is used in the physical switch.

The *Load balancing mode* option in vSphere vDS (see Figure 16-3) determines how traffic is distributed across the physical uplinks within a LAG. It controls the algorithm used to determine which uplink is used for transmitting traffic from virtual machines. Several *Load balancing mode* options are available in vSphere vDS, but since we will be selecting the **Route based on the IP hash** option in our vDS, select the **Source and destination IP address** (default) here.

This load-balancing mode is helpful for traffic that flows between the same source and destination IP addresses. The source and destination IP addresses are used to create a hash value in this mode. The hash value is then used to determine the traffic's uplink.

Moving down to the *Port policies* section of Figure 16-3, we are not using port policies in our LAG example, but I'll quickly explain how port policies work.

In vSphere, a LAG combines multiple physical network connections into a single logical connection, increasing bandwidth and redundancy. LAG port policies are a set of rules that define how the LAG is configured for each port.

When configuring LAG port policies, you can specify VLAN policies and NetFlow policies for individual LAGs within the same uplink port group. This allows you to apply different policies to different LAGs within the same group based on their specific requirements.

By default, the policies defined at the uplink port group level will be applied to all LAGs in the group. However, if necessary, you can override these policies for individual LAGs by specifying different policies at the LAG level. For example, you may want to apply a different VLAN policy to a particular LAG to isolate traffic from other LAGs in the same port group. Alternatively, you might want to apply a different NetFlow policy to a specific LAG to monitor traffic flow more closely.

Overall, LAG port policies provide a flexible and granular approach to configuring LAGs in vSphere, allowing you to tailor your network configuration to meet the specific needs of your environment.

Now that we have a vDS, a port group, and a LAG, we must set our Teaming from the vDS uplink to our LAG created in the previous step. Right-click the LACP-LAG vDS, click **Edit Settings**, and then select **Teaming and failover**, as shown in Figure 16-4. We need to move down the vDS uplinks to unused and move the LAG to active.

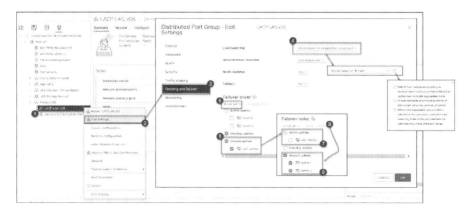

Figure 16-4. *(LACP in vSphere vDS 3 of 13)*

As previously explained, when using LACP, you need to set the vDS *Load balancing* field to **Route based on IP hash**, as shown in Figure 16-4.

Figure 16-5 shows the final result after finishing our vDS reconfiguring to use LAG.

Figure 16-5. *(LACP in vSphere vDS 4 of 13)*

Now that we have our LAG configured in our new vDS, we will add ESXi hosts to our vDS.

Right-click the vDS and click **Add and Manage Hosts** in the context menu. See Figure 16-6. Since this is a new vDS, select the **Add hosts** option in the wizard that opens; If this was to be done in a vDS that already exists, in this case we need to create one, so extra steps are needed, then you would need to use the **Manage host networking** option (as described in Chapter 15 in the "Migrate from a Standard vSwitch to vSphere Distributed Switch" section). Click **Next**.

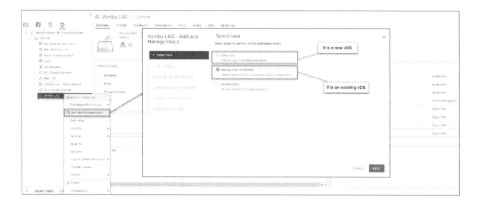

Figure 16-6. *(LACP in vSphere vDS 5 of 13)*

In step 2 of the wizard, select the ESXi hosts to add to this vDS, as shown in Figure 16-7. Click **Next**.

Figure 16-7. *(LACP in vSphere vDS 6 of 13)*

Next, select the vmnics connected to the physical switch ports and configured with LACP—in our case, `vmnic1` and `vmnic7`, as shown in Figure 16-8. Click **Next**.

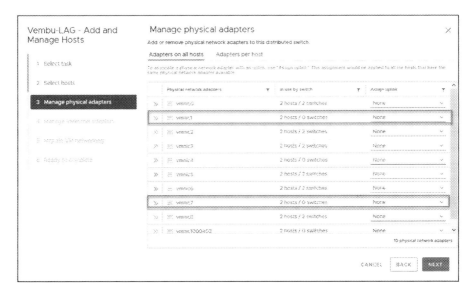

Figure 16-8. *(LACP in vSphere vDS 7 of 13)*

Note   Don't forget that all your ESXi hosts' network interface connections need to be set as LACP in your physical switch.

In step 3 of the wizard, bind the vmnics with the LAG that you previously created, as shown in Figure 16-9. Click **Next**.

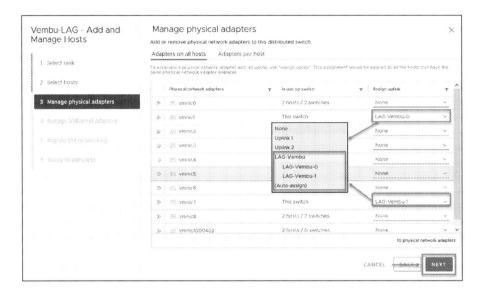

Figure 16-9. *(LACP in vSphere vDS 8 of 13)*

Step 4, shown in Figure 16-10, is about migrations of the VMkernel networks. In the next option we will skip this step, since this is only if you have VMkernel with LAG enabled, since is not the case we skip it. Click **Next**.

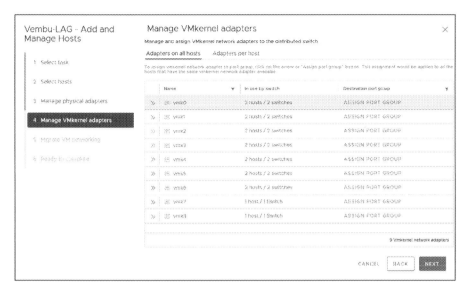

Figure 16-10. *(LACP in vSphere vDS 9 of 13)*

In step 5 of the wizard, you migrate existing VMs connected to this vDS to use the LAG port group. As shown in Figure 16-11, check the **Migrate virtual machine networking** check box and click the **Configure per virtual machine** tab.

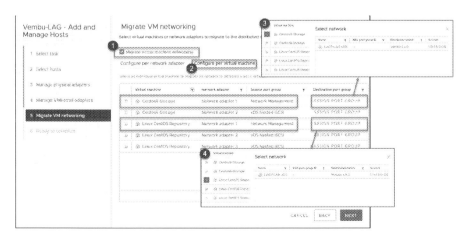

Figure 16-11. *(LACP in vSphere vDS 10 of 13)*

315

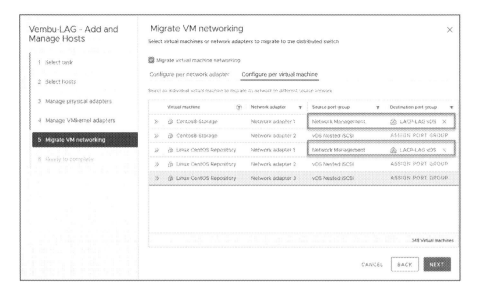

Figure 16-12. *(LACP in vSphere vDS 11 of 13)*

Note   If your VMs have more than one virtual network adapter and are in different networks (one using LAG and the other not), but all are in the same network (for example, `nic1` is management and `nic2` is production), then you would use the *Configure per network adapter* tab.

In our test lab design, all VMs have more than one network adapter, but we want to change only the VM network management. Select the VM and the network adapter, click **Assign Port Group**, and **Assign**. Then click **Next**.

After VMs are connected to LAG, and will use an LACP network. Click **Next**.

In the final wizard step, shown in Figure 16-13, verify the details and click **Finish** to complete the port group configuration for utilizing LAG.

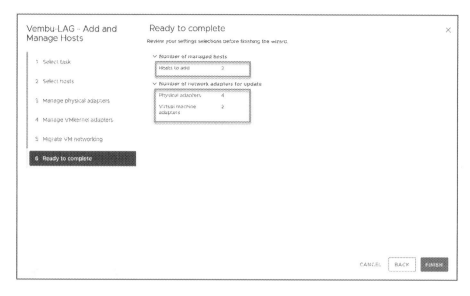

Figure 16-13. *(LACP in vSphere vDS 12 of 13)*

With the completion of all LACP configurations, you have successfully executed the following steps:

- Create a vDS for LACP.

- Create a LAG (link aggregation group).

- Set up the port group with LAG.

- Associate the LAG uplinks with vmnics.

- Transfer the VMs' networks to the LAG port group.

Now we can check the ESXi host console to see if the host uses LACP and is enabled on the physical switch. To do so, running the following command:

```
esxcli network vswitch dvs vmware lacp status get
```

If we see the physical switch and the physical ports number, as in Figure 16-14, then LACP is active and working.

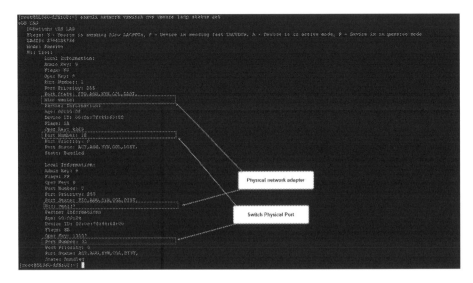

Figure 16-14. *(LACP in vSphere vDS 13 of 13)*

This command shows us the configuration of our vDS with the LAG:

```
esxcli network vswitch vmware lacp config get
```

With the information, we have the guarantee that our LACP is adequately configured and active on both sides (in the vDS and the physical switch).

16.4 Migrate vDS VMkernel Network to vDS LACP

When enabling LACP (LAG) in our vDS and using LACP on our VMkernel, we need to consider the timeout or even losing communication while LACP is enabled.

In the previous section, we already checked how the LACP runs on both sides (physical and virtual), meaning that the LACP is working on your vSphere with LAG. But to migrate a VMkernel (that could be using Active/Passive Teaming or even Active/Active Teaming), one physical adapter must be done each time. If not, you could lose connection to your ESXi host or to your Datastores if using NFS.

Note   Before starting the migration, if you have two new physical adapters (vmnics) configuring a vDS with LACP, this migration is more straightforward. But if you plan to use vmnics that are in use, the migration must be done one vmnic at a time.

Migrate VMkernel and vmnics to a new vDS with LACP using the same vmnics.

As previously explained, when migrating to an LACP but using the same physical network adapters, the process must be done differently, one vmnic at a time. If we enable LACP on both ports in the physical switch, we will automatically lose the connection in the Virtual Switch (a Standard Switch or a vDS) because we didn't change the settings in the vSphere. If we are doing this for a management VMkernel, then we don't have access to the ESXi host to make these changes.

Whenever there is a networking modification, it is advisable to allocate a maintenance window due to the potential for network disruptions. This is particularly crucial when working with a vDS since the vDS is controlled by vCenter, and individual hosts cannot make alterations to the vDS without a connection to vCenter.

Implementing LACP can introduce complications for restoring vCenter or host management functionality during critical situations, since the LACP connection may need to be terminated to revert to a Standard Switch if required (as LACP is not compatible with a Standard Switch).

How do we do this?

Note   Since LACP is not supported in nested environments, we will not use the nested environment that we are using throughout the book. We will use a physical environment for these tasks.

First, this process is recommended with the ESXi in maintenance mode.

Figure 16-15 shows our network vDS for the physical environment: two ESXi hosts with a management vDS.

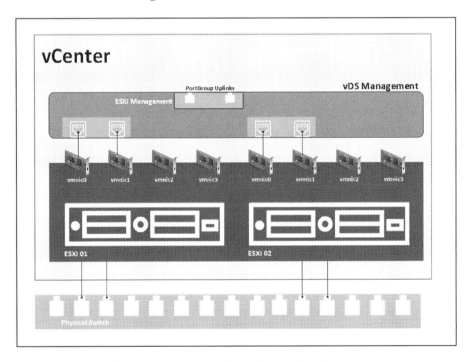

Figure 16-15. *(Migrate VMkernel LACP 1 of 11)*

As mentioned, we will use vmnic0 and vmnic1 for this migration. So our first step is to shut down the port in the physical switch where vmnic0 is connected to the ESXi 01.

Note   I will use my HPE ProCurve switch for the physical switch example. Don't forget that other switch vendors' commands are different to perform these tasks.

The following command are to shutdown the physical port in the Switch.

There were no number in my initial writing, only bullet points. But each number here is a step a command that needs to be done in physical switch, nothing related to what you see in the next image. Next image is a consequence of the steps, vmnic down. As is explained in the first paragraph.

This was done in a HPE physical switch, that is not discuss in this book, reader can have different devices, he just need to see what happen when we shutdown the port that is show in the Figure 16-16:

1. `conf` (enter the configuration shell).

2. `interface 13 disable` (shut down port 13 where vmnic0 is connected).

   After the port is disabled, you should see it in the vDS. See Figure 16-16.

Figure 16-16. *(Migrate VMkernel LACP 2 of 11)*

3. `interface 13 LACP` (add port 13 or `vmnic0` to the LACP/EtherChannel configuration).

   In the vDS Management, create a LAG. See Figure 16-17.

321

Figure 16-17. *(Migrate VMkernel LACP 3 of 11)*

Now let's us add the `vmnic0` to the LAG uplinks.

On the vDS Management, select **Manage host networking** and then click **Next**. See Figure 16-18.

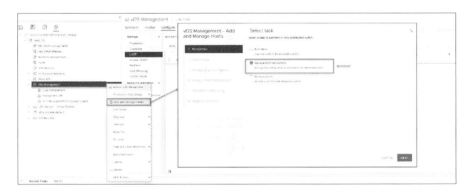

Figure 16-18. *(Migrate VMkernel LACP 4 of 11)*

Then select the ESXi host on which you disabled the vmnic, in our case ESXi 01, and click **Next**. See Figure 16-19.

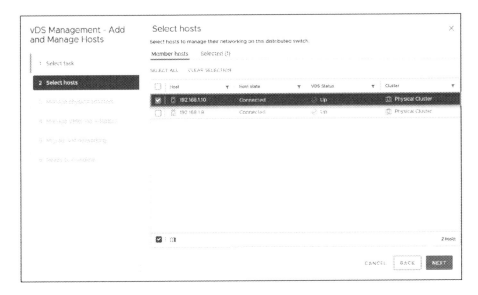

Figure 16-19. *(Migrate VMkernel LACP 5 of 11)*

Next, select `vmnic0` and that interface to the LAG
uplink (the vDS LACP). See Figure 16-20.

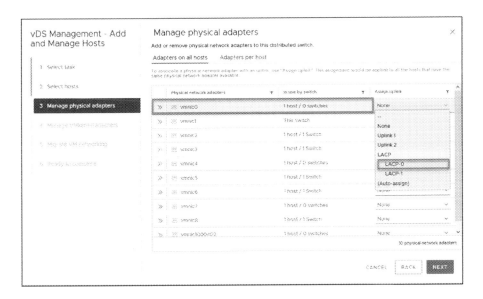

Figure 16-20. *(Migrate VMkernel LACP 6 of 11)*

Do not change anything else: click **Next** until the final wizard step and then click **Finish**.

Return to the physical switch and reenable the port 13 (vmnic0).

4. `interface 13 enable`

Now edit the vDS LACP, and in the *Teaming and failover* section, move the LACP group to the *Active uplinks* and move the Uplinks to the *Unused uplinks*. See Figure 16-21.

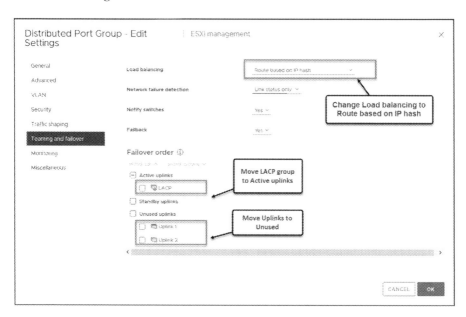

Figure 16-21. *(Migrate VMkernel LACP 7 of 11)*

Note   While doing these changes, ensure the ESXi host doesn't lose its connection.

In the Figure 16-22, we show the process that we created above witht the commends in your physical switch.Moving from a Standalone port, to an LACP port, by disabling ports and enabling the ports with LACP.

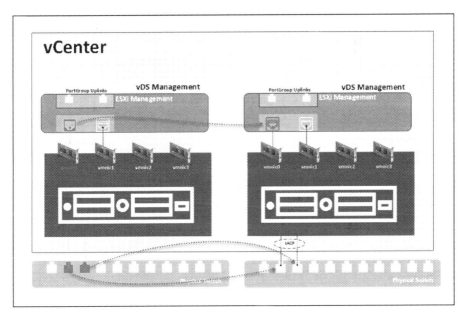

Figure 16-22. *(Migrate VMkernel LACP 8 of 11)*

Now let's disable the second port (vmnic1)

5. interface 12 disable (shut down port 12 where vmnic1 is connected)

As you can see in Figure 16-23, vmnic1 is down in vCenter.

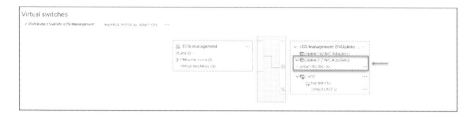

Figure 16-23. *(Migrate VMkernel LACP 9 of 11)*

Next, following the same procedure previously
described, move the `vmnic1` to the LAG link. See
Figure 16-24.

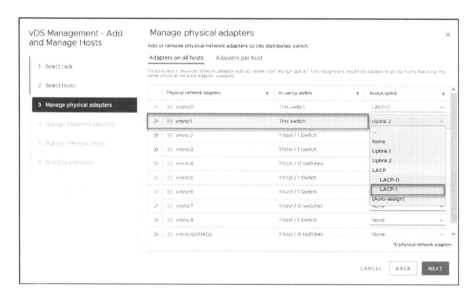

Figure 16-24. *(Migrate VMkernel LACP 10 of 11)*

Again, do not change anything else; click **Next** to proceed through the
wizard steps and then click **Finish** in the last step.

Finally, add port 12 (`vmnic1`) to LACP in the physical switch.

6. `interface 12 LACP` (add port 12 or `vmnic1` to LACP/EtherChannel configuration).
   To finalize the VMkernel migration, reenable the port for the `vmnic1`.

7. `interface 12 enable`
   We have migrated our VMkernel to a vDS with LACP without losing any connection to our ESXi host.
   We did this process for ESXi 01, but you also need to do this for all ESXi hosts in the Cluster that are added to this vDS Management.
   For a final check to see if LACP is running on your ESXi hosts, run the following commands (see Figure 16-25):

   • `esxcli network vswitch vmware lacp config get`

   • `esxcli network vswitch dvs vmware lacp status get`

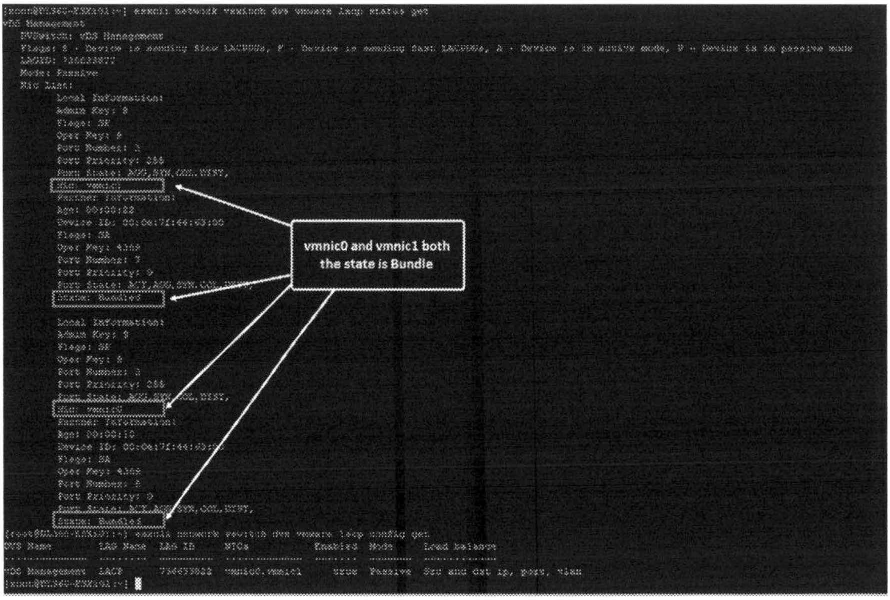

Figure 16-25. (*Migrate VMkernel LACP 11 of 11*)

16.5 Summary

This chapter explored the intricacies of configuring LACP in vSphere Distributed Switch and explained its core concepts, requirements, and the necessary steps for implementation and migration. In Chapter 16, we shift our focus to gaining a deeper understanding of advanced configurations in vSphere Distributed Switch. Our next topic is the utilization of VLANs within vDS, which plays a role in improving network segmentation and performance. Furthermore, we will also explore the process of migrating from a Standard vSwitch to vDS—a step for network advancement in VMware environments. This phase aims to enhance your expertise in managing networks by leveraging the capabilities of vDS within VMware vSphere.

CHAPTER 17

vSphere Advanced Features

Now that we have our vCenter/vSphere network set up and configured, we are ready to explore the numerous advanced features of vSphere that we may customize while using vCenter. Some of these features have been mentioned in previous chapters, but now we will go over them in depth and examine how they function and how to set and activate advanced options on those features.

17.1 vSphere vMotion

VMware vSphere vMotion allows you to migrate workloads from one server to another without downtime. This seamless process ensures that users experience no disruption, as the VMs remain operational during the migration.

While vMotion facilitates uninterrupted service during migrations, it is distinct from vSphere High Availability (HA). HA is focused on providing continuous availability by automatically restarting VMs on other available servers in the event of a server failure. Unlike HA, vMotion does not involve VM restarts and is used primarily for balancing workloads and performing maintenance without downtime.

© Luciano Patrão 2024
L. Patrão, *VMware vSphere Essentials*, https://doi.org/10.1007/979-8-8688-0208-9_17

17.1.1 How Do Live Migrations Work?

If you know ahead of time when system downtime is expected, such as for maintenance, you can vMotion the VMs on that server to a different one. That way, your workload will still be available if a server goes down or needs to be shut down.

vSphere vMotion makes it possible to move workloads from one server to another without ever stopping the application. Your application still runs during the live migration, and users can still access their systems. No downtime means your productivity never stops!

- Automatically optimize virtual machines within resource pools

- Perform hardware maintenance without scheduling downtime or disrupting business operations

- Move virtual machines away from failing or underperforming servers

You can vMotion between ESXi hosts, Clusters, Datacenters, and vCenters. It is also possible between sites with Advanced Cross vCenter vMotion.

Figure 17-1 shows a vMotion between ESXi hosts in the same Cluster, but it can also be between Clusters or Datacenters inside the same vCenter.

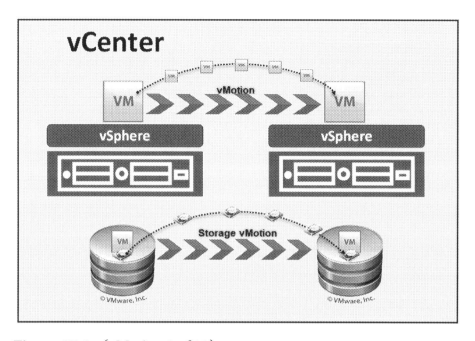

Figure 17-1. *(vMotion 1 of 11)*

Figure 17-1 also shows an example of Storage vMotion (SvMotion). SvMotion enables a VM to be migrated between Datastores. The VM stays in the same ESXi host, only migrating the virtual disks and VM configuration files to another Datastore shared between the ESXi hosts.

The next example, shown in Figure 17-2, is a vMotion from one vCenter to another vCenter (which can be in the same physical Datacenter or between two different sites/buildings) by using the Long Distance vMotion option.

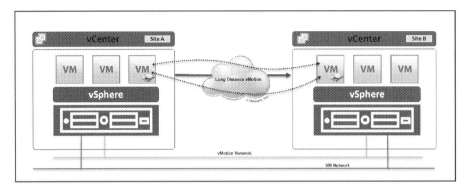

Figure 17-2. *(vMotion 2 of 11)*

When planning for cross-vCenter vMotion, it is important to be aware of this two specific requirements:

- **Network latency:** For Long Distance vMotion to be successful, network latency should typically be 150 milliseconds RTT (Round-Trip Time) or less. This is crucial for ensuring the integrity and performance of the live migration.

- **Licensing:** Ensure the source and destination vCenters have the appropriate licensing level. Cross-vCenter vMotion requires higher-tier licenses, such as Enterprise Plus.

Using the vMotion feature, you can migrate any VM inside or outside the infrastructure without the need to power off the VM.

The previous designs and explanations should give you an idea of vMotion and how live migrations work. Additionally, it is important to mention XvMotion, which represents an advanced use of this technology. XvMotion allows for the live migration of both compute resources and storage simultaneously. This is particularly useful in scenarios without shared storage between the compute hosts. With XvMotion, a VM can be moved to another host and its associated storage with brief interruption (one or two pings). This capability significantly enhances flexibility in resource management and infrastructure maintenance.

17.1.2 Create a vMotion VMkernel Network

To create a VMkernel network, we need to create a VMkernel as we created in iSCSI/NFS in Chapter 7, but this time for vMotion service.

We need an IP address for each ESXi host that uses this vMotion network—in this case, for all the ESXi hosts in the Cluster. That means we need three IP addresses.

A vMotion network should be isolated from any other network, so we'll use a unique subnet (or, if you want, you can use a VLAN).

The vMotion network is primarily used for internal traffic, with data transfer occurring exclusively between ESXi hosts. This remains true even in Cross vCenter vMotion scenarios. As such, the vMotion network typically does not require a gateway when set up in a single Layer 2 (L2) network configuration. However, this is often not the case in more complex environments, especially for cross-datacenter migrations.

In many real-world applications, especially those involving cross-datacenter vMotion, the network is configured over Layer 3 (L3). This setup involves local routing and can be routed across different datacenters. Recognizing the need for flexibility in such scenarios, VMware introduced the vMotion networking stack. This feature allows for a separate, potentially dedicated gateway for the vMotion service, accommodating more complex network topologies and ensuring efficient, secure migrations across various network configurations.

In our configuration, we will use the subnet 192.168.0.0/24.

As shown in Figure 17-3, select the ESXi host, click the **Configure** tab, select **VMkernel adapters**, click **Add Networking**, and select **VMkernel Network Adapter** in the first step of the wizard. Click **Next**.

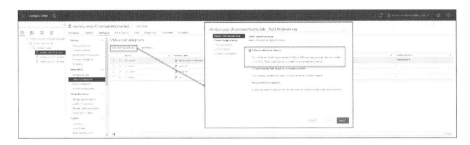

Figure 17-3. *(vMotion 3 of 11)*

In step 2 of the wizard (see Figure 17-4), choose **Select an existing standard switch** and (for purposes of the test lab) specify **vSwitch1**. Since vMotion needs good bandwidth, we will use the Storage vSwitch to add our vMotion.

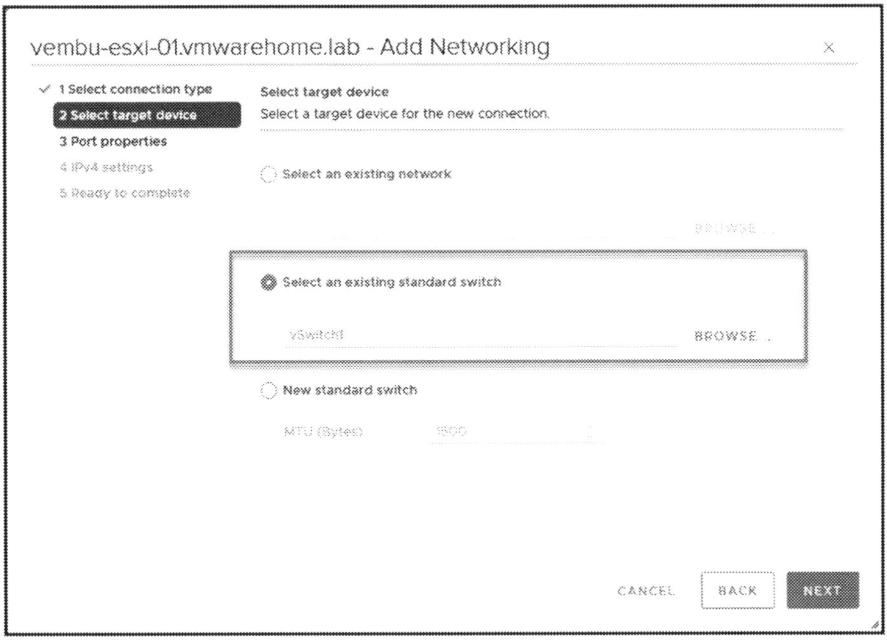

vembu-esxi-01.vmwarehome.lab - Add Networking   ×

✓ 1 Select connection type   Select target device
2 Select target device   Select a target device for the new connection.
3 Port properties
4 IPv4 settings   ◯ Select an existing network
5 Ready to complete
                                                                    BROWSE

                               ◉ Select an existing standard switch

                                   vSwitch1   BROWSE

                               ◯ New standard switch

                                   MTU (Bytes)   1500

                                         CANCEL   BACK   NEXT

Figure 17-4. *(vMotion 4 of 11)*

If you have extra vmnics, you should create a new Virtual Switch and use the new vmnics so that vMotion works appropriately with less latency. Even 10/20GB network interfaces are enough for most cases for Storage and vMotion.

Note   Don't forget that as a best practice for the vMotion network, you should use 10GB or 25GB connections.

After you select your vSwitch and click **Next**, enable the vMotion service for this VMkernel by checking the corresponding check box, as shown in Figure 17-5. Click **Next**.

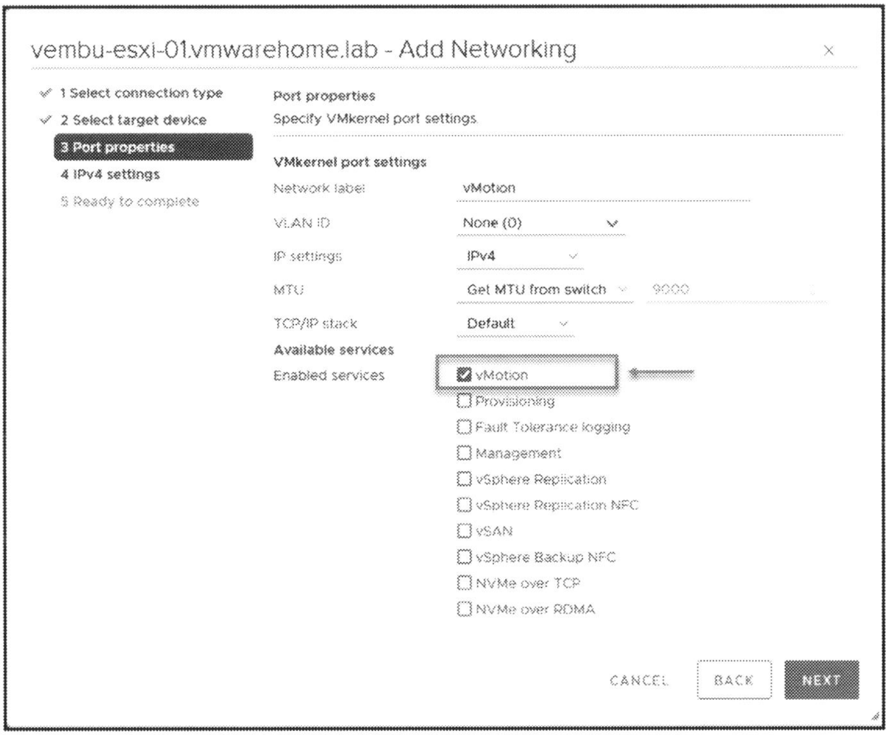

Figure 17-5. *(vMotion 5 of 11)*

In step 4 of the wizard, shown in Figure 17-6, select **Use static IPv4 settings** add your IP. Click **Next**.

Note   I've seen some deployments where customers used DHCP for vMotion or even vSAN. In one case, a firmware upgrade of physical switches cleaned out all DHCP table entries, and systems stopped working because all DHCP were lost. You can use DHCP, but it should continuously be monitored. But to bypass any future issues, we won't use DHCP in our test lab for this type of service.

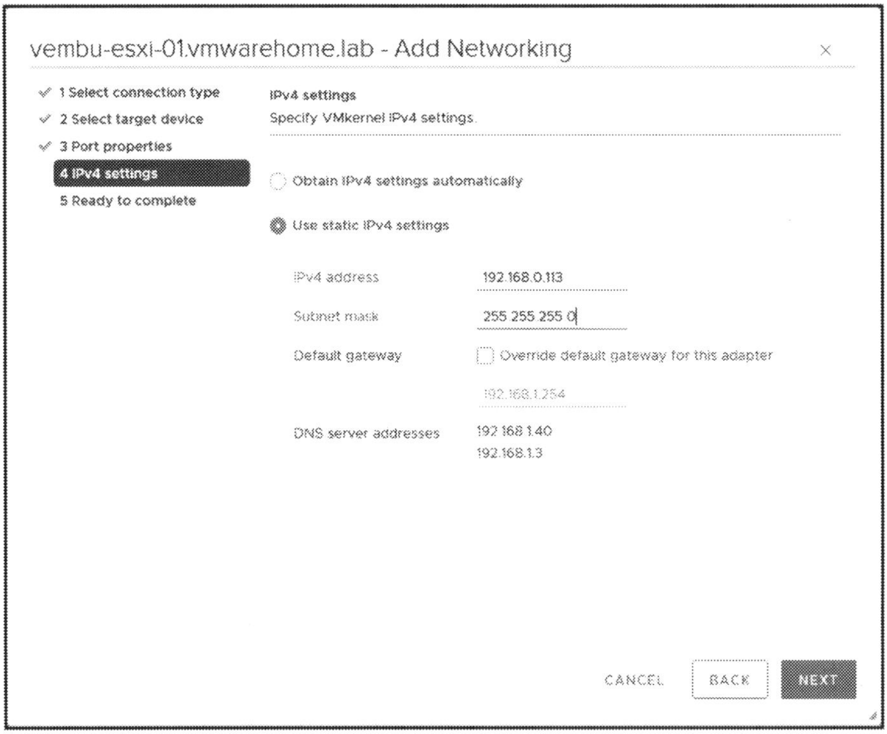

Figure 17-6. (vMotion 6 of 11)

For the final wizard step, check that the information is correct, as shown in Figure 17-7. If all is correct, click **Finish**.

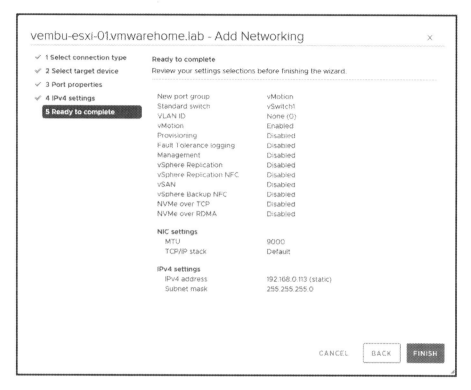

Figure 17-7. (vMotion 7 of 11)

Figure 17-8 shows that we now have a new VMkernel for vMotion.

Note   Although we will not configure a vMotion TCP/IP stack for our test lab, having a dedicated TCP/IP stack for vMotion can be particularly beneficial in environments where routed vMotion is required. This setup allows for more granular control over vMotion traffic, and can help manage network policies and routes more effectively. Especially in complex network architectures, where vMotion traffic needs to be routed across different network segments or datacenters, utilizing a dedicated TCP/IP stack can enhance network organization and potentially improve overall management of vMotion processes.

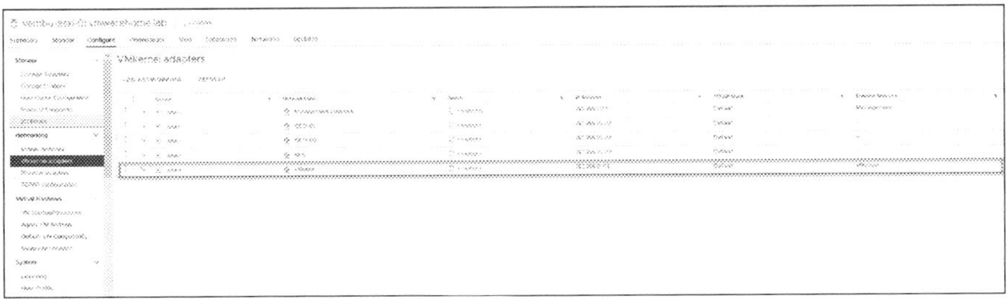

Figure 17-8. *(vMotion 8 of 11)*

Note   For better performance, if there are vmnics available, you can create multiple vMotion VMkernels.

After you create a vMotion VMkernel and repeat the process in every ESXi host, let's us test our new vMotion Network.

As covered in Chapter 12, we use the ESXi command vmkping to test the VMkernel networks. So, from one ESXi host, we will ping all the VMkernels in other ESXi hosts.

First, to make sure we are pinging the right VMkernerl (in this case vmk interface), identify the vMotion VMkernel with the command: esxcli-vmknic -l. Then, ping all the ESXi hosts' VMkernel IPs using jumbo frames (Chapter 11 introduced jumbo frames and MTU 9000).

Figure 17-9 shows that all pings were successful, so the vMotion network is working without issues.

Figure 17-9. *(vMotion 9 of 11)*

Figure 17-10 shows that the following types of vMotion migrations are possible:

1. It migrates only the VM to another ESXi host and doesn't change the Datastore location.

2. It migrates the VM to another Datastore and doesn't change the ESXi host location.

3. It migrates the VM location, ESXi host, and Datastore.

4. It migrates the VM to another vCenter (explained in the previous design).

Figure 17-10. *(vMotion 10 of 11)*

17.1.3 Encrypted Migration with vMotion

Before we finish this section about vMotion, let's see how to set up an encrypted migration with vMotion.

You set vMotion encryption in the VMs that you want to encrypt. We need to go to VM encryption section and encrypt our vMotion for this particular VM.

As Figure 17-11 shows, the *Encrypted vMotion* drop-down list has three encryption options:

- **Disabled:** Do not use encrypted vMotion, even if available.

- **Opportunistic:** Use encrypted vMotion if source and destination hosts support it, fall back to unencrypted vMotion otherwise. This is the default option.

- **Required:** Allow only encrypted vMotion. If the source or destination host does not support vMotion encryption, do not allow the vMotion to occur.

As noted, the default option is **Opportunistic**, if source and destination hosts are supported (meaning if they all have the key provider configured, then it will use encryption; if just one host doesn't have the key provider configured, it will not use encryption).

If the **Required** option is set, the source and destination hosts must have the key provider configured to start the migration using vMotion; if not, it will not migrate.

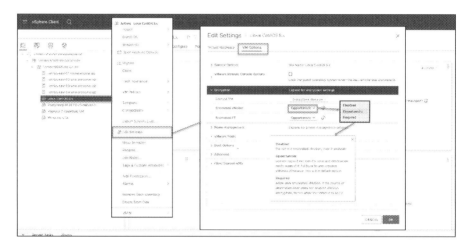

Figure 17-11. *(vMotion 11 of 11)*

After configuring encrypted vMotion, it is important to conduct tests to verify that migrations are happening securely and without performance degradation.

By configuring encrypted vMotion, you add a critical security measure to your vMotion migrations, protecting data in transit between hosts. This configuration is especially crucial in environments where data privacy and compliance are paramount.

17.2 vSphere Distributed Resource Scheduler

Now that we have our vMotion network created, we can start enabling vSphere Distributed Resource Scheduler (DRS).

vSphere DRS offers the resources that you need for your network to run reliably. This utility works on a cluster of ESXi servers and ensures appropriate resource distribution in the virtual machine placement. DRS also honors resource allocation policies at the cluster level while supporting system-level constraints.

17.2.1 How DRS Works

vSphere DRS is a function of VMware vSphere that ensures virtual machines and their applications have access to the CPU, memory, and disks (in sDRS) they need to run at optimal efficiency. In other words, DRS always tries to keep your VMs happy by providing them with the required compute resources as soon as they are powered on so that each VM's performance requirements are always met across the entire cluster.

If a VM's workload changes, it can have an impact on the balance in the Cluster. DRS monitors the Cluster at regular intervals (once every few minutes) to prevent bad performance and takes the necessary actions to restore balance. For example, when DRS detects an imbalance, it migrates the virtual machines from one host to another using vMotion.

Automatic DRS ensures that each virtual machine in the Cluster has adequate host resources, such as memory and CPU, at all times.

17.2.2 Create a Cluster DRS

At the Cluster level, click the **Configure** tab, select **vSphere DRS** (under Services on the left), click **Edit** (in the upper-right corner of the window), and enable the **vSphere DRS** option, as shown in Figure 17-12. The *Automation* tab of the Edit Cluster Settings window has the following options to configure in DRS:

- **Automation Level:** There are three levels of automation from which to choose:

    - **Fully Automated:** DRS applies both initial placements and load-balancing recommendations automatically.

    - **Partially Automated:** DRS applies recommendations only for initial placement. Any VM that is Power on, DRS asks and recommends in witch ESXi host should run.

    - **Manual:** The administrator must apply both initial placement and load-balancing recommendations. An administrator needs to apply those recommendations manually.

- **Migration Threshold:** DRS can regulate migration and rebalancing behavior by adjusting the level of aggression. DRS has five levels ranging from 1 (most conservative) to 5 (most aggressive). The more aggressive the level, the less disparity is tolerated in the Cluster. The more conservative the level, the more parity is tolerated. As a result, DRS might initiate more migrations when you increase aggression.

    By default, DRS aggression is set at 3. This number seems to be sufficient and balances peaks equally across all nodes in the Cluster. For most Clusters, this level of DRS works best.

- **Example:** You have 3 three ESXi hosts that have many workloads, and ESXi hosts constantly reach the 100% capacity used. In that case, a more aggressive Migration Threshold level could be set to migrate VMs and have more-balanced resources used.

  But consider that a more aggressive Migration Threshold means more vMotion migrations and puts more stress on the vMotion network and the Storage. So always set the Migration Threshold wisely, considering the benefits and downsides of the selected option.

- **Predictive DRS:** Predictive DRS makes VM placement more accurate by utilizing VMware vRealize Suite data (now VMware Aria). Predictive DRS also provides automatic load balancing in hosts or VM OS power control features that can minimize potential failures.

  Enabling this option is unnecessary if you are not using VMware vRealize Suite data (now VMware Aria).

- **Virtual Machine Automation:** When enabled, individual virtual machine automation levels can override the cluster-level settings for individual VM settings. This means that you cant set the DRS per VMS or per VM groups.

  Example: If you have sensitive VMs or applications that should not vMotion because it will impact VM performance, you should enable Virtual Machine Automation. The VM settings always override the DRS Cluster settings.

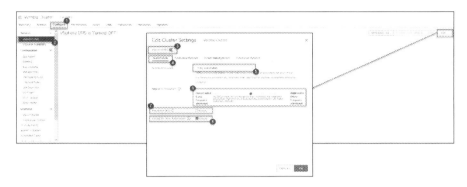

Figure 17-12. *(Distributed Resource Scheduler 1 of 4)*

The following additional DRS options are available on the Additional Options tab of the Edit Cluster Settings window, as shown in Figure 17-13.

- **VM Distribution:** This is a DRS feature that helps ensure that the number of VMs is evenly distributed across the hosts in a cluster. This can help to improve performance and availability by reducing the impact of host failures.

  When VM Distribution is enabled, DRS will monitor the number of VMs on each host and recommend migrating VMs to other hosts if the load is unbalanced. The recommendations are made based on several factors, including the current resource usage of the hosts and the expected future workload of the VMs.

- **CPU Over-Commitment:** CPU over-commitment is a technique for allocating more CPU resources to a VM than are physically available on the host. This can be beneficial in situations where there is much variability in VM workloads, or where there is a need to

maximize resource utilization. However, it is important
to use CPU over-commitment cautiously, as it can
lead to performance problems if the VMs are not
well-behaved.

Caution   While CPU over-commitment can be a powerful tool in
resource management, it's important to approach it cautiously.
Overcommitting CPU resources means allocating more virtual CPU
resources than the physical CPUs available, which can lead to
contention and performance degradation if not managed carefully. In
environments where high CPU demand is consistent, overcommitting
can strain the system, potentially impacting the performance of all
VMs on the host. Therefore, it's crucial to monitor the environment
closely and use CPU over-commitment judiciously, ensuring that it
aligns with the specific needs and capabilities of your infrastructure

---

- **Scalable Shares:** Scalable Shares is a feature of DRS
  that allows you to define a priority for each VM. VMs
  with higher scalable shares will be given more CPU
  resources when competing for resources with VMs with
  lower scalable shares. This can be useful for ensuring
  critical VMs always have the necessary resources.
  Scalable shares can be a useful tool for managing
  resource contention between VMs.

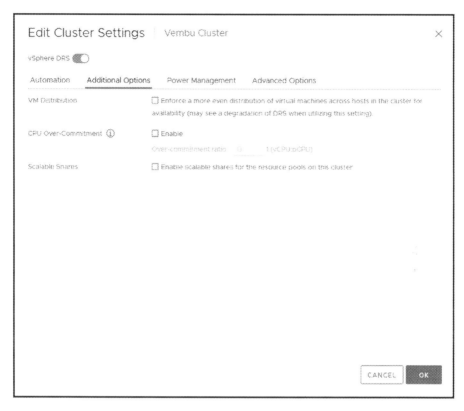

Figure 17-13. *(Distributed Resource Scheduler 2 of 4)*

17.2.3 Power Management Options for DRS

Continuing with the Edit Cluster Settings window, the Power Management tab provides options for configuring DPM, as shown in Figure 17-14. With vSphere Distributed Power Management (DPM), a DRS cluster can reduce its power consumption by powering off hosts when their usage is low. The feature monitors the demand for memory and CPU resources across the whole Cluster and turns off one or more hosts once enough excess capacity is found. Once this has been completed, vSphere DPM migrates virtual machines to other hosts in order to maintain availability while conserving power.

Figure 17-14. *(Distributed Resource Scheduler 3 of 4)*

When there isn't enough capacity, DRS can power on hosts that are in standby mode and migrate virtual machines to them. DPM even takes into account resource reservations you make for your virtual machines.

As an example of how DPM works, suppose that you have three ESXi hosts in the Cluster and 20 VMs and that two ESXi hosts are enough to run those 20 VMs. DPM will power off one ESXi host to save power.

DPM saves power while providing enough processing power to keep the environment running without a lack of resources.

And with these last details about vSphere DRS and its options, we have finished and configured DRS for our test lab environment, as shown in Figure 17-15.

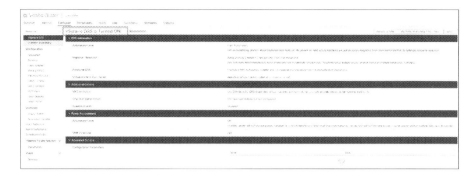

Figure 17-15. *(Distributed Resource Scheduler 4 of 4)*

17.3 Summary

In this chapter, we explored two advanced features of vSphere, vMotion and Distributed Resource Scheduler (DRS). Next we'll explore vSphere Cluster Services (vCLS). Chapter 18 introduces vCLS and explains its important role within the VMware ecosystem. We'll discuss how vCLS operates to ensure the health of clusters and the quality of services. Additionally, we'll delve into aspects such as moving vCLS VMs to datastores and creating anti-affinity rules. This transition aims to deepen your knowledge in managing vSphere clusters, which is crucial for maintaining robust virtual environments.

CHAPTER 18

vSphere Cluster Services (vCLS)

vSphere vCLS was briefly covered in Chapter 10. This chapter provides additional information about this vSphere feature, including how to move vCLS VMs to a different datastore and how to create an Anti-Affinity rule for vCLS VMs.

18.1 What Is vCLS?

vSphere vCLS is a set of services that run on vSphere clusters to provide cluster-level functionality even when the vCenter is unavailable. vCLS services include the following (both of which are discussed in Chapter 17):

- **vSphere Distributed Resource Scheduler (DRS):** vSphere DRS is a service that automatically balances workloads across hosts in a cluster.

- **vSphere vMotion:** vSphere vMotion is a service that enables you to move VMs from one host to another without downtime.

In recent versions of vSphere, vCLS doesn't directly manage other services like vSphere Fault Tolerance (FT) or vSphere High Availability (HA). These services operate independently of vCLS, each with its specific mechanisms and operational requirements.

© Luciano Patrão 2024
L. Patrão, *VMware vSphere Essentials*, https://doi.org/10.1007/979-8-8688-0208-9_18

vCLS services are enabled by default on all vSphere clusters. If vCenter Server becomes unavailable, vCLS services continue to run and provide cluster-level functionality.

Here are some of the benefits of using vCLS:

- **Increased availability:** vCLS services help to ensure that workloads in a cluster remain available even if vCenter Server becomes unavailable.

- **Simplified management:** vCLS services are managed through the vSphere Client, which makes it easy to configure and monitor them.

- **Improved performance:** vCLS services are designed to minimize the impact on performance, so you can be confident that your workload continues to run smoothly even when vCenter Server is unavailable.

If you are running vSphere clusters, I recommend enabling vCLS services to help improve the availability and performance of your workloads.

There are three ways to measure the health of a cluster service:

Healthy: When at least one worker VM is running in the cluster, the vCLS health is green. A cluster group of three agent VMs is set up to ensure that agent VMs are always available.

Degraded: This is a temporary state that happens when at least one of the agent VMs isn't available, but DRS hasn't skipped its logic because the agent VMs aren't available. The cluster could be in this state when vCLS VMs are being redeployed or when they are being turned back on after something happened to the VMs that were already running.

Unhealthy: A vCLS is in an unhealthy state when the next run of the DRS logic (load placement or load balancing) is skipped because the vCLS control plane is unavailable (at least one agent VM).

vCLS is linked to DRS. If you disable DRS, vCLS will also be disabled. Also if you Disable vCLS, your RDS cluster loses some of its self-maintenance capabilities, like ensuring that services critical for cluster health are running. However, this doesn't affect the operational status of DRS. DRS can still balance workloads across your cluster, but the overall health and efficiency of the cluster might be impacted without the support services provided by vCLS.

18.1.1 What is vCLS Retreat Mode

When a vSphere cluster is running low on resources, cluster and ESxi hosts faces a limitation that could impact its performance, then is when vCLS Retreat Mode comes into play. This mode is activated to reduce the resource usage of vCLS VMs allowing critical workloads, on the cluster to run smoothly. It's like putting these service VMs in a "power mode" to ensure they operate with minimal resources while still functioning.

Retreat Mode kicks in automatically depending on the clusters resource levels. Once the resource situation improves, the vCLS VMs exit Retreat Mode on their own. Go back, to operation. This feature showcases vSpheres resilience and efficiency design aiming to minimize service disruptions and enable the cluster to adjust to resource availability scenarios.

18.2 How vCLS Works

The vCLS agents in each cluster will establish a cluster quorum if vCenter Server becomes unavailable. This quorum enables the vCLS agents to continue providing cluster-level functionality, including DRS and vMotion.

The vCLS agents exchange messages using a lightweight messaging protocol. This protocol is designed to be highly efficient, so its impact on performance is minimal.

If a vCLS agent fails, the other agents in the cluster will detect the failure and replace it automatically. This ensures that the cluster quorum is always maintained, even if one or more vCLS agents fail.

Here are some of the key features of vCLS:

- **Lightweight:** vCLS agents are lightweight VMs with little performance effect.

- **Redundant:** vCLS agents are redundant, so cluster-level functionality will still be provided even if one agent fails.

- **Efficient:** vCLS makes use of a communications protocol that is both lightweight and exceedingly efficient.

- **Scalable:** Large clusters can be supported by vCLS at scale.

Each vCLS VM is created with the following size:

Memory	128 MB
Memory reservation	100 MB
Swap Size	256 MB
vCPU	1
vCPU reservation	100 MHz
Disk	2 GB
Guest VMDK Size	245 MB
Storage Space	480 MB

18.2.1 Architecture Fundamentals

The core architecture of the vCLS control plane comprises a maximum of three VMs, which may also be called system VMs or agent VMs. These VMs are installed on distinct hosts that are part of a cluster.

These are lightweight agent virtual machines that come together to establish a quorum for the cluster. On clusters with less than three ESXi hosts, the number of agent VMs is always proportional to the total number of hosts in the cluster.

vSphere Cluster Services is in charge of managing the agent virtual machines. It is not the responsibility of the users to monitor the lifetime or condition of the agent virtual machines, and these VMs should not be handled as the conventional workload VMs.

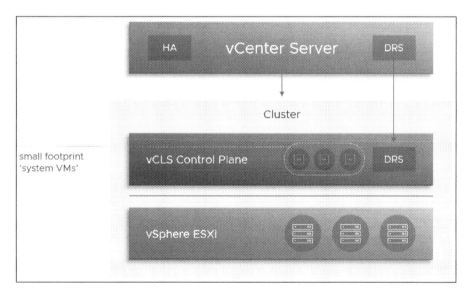

Figure 18-1. *(vSphere Cluster Services 1 of 6)(Image source: VMware)*

When a host is placed into maintenance mode, the vCLS agent VMs are migrated to other hosts within the cluster like ordinary VMs. To maintain the viability of the cluster services, customers should not delete or rename agent VMs or their folders.

Virtual machines in a vSphere cluster have their resources, power status, and availability handled by vSphere Cluster Services. These VMs are crucial to the smooth operation of vSphere Cluster Services. The DRS functioning of the cluster may be affected if the power status or resources of these VMs are altered in any way.

vSphere ESX Agent Manager (EAM) manages the life cycle of vCLS agent VMs. ESX Agent Manager automatically creates or re-creates/re-powers on VMs when users attempt to power them off or delete them.

vCLS is a relatively new feature, and it is still being improved in the latest versions, with more options added to handle these VMs. Some issues were handling these VMs or moving them to other Hosts/Datastores in the initial version. In each vSphere update, VMware fixes that and gives more flexibility to customers to handle these vCLS VMs.

vCLS VMs should not be backed up or the VM vHardware updated.

18.3 Move vSphere vCLS VMs Datastore

For better Storage management, some organizations want to customize the placement of their vCLS.

The option to move or customize vCLS datastores was added in vSphere 7 Update 3, together with the option to create an Anti-Affinity rule for vCLS VMs not running with specific VMs.

Moving a vCLS Datastore can be done at the Cluster level (every Cluster with DRS and HA will have one to three vCLS VMs depending on the size of your Cluster).

As shown in Figure 18-2, select the Cluster, click the **Configure** tab, select **Datastores**, and you will see a section **vSphere Cluster Services** *and* **Datastores**.

Figure 18-2. *(vSphere Cluster Services 2 of 6)*

Here you have option 3 have the Datastores and vCLS: Datastores where vCLS are allowed to run, and Datastores where vCLS are not allowed to run. In this case, we will only move the vCLS VMs to run in a particular datastore (for security, you should add a second datastore if the first one is not available).

Select your Datastore(s) and click **Add**.

You have it configured after you add your Datastore(s); there is no need to do anything else. After you select and add the Datastore above, the vCLS VMs are now bound to the Datastore, or blocked to be used by the vCLS VMs (depending on your selections) and all if configured as we can see in Figure 18-3.

Figure 18-3. *(vSphere Cluster Services 3 of 6)*

The vCLS VMs will automatically move to the Datastore(s) you added, as shown in Figure 18-4.

Figure 18-4. *(vSphere Cluster Services 4 of 6)*

The Datastore move of vCLS is done.

18.4 Create an Anti-Affinity Rule for vCLS VMs

Anti-affinity rules in a vSphere environment are settings used to prevent specific virtual machines (VMs) from running on the same physical host. This is done to improve application availability and reduce the risk of simultaneous downtime. These rules are essential for critical applications that require high availability. However, we are not discussing or implementing anti-affinity rules on normal VMs, but the concept is the same how you implement for your vCLS agent VMS.

Important to note is that the rule is only to set vCLS VMs, not to run with specific VMs using TAGs. There is no other option to set this. I don't know why VMware only added this option and not the same option we use for DRS Anti-Affinity for Hosts/VMs rules.

So to use this option, you need to implement TAGs in your Center. A couple of years ago, I wrote a blog post on implementing and creating TAGs. Check it out if you want to implement this feature in your environment: `https://www.provirtualzone.com/vmware-how-to-create-and-use-tags-part-1/`.

On the vCenter main menu, go to **Policies and Profiles**, select **Compute Policies**, click **Add**, and create the Anti-Affinity vCLS rule. As shown in Figure 18-5, there is only one option in the *Policy type* field: Anti-affinity for vCLS.

Figure 18-5. *(vSphere Cluster Services 5 of 6)*

Next, you need to select options in the *VM tag* category. Figure 18-5 shows the rule configured so that vCLS VMs never run in the same ESXi host where VM Guest OS is classified as Other OS (like Oracle, other DBS, etc.). This is an example where a VM (like Oracle, SAP, or other DBs) must run isolated in an ESXi host, and no other VMs can run on the ESXi host.

Click **Create**, and you have your Anti-Affinity rule created for vCLS VMs. See Figure 18-6. You can delete this rule when you want, with no impact on the vCLS performance or configuration.

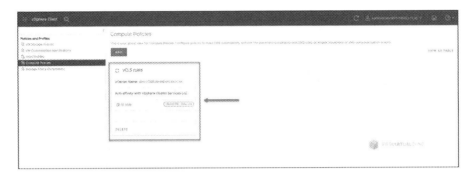

Figure 18-6. *(vSphere Cluster Services 6 of 6)*

18.5 Summary

This chapter covered the basics of vSphere Cluster Services (vCLS) and its important role in managing clusters. In Chapter 19 we turn our attention to another component of VMware infrastructure, vSphere High Availability (HA), a feature that improves the reliability and resilience of your virtual environment. We'll explore how vSphere HA works, the situations it addresses on hosts, and the steps to enable HA in your setup. Additionally, we'll dive into the features of vSphere HA, including admission control, to give you an understanding of how it ensures uninterrupted service availability and reduces downtime in virtual environments.

CHAPTER 19

vSphere High Availability (HA)

VMware vSphere High Availability (HA) is one of the most important features in vCenter and is a significant and extensive feature in your VMware environment. This chapter explores what vSphere HA is, how it works, and some of its key benefits.

19.1 What Is vSphere HA?

vSphere HA is a vital component of the vSphere platform, providing cost-effective high availability for business-critical applications. vSphere HA protects your virtual machines from host failures by restarting them on other available hosts in the Cluster. If a physical server in your Cluster goes down, vSphere HA automatically restarts the virtual machines on other hosts in the Cluster.

vSphere HA is transparent to users and requires no changes to your applications. It is easy to set up and requires no additional networking configuration (except the vMotion network to migrate VMs between ESXi hosts). This ensures that your applications remain available in case of a host failure.

19.2 How Does vSphere HA Work?

vSphere HA is a datacenter feature that reduces downtime for applications and services in the event of a hardware or software failure. When a failure occurs, vSphere HA automatically restarts any affected virtual machines on alternative hosts. This ensures your applications and services remain available even when individual components fail.

vSphere HA constantly monitors each virtual machine's and host's health in your Cluster. If a virtual machine or host fails, vSphere HA immediately detects the failure and starts the affected virtual machines on other hosts in the Cluster. This process is automatic and requires no administrator intervention.

When a vSphere Cluster is configured with HA, ESXi hosts communicate. This periodic message tells the primary host that the node or VM is running as expected. If it doesn't detect the heartbeat signal from another host or VM, vSphere HA takes corrective actions such as restarting VMs.

In addition to providing high availability for individual virtual machines, vSphere HA can protect your entire application by restarting virtual machines in accordance with a predefined order. This ensures that critical components are always started first, followed by less important components. By starting virtual machines in this order, you can minimize downtime and ensure that your applications are always available.

vSphere HA is an essential datacenter feature that can help you avoid costly downtime for your applications and services. By automatically restarting affected virtual machines on alternative hosts, vSphere HA ensures that your applications remain available even when individual components fail.

Key features:

- Monitor VMware vSphere hosts and virtual machines to identify hardware or guest operating system failures.

- vSphere HA continuously monitors if any of the ESXi hosts are down. If it detects an outage, HA restarts virtual machines on other vSphere hosts in the Cluster without any intervention necessary.

- Virtual machines automatically restart when VM Monitoring detects an operating system failure. This keeps applications up and running, which reduces downtime.

19.3 Types of vSphere HA Host Failure Scenarios

A VMware vSphere High Availability cluster's primary host is responsible for monitoring secondary hosts for failures. Virtual machines running on the hosts may need to be failed over, depending on the type of failure detected.

In a vSphere HA cluster, three types of host failure are detected: failure, isolation, and partition.

vSphere uses datastore heartbeat and gateway ping monitoring to quickly detect host failures or network isolation by checking for regular signals to shared storage and pings to a network gateway.

19.3.1 Host Failure

A host failure occurs when a host stops functioning. When an ESXi host fails, VM failover is triggered. All VMs from the failed ESXi host move to and restart on an available ESXi host.

In the example depicted in Figure 19-1, after the ESXi host fails, VMs 1 and 2 are migrated from the ESXi host to the next available ESXi host. All the VMs' files are stored in shared storage that all ESXi hosts have access to (HA requires this).

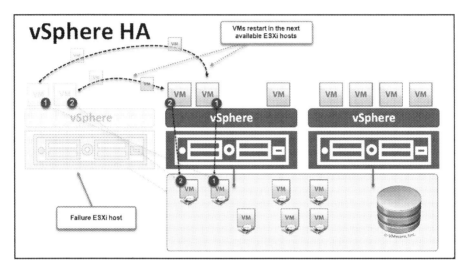

Figure 19-1. *(vSphere High Availability 1 of 3)*

19.3.2 Host Isolation

Host isolation occurs when a host becomes isolated from the network. When a host becomes isolated from the network, it can no longer communicate with other hosts in the Cluster. This can happen for many reasons, including the following:

- The host has lost network connectivity.

- The host has been manually isolated.

- The host is in a network partition.

If a host becomes isolated, vSphere HA protects any virtual machines running on the host. If the host is part of a cluster with vSphere HA enabled, the other hosts in the Cluster continue to provide resources and services to the virtual machines on the isolated host.

Host Failure Response in HA is disabled by default (see Figure 19-2 in the next section), and if you want HA to protect your VMs in case of an ESXi host isolation, then you need to configure and enable it with one of the following options:

- **Power off and restart VMs:** All affected VMs will be powered off and vSphere HA will attempt to restart the VMs on hosts that still have network connectivity.

- **Shut down and restart VMs:** All affected VMs will be gracefully shut down and vSphere HA will attempt to restart the VMs on hosts that are still online.

19.3.3 Host Partition

A host partition occurs when a host loses network connectivity with the primary host. When this occurs, vSphere HA detects the partition and restarts any affected virtual machines on other hosts in the Cluster. This failover is transparent to users because the virtual machines are restarted on other hosts in the Cluster.

When a host loses network connectivity with the primary host, it automatically attempts to connect to a secondary host in the Cluster. If the host cannot connect to the secondary host, it restarts any virtual machines running on the primary host.

If we have a vSphere Cluster with three ESXi hosts, and let's say host number 2 or number 3 experiences a failure or becomes unreachable through gateway ping, datastore heartbeats, or VM Monitoring, then the virtual machines from the affected host are automatically restarted on the next available ESXi host to ensure continuous operation.

Note   Even when an ESXi host agent or gateway becomes unreachable, virtual machines (VMs) may continue to operate and remain accessible. This scenario underscores the importance of implementing VM Monitoring. However, for VM Monitoring to function effectively, VMware Tools must be installed on the VMs.

19.4 How to Enable vSphere HA

It's easy to enable vSphere HA, but that's just the first step in setting up vSphere HA. There are a lot of choices and features in vSphere HA. Some must be set up, while others are turned off by default. In this section, we'll look at all these options and discuss each one in depth.

As shown in Figure 19-2, to start and enable vSphere High Availability, go to vCenter, select the Cluster (**Vembu Cluster** in the example), click the **Configure** tab, select **vSphere Availability**, click **Edit** in the upper-right corner of the window, and then enable **vSphere HA**.

Figure 19-2. *(vSphere High Availability 2 of 3)*

19.5 vSphere HA Feature Details

Let's go through all the options that are available when configuring vSphere HA. The following sections correspond to the four tabs in the Edit Cluster Settings window.

19.5.1 Failures and Responses

As shown in Figure 19-2, the *Failures and responses* tab has the options described next. First, turn on **Enable Host Monitoring**.

Host Failure Response

This option determines what vSphere HA will do when a host fails. As previously discussed regarding the failure types, there are different types of failures. You only have two options for what to do when a host fails:

- **Disabled:** When Host Failure Response is set to "Disabled," it means that the automatic response to host failures, such as restarting VMs on another host, is turned off. However, Host Monitoring itself remains active, allowing vCenter to detect host failures but not take action to automatically migrate or restart the affected VMs.

- **Restart VMs:** When a host failure is detected, VMs will be restarted in the order determined by their restart priority. Select this option to get the full benefit of vSphere HA.

Response for Host Isolation

This option is used to configure what vSphere HA should do if you have an isolated host. You have three options:

- **Disabled:** No action will be taken on the affected VMs.

- **Power off and restart VMs:** All affected VMs will be powered off, and vSphere HA will attempt to restart the VMs on hosts that still have network connectivity.

- **Shut down and restart VMs:** All affected VMs will be gracefully shut down, and vSphere HA will attempt to restart the VMs on hosts that are still online.

  Shutdown and restarting VMs is the default option and the best practice. vSphere HA tries to shut down gracefully all the VMs and power them on in the next available ESXi host. This is important if you have applications on your VMs that could be corrupt with a hard restart. So, trying to gracefully shut down is essential.

Note   Gracefully shutting down only works if you have VMware Tools installed in your VM. If not, vSphere HA will power off the VM and restart VM in the next available ESXi host.

Datastore with PDL

A Datastore with Permanent Device Loss (PDL) occurs in the following situations:

- **Unavailable datastore**: The datastore appears as unavailable in the Storage view.

- **Lost communication**: The storage adapter reports the Operational State of the device as Lost Communication.

- **Dead paths**: All paths to the device are marked as Dead.

It's crucial to understand that a PDL is specifically flagged based on certain SCSI sense codes, which indicate that a storage device has been permanently removed. This situation differs from an All Paths Down (APD) condition, where the storage paths are down but the device is not necessarily permanently lost. In this case, a host has a PDL where VMs are running, and vSphere HA needs to address the problem since VMs are running on the Datastore.

Note   In the case of a Permanent Device Loss (PDL) with VMs still running, the focus is solely on addressing situations where a host has problems connecting to a Datastore but still have VMs runnings.

The Datastore with PDL setting has also has three options:, disable, only log the events, or Power off and restart VMs.

- **Disabled:** No action will be taken to the affected VMs.

- **Issue events:** No action will be taken to the affected VMs; events will be generated.

- **Power off and restart VMs:** All affected VMs will be terminated, and vSphere HA will attempt to restart the VMs on hosts that still have connectivity to the datastore.

The last option is the default and is the best practice.

Datastore with APD

A Datastore with All-Paths-Down (APD) occurs in the following situations:

- A datastore is shown as unavailable in the Storage view.

- A storage adapter indicates the Operational State of the device as Dead or Error.

- All paths to the device are marked as Dead.

- You are unable to connect directly to the ESXi host using the vSphere Client.

- The ESXi host shows as Disconnected in vCenter Server.

A Datastore with APD is one of the most severe issues that you can have in your Cluster with your ESXi hosts. All VMs will be unavailable, mainly if this happens in more than one ESXi host (depending on how many host failures your Cluster tolerates), the Cluster can be unavailable or ESXi hosts can be unstable.

As described in the following list, there are four options on how vSphere HA handles a Datastore with APD. I do not recommend the first and second options since an APD can be a considerable environmental issue, which leaves you with the choice between a more conservative option and a more aggressive option. The choice all depends on how you want to configure your environment, and service level agreements (SLAs) are very important to take into account (again, any VMs with critical applications restart and power on in the next ESXi host available) since an aggressive policy restarts the VM as long there is no connection.

By default, vSphere HA selects the third, conservative option described next.

- **Disabled:** No action will be taken on the affected VMs.

- **Issue events:** No action will be taken on the affected VMs. Events will be generated.

- **Power off and restart VMs - Conservative restart policy:** If HA determines the VM can be restarted on a different host, a VM will be powered off.

- **Power off and restart VMs - Aggressive restart policy:** A VM will be powered off if HA determines the VM can be restarted on a different host, or if HA cannot detect the resources on other hosts because of network connectivity loss (network partition).

   In the same APD option, we have a second option where we can select the Response Recovery and Response delay for the VMs. It is disabled by default, but you can set 2/3m (example), the number of minutes VM Component Protection (VMCP) waits before taking action. vSphere HA waits that time and waits for Cluster and ESXi hosts to recover from the APD before restarting VMs in another host.

VM Monitoring

VM Monitoring is a feature within vSphere High Availability (HA) designed to improve the resilience of virtual machines running in a cluster. It continuously checks the health of VMs, using VMware Tools to detect if a VM has stopped responding. This proactive monitoring allows vSphere to take corrective action, such as restarting a VM, to minimize downtime and ensure continued service availability.

VM Monitoring monitors the VM, the in-guest OS and also applications (here it needs an SDK or supported applications).

As previously discussed, VMware Tools must be installed in your virtual machines to use this feature. It is disabled by default, and the other options are Monitor the Virtual Machine only or Monitor the Virtual Machine Application.

Note   To enable VMware Application Monitoring, you must first obtain the appropriate SDK (or be using an application that supports VMware Application Monitoring).

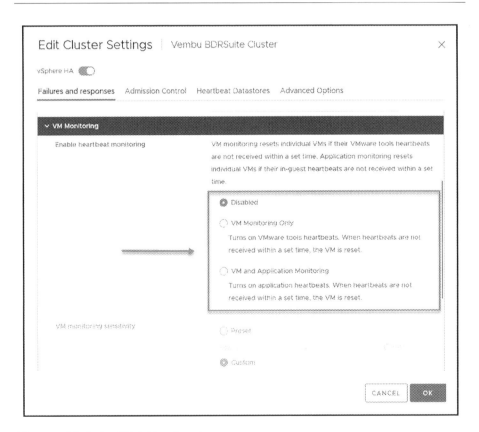

Figure 19-2.1. VM Monitoring

Occasionally, when a virtual machine or application works as expected, it ceases to send heartbeats.

The VM Monitoring service also oversees a virtual machine's I/O activity to keep unnecessary resets at bay. If no heartbeats are detected within the failure interval, then the I/O stats interval (a cluster-level attribute) is consulted. This I/O stats interval registers any disk or network activity that has taken place during the last two minutes (120 seconds). And if there is nothing to show for it, then the virtual machine gets reset. This default value (120 seconds) can be altered by employing an advanced option `das.iostatsinterval`.

Enable heartbeat monitoring:

- **Disabled:** No heartbeat monitoring in the selected VMs.

- **VM Monitoring Only:** Turns on VMware Tools heartbeats. The VM is reset when heartbeats are not received within a set time.

- **VM and Application Monitoring:** Turns on application heartbeats. The VM is reset when heartbeats are not received within a set time.

The last option in VM Monitoring is the VM monitoring sensitivity. You can adjust the monitoring sensitivity to best suit your needs. If you choose a high level, it will enable faster detection of failures. However, this setting has a higher risk of mistakenly concluding that a virtual machine or application has failed when it is still operational due to resource constraints.

On the other hand, selecting a lower sensitivity option will mean service interruptions between actual failures, and resetting of VMs may last longer. Consider what option works best for you before making a selection.

You can use the vSphere HA automatically configured default settings or configure the settings manually. For the auto-settings, these are the defaults.

Note   The interval and reset times option is only available if you select **Custom**.

VM Monitoring Settings

Setting	Failure Interval (seconds)	Reset Period
High	30	1 hour
Medium	60	24 hours
Low	120	7 days

Figure 19-3. *(vSphere High Availability 3 of 3)*

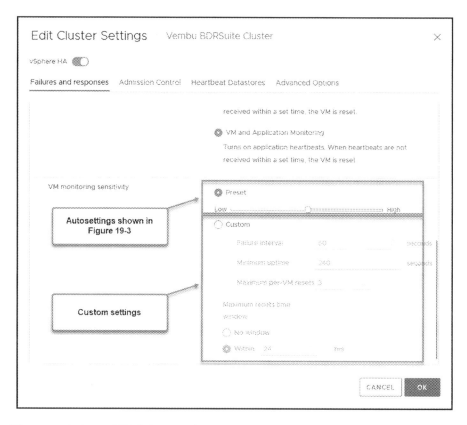

Figure 19-3.1. *VM Monitoring*

You can set the number of times a VM can be reset in a period of time.

When failures are detected, vSphere HA resets virtual machines to ensure services remain available. To prevent continual restarts due to persistent errors, vSphere HA has a specific setting to limit the number of resets done in a specific configurable time interval. This setting, *Maximum per-VM resets*, can be configured by the user, and after three attempts, no further retries occur until the set interval has passed.

Note The reset statistics are cleared when a virtual machine is powered off and back on or migrated using vMotion to another host. A VM reboot typically occurs due to a reset or power state change. The heartbeat mechanism in vSphere HA is used to detect the health of a VM. If a VM is unresponsive, it may trigger a reset or restart, depending on the HA configuration, but it is not the same as a "restart" in which the virtual machine's power state is changed.

Now that we've addressed all the options on the *Failures and responses* tab, we are ready to check out the options on the *Admission Control* tab.

19.5.2 Admission Control

vSphere HA Admission Control is a feature that is part of vSphere HA. This section describes how to configure admission control on the *Admission Control* tab of the Edit Cluster Settings window, shown in Figure 19-4.

Figure 19-4. *(vSphere HA Admission Control 1 of 5)*

What Is Admission Control in vSphere HA?

In a VMware vSphere HA cluster, admission control is a feature that ensures enough resources are available to restart virtual machines on other hosts in the event of a host failure. Admission control also prevents the over-commitment of resources in a cluster.

These are two of the existing types of admission control:

- **Host failures cluster tolerates:** This setting ensures that a certain number of hosts can fail, and there will still be enough resources to restart all the virtual machines on those hosts. The number of hosts that can fail is determined by the number of spare capacity slots that are calculated by the admission control algorithm.

- **Percentages Of Cluster Resources Reserved:** With this setting, you specify a percentage of cluster resources that must be reserved for failover. This takes into account not only host failures but also capacity contention within the Cluster itself.

You can configure admission control using either setting or a combination of both. In most cases, it is recommended to use a combination of both settings to provide the best protection for your environment.

The following sections describe the three settings on the Admission Control tab.

Host Failures Cluster Tolerates

In a vSphere HA cluster, host failures are tolerable. The maximum number of failures that can be tolerated is one less than the number of hosts in the Cluster, (as stated below the *Host failures cluster tolerates* field in Figure 19-5). This means that vSphere HA can tolerate a single host failure if you have a three-node cluster.

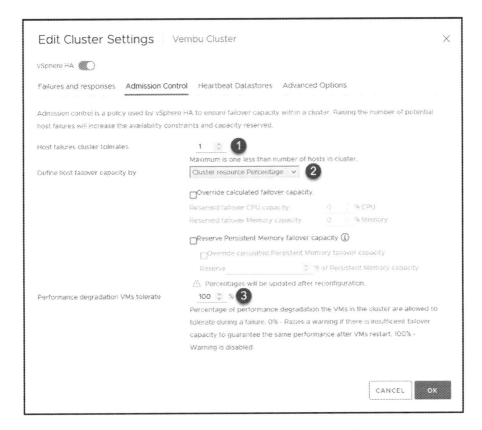

Figure 19-5. *(vSphere HA Admission Control 2 of 5)*

As we conclude our discussion on the resilience of a vSphere HA cluster to tolerate host failures, we have emphasized how it ensures operational stability even when a host has a failure. An essential part of this mechanism involves the management of cluster resources through a concept known as "slots."

Slots in vSphere HA are the minimum resources required for the most resource-intensive virtual machine in the cluster. This concept is critical as it defines the baseline amount of CPU and memory needed to guarantee that the cluster can gracefully handle failures. By using slots, HA effectively allocates resources to maintain service availability during a host failure, ensuring the cluster's overall health and functionality.

How HA Calculates the Number of Slots

A memory component is calculated by obtaining each powered-on virtual machine's memory reservation, plus memory overhead, and selecting the largest value.

The CPU component of a slot within a vSphere HA setup is determined by assessing the CPU reservation of each virtual machine that is powered on within the cluster. The highest reservation value is selected to define the slot size. If no specific CPU reservation has been set for a virtual machine, a default value of 32 MHz is used. This default can be adjusted to suit different needs through the das.vmcpuminmhz setting in the Advanced Settings tab, which will be explored later in this chapter.

The following list details the process and critical steps involved in calculating and managing slots within a vSphere HA environment. Here's what each point in the list signifies:

- The first size Slot is Calculated: This step involves determining the size of a "slot" based on the largest CPU and memory reservations among all the VMs. This calculation sets the baseline for resource requirements per VM in the event of a host failure.

- vSphere HA determines how many slots can be held by each ESXi host within a Cluster: After defining the slot size, HA calculates how many such slots each host in the cluster can support, effectively determining how many VMs can run simultaneously on a single host under maximum load.

- Calculates the Current Failover Capacity of the Cluster (how many ESXi hosts): This involves assessing how many hosts can fail within the cluster while still maintaining the ability to power on all VMs on the remaining hosts. This calculation is crucial for understanding the resilience of the cluster.

- Compares the Current Failover Capacity of the Cluster
  with the Configured Failover Capacity: Finally, HA
  compares the actual failover capacity (the number of
  hosts that can fail without impacting service continuity)
  with the pre-configured or desired failover capacity set
  by the administrators. This comparison helps ensure
  that the cluster is configured to meet the desired levels
  of availability.

These steps collectively ensure that vSphere HA can adequately prepare for and respond to host failures, maintaining service availability and minimizing downtime in virtual environments.

As an example of how HA calculates the number of slots, suppose we have VM-01 with 4 GHz but only 2GB of vMemory, and VM-02 with only 2GHz and 4GB of vMemory. In this case, a slot for this Cluster will be 4 GHz + 4GB (plus memory overhead). Then divide this slot for each ESXi host resource.

An example host with 68 GHz (26 Cores with 2.6 GHz each) CPU and 192GB of Memory will be divided by the slot size:

$$68 \text{ GHz} / 4 \text{ GHz} = 17 \text{ slots and } 192\text{GB} / 4\text{GB} = 48 \text{ slots}$$

Since we need to consider the CPU, we only have 17 slots on this type of host, meaning, we can only Power on 17 VMs on each ESXi host when Admission Control is enabled.

So, every powered-on VM declared as a slot will be divided by the slots that we have in our ESXi host. If we have three ESXi hosts, then there are three hosts with 17 slots each that need to be divided by each powered-on VM we have on each host.

Let's say we have a maximum of six VMs powered on in one host, and we will have 11 slots free on that host. If that host fails, it will move those six VMs to the next two ESXi hosts and must have free slots to store those six VMs.

In the example shown in Figure 19-6, we see that Host 1 and moving the six VMs into Host 2 with nine slots free and Host 3 with seven slots free. So in this Cluster, we can afford one ESXi failure without any problem. Since vSphere HA needs a minimum of two ESXi hosts to work, we cannot afford a second ESXi failure.

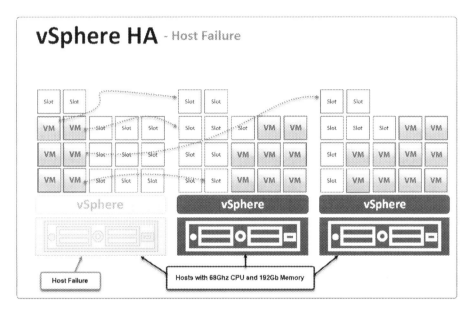

Figure 19-6. *(vSphere HA Admission Control 3 of 5)*

But if we had four ESXi hosts and lost two hosts, each of which had 30 VMs powered on, then we could have a problem. Even if we have free slots for all VMs, we must add 20% to the overhead. vSphere HA, by default, reserves 33% for any host failures.

So always divide your VMs per slot and divide again per host, and you will get the number to set for *Hosts failures cluster tolerates.*

Define Host Failover Capacity By

The *Define host failover capacity by* drop-down list includes the following four options:

- **Cluster resource Percentage:** In this option, you select if you want to use the above calculation using the Cluster resource percentage (default). You can also select the following override options:

  - By default, vSphere HA will reserve 33% of the Cluster resources for the host failures when using override calculation.

  - If the percentage is very high, you will not have enough resources to power on VMs, since it will reduce the number of free slots.

- **Slot Policy (powered-on VMs):** This option will use the previously described calculation to check how many slots and how many VMs are allowed to power on on each ESXi host. Don't forget, powered-on VMs = used slots. You can also calculate how many VMs require multiple slots (in the same host or different hosts).

- **Dedicated failover hosts:** This option reserves a specific ESXi host for any host failure. vSphere HA will put the ESXi host on standby and use it only if any host fails. This option is only for situations in which you have many hosts and resources and can put one (or more) hosts on standby for ESXi host failure. The host cannot be used for anything else than vSphere HA host failures. No VMs can be powered on on this ESXi host (unless there is a host failure).

When you try to move a VM to this standby ESXi host, you get the following error: "The current operation cannot be performed on the host 'esxi-01.domain.local' because it has been configured as a failover host for a cluster."

- **Disable:** Select this option to deactivate admission control and allow virtual machine power on that violates availability constraints. Disabling will allow you to power on any VMs regardless if you are violating the *Hosts failures cluster tolerates* setting.

Note   Use the **Disable** option very carefully and only if you are sure you are not breaking any company's SLA or Hight Availability policy. If an ESXi host fails and there are not enough resources for the vSphere HA restart the VMs from the failures host, VMs will not be accessible until the host failure is fixed.

Performance Degradation VMs Tolerate

This admission control setting determines the percentage of performance degradation the VMs in the Cluster can tolerate during a failure. If there is a high resource request from VMs, Cluster cannot provide proper CPU or Memory, and VMs performance will be impacted.

Note   Always do your math. Check Cluster resources and how many VMs you have, how many slots you have, and how many ESXi hosts you can afford to lose in case of a host failure.

If you incorrectly calculate your settings and how many host failures your Cluster tolerates, you get a warning like this: "Insufficient resources to satisfy vSphere HA failover level on cluster."

19.5.3 Heartbeat Datastores

The *Heartbeat Datastores* tab includes the rest of the normal (i.e., not advanced) vSphere HA Cluster settings. As Figure 19-7 shows, there is nothing special to set on this tab. As discussed earlier in the chapter, vSphere HA uses the Datastore Heartbeat to check if a host is failing or if an APD or PDL situation exists.

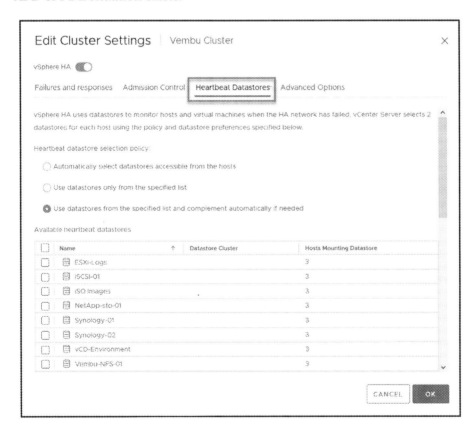

Figure 19-7. *(vSphere HA Admission Control 4 of 5)*

The default setting is **Automatically select datastores accessible from the hosts**, meaning vSphere HA selects automatically any Datastore connected to the ESXi hosts in the Cluster. The other two options allow you to select manually which Datastores to use. Unless you want to use specific Datastores for the heartbeat, you should leave it in automatic mode.

19.5.4 Advanced Options

The last tab in the vSphere HA Edit Cluster Settings window is *Advanced Options*, where you can configure different settings for the maximum slot resources, as discussed earlier.

The *Advanced Options* tab presents many parameters that you can configure for your vSphere HA Cluster and how it should behave in case the host becomes network isolated. This is where you can fine-tune settings like isolation response and gateway parameters. These specific settings, such as das.isolationaddress and das.isolationgateway, are crucial, as they define how HA responds if a host becomes network isolated. Tailoring these parameters to your environment ensures that HA behaves optimally during such scenarios, which are common in many setups.

As stated, you can add many parameters in this tab, but discussing them all would be beyond the scope of this book, so I will present only the two most commonly used, highlighted in Figure 19-8.

The das.isolationaddress option in vSphere HA is used to set specific IP addresses that a host pings to determine if it is isolated from the network. This is especially relevant when a host does not receive heartbeats from other hosts in the cluster. By default, the management network's default gateway is used for this purpose. However, you can specify up to ten custom isolation addresses using das.isolationaddress0 to das.isolationaddress9. This flexibility allows for more accurate isolation detection, particularly in complex network environments. The example in Figure 19-8 shows only one IP address being used, the IP 192.168.1.254, to check if the ESXi hosts was isolated from the network.

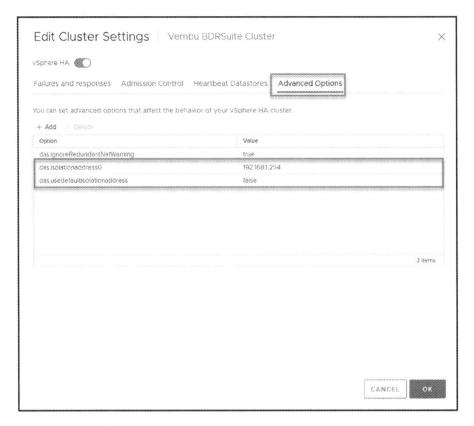

Figure 19-8. *(vSphere HA Admission Control 5 of 5)*

The das.usedefaultisolationaddress option in vSphere HA determines whether the default gateway of the console network is used as an isolation address for host isolation response. By default, this option is set to true, meaning the default gateway is used. If set to false, vSphere HA will not use the default gateway as an isolation address, and you should specify custom isolation addresses using the das.isolationaddress options. This setting is crucial for defining how a host should verify its network isolation in a vSphere HA environment.

So, both parameters needs to be use together.

I could explain more details about the Admission Control feature and other options, but I think I've discussed the most important options to give you an advanced overview of vSphere HA and all its options.

19.6 Summary

In this Chapter about vSphere Availability (HA) you you learn how this important feature in vCenter safeguards virtual machines from host failures by restarting them on other hosts in the cluster. It explained how to set up and use HA showing how user friendly and easy it is to configure without needing changes to applications or extra networking setups.

The chapter details on how vSphere HA keeps an eye on both host and virtual machine health automatically handling issues to minimize downtime. It discussed host failure scenarios demonstrating how vSphere HA distinguishes between hardware failures, network problems and partitions to keep services running smoothly.

This basic understanding helps readers grasp how vSphere HA plays a role, in ensuring availability in the virtual environment.

CHAPTER 20

vSphere Proactive HA

vSphere Proactive HA is not a service of vSphere HA but rather a hardware monitoring feature that is available only when vSphere HA is enabled (as described in Chapter 19).

In this chapter, we will discuss the features and benefits of Proactive HA, how it works, and how you can use it to keep your virtual infrastructure up and running.

20.1 What Is vSphere Proactive HA?

vSphere Proactive HA is a feature that provides enhanced high availability protection for virtual machines by monitoring the health of the underlying physical servers and taking proactive measures to prevent potential failures.

Proactive HA monitors server hardware components, such as memory, CPU, and storage, for potential issues that could lead to failure. It then uses this information to predict when a server could fail and takes proactive measures to avoid that failure.

For example, suppose Proactive HA detects that a physical server is running low on memory because of a hardware memory failure. In that case, Proactive HA can automatically migrate VMs from one ESXi host to another ESXi host in the same Cluster with more available memory. This process allows the VMs to continue running without interruption, even if a server failure occurs.

© Luciano Patrão 2024
L. Patrão, *VMware vSphere Essentials*, https://doi.org/10.1007/979-8-8688-0208-9_20

Built on the core of vSphere HA, Proactive HA provides advanced monitoring and remediation capabilities to help prevent downtime and disruptions due to hardware failure.

20.2 How Does Proactive HA Work?

Proactive HA detects when an ESXi host is about to fail and then takes action to protect the VMs running on that host. It does this by using vSphere HA and Distributed Resource Scheduler (DRS) to monitor the health of each ESXi host in a cluster.

Proactive HA has the following four stages:

- **Monitoring:** Proactive HA monitors hardware components of physical servers, such as memory, CPU, storage, and network. It also monitors environmental factors like temperature, power consumption, and other server health conditions.

- **Predictive Analysis:** The monitoring data is analyzed by vSphere to predict potential hardware failures that might happen soon. For example, if memory usage runs high or the temperature rises above the acceptable limit, Proactive HA predicts that the server will soon encounter a problem.

- **Remediation:** Once Proactive HA detects an impending hardware failure, it takes proactive measures to prevent it. For example, if a server is predicted to run out of memory, Proactive HA can automatically migrate VMs to other servers in the Cluster with more available memory. This ensures the VMs continue running without disruption, even if a server fails.

- **Notification:** Proactive HA sends notifications to administrators when it detects an issue and takes action. The notification includes details of the problem and what action was taken, allowing administrators to quickly respond if further action is necessary.

Proactive HA provides additional protection for VMs in the vSphere HA and vSphere DRS by proactively identifying and mitigating potential issues before they cause downtime or data loss. It helps to increase the reliability of vSphere environments by detecting and addressing hardware issues early on.

20.3 How to Configure Proactive HA

To enable and configure Proactive HA, go to vCenter, select the Cluster for which you want to enable Proactive HA, click the **Configure** tab, select **vSphere Availability**, and click **Edit** (directly below the Edit button for vSphere HA), as shown in Figure 20-1.

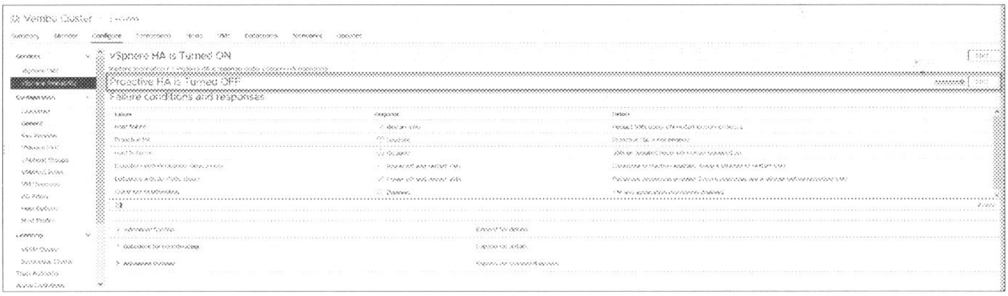

Figure 20-1. *(vSphere Proactive HA 1 of 3)*

In the Edit Proactive HA dialog box, enable **Proactive HA** and select options for *Automation Level* and *Remediation*. Figure 20-2 shows the expanded drop-down lists for each setting, described next.

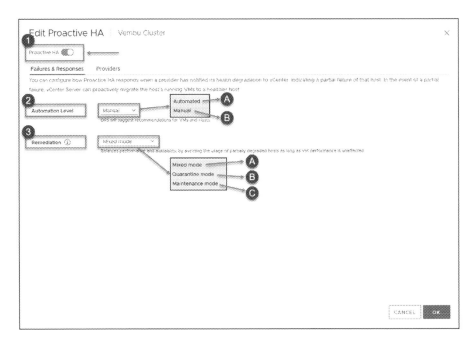

Figure 20-2. *(vSphere Proactive HA 2 of 3)*

- **Automation Level:** Determines whether host quarantine, maintenance mode, and VM migrations are recommendations or automatic.

- **Manual:** DRS will suggest recommendations for VMs and hosts.

- **Automated:** Virtual machines will be migrated to healthy hosts, and degraded hosts will be entered into quarantine or maintenance mode depending on the configured Proactive HA automation level.

- **Remediation:** There are three types of Remediation mode in Proactive HA:

- **Quarantine Mode:** This mode is applicable for all types of failures. It aims to strike a balance between performance and availability by limiting the use of partially degraded hosts. The system will continue to utilize these hosts as long as doing so does not impact VM performance. This approach is beneficial for ensuring availability while avoiding the potential overreaction of moving all operations from a host that is still capable of functioning adequately.

- **Mixed Mode:** Designed for varying levels of failure, this mode uses a tiered approach. For moderate failures, it behaves similarly to Quarantine Mode by avoiding the use of moderately degraded hosts unless it impacts VM performance. For severe failures, it escalates the response to Maintenance Mode, ensuring that VMs are not run on hosts that are considered severely compromised.

- **Maintenance Mode:** The most conservative of the three, Maintenance Mode is triggered for any level of failure. It guarantees that no VMs will continue to operate on a failing host by completely offloading all operational capabilities from the affected host to ensure maximum protection and stability.

For purposes of the test lab, set the options to fully automatic, as shown in Figure 20-3: *Automation Level* to **Automated** and *Remediation* to **Mixed mode**.

Figure 20-3. *(vSphere Proactive HA 3 of 3)*

20.4 The Difference Between Proactive HA and DRS

Distributed Resource Scheduler (DRS), discussed in several previous chapters, is sometimes confused with Proactive HA. They are not the same thing.

Proactive HA and DRS serve different purposes, but as previously discussed, DRS must also be enabled to enable Proactive HA.

Proactive HA primarily focuses on identifying and mitigating potential hardware failures before they occur, such as predicting server component failures (like power could be a failure in a power supply, storage, disks, and network) and monitoring issues with server temperature. Proactive HA takes proactive actions to avoid this type of service disruption.

On the other hand, DRS is a feature that provides intelligent resource management for virtualized environments. DRS is designed to optimize resource utilization and balance workloads across ESXi hosts by automatically migrating VMs to hosts with more available resources, such as CPU, memory, and storage. DRS helps to ensure that resources are used efficiently and workloads are evenly distributed, which can help to improve performance and reduce the risk of performance bottlenecks.

In summary, while Proactive HA and DRS are designed to improve virtualized environments' performance and reliability, Proactive HA focuses on identifying and mitigating hardware failures before they occur, while DRS focuses on optimizing resource utilization and balancing workloads across ESXi hosts inside the Cluster.

Proactive HA is a valuable feature in VMware's vSphere virtualization platform that provides enhanced high-availability protection for virtual machines by monitoring the health of the underlying physical servers and taking proactive measures to prevent potential failures.

Proactive HA helps to ensure that VMs continue running without disruption, even if a server failure occurs. Proactive HA can predict any hardware failures automatically in your VMware environment and takes remedial actions. This feature provides an additional layer of protection for your vSphere HA and vSphere DRS, helping to increase their reliability and minimize the risk of downtime or data loss.

vSphere Proactive HA is a powerful feature for VMware administrators to ensure their virtual machines remain highly available, even when faced with hardware outages.

Note   It is important to note that for Proactive HA to operate correctly, it requires integration with a specific hardware provider. This integration allows Proactive HA to receive detailed insights about the health and status of physical hardware components.

20.5 Summary

In this Chapter we explored vSphere Proactive HA, a feature that enhances the availability of virtual machines by monitoring the health of physical server components to predict and preempt potential failures. Proactive HA operates through stages of monitoring, predictive analysis, remediation, and notification to prevent server issues from disrupting virtual environments. It enables proactive VM migrations to healthier hosts, ensuring continuous operations.

The chapter also detailed how to configure Proactive HA, including setting automation levels and choosing remediation strategies to manage server health effectively. Additionally, it distinguished Proactive HA from vSphere DRS, emphasizing that Proactive HA focuses on preventing hardware failures, while vSphere DRS optimizes resource distribution and workload balance across ESXi hosts. This distinction underlines Proactive HA role in preemptively securing infrastructure, maintaining high availability, and minimizing downtime in your vSphere Cluster.

Chapter 21 introduces vSphere Fault Tolerance (FT). We'll explore how it enhances the resilience of VMware environments by ensuring availability of virtual machines by creating duplicate instances. We will delve into the mechanism of FT, its advantages and limitations, and the requirements needed to implement it successfully. Moreover, we will discuss the configuration of FT.

CHAPTER 21

vSphere Fault Tolerance

VMware vSphere Fault Tolerance (FT) is directly bound to vSphere HA: you cannot use vSphere FT without vSphere HA enabled.

vSphere FT, much like vSphere HA, is a complex topic that requires extensive coverage to fully explain all the configuration options and use cases. Therefore, a comprehensive exploration of vSphere FT capabilities and functionalities exceeds the scope of this book. It's important to note that vSphere FT cannot be used without vSphere HA enabled, as FT is intricately linked to HA mechanisms.

This chapter will focus on vSphere Fault Tolerance (FT), explaining what it is, how it works, and how to configure and perform a simple VM fault tolerance setup with failover capabilities.

21.1 What Is vSphere Fault Tolerance?

vSphere Fault Tolerance is a feature of VMware's vSphere virtualization platform that provides continuous availability for virtual machines. It creates a secondary copy, or "shadow instance," of a running VM that is synchronized with the primary instance in real time.

The secondary instance is kept in lockstep with the primary instance using a technology called vLockstep, which mirrors all of the actions taken on the primary VM to the secondary VM. If the primary VM fails for any reason, the secondary VM seamlessly takes over without disrupting the applications or services running on it. This provides a higher level of availability than traditional failover solutions, which typically require some amount of downtime during the failover process. With vSphereFT there is no need for manual intervention or restarts, ensuring that critical applications and services remain continuously available to end-users.

With vSphere FT, you can create an online replica of your virtual machine, allowing for zero downtime and full high availability. This ensures that your applications are always operational, even in the event of hardware failures.

vSphere FT eliminates even the most minor disruptions caused by server hardware failures. In the event of server failure, vSphere FT provides instantaneous, nondisruptive failover, protecting organizations from even the slightest interruption or data loss and the corresponding downtime costs, which can reach thousands of dollars.

vSphere FT also provides continuous availability for critical applications. When hardware fails, applications continue to run without interruptions, user disconnections, or data loss because vSphere FT provides automatic failure detection and seamless failover. vSphere Fault Tolerance can protect even homegrown and custom applications, ensuring continuous availability.

21.2 How Does vSphere Fault Tolerance Work?

vSphere Fault Tolerance works by creating and maintaining a synchronized copy of a running VM on a secondary host. The secondary VM is kept in a "shadow instance" continuously synchronized with the primary VM using a technology called vLockstep.

When vSphere FT is enabled for a VM, the primary VM and its shadow instance are kept on separate hosts in the vSphere cluster. The shadow instance is continuously synchronized with the primary VM in real time, mirroring all of its CPU and memory operations.

Suppose the primary VM fails for any reason, such as a hardware failure or an operating system crash. In that case, the shadow instance takes over seamlessly without disrupting the applications or services running on it. This is because the shadow instance has the same state as the primary VM, including its CPU and memory contents. It can immediately continue processing from where the primary VM left off.

The takeover process is automatic and transparent to end users, without manual intervention or restarts. Once the secondary VM takes over, it becomes the new primary VM, and a new shadow instance is created on another host in the cluster to ensure continuous availability.

vSphere FT provides a higher level of availability than traditional failover solutions, which may incur some downtime during the failover process. By keeping a continuously synchronized copy of the primary VM, vSphere FT ensures that critical applications and services remain available to end users at all times.

Figure 21-1 shows how vSphere Fault Tolerance works in your infrastructure.

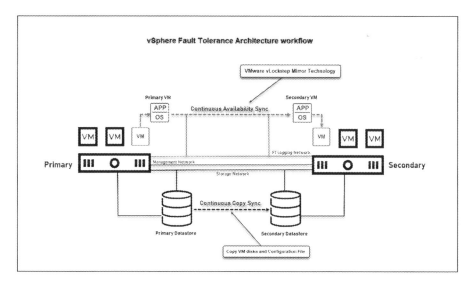

Figure 21-1. *(vSphere Fault Tolerance 1 of 13)*

Figure 21-2 shows an example of vSphere Fault Tolerance failover. When an ESXi host has a problem, or the VM stops working, vSphere FT automatically puts the secondary VM online, promotes it to primary VM, and creates a secondary ESXi host in the next available ESXi host. vSphere FT workflow rebuilds a new mirror and creates a new primary VM and a new secondary VM.

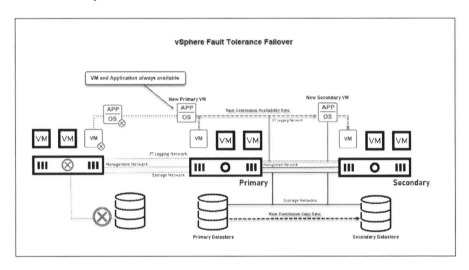

Figure 21-2. *(vSphere Fault Tolerance 2 of 13)*

21.3 vSphere Fault Tolerance Restrictions

When you're considering implementing vSphere Fault Tolerance to improve the availability of your virtual machines, it's important to understand its restrictions. While vSphere FT greatly enhances the resilience of your VMs, being aware of these restrictions is crucial in order to successfully deploy it in your VMware environment. In this section we discuss the constraints of vSphere FT, which will help you to navigate its requirements and make choices about how to apply it within your virtual infrastructure.

The following are several restrictions that you should be aware of before implementing vSphere FT:

- **Limited to eight vCPUs:** Fault Tolerance is limited to virtual machines with two vCPUs or eight vCPUs (depending on the license). This means that if your VM has more than that number of vCPUs, you'll need to reduce the number of vCPUs to use vSphere FT.

- **Limited to four vSphere FT VMs per host in the cluster:** Both primary VMs and secondary VMs count toward this limit. However, you can use larger numbers if the workload performs well in FT by configuring necessary advanced parameters. Setting this in the advanced parameters.

- **System requirements:** To configure vSphere FT, your system must meet specific requirements. This includes having sufficient CPU resources, meeting virtual machine limits, and ensuring the correct licensing. When setting up vSphere FT, you should also consider other factors, such as the type of workloads, the size of the VMs, and the overall performance and scalability of the environment.

- **Limited to certain types of VMs:** Fault Tolerance is not available for all types of virtual machines, such as VMs with specific devices or configurations. vSphere FT cannot be used on the following:

- VMs with more than 16 virtual disks and 2TB size disks

- VMs with more than 128GB of memory

- VMs with more than eight vCPUs

- VMs with physical Raw Device Mapping (RDM) disks

- VMs with virtual RDMs in physical compatibility mode

- VMs with CPU affinity configured

- VMs with specific virtual devices, such as USB devices, parallel ports, and SATA controllers

For example, virtual machines with the following devices or configurations cannot be protected with Fault Tolerance:

- USB devices

- Parallel ports

- SATA controllers

Table 21-1 outlines the vSphere Fault Tolerance maximums for each license type.

Table 21-1. *vSphere Fault Tolerance Maximums*

| | vSphere License Type | | |
	vSphere Standard	vSphere Enterprise Plus	vSphere+
vCPUs per VM	2	8	8
Virtual disks	8	16	16
Disk size	2TB	2TB	2TB
RAM per FT VM	128GB	128GB	128GB
VMs per host	4	4	4
vCPUs per host	8	8	8

21.4 vSphere Fault Tolerance Requirements

Before you can effectively use vSphere Fault Tolerance in your environment, you need to ensure several prerequisites are met. This section outline these requirements, giving you an understanding of what's necessary for the successful deployment and maintenance of vSphere FT. It's crucial to comprehend and fulfill these requirements in order to make the most of this feature and improve the resilience and availability of your machines.

To use vSphere Fault Tolerance, you must ensure that your environment meets the following requirements:

- **Compatible hardware:** Fault Tolerance requires specific hardware configurations to function correctly. Consult the VMware Compatibility Guide to ensure your hardware is compatible with this feature. At the host level, the CPUs in the host machines must be compatible with vSphere vMotion and must also support Hardware MMU virtualization (Intel EPT or AMD RVI).

- **Network requirements:** Fault Tolerance generates additional network traffic to keep the primary and secondary VMs in sync. You should ensure that your network infrastructure can handle this increased traffic and that your hosts are connected to the same network switch.

- **Storage requirements:** Fault Tolerance requires additional storage resources to store the shadow instance of the VM. You should ensure that you have enough storage capacity to accommodate the additional overhead. The hosts must have an FT-compatible storage device, such as a shared storage system, so that the FT-enabled VMs can be replicated across hosts.

- **Host requirements:** For Fault Tolerance, the primary and secondary VMs must be on separate hosts within a vSphere HA cluster. While these hosts need access to shared storage, this requirement pertains to the virtual machine configuration files. It's important to note that the virtual disks (VMDKs) of the VMs do not necessarily need to be on shared storage.

The following CPUs are supported:

- Intel Sandy Bridge or later. Avoton is not supported.

- AMD Bulldozer or later.

Ensuring that your environment meets these requirements allows you to successfully implement vSphere FT and provide continuous availability for your virtual machines.

21.5 Configure vSphere Fault Tolerance

Before enabling vSphere Fault Tolerance in your VMs, you need to create a network that will support this feature and is used for VMs sync. Therefore, you need to create a VMkernel for *Fault Tolerance logging*.

Note   Chapter 5 describes how to create a VMkernel.

As shown in Figure 21-3, select your ESXi host, click the **Configure** tab, select **VMkernel adapters**, and click **Add Networking**. In the first step of the Add Networking wizard, select **VMkernel Network Adapter**. Click **Next**.

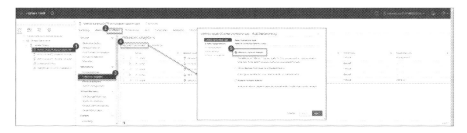

Figure 21-3. *(vSphere Fault Tolerance 3 of 13)*

In step 2 of the wizard, shown in Figure 21-4, click the **Select an existing standard switch** option, click **Browse**, and choose the Virtual Switch that this VMkernel will be using. For the test lab, use the Switch that we are using for Storage, **Switch1**. Click **Next**.

Note   You learned how to create a vmkernel in a Distributed Virtual Switch in Chapter 5, but we will use a Standard Switch for this case.

If you plan to use a vDS, you can follow the vSphere network in vDS chapter regarding vmkernel.

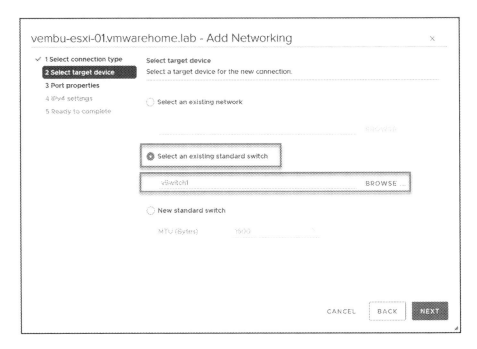

Figure 21-4. _(vSphere Fault Tolerance 4 of 13)_

In step 3, shown in Figure 21-5, add a name for the port group (not mandatory; you can use the default) and enable the vSphere **Fault Tolerance logging** service. Click **Next**.

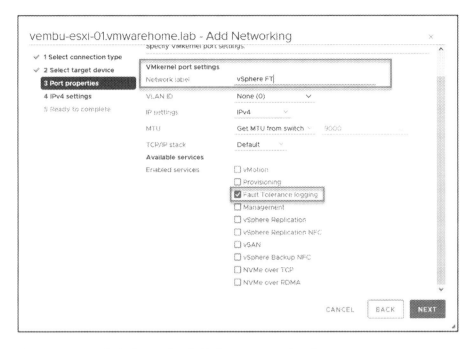

Figure 21-5. *(vSphere Fault Tolerance 5 of 13)*

Next, add an IP address for your vSphere Fault Tolerance network. See Figure 21-6. Click **Next**.

Note   You can separate and isolate the network using VLANs or a different subnet.

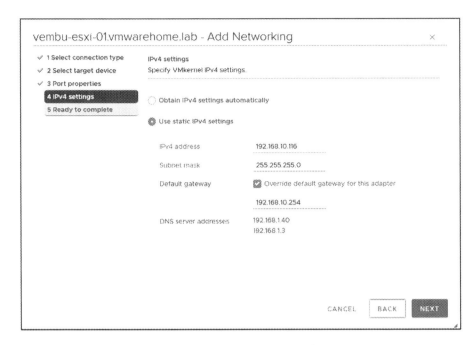

Figure 21-6. *(vSphere Fault Tolerance 6 of 13)*

Check all the configuration information in the final step of the wizard, shown in Figure 21-7; if all is in order, click **Finish**.

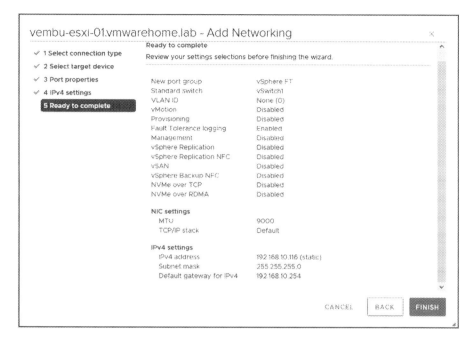

Figure 21-7. *(vSphere Fault Tolerance 7 of 13)*

Note   As you learned in Chapter 5, the process just described must be done in all ESXi hosts in the Cluster.

Now that you have created your vSphere Fault Tolerance network, you can enable it on your virtual machines.

As shown in Figure 21-8, select in the VM menu the virtual machine for which you want to enable vSphere FT, right-click it, select **Fault Tolerance** from the context menu, and then click **Turn On Fault Tolerance**.

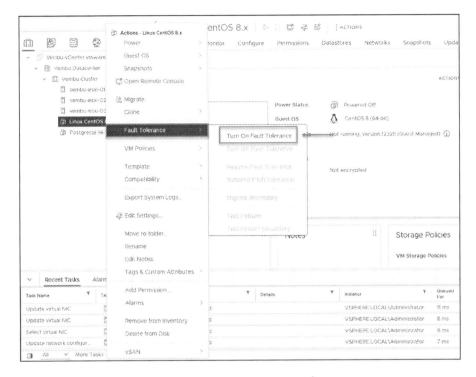

Figure 21-8. *(vSphere Fault Tolerance 8 of 13)*

In the Turn On Fault Tolerance wizard that opens, select the datastore for the secondary VM, as illustrated in Figure 21-9. As discussed earlier in this chapter, the Datastore chosen for the secondary VM must be a shared datastore. Additionally, it should be different from the Datastore where the primary VM is stored to ensure redundancy. Click '**Next**'.

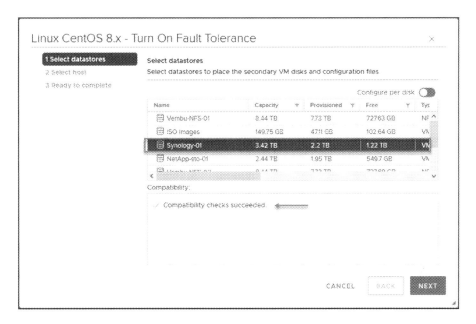

Figure 21-9. *(vSphere Fault Tolerance 9 of 13)*

Next, select the ESXi host in which to place this secondary VM. See
Figure 21-10. Click **Next**.

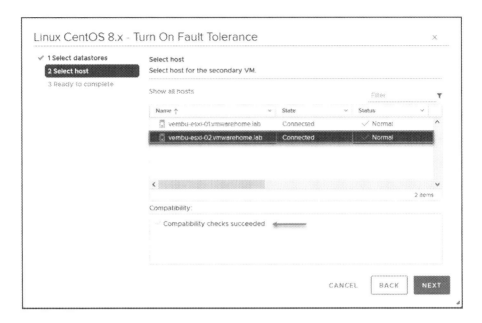

Figure 21-10. *(vSphere Fault Tolerance 10 of 13)*

In final wizard step, shown in Figure 21-11, double-check the information and click **Finish**.

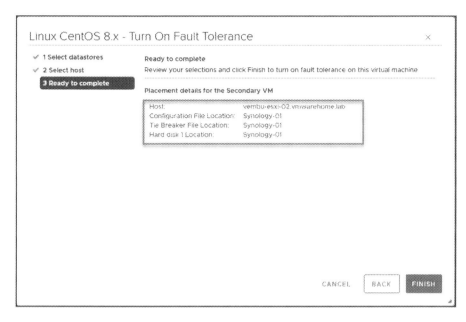

Figure 21-11. *vSphere Fault Tolerance 11 of 13)*

As you can see in Figure 21-12, vSphere Fault Tolerance created a secondary VM.

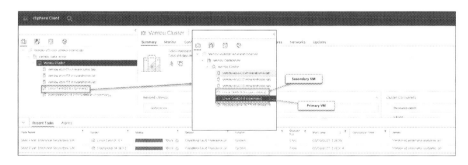

Figure 21-12. *(vSphere Fault Tolerance 12 of 13)*

The two VMs for which we have enabled vSphere FT are now configured for Fault Tolerance. Both are protected against failures. In the event of a failure, the secondary VM will seamlessly take over, ensuring continuous operation without any downtime in the guest operating system or applications.

If you check the Fault Tolerance options in the virtual machine, as shown in Figure 21-13, you see some management options to check the Fault Tolerance implementation:

- **Migrate Secondary:** Migrate the secondary VM to another ESXi host.

- **Test Failover:** Test failover to check if vSphere FT will work if the VM fails.

- **Test Restart Secondary:** Restart the secondary VM to make sure it works.

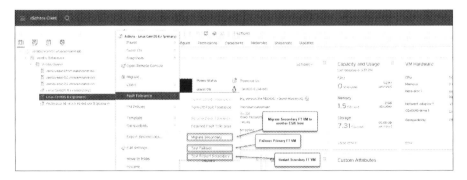

Figure 21-13. *(vSphere Fault Tolerance 13 of 13)*

Note that in the same context menu you can also suspend or turn off vSphere Fault Tolerance for this VM.

As discussed in the initial section on vSphere FT, this highly available vSphere service is crucial for maintaining business continuity. vSphere FT is particularly useful for applications or guest operating systems that cannot be clustered. FT effectively provides high availability for applications and VMs that cannot be clustered due to hardware or software limitations.

When using FT, you can create a "live shadow instance" of the primary VM and run both copies simultaneously. If one of the machines fails, the other will take over. This eliminates the need to manually manage and configure failover processes while providing increased reliability, improved performance, and cost savings.

It is important to note that specific workloads are not eligible for FT. Let's now turn to the pros and cons of using vSphere Fault Tolerance.

21.6 Pros and Cons of vSphere Fault Tolerance

Like any technology, VMware vSphere Fault Tolerance has both pros and cons. When considering vSphere FT, it is essential to consider both its advantages and disadvantages. This section includes coverage of the negative aspects of Fault Tolerance so that you have a more rounded view of how it affects the uninterrupted availability of virtual machines. Having an understanding of both the benefits and limitations of this technology is crucial for making choices regarding its integration in your virtual environment.

21.6.1 Pros of vSphere Fault Tolerance

The primary benefit of using vSphere Fault Tolerance (FT) is its ability to provide continuous uptime in case of hardware or software failure. With vSphere FT, users can keep their applications running without experiencing any downtime due to unexpected outages. Additionally, vSphere FT offers many performance benefits, including the following:

- **Increased reliability:** By providing automated failover in the event of hardware or software failure, vSphere FT allows applications to continue running without disruption.

- **Improved performance:** Through its live shadow instance of the primary virtual machine, vSphere FT provides faster response times and improved application throughput.

- **Cost savings:** By manually eliminating the need to manage failover processes, vSphere FT reduces the cost of IT personnel to maintain operations. Additionally, by reducing downtime, vSphere FT helps to minimize lost revenue due to outages.

- **Reduced complexity:** vSphere FT simplifies the process of configuring and managing application availability, allowing users to focus on core tasks and activities.

Overall, vSphere FT provides a reliable and cost-effective solution for ensuring the availability of applications and services. By providing a live shadow instance of a virtual machine, vSphere FT ensures that any outages are quickly mitigated and that applications remain operational. Additionally, vSphere FT offers a number of performance and cost benefits to help organizations maximize the return on investment of their IT infrastructure.

21.6.2 Cons of vSphere Fault Tolerance

The main disadvantage of vSphere FT may be its increased resource usage. Since FT creates a live shadow instance of the primary VM, it requires double the resources usually needed for a single VM. This can be a concern if resources are limited or multiple FT-protected VMs run on the same host.

Additionally, as previously discussed, there are two important limits for FT that must be considered: each host in the cluster can support a maximum of four Fault Tolerant VMs, and while the number of FT VMs per host is technically unlimited, it varies depending on the workload. Each ESXi host can support up to eight vCPUs allocated to Fault Tolerant VMs. If your VM has multiple vCPUs, you need to ensure it has no more than eight vCPUs to utilize vSphere Fault Tolerance effectively.

Furthermore, vSphere FT cannot protect specific virtual machines with raw device mapping, memory reservations, and more than four virtual CPUs. Also, when using FT, some features, such as snapshots, DRS, and High Availability, may not be available or may have limited functionality.

Moreover, troubleshooting FT-protected VMs may be more complicated than troubleshooting other VMs due to the complex architecture of vSphere FT.

21.7 Summary

vSphere Fault Tolerance is a powerful feature of VMware vSphere that provides continuous availability for virtual machines. By maintaining a synchronized copy of the VM on a secondary host, Fault Tolerance ensures that critical applications and services remain available to end users at all times, even during a primary VM failure.

While vSphere FT offers many benefits, there are also several restrictions and limitations to consider, such as the requirement for compatible hardware and software, limited virtual machine configurations, and increased network and storage requirements.

By carefully evaluating the pros and cons of vSphere FT in your environment, you can decide whether to implement this feature and how best to configure it to meet your needs.

Having examined the intricacies of vSphere FT, including its strengths and limitations, we now shift our focus to another aspect of VMware management: virtual machine snapshots. In Chapter 22 we will begin with an overview of what VM snapshots are and then delve into the specifics of files. We will also explore how snapshots function and I'll provide guidance on creating and managing them.

Furthermore, we will discuss practices for utilizing snapshots while considering their impact on VM performance and storage. A vital part of this discussion involves identifying and resolving any issues related to snapshots to ensure the operation of your environment. Lastly, we will address the setup of alarms in vSphere for monitoring and receiving alerts regarding snapshot-related issues—a measure to maintain the health and efficiency of your machines.

CHAPTER 22

Virtual Machine Snapshots

The virtual machine snapshots feature in the VMware vSphere environment often acts as a lifeline for system administrators and IT professionals. VM snapshots allow you to capture the state of a virtual machine at any given moment, offering a safety net for troubleshooting, testing new configurations, and guarding against potential errors.

This chapter explores the intricacies of creating, managing, and deleting snapshots. Additionally, we will explore some considerations to keep in mind throughout the process.

22.1 What Are Virtual Machine Snapshots?

Virtual machine snapshots are essentially "point-in-time" captures of a virtual machine's state, including its settings, disk data, and system memory. Think of them as being like a camera snapshot of your VM at a specific moment. They let you go back to that state whenever you need to, which can be very helpful for troubleshooting, trying software updates, or backing out changes.

Snapshots are not full backups, but they offer a quick way to save your VM's state without cloning the entire machine. However, they can consume a lot of storage and degrade performance if not managed properly, so it's important to use them judiciously.

© Luciano Patrão 2024
L. Patrão, *VMware vSphere Essentials*, https://doi.org/10.1007/979-8-8688-0208-9_22

One of the problems when using snapshots is that administrators often will start using them as backups, which is a big mistake.

Here are some of the benefits of using virtual machine snapshots:

- They can be used to revert a virtual machine to a previous state. This can be useful if you make changes to a virtual machine and don't like them or experience a problem with the virtual machine.

- They can be used to test software or configurations without affecting the production environment. This can be done by creating a snapshot of the virtual machine, making the changes, and then reverting to the snapshot if the changes are unsuccessful.

- They can be used to create a backup of a virtual machine. This can be useful to protect the virtual machine from data loss.

Here are some of the limitations of using virtual machine snapshots:

- They can degrade performance, because the virtual machine's disks are marked as read-only when a snapshot is created.

- They can lead to snapshot management problems, because keeping track of multiple snapshots can be challenging.

- They are not a complete backup solution. Snapshots only capture the virtual machine's state at the time the snapshot is created. They do not capture changes made to the virtual machine after the snapshot is created.

In a word, snapshots provide a safety net that makes fixing mistakes or other problems easier without affecting the whole system.

22.2 Snapshot Files

The types of files for snapshots are described next (previously introduced in Chapter 7).

22.2.1 Delta Disk Files

A delta disk file (.vmdk) is a writeable file accessible by the guest operating system. The delta disk represents the virtual disk's current state and that state when the previous snapshot was taken. The guest operating system stops writing to the virtual disk, and a delta or child disk is created when you take a snapshot, which also preserves the state of the virtual disk.

Two files are on a delta disk. One is a brief descriptor file that provides details about the virtual disk, including its geometry and parent-child relationships. The raw data is in a corresponding file, which is the other one.

The child disks or redo logs are the names of the files that make up the delta disk. Figure 22-1 shows one of the snapshot .vmdk files that belongs to the delta files group. It has all the information about the snapshots, parent, and child for Content ID (CID) and snapshot disk files used.

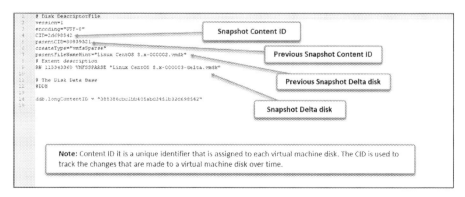

Figure 22-1. *(Snapshots 1 of 14)*

421

Note In managing virtual machine snapshots within VMware, there are several key details to keep in mind that affect how snapshots are handled and stored. These points are crucial for understanding the behaviors and limitations of snapshot technology, particularly in relation to storage and file management. Note the following specifics:

- The value may not be consistent across all child disks from the same snapshot. The file names are chosen based on file name availability.

- If the virtual disk is larger than 2TB in size, the delta file is `--sesparse.vmdk` format.

- With VMFS6, all snapshots will be sesparse regardless of the size.

22.2.2 Flat Files

A flat file is one of the two files that make up the base `disk.vmdk` file. The raw data for the base disk is on the flat disk. This file is not shown in the Datastore browser. You need to use the vSphere console and check in the Virtual Machine folder. This is how you see snapshot files in your vSphere Datastore browser. In Figure 22-2 in the vSphere Datastore browser illustrates how snapshot files are displayed.

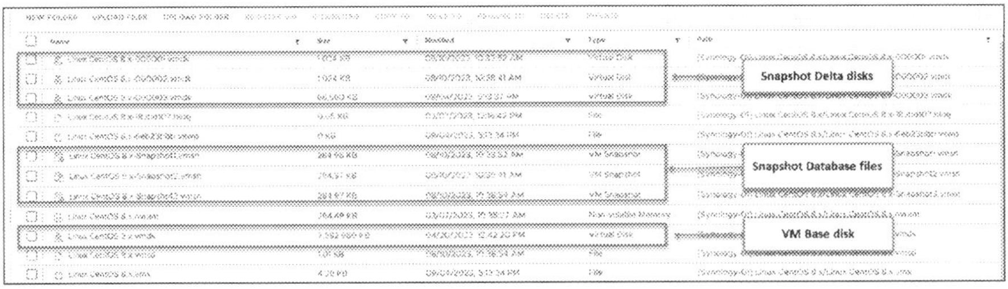

Figure 22-2. (*Snapshots 2 of 14*)

Figure 22-3 shows the files in the Virtual Machine folder. As you can see, the flat file is not shown when you use vSphere Datastore browser. Figure 22-3 also shows the snapshots .vmdk files. Those are the files with the CID shown in Figure 22-1.

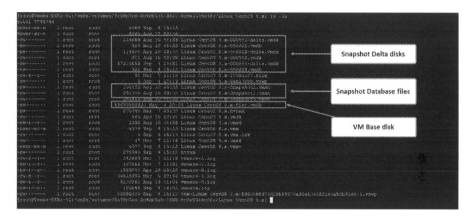

Figure 22-3. *(Snapshots 3 of 14)*

22.2.3 Database Files

A database file is a .vmsd file is a file that serves as the primary data source for the Snapshot Manager and contains information about the virtual machine's snapshot. This file contains line entries that describe the connections between each snapshot's child disks and previous snapshots.

22.2.4 Memory Files

A memory file is a .vmsn file that contains the virtual machine's active state. You can go back to a virtual machine state where it is turned on by capturing the virtual machine's memory state. You can return to a virtual machine that is turned off only when using nonmemory snapshots. Compared to nonmemory snapshots, memory snapshots require more time to create. The amount of memory the virtual machine is set to use determines how long it takes the ESXi host to write memory to the disk.

423

22.3 How Snapshots Work

When you create a snapshot, VMware vSphere takes a copy of the virtual machine's disks and memory. The original disks and memory are then marked as read-only. Any changes made to the virtual machine after creating the snapshot are stored in a separate delta file.

When you revert a virtual machine to a snapshot, VMware vSphere restores the virtual machine's disks and memory to their state when the snapshot was created. This means that the virtual machine will be restored to the same state it was in when the snapshot was created.

Figure 22-4 shows a simple example of how snapshots and delta files are handled in different situations. When the first snapshot is created, the virtual machine base disk (vmdk) will now be read-only, and then the snapshot creates new .vmdk files (delta files) where all the changes are written.

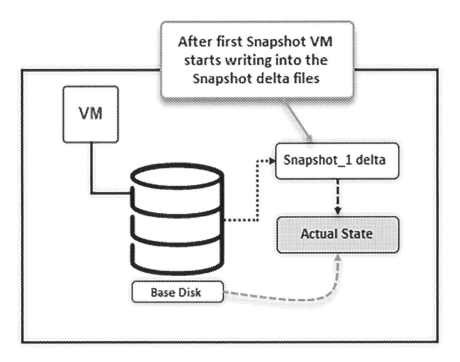

Figure 22-4. *(Snapshots 4 of 14)*

In the example shown in Figure 22-5, we have three snapshots and a VM base disk; the delta files from Snapshots 1 and 2 are read-only, and all the writes are written to Snapshot 3.

But what happens when we delete one of the snapshots? All the snapshot files are deleted and the VM state saved is lost. The change we did in Snapshot 1 should be in Snapshot 2; consequentially, the changes in Snapshot 2 are in Snapshot 3 when we created the latest snapshot. Also, as shown in point 1, VMs only write to the latest snapshot.

What happens when you revert a VM to a snapshot? -e process of restoring a virtual machine to a previous state. When you revert to a snapshot, the virtual machine is rolled back to the point in time when the snapshot was taken. All changes that were made to the virtual machine since the snapshot was created are lost.

Reverting to a snapshot is the process of restoring a virtual machine to its state at a previous point in time. When you revert to a snapshot, the virtual machine rolls back to the moment when that snapshot was taken, and all changes made to the virtual machine after the snapshot was created are discarded. For example, suppose you were working with Snapshot 2 and created a file named 'file nr 1' in the VM's guest operating system (e.g., Windows). After this, you created Snapshot 3. All the changes, including the creation of 'file nr 1,' are now part of Snapshot 3, which represents your current state.

Understanding the mechanics of snapshots is crucial. It ensures that you don't lose critical data during the revert process and maintains the integrity of your VM's state. With this understanding, let's look at Figure 22-6, which visually demonstrates how snapshot files are organized and how reverting to a specific snapshot affects the current state of a virtual machine.

Then, while in Snapshot 3, you create more files (file nr 2 and file nr 3). Now, you have file nr 1, nr 2, and nr 3 in that VM. If you revert from Snapshot 3 to Snapshot 2, you will not see 'file nr 1' because it was created after Snapshot 2 was taken and is therefore included in the delta files of Snapshot 3. This change, specifically the addition of 'file nr 1,' was saved in the delta files associated with Snapshot 3.

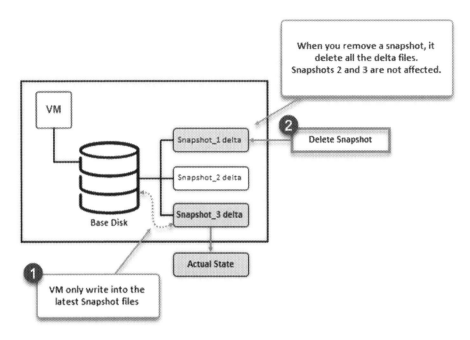

Figure 22-5. *(Snapshots 5 of 14)*

What happens when you revert to Snapshot 3? You will only see the file nr 1. Files nr 2 and nr 3 are lost when you revert to Snapshot 2.

You can only save files nr 2 and nr 3 before reverting to Snapshot 2, by creating a Snapshot 4. Then, on Snapshot 4 you have files nr 1, nr 2, and nr 3, even if you revert to Snapshot 2.

So, that is why it is crucial to understand how snapshots work.

22.4 Creating and Managing Snapshots

In this section, we will cover the steps for creating and managing snapshots. Managing snapshots carefully is crucial to avoid issues like snapshot sprawl. We will detail the options available when taking a snapshot, including capturing the virtual machine's memory and quiescing the guest file system for data consistency.

The process of deleting and reverting snapshots will be explained, highlighting the importance of understanding their impact on your virtual machines. The discussion will also extend to disk consolidation, which is necessary when dealing with issues such as orphaned snapshot files or failed snapshot operations. Mastery of these practices is key to ensuring an organized and recoverable virtual machine environment.

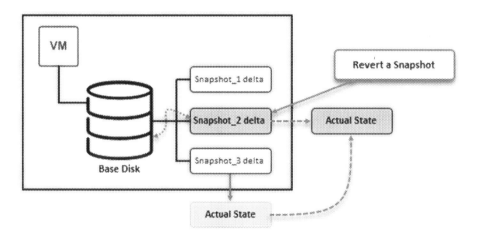

Figure 22-6. *(Snapshots 6 of 14)*

22.4.1 Create a Snapshot

Creating a snapshot is a straightforward process. However, don't let the ease of the process lead to snapshot sprawl.

To create a snapshot, right-click your VM, select **Snapshots** in the context menu, and click **Take Snapshot**. Then, as shown in Figure 22-7, you have two options for your snapshot:

- **Include virtual machine's memory**: This option captures the virtual machine's memory state at the time the snapshot is created. This allows you to revert the virtual machine to a specific point in time, even if it was powered off or suspended when the snapshot was taken. This option is enabled by default.

- **Quiesce guest file system**: This option pauses all writes to the guest file system before the snapshot is created. This ensures that the snapshot captures a consistent view of the file system. This option is disabled by default.

The following are some of the benefits of enabling the *Quiesce guest file system* option:

- It ensures that the snapshot captures a consistent view of the file system.

- It can help to prevent data corruption.

- It can improve the performance of the snapshot operation.

And these are some of the drawbacks of enabling the *Quiesce guest file system* option:

- It can slow down the virtual machine.

- It can disrupt any ongoing operations in the virtual machine.

- It requires VMware Tools to be installed on the virtual machine.

Whether or not to enable the *Quiesce guest file system* option depends on your specific needs. If you need to ensure that the snapshot captures a consistent view of the file system, then you should enable this option. However, if you are concerned about the performance impact or the virtual machine is not actively used, you may want to disable this option and select only the default option. After you make your choice, click **Create**.

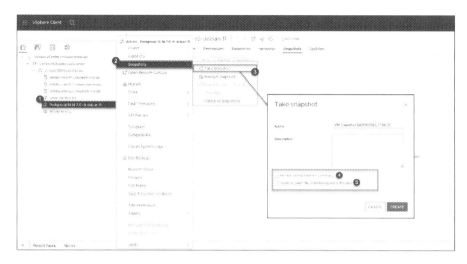

Figure 22-7. *(Snapshots 7 of 14)*

Then, you should see your snapshot in the VM *Snapshots* tab. Figure 22-8 shows the example from the previous section, with three snapshots, and text below Snapshot 3 saying "You are here," referring to the active snapshot.

Figure 22-8. *(Snapshots 8 of 14)*

22.4.2 Delete a Snapshot

Deleting a snapshot is as easy as creating one. As shown in Figure 22-9, go to the VM **Snapshots** tab, select the snapshot (Snap 02 in the example), and click **Delete**. Confirm your decision by clicking **Delete** in the dialog box.

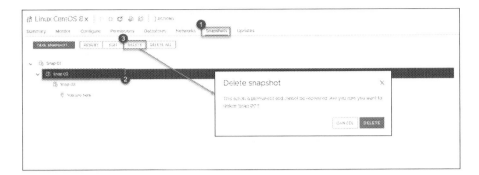

Figure 22-9. *(Snapshots 9 of 14)*

As shown in Figure 22-10, once the snapshot is deleted, the virtual machine is left with only two remaining snapshots. Whether a virtual machine has one, two, or three snapshots, the deletion process is consistent for any number of snapshots.

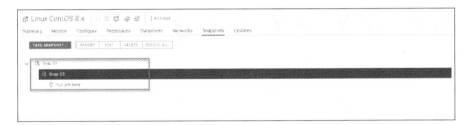

Figure 22-10. *(Snapshots 10 of 14)*

22.4.3 Revert to a Snapshot

The earlier section "How Snapshots Work" discussed how reverting to a snapshot works. Here, you will learn how to do it.

On the **Snapshots** tab, select the snapshot and click **Revert**. Before you confirm that you want to revert to the selected snapshot, make sure that you understand how the VM is handled after the reversion (see Figure 22-11):

- When reverting to the snapshot, if you select the
  option **Suspend this virtual machine when reverting
  to selected snapshot**, the VM will always revert to
  suspended regardless of whether the snapshot was
  taken with the VM powered on or powered off.

Note   The suspended option is only when you are reverting a
powered-on VM. This option is not shown if you are reverting a
powered-off VM.

- If you create a snapshot with the VM powered on, it will
  revert with the VM power on, but if the snapshot was
  created with the VM power off, then the revert will also
  revert with the VM powered off (VM may reboot).

It is not mandatory, and regardless of how the snapshot was created
and how the revert is done, it is always recommended to reboot your VM
before making any changes.

As explained in the "Delete a Snapshot" section, you will lose any
changes you made to the VM state. To save any changes, create another
snapshot before reverting to another snapshot.

431

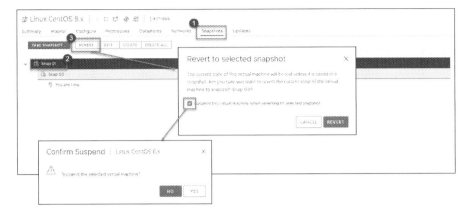

Figure 22-11. *(Snapshots 11 of 14)*

After you revert the VM to the snapshot, the Actual State will change for the specific snapshot.

22.4.4 Consolidate Disks

The option to consolidate disks is available only when there is an issue with the snapshots or the delta files.

The *Consolidate* option is used to merge snapshot delta disk files into the main virtual machine disk file when certain conditions arise. Here are the scenarios when you might need to use the *Consolidate* option for a virtual machine:

- **Orphaned snapshot delta files**: Sometimes, due to various reasons like backup operations or failed snapshot deletions, delta disk files (snapshots) can remain even after the Snapshot Manager shows no existing snapshots. These are often referred to as "orphaned snapshots."

- **Backup software**: Many backup solutions use VMware's snapshot technology to capture a point-in-time state of a VM. If the backup software does not correctly delete the snapshot after the backup, you might need to consolidate the disks.

- **Failed snapshot operations**: If a snapshot operation (create, delete, or revert) fails, it might leave behind delta files. In such cases, you might see a warning in the vSphere Client indicating that disk consolidation is needed.

- **Performance issues**: If you notice performance degradation and find multiple snapshot files in the VM's datastore, it might be time to consider consolidation, especially if these snapshots are not actively needed.

- **Storage warnings**: If you receive warnings about the VM's datastore running out of space and you identify unnecessary snapshot files consuming space, consolidating can help free up Storage.

To check if consolidation is needed, in the vSphere Web Client, you can check the virtual machine's *Tasks and Events* tab for messages indicating that disk consolidation is needed. The *Summary* tab for a VM will also show a warning if consolidation is required.

The following are things to keep in mind when consolidating snapshots:

- The consolidation process will generate IOPS on the underlying storage array. If the process is started while the virtual machine is powered on and if the virtual machine requires intensive I/O, performance degradation may be noticed.

- If you have multiple snapshots, you can consolidate them all at once. However, it is recommended to consolidate them one at a time so that you can monitor the virtual machine's performance after each consolidation.

- Consolidation can take many hours to complete depending on the size of VM disks and the snapshot delta file size.

While consolidating, there will be some storage I/O, so performing this operation during off-peak hours or maintenance windows is a good idea to minimize any potential performance impact.

22.4.5 Delete All Snapshots

Suppose you need or want to merge all the snapshots into the VM disk and the *Consolidate* option is not available (as just described, it is only available in case of one of the listed errors). In that case, you can select the option **Delete All** on the *Snapshots* tab, as shown in Figure 22-12.

Figure 22-12. *(Snapshots 13 of 14)*

22.4.6 Consolidate Disks vs. Delete All Disks

The *Delete all* disks option is similar to the *Consolidate disks* option insofar as both options are available to manage virtual machine disk files, but they serve different purposes. Let's break down the differences:

- **Delete all snapshots**

  - **Purpose**: This option removes all snapshots of a virtual machine, and the changes stored in the snapshot delta disks are committed back to the original base disk.

  - **How it works**: When you choose this option, vSphere commits the most recent snapshot disk changes into the base disk. Once that's done, it moves to the next snapshot in the hierarchy, and so on, until all snapshot delta disks are committed and deleted.

  - **Use case**: This option is typically used when you no longer need any of the snapshots you have created. For instance, after testing a software patch, if everything works fine, you might decide to delete all snapshots to reclaim storage space and reduce complexity.

- **Consolidate disks**

  - **Purpose**: This option is used when orphaned snapshot delta disk files are not associated with any snapshot entry in the Snapshot Manager. This can happen due to failed snapshots or backup operations.

435

- **How it works**: When you choose this option, vSphere checks for any orphaned delta disks and, if found, merges the changes from those delta disks back into the base disk or parent snapshot disk.

- **Use case**: This option is used when there is a discrepancy between the Snapshot Manager and the actual snapshot files present in the datastore. For instance, if the Snapshot Manager shows no snapshots, but there are still delta disk files in the datastore, you use *Consolidate* to clean up and merge those files.

Delete all snapshots is a proactive action you take when you want to remove all snapshots and their associated delta disks.

Consolidate is more of a corrective action used to resolve inconsistencies between the Snapshot Manager and the actual snapshot files on the datastore.

The following image provides a quick guide to the differences:

Feature	Delete All Snapshots	Consolidate Disks
Removes snapshots	Yes	No
Removes delta disk files	Yes	Yes (redundant only)
Revert to snapshots	No	Yes (not deleted)
Frees up storage space	Yes	Yes (if redundant delta disk files are large)
Performance impact	May impact performance	May impact performance if started while VM is powered on

One trick when it is not possible to consolidate the disks (error or files not properly deleted) is to create a new snapshot (even if there are no snapshots in the Snapshot Manager) and after the snapshot is created, select the option **Delete all snapshots**.

This trick can fix the problem and bypass the issue with the consolidation disks.

As previously explained, all files are merged to the VM disk in both scenarios, but in a different way.

Figure 22-13 provides a schematic view of a VM with multiple snapshots and the base disk. It illustrates the consolidation process, where all delta disks associated with the snapshots merge back into the base disk of the VM. This diagram is particularly helpful in understanding the concept of snapshot consolidation and the 'Delete all Snapshots' method, which is useful for resolving certain consolidation issues.

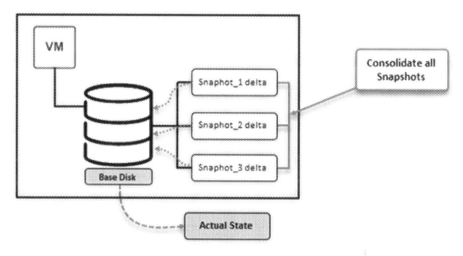

Figure 22-13. *(Snapshots 14 of 14)*

Monitoring the progress and ensuring storage capacity in the datastore is crucial to prevent any problems. Furthermore, carrying out these tasks during periods is advisable to minimize any potential impact on performance.

While consolidating disks or deleting all snapshots, there will be some storage I/O, so performing this operation during off-peak hours or maintenance windows is an excellent idea to minimize any potential performance impact.

22.5 Snapshot Best Practices

First and foremost, it's essential to reiterate: *snapshots are not backups.* They are meant to capture the state of a VM at a specific point in time, providing a temporary safety net for short-term tasks like testing or troubleshooting. They are not designed for long-term data retention or recovery.

The following are some guidelines to create and manage your snapshots:

- **Limit the number**: Avoid having too many snapshots for a single virtual machine. It's generally recommended to keep only a few snapshots and not to rely on them as long-term backups.

- **Retain them no longer than 48 hours**: Best practices recommend that snapshots be retained for no longer than 24 to 48 hours, for the following reasons:

  - **Performance**: The longer a snapshot is kept, the larger its associated delta file grows. This growth can lead to increased I/O operations, impacting the performance of the VM and potentially the entire datastore.

  - **Storage**: Extended retention of snapshots can consume significant storage space, leading to potential issues if the datastore runs out of space.

  - **Complexity**: The more snapshots you have, especially in a chain, the more complex and time-consuming the consolidation process becomes.

  - **Reality check**: Despite these guidelines, it's not uncommon to find VMs with snapshots that have been retained for weeks or even months.

- **Lack of awareness**: Some administrators might not fully understand the implications of retaining snapshots for extended periods.

- **Forgetfulness**: In busy IT environments, administrators might create a snapshot and then forget to delete it after the intended task is completed.

- **Misuse**: Sometimes, due to misconceptions or lack of proper backup solutions, snapshots are incorrectly used as a pseudo-backup mechanism.

Snapshots are best used for short-term purposes, like testing a new patch or configuration. It's a good idea to delete snapshots once they're no longer needed, to free up Storage and maintain performance.

- **Monitor storage**: Snapshots can quickly consume storage space, especially if there's a lot of disk activity. Regularly monitor your Storage to ensure you don't run out of space.

- **Avoid chain reactions**: Try not to create long chains of snapshots. The longer the chain, the more complex the merge process becomes when you decide to delete or revert.

- **Document**: Always document the reason for creating a snapshot, its expected lifespan, and any other relevant details. This makes management easier, especially in environments with multiple VMs and administrators.

- **Regularly review**: Periodically review and manage your snapshots. Old and unnecessary snapshots can be deleted to reclaim Storage and improve performance.

Remember, snapshots are resource-intensive and can affect performance if not managed well, so it's best to use them wisely.

22.6 Impact on VM Performance and Storage Performance

As discussed in previous section, snapshots can significantly impact your VM and Storage performance. Snapshots, while incredibly useful, come with their own set of challenges, especially when not managed appropriately. The impact on both VM performance and Storage can be significant, and understanding these implications is crucial for any administrator.

22.6.1 Impact on VM Performance

When not managed correctly, snapshots can introduce several performance-related challenges for virtual machines.

When a snapshot is created, the virtual machine's disk is split into two parts: the base disk and the delta disk. The base disk contains the original state of the virtual machine's disk, and the delta disk contains the changes made to the disk since the Snapshot was created.

When the virtual machine is running, all writes to the disk are first written to the delta disk. The delta disk is then periodically merged back to the base disk. This process can slow down the virtual machine's performance, especially if many changes are being made to the disk.

The number of snapshots taken can further exacerbate the performance impact of snapshots. Each snapshot creates a new delta disk, adding up to a significant amount of disk space. This can lead to storage fragmentation, further slowing down the virtual machine's performance.

Understanding the impacts of snapshots on VM performance is crucial for effective virtual infrastructure management. Here are some key factors to consider:

- **Disk I/O overhead**: With the creation of a snapshot, a new delta file is formed. All new writes to the VM's disk are redirected to this delta file, while the original disk becomes read-only. This redirection process adds extra I/O operations, potentially slowing down the VM, especially when multiple chained snapshots exist.

- **Snapshot consolidation**: When you decide to delete or consolidate snapshots, the data from the delta files needs to be merged back into the main disk. This merging process is I/O intensive, which can lead to noticeable performance degradation for the VM during the consolidation period.

- **Memory overhead**: If the VM's memory state is included in a snapshot, it can impact the VM's performance, because the snapshot will consume additional Storage equivalent to the VM's allocated RAM, which can affect the VM's operations, especially if memory resources are constrained.

- **Fragmentation**: As snapshots are created and deleted, disk fragmentation can occur. Fragmented snapshot delta files can result in slower disk access times, which in turn affects the VM's responsiveness.

22.6.2 Impact on Storage Performance

The implications of snapshots extend beyond just the VM's performance. Snapshots can also have a significant impact on Storage.

A new file is created on the storage device when a snapshot is created. This file can be quite large, especially if many changes have been made to the virtual machine's disk since the last snapshot was created.

The creation of new snapshot files can put a strain on the storage device, especially if there are a lot of snapshots being created. This can lead to performance degradation, such as increased latency and reduced throughput.

In addition, the need to merge delta disks back to the base disk can also put a strain on the storage device. This process can be especially time-consuming if there are a lot of delta disks to merge.

Considering the impact of snapshots on storage utilization is essential for maintaining a healthy virtual environment. Here are some factors to keep in mind:

- **Storage space consumption**: Delta files grow as they accumulate changes. If snapshots are retained for long durations, these delta files can consume a large portion of storage space. This diminishes available space in the datastore and can lead to scenarios where VMs might pause or even crash if the datastore runs out of space.

- **Memory storage**: Snapshots that include the VM's memory state will use additional Storage equivalent to the VM's allocated RAM. In environments with multiple memory-intensive VMs, this can quickly consume significant Storage.

To mitigate these performance and storage issues, follow these (previously discussed) best practices:

- Limit the duration and number of snapshots.

- Monitor Storage regularly to ensure adequate free space.

- Delete old snapshots regularly.

- Schedule snapshot-related tasks during off-peak hours to minimize disruption.

- Consider using faster storage solutions, like SSDs, for datastores that frequently use snapshots.

22.7 Identifying and Resolving Snapshot Issues

Snapshots of machines are incredibly useful in managing VMware, as they provide flexibility in performing operations on VMs. However, it's important to be aware of issues that may arise when using them. In this section we will explore problems related to snapshots and practical solutions for resolving them. By understanding the strengths and limitations of snapshots, you can effectively utilize them while minimizing any impact on your virtual environment. This knowledge is crucial for maintaining the health and performance of your VMs, ensuring that snapshots serve as an asset rather than a hindrance in your infrastructure.

22.7.1 Orphaned Snapshots

As previously introduced, orphaned snapshots are snapshots that, for various reasons, exist on the datastore but don't appear in the Snapshot Manager. Navigating through the Datastore browser can help locate these elusive files. Once identified, they can be manually deleted, but always ensure you have a backup before taking such actions. In situations where the path forward isn't clear, consolidating the VM's disks can be a safer approach, as it should integrate any data from orphaned snapshots.

22.7.2 Datastore Space Depletion

Datastore space depletion can be due to snapshots that have grown too large or have been retained for extended periods. When the datastore's space starts running low, VM operations can be interrupted, leading to potential downtime or data loss. Regularly monitoring the size and age of snapshots and being proactive in deleting those no longer needed can help mitigate this risk. In more dire situations, moving VMs to a different datastore might be necessary to free up space.

22.7.3 Performance Dips

Performance dips result from long snapshot chains or extended snapshot durations. In such cases, the VM might become sluggish, particularly in tasks that involve disk operations. Deleting or consolidating these snapshots can often alleviate performance issues and improve VM responsiveness. However, it's worth noting that certain snapshot operations, especially those involving quiescing the file system or capturing the VM's memory state, can cause the VM to momentarily "stun" or freeze. While this is expected behavior, it can be minimized by scheduling these operations during times when the VM's workload is light.

22.7.4 Failed Snapshot Operations

Sometimes, for various reasons such as lack of space, file locks, or other processes interfering, snapshot operations like creation, deletion, or reversion might fail. When this happens, it's essential to check the VM's logs to get a clearer picture of the underlying issue. Resolving the problem might involve freeing up space, releasing file locks, or using command-line tools to manage the snapshot.

22.7.5 Backup Software Clashes

Some backup solutions leverage VMware's snapshot technology to capture a point-in-time state of a VM. If not configured correctly, these tools might leave behind snapshots after the backup is completed. Regularly checking the backup software's logs and ensuring it's set up to delete snapshots post-backup can prevent this issue.

22.7.6 Misconfigured Alarms and Notifications

Ensuring that alarms and notifications related to snapshots are correctly configured is essential. These alarms can be invaluable in alerting administrators to potential issues, such as snapshots that have grown too large or retained for too long. Ensure correct configuration for timely alerts.

22.8 Summary

In this chapter you explored the intricacies and practical aspects of virtual machine snapshots, including how to manage and troubleshoot them.

We now shift our focus to a topic that greatly impacts the functioning of different VMware environments: Enhanced vMotion Compatibility (EVC) mode. Chapter 23 begins by explaining what EVC mode is and what purpose it serves in virtualized environments. This will involve examining the advantages and limitations of EVC mode, providing an understanding of how it optimizes VM migrations.

Next, we will explore the requirements for implementing EVC mode to ensure an understanding of what is needed for its effective use. We will then move on to discussing the aspects of enabling and configuring EVC mode. I'll provide you with step-by-step guidance to help you seamlessly integrate EVC into your VMware setup.

Finally, I'll cover some practices and considerations when working with EVC mode. We'll focus on maximizing its benefits while addressing any challenges. This chapter aims to equip you with the knowledge and skills to leverage EVC mode for enhanced compatibility and flexibility in your virtual machine operations.

CHAPTER 23

Enhanced vMotion Compatibility (EVC) Mode

23.1 What Is EVC Mode and Its Purpose?

VMware Enhanced vMotion Compatibility (EVC) mode is a feature that helps ensure that virtual machines can be moved from one host server to another without compatibility issues. It does this by creating a baseline of CPU features that all hosts in a cluster must adhere to. This way, VMs can easily move around without administrators having to worry about the underlying CPU differences between hosts.

When you enable EVC mode, the CPUs on all hosts basically "pretend" to be the same type, masking off any extra features not shared across all CPUs in the Cluster. This makes migrating of VMs (using a feature like vMotion) much smoother. However, the downside is that you might not use all the advanced CPU features if they are not part of that common baseline.

© Luciano Patrão 2024
L. Patrão, *VMware vSphere Essentials*, https://doi.org/10.1007/979-8-8688-0208-9_23

EVC usefulness during hardware upgrades is a significant additional benefit. To ensure that VMs work with all hosts when adding new hardware to an existing environment, enable EVC. This enables phased hardware upgrades because VM operations won't be interrupted even if you add newer hosts to a cluster with older hardware.

EVC also offers a defense against potential VM downtime. A VM might not start if it uses CPU features specific to one host and then moves to a host without those features. This is avoided by EVC mode, which makes sure all VMs in a cluster use only the features that it specifies.

As a bridge, EVC mode ensures flexibility and compatibility in different virtual environments. This feature is essential for high availability, load balancing, and hardware upgrades because it ensures that virtual machines can move and function consistently across all hosts, regardless of hardware differences.

Overall, EVC helps increase the flexibility and manageability of your virtual environment, mainly if your Cluster contains a mix of different server and CPU generations.

23.2 EVC Mode Benefits and Limitations

EVC mode in VMware vSphere is a feature that simplifies the management of environments with hosts running CPU generations. It offers advantages such, as improved compatibility and flexibility when migrating VMs. However, it's important to be aware of the limitations associated with EVC mode. In this section we'll explore both its benefits and the constraints it may introduce to your environment. Having an understanding of these aspects will help you effectively plan and implement EVC mode, allowing you to leverage its advantages while proactively addressing any challenges that may arise.

23.2.1 EVC Mode Benefits

The following are the primary benefits of using EVC mode:

- **Consistent VMotion across hosts**: EVC mode ensures that VMotion migrations between hosts are seamless, irrespective of the CPU generations. By standardizing the CPU features available to virtual machines, potential compatibility issues during VMotion are effectively eliminated.

- **Simplified Cluster management**: EVC mode allows for easier management of clusters that have a mix of CPU generations. All hosts in the Cluster offer a consistent set of CPU features to the VMs, making VM deployment and migration within the Cluster more straightforward.

- **Facilitated hardware upgrades**: When introducing newer server hardware into existing clusters, EVC ensures that VMs remain compatible across both old and new hosts. This feature permits phased hardware upgrades without disrupting VM operations.

- **Protection against VM downtime**: EVC minimizes the risk of a VM failing to start due to CPU feature discrepancies between hosts. Ensuring all VMs in a cluster utilize only the CPU features defined by EVC mode prevents unexpected downtimes.

- **Optimized resource utilization**: EVC provides the confidence to move VMs freely across hosts without compatibility concerns, allowing for better resource balancing based on VM demands.

- **Reduced administrative overhead**: EVC mode reduces the need for administrators to track which VMs can run on specific hosts based on CPU features, simplifying overall management.

23.2.2 EVC Mode Limitations

The EVC mode limitations that you should be aware of are as follows:

- **Vendor lock-in**: EVC mode works within the same CPU vendor family. This means you can't use EVC to migrate VMs between, for example, Intel and AMD hosts.

- **Baseline restrictions**: When EVC is enabled, the hosts might be restricted from using some of the newer CPU features if the EVC mode caters to older CPU generations.

- **Initial setup constraints**: EVC can't be enabled on a cluster if there are VMs already running and using CPU features not included in the desired EVC mode. In such cases, VMs might need to be powered off or migrated out of the Cluster to enable EVC.

- **Not a substitute for planning**: EVC provides flexibility but shouldn't replace proper hardware planning and standardization in large environments.

Overall, EVC mode is a valuable feature that can help simplify managing your vSphere environment and ensure that your VMs are always compatible with the host they are running on.

23.3 EVC Mode Requirements

EVC mode comes in different "levels" corresponding to various generations of Intel and AMD processors. When you set up an EVC mode, you are essentially picking your Cluster's lowest common denominator CPU. This ensures that all VMs can run on all hosts within that Cluster.

EVC mode ensures that VMotion can occur between different generations of CPUs by presenting a consistent baseline set of CPU features to the VMs. The type of EVC mode you can enable depends on the CPU vendor (Intel or AMD) and the generations of CPUs you have in your hosts.

EVC has different modes for AMD and Intel, each for a specific CPU model. Figure 23-1 shows a matrix of EVC modes for Intel and AMD and the features available in each EVC mode.

CPU	Supported CPUs	Features
AMD EVC Modes		
Opteron Generation 1	Opteron Rev. E and newer	All features of AMD Opteron Rev. E CPUs
Opteron Generation 2	Opteron Rev. F and newer	CMPXCHG16B, RDTSCP
Opteron Generation 3	Opteron Greyhound series and newer	SSE4A, MisAlignSSE, POPCOUNT, ABM (LZCNT)
Opteron Generation 3 (no 3DNow!)	Opteron Greyhound series without 3DNow!	Same as Gen 3 but without 3DNow! support
Opteron Generation 4	Opteron Bulldozer series and newer	SSSE3, SSE4.1, AES, PCLMUL-QDQ, XSAVE, AVX, XOP, FMA4
Opteron "Piledriver" Generation	Opteron Piledriver series and newer	FMA3, BMI1, TBM
Opteron "Steamroller" Generation	Opteron Steamroller series and newer	XSAVEOPT, FSGSBASE
Zen Generation	Zen series and newer	XSAVEOPT, RDFSBASE, RDGSBASE, WRFSBASE, WRGSBASE, FSGSBASE
Zen 2 Generation	Zen 2 series and newer	CLWB, UMIP, RDPID, XGETBV with ECX = 1, WBNOINVD, GMET
Intel EVC Modes		
Merom Generation	Intel Xeon Core 2 and newer	All features of Intel Core 2 CPUs
Penryn Generation	Intel Xeon 45nm Core2 and newer	SSE4.1
Nehalem Generation	Intel Xeon Core i7 and newer	SSE4.2, POPCOUNT
Westmere Generation	Intel Xeon 32nm Core i7 and newer	AES, PCLMULQDQ
Sandy Bridge Generation	Intel Sandy Bridge series and newer	AVX, XSAVE, ULE
Ivy Bridge Generation	Intel Ivy Bridge series and newer	RDRAND, ENFSTRNG, F16C, FSGSBASE, SMEP, CPUID Faulting
Haswell Generation	Intel Haswell series and newer	Advanced Vector Extensions 2, fused multiply adds, Transactional Synchronization Extensions, new bit manipulation instructions
Broadwell Generation	Intel Broadwell series and newer	ADCX/ADOX, RDSEED, SMAP, PREFETCHW, RTM, HLE
Skylake Generation	Intel Skylake series and newer	Advanced Vector Extensions 512, Persistent Memory Support instructions, Protection Key Rights, and more
Cascade Lake Generation	Intel Cascade Lake series and newer	VNNI, XGETBV with ECX = 1
Ice Lake Generation	Intel Ice Lake series and newer	SHA extensions, Vectorized AES, User Mode Instruction Prevention, Read Processor ID, and more

Figure 23-1. *(Enhanced vMotion Compatibility 1 of 7)*

Choosing an EVC mode is a balance between compatibility and performance. Pick a mode that is too old, and you are not using your hardware to its fullest potential. Pick one that is too new, and older hosts won't be able to join the Cluster.

Here are some additional factors to consider when choosing an EVC mode:

- The CPU features that are required by your workloads

- The CPU features that your hosts support

- The need for vMotion compatibility between your hosts

- The need to support older or newer hardware

If you have a mix of older and newer hardware, you may want to choose an EVC mode that is compatible with all your hosts. This allows you to vMotion virtual machines between all your hosts without worrying about CPU compatibility.

So, the available EVC modes allow you to align the capabilities of different hosts, making it easier to manage and migrate VMs.

Intel EVC modes are generally more restrictive than AMD EVC modes due to their capability to expose a broader array of CPU features. This difference stems from Intel CPUs typically incorporating a more extensive range of capabilities compared to AMD CPUs, which can influence the flexibility and limitations of the EVC mode applied.

The selection of an EVC mode is critical and should be based on the specific requirements of your VMware environment. If there is any uncertainty about the most appropriate EVC mode for your setup, it is highly recommended to consult with VMware support to ensure optimal configuration and performance:

- Generally, Intel EVC modes are more limited compared to AMD EVC modes because they expose more CPU features. The reason is that Intel CPUs tend to have a broader range of features than AMD CPUs.

- The choice of EVC mode depends on the needs of your environment. If you are uncertain about which EVC mode to select, it is advisable to seek guidance from the VMware support team.

23.4 Enabling and Configuring EVC Mode

Enabling and setting up Enhanced vMotion Compatibility mode is a task to optimize your environment, especially when working with hosts that have different CPU generations. While the process itself is straightforward, it's crucial to approach it with an understanding of the steps. This section offers guidance on enabling and configuring EVC mode. By following these instructions you can ensure that EVC mode is properly configured, allowing for VM operations and improving compatibility and flexibility within your VMware infrastructure.

Here are some considerations before enabling EVC mode:

- **Check prerequisites**: Ensure all hardware is compatible and you have the necessary virtualization software updates.

- **Cluster creation**: If you haven't done so, create a new cluster in vSphere. If a cluster already exists, you can configure EVC on it.

- **Plan downtime**: Although EVC can be enabled without downtime on some systems, it's often safest to plan a brief maintenance window.

- **Identify ESXi hosts**: All hosts in the Cluster must support the selected EVC mode.

- **Maintenance mode**: You cannot enable EVC mode on a cluster containing any ESXi hosts in maintenance mode.

- **Virtual machines**: You cannot enable EVC mode on a cluster containing any virtual machines powered on and running on a host that does not support the selected EVC mode.

Finally, if you disable EVC mode on a cluster, all hosts in the Cluster will be unmasked and will expose all of their CPU features. New virtual machines created on the Cluster will be able to access all of the CPU features available on the hosts in the Cluster.

Existing virtual machines will not be affected by disabling EVC mode. You can choose to power off and power on existing virtual machines to make them use all of the CPU features available on the cluster hosts.

To enable EVC mode, select your Cluster, go to the **Configure** tab, click the **VMware EVC** option, and then enable EVC according to your CPU, as shown in Figure 23-2.

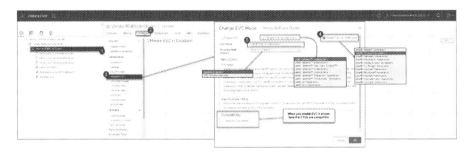

Figure 23-2. *(Enhanced vMotion Compatibility 2 of 7)*

Always check the message(s) in the *Compatibility* section to make sure you have a compatibility mode. If you get an incompatible CPU mix or use the wrong *Graphics Mode (vSGA)* option, you will see something similar to the message shown in the Figure 23-3.

Note   If you plan to use the **D3D 11.0 class features** option for *Graphics Mode(vSGA)*, which is a best practice, you should first select your compatibility EVC mode and, when it is all set and green (compatible), then change to the **D3D 11.0 class features** setting for *Graphics Mode (vSGA)*.

Do not start by selecting the Graphics Mode (vSGA) after you select any EVC mode.

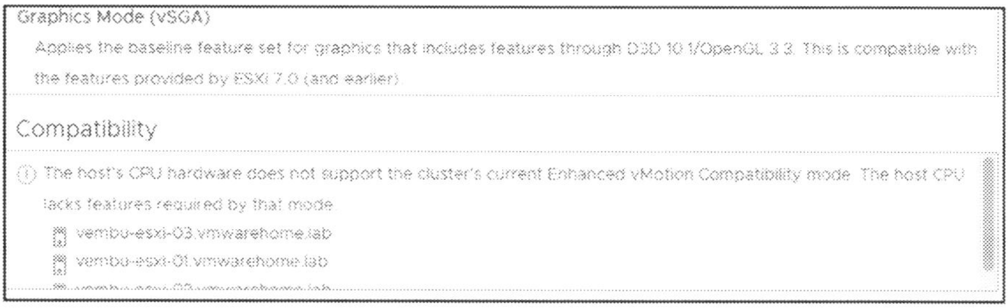

Figure 23-3. *(Enhanced vMotion Compatibility 3 of 7)*

In Figure 23-2, the "*Graphics Mode (vSGA)x*" option refers to VMware's Virtual Shared Graphics Acceleration (vSGA). This technology enables the sharing of GPU resources among multiple virtual machines. Through vSGA, all virtual machines within the environment gain access to essential graphics features, ensuring consistent performance across hosts with varying hardware capabilities. This ensures that even virtual machines on less capable hosts can still perform graphically intensive tasks.

This feature is crucial for workloads that require graphics acceleration, such as specialized applications in design, gaming, and video editing. With vSGA, commonly referred to as "Graphics Mode," you can establish a cluster of hosts equipped with graphics hardware, allowing seamless VM migrations between them using vMotion without worrying about graphics compatibility.

Advantages of vSGA include:

- **Enhanced flexibility and scalability**: Creates a cluster of graphics-enabled hosts, facilitating smooth scalability and leveraging hardware advancements.

- **Improved performance**: Ensures VMs operate on hosts with the most suitable graphics hardware, enhancing performance.

- **Minimized downtime**: Allows for host maintenance with minimal VM disruptions, reducing downtime.

The *Graphics Mode (vSGA)* drop-down list box has two options:

- **Baseline Graphics**: Applies the baseline feature set for graphics that includes features through D3D 10.1/ OpenGL 3.3. This is compatible with the features provided by ESXi 7.0 (and earlier). This option usually represents the minimum set of graphics capabilities that all the GPUs in the Cluster can support. Choosing this option ensures you get a compatible feature set across all your VMs, making it easier to use vMotion. However, this baseline would generally limit you to less advanced graphical features.

  The **Baseline Graphics** option is the default EVC Graphics Mode option. It is compatible with all ESXi hosts that support vSGA.

- **D3D 11.0 class features**: Applies the baseline feature set for D3D 11.0/OpenGL 4.1 Graphics support. This option exposes additional graphics features, such as Direct3D 11.0, DirectCompute 11.0, and Shader Model 5.0. This option is only available on ESXi hosts that support Direct3D 11.0. When using this option, VMs benefit from D3D 11.0 class features. Some examples:

- 3D graphics applications, such as CAD and video-editing software

- Games that require Direct3D 11.0 or higher

- Virtual machines that are used for machine learning or artificial intelligence

---

Note   Your choice between these two options depends on the specific graphical needs of your applications and the hardware capabilities of your VMs.

23.4.1 Enabling Enhanced vMotion Compatibility

If you attempt to enable EVC on a cluster that has VMs powered on which are not already supported or enabled for EVC, you may encounter an error as illustrated in Figure 23-4. EVC cannot be enabled until these VMs are powered off or migrated out of the cluster. This section focuses on the requirements and steps necessary for enabling EVC effectively in your VMware environment.

Figure 23-4. *(Enhanced vMotion Compatibility 4 of 7)*

After you enable EVC, you will see it enabled at the Cluster level and in the VMs. Next are some examples of where you can see the EVC enabled and all the information about the EVC mode.

In the Figure 23-5 at Cluster level and in the VMware EVC section we notice that we are not using any special vSGA graphics, but only the default configuration that is the Baseline Graphics. If you configure EVC with a special vSGA you would see here.

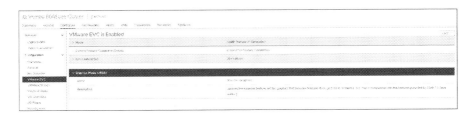

Figure 23-5. *(Enhanced vMotion Compatibility 5 of 7)*

In the Figure 23-6 we see the EVC mode is enabled at the Cluster level and what type of CPU mode is using. In this case is "Nehalem" for Intel Xeon Core 7i.

Figure 23-6. *(Enhanced vMotion Compatibility 6 of 7)*

In the Figure 23-7 is a bit different, here we see when the EVC mode is enabled, we see it at in the VM level. So if you have EVC enabled, in all your VMs you will that they are also enabled for EVC mode and will the CPU compatibility when needs to migrate between the ESXi hosts. In case you have different CPU models in your Cluster.

Figure 23-7. *(Enhanced vMotion Compatibility 7 of 7)*

Remember, once EVC is enabled, all hosts in the Cluster are restricted to the CPU features of the EVC mode you selected. Make sure this is compatible with any software you plan to run on the virtual machines.

23.5 Best Practices and Considerations for EVC Mode

We've already covered a lot of useful tips and things to keep in mind when using the EVC mode, but this section will summarize them in terms of best practices and considerations.

When setting up EVC mode in vSphere, making informed decisions is crucial for compatibility and performance. Each choice has nuances, from selecting the appropriate baseline for AMD and Intel CPUs to understanding Graphics Mode (vSGA) implications. The following are detailed best practices and considerations to guide you.

- **General EVC mode**

  - **Choose the right baseline**: Opt for the highest EVC mode that your current and future CPUs can support.

  - **Test before deployment**: Use a test environment to ensure that chosen EVC modes work as expected.

- **AMD and Intel specifics**

  - **Feature matching**: Check what features each EVC mode exposes for AMD and Intel, which is crucial when mixing CPU brands.

  - **Future-proofing**: Choose an EVC mode compatible with your current and future CPUs.

- **Graphics Mode (vSGA)**

  - **Application needs**: If you have graphic-intensive apps, the *D3D 11.0 class features* option may be better than the *Baseline Graphics* option.

  - **Compatibility vs. performance**: Choose *Baseline Graphics* for excellent compatibility but potentially lower performance.

- **Miscellaneous**

  - **Documentation**: Keep records of your EVC configurations.

  - **Consult vendor**: Double-check any CPU requirements for your software.

- **EVC mode restrictions and limitations**

  - **Compatibility issues**: EVC can't make incompatible CPUs work together and doesn't address Storage or other hardware compatibility.

  - **Limited features**: Choosing a lower EVC mode or *Baseline Graphics* in vSGA limits CPU and graphics capabilities, potentially affecting performance and software functionality.

- **No downgrading**: You can upgrade to a more inclusive EVC mode without shutting down VMs, but downgrading isn't straightforward.

- **Software dependencies**: Some applications may require CPU or graphic features that your chosen EVC mode doesn't support.

Here are a few important additional reminders when planning to use EVC mode:

- Use EVC mode only if it is essential, as it can complicate your setup and impact performance.

- Always plan and test any changes to a Cluster EVC mode before applying them in an environment. Changing the EVC mode can cause disruptions.

- EVC mode is not meant to hide CPU compatibility issues. It's important to address the root causes of CPU compatibility problems by relying on EVC mode as a workaround.

23.6 Summary

In this chapter, we explored the particulars of EVC mode, including its benefits, limitations, and how to configure it. The chapter highlighted the role of EVC mode in bridging technological gaps. EVC provides administrators with a more flexible environment, allowing diverse hardware to coexist seamlessly within a cluster.

A remarkable advantage of EVC is its ability to enable VMotion across CPU generations. This ensures businesses can maintain operations when their infrastructure combines old and new components. By standardizing the CPU features presented to ESXi hosts, EVC eliminates the obstacles that typically impede migrations between hosts with different CPU architectures.

Additionally, EVC mode proves beneficial for organizations aiming to be budget conscious of incurring expenses to replace older hardware. EVC offers a cost-effective alternative for compatibility reasons. It allows businesses to integrate server models into their existing clusters without requiring a hardware overhaul. This extends the lifespan of investments and ensures that organizations can scale and adapt without being weighed down by excessive costs.

As we conclude our exploration of EVC mode, it is essential to recognize the value of EVC mode beyond its merits. Still, it also is essential to consider its limitations to your environment.

Now let's shift our focus to another aspect of VMware vSphere management: Host Profiles. Chapter 24 delves into what Host Profiles are and how they simplify and standardize the configuration of ESXi hosts. We'll explore the process of creating and applying these profiles to streamline host settings management across your environment.

Furthermore, Chapter 24 covers aspects like applying Host Profiles to ESXi hosts or clusters, troubleshooting common issues, and editing profiles for specific requirements. We'll also discuss importing and exporting Host Profiles and their integration with Auto Deploy. This will showcase how versatile and efficient Host Profiles are in maintaining configurations while easing burdens. Moving from EVC mode to Host Profiles represents a progression from enhancing VM compatibility to optimizing and standardizing host configurations—both for vSphere environment management.

CHAPTER 24

Host Profiles in vSphere

This chapter explores the ins and outs of Host Profiles in vSphere and the role they play in automating and standardizing host configurations across your vCenter and Clusters. You'll learn everything from creating profiles to monitoring compliance. We will also highlight practices for optimizing resource usage while keeping an eye on any limitations. The aim of this chapter is to equip you with the know-how to manage and expand your virtualized environments using Host Profiles.

24.1 What Are Host Profiles?

Host Profiles are a feature in vSphere that allow for the standardization and automation of host configurations. They enable administrators to define a reference configuration for ESXi hosts and Clusters. Once a Host Profile is created, it can be applied to new and existing hosts to ensure configurations are consistent and compliant with the defined standards, simplifying management tasks and improving compliance across the infrastructure.

This proves advantageous in large-scale environments where manually configuring each host could become burdensome and prone to errors. Host Profiles incorporate networking, Storage, and security policies, guaranteeing operation across the Cluster or ESXi hosts.

Basically, Host profiles are templates that can be used to standardize and automate the configuration of ESXi hosts.

24.2 Benefits of Using Host Profiles

The use of Host Profiles in ESXi hosts provides advantages such as making operations more efficient and contributing to the stability of the system. These profiles act as a tool for managing and standardizing configurations across your VMware environment. By implementing Host Profiles, administrators can save time and effort on tasks while ensuring consistent settings across different hosts. In this section we will explore the benefits of utilizing Host Profiles, including simplified configuration management and improved performance and reliability of the system. Understanding these advantages will enable you to make the most of Host Profiles, enhancing your ESXi host operations and creating a stable virtual environment.

Using host profiles offers advantages such as the following:

- **Automation and consistency:** Host Profiles streamline the setup of ESXi hosts, ensuring that all hosts are configured consistently. This reduces the chances of error during the setup process.

- **Time savings:** Configuring each ESXi host manually can be time consuming. With Host Profiles, the time required to align hardware or virtual environments with standards is significantly reduced.

- **Efficiency:** Host profiles automate ESXi hosts' configuration process, saving time and effort— especially in environments with numerous hosts.

- **Ease of management:** With Host Profiles, changes can be done centrally and can be applied effortlessly to all hosts. This simplifies management and minimizes the potential for errors.

- **Compliance:** Host profiles help enforce compliance with policies and standards.

Host profiles add benefits in scenarios such as:

- **Deploying hosts:** Host profiles facilitate the deployment of new hosts into a cluster while maintaining consistent configurations.

- **Upgrading hosts:** Host profiles ensure controlled and consistent upgrades for all hosts by aligning them with the desired configuration.

- **Troubleshooting:** By comparing the configuration to the good configuration stored in the host profile, troubleshooting configuration issues on ESXi hosts becomes more efficient.

Host profiles are used to ensure that all hosts comply with policies and standards. To begin using host profiles, you must first create one. You can do so either by starting from scratch or by duplicating an existing host profile. After you create a host profile, it can be applied to hosts or groups of hosts.

Applying a host profile to a host will configure it to match the settings specified in the profile. If the host is already configured, any settings that differ from those in the profile will be overwritten.

Host profiles are a vCenter and ESXi host feature for enhancing efficiency, reliability, and security in vSphere environments.

These advantages make Host Profiles a valuable tool for administrators looking to optimize and standardize their vSphere environments.

24.3 Creating and Applying Host Profiles

You have two options for accessing the Host Profiles section from the vCenter main menu in the vSphere Client (see Figure 24-1): click **Shortcuts** and then click **Host Profiles**, or click **Policies and Profiles** and select **Host Profiles**. Both options will show you the Host Profiles section.

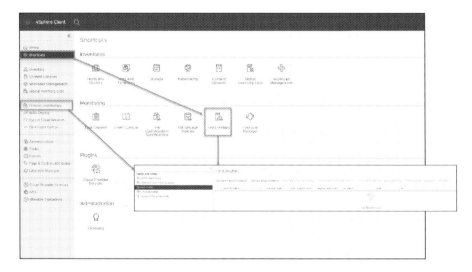

Figure 24-1. *(Host Profiles 1 of 30)*

You can check all the Host Profiles in your vCenter in this section. For each Host Profile, you can extract it, import it, export it, duplicate it, copy its settings, and manage its settings.

To create your first Host Profile, you first need to extract your ESXi host configuration to a Host Profile. As shown in Figure 24-2, right-click the name of your ESXi host template (the one you will use as the source for all ESXi host template configurations; for purposes of the test lab, right-click vembu-esxi-01.vmwarehome.lab), select **Host Profiles** in the context menu, click **Extract Host Profile**, give it a name, and click **OK**. For purposes of this example, name the Host Profile **VMware vSphere Essentials Profiles**.

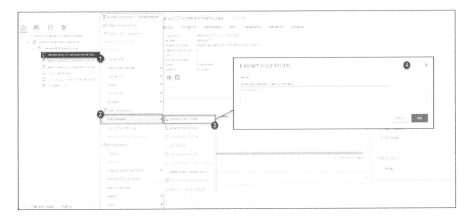

Figure 24-2. *(Host Profiles 2 of 30)*

Now you have a Host Profile based on that ESXi host, as shown in Figure 24-3. Also note in the toolbar all the options to manage this and other Host Profiles.

Figure 24-3. *(Host Profiles 3 of 30)*

Note   Although you can change/update your Host Profile after you extract it, as a best practice you should extract a Host Profile only after all the settings and configuration are finished on the source ESXi host (configurations such as network, Storage, Security, and Advanced settings, if you have any).

Before we go through all the Host Profile settings and configurations, let's attach our new Host Profile to an ESXi host. We don't want to change configurations from other ESXi hosts, so we apply the Host Profile to the same ESXi host we created it from.

Again, right-click the ESXi host, select **Host Profiles**, click **Attach Host Profile**, and select your Host Profile, as shown in Figure 24-4. (At this point, we have only one Host Profile, but after you create more Host Profiles, you will see them listed here.) Click **OK**.

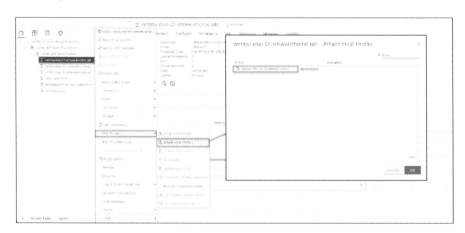

Figure 24-4. *(Host Profiles 4 of 30)*

When you attach a Host Profile to an ESXi host, you are linking the ESXi host to that Host Profile.

The ESXi host *Summary* tab shows the Host Profile attached to this ESXi host, as shown in Figure 24-5. Currently, the *Status* is Unknown, and we will discuss these options and information later in this section.

Figure 24-5. *(Host Profiles 5 of 30)*

Now, go back to the Host Profiles section and click your Host Profile to enter the settings and configurations section shown in Figure 24-6.

Figure 24-6. *(Host Profiles 6 of 30)*

Let's discuss all the options shown in Figure 24-6 so that you understand how they work and how to use them to manage your Host Profiles and ESXi hosts.

In the Figure 24-6 in the Summary Tab we see the summary at the right side where shows ESXi hosts that are Not Compliant, Compliant, or Unknown with this Host Profile.

This shows how many ESXi hosts need to run the remediation to apply all changes and configurations in the Host Profile.

1. The panel on the left shows how many ESXi hosts and Clusters this particular Host Profile is attached to. Thus far in our example, we've attached the Host Profile only to our source ESXi host, so only one ESXi host is attached.

2. The Monitor tab enables you to monitor any task or information about the ESXi host connected to your Host Profile, check its compliance status, and edit it to make any customizations (e.g., add IPs to your vmkernel, etc., as shown in Figure 24-7).

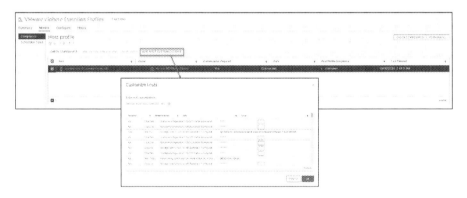

Figure 24-7. *(Host Profiles 7 of 30)*

It is also possible to create scheduled tasks by selecting **Schedule Tasks** on the left side of the Monitor tab. You can configure vCenter to check periodically that Host Profile Compliance is set with the ESXi host configuration.

3. The Configure tab enables you to configure the full Host Profile. As with the Monitor tab, you can edit the Host Profile's settings and customize the configuration.

    For example, if you want to change a Distributed Switch port group (change the vmnic name or uplink), you can change it here, as shown in Figure 24-8, and then run the *Remediate* option (discussed in the next section) to apply it to all the ESXi hosts with this Host Profile attached.

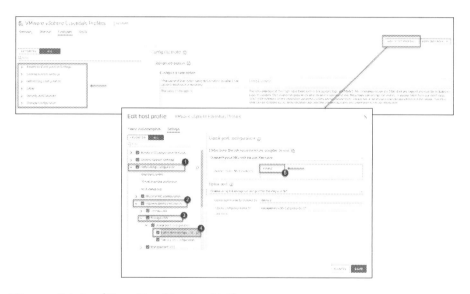

Figure 24-8. *(Host Profiles 8 of 30)*

4. The Hosts tab lists all ESXi hosts and Clusters attached to this Host Profile, as shown in Figure 24-9.

Figure 24-9. *(Host Profiles 9 of 30)*

5. Figure 24-9 shows the Host Profiles section in
   vSphere, listing all the ESXi hosts attached to a
   Host Profile, regardless of their current compliance
   status, be it Compliant, Not Compliant, or
   Unknown. This provides administrators with a clear
   view of the Host Profile and the attached ESXi hosts.

24.4 Applying a Host Profile to an ESXi Host or Cluster

Now that you understand a bit about Host Profiles and the options, we will
apply a Host Profile to a new ESXi host that we will add to our Cluster.

First, remember that we can apply a Host Profile per ESXi host or
Cluster. We can apply a Host Profile to an existing ESXi host or a new one
we deployed in our vCenter/Cluster.

Added the new ESXi host to vCenter/Cluster and attached the Host
Profile you learned in the previous section in Figure 24-4. Also, as you
learned in the previous section, after we attach a Host Profile to an ESXi
host, its compliance status is Unknown, as shown in Figure 24-10.

Figure 24-10. *(Host Profiles 10 of 30)*

To change the compliance status (you don't need to do this initial step to apply the Host Profile, right-click the ESXi host, select **Host Profiles**, and click **Check Host Profile Compliance**. As shown in Figure 24-11, the status has changed from *Unknown* to *Not Compliant*. This makes sense because we have not yet run the *Remediate* option that will apply all the changes that this ESXi host needs to comply with the Host Profile and the source ESXi host.

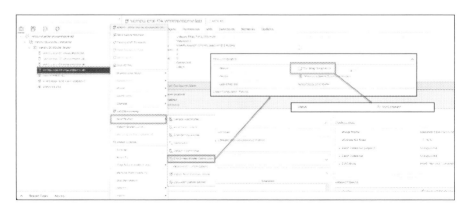

Figure 24-11. *(Host Profiles 11 of 30)*

473

Before we go further, I will show some of the settings that in the source ESXi host that need will set in the new ESXi host we apply and remediate the Host Profile.

In the Figure 24-12 we see all the Virtual Switches that exists in the ESXi host that we used to create the Host Profile.

- **Virtual Switches:** Host Profile will create all this existing Standard Switches and port groups in the ESXi host we attached the Host Profile. It will also create all the existing vDS.

Note   Host Profile only creates the Standard or vDS Switches is they do not exist in the ESXi host, if they already exist (with the same name and settings) Host Profile will skip this. This applies to all settings or objects that Host Profile needs to create in the destination ESXi host.

Figure 24-12. (*Host Profiles 12 of 30*)

- **Storage and vmkernel:** It will create or add the
  destination ESXi any NFS or iSCSI volumes/LUNS
  existing in the Cluster. It will also create all the
  vmkernels (management, vMotion, Fault Tolerance,
  etc.), but it will not automatically add the IPs for those
  vmkernels. This needs to be one with the option,
  Customization.

Figure 24-13. *(Host Profiles 13 of 30)*

Now the next step should be starting remediation to apply Host Profile
and make all the changes to the ESXi host. But if we try to do this now
before customization, we get this message shown in Figure 24-14.

Since we have Network settings per ESXi host, like IP addresses,
VMkernel, etc, we need to provide this information, as we see in the
Figure 24-15, before apply the changes, so that Host Profile applies all this
network settings per ESXi host.

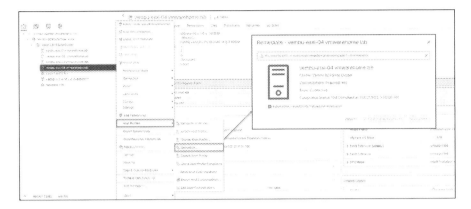

Figure 24-14. *(Host Profiles 14 of 30)*

This message appears because we have customized options to set before applying the changes (via *Remediate*). What are those customized options? The vmkernels we discussed previously have IPs, and since the Host Profile cannot apply the same IPs we have in the Host Profile ESXi host, we need to add them manually. To do so, right-click the ESXi host, select **Host Profiles**, click the option **Edit Host Customizations**, and add all the customized information, as shown in Figure 24-15. In this case, this information includes IPs and subnet masks for all the vmkernels.

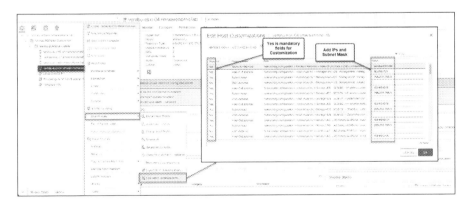

Figure 24-15. *(Host Profiles 15 of 30)*

Next, we can reapply the *Remediate* option. However, before we click *Remediate*, we can click **Pre-Check Remediation** to do a manual check to ensure that all customized options are filled and the Host Profile doesn't need any more information to apply the changes. See Figure 24-16.

Figure 24-16. *(Host Profiles 16 of 30)*

Figure 24-16 shows that our pre-check was complete without any warnings. Then, we can click **Remediate** again. It will do a Pre-Check before starting the Remediation.

The Host Profile will put the ESXi host in Maintenance mode, and the remediation starts. Then, a batch task is launched.

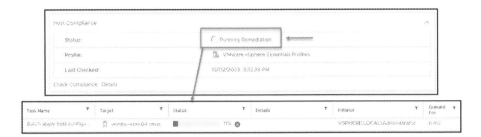

Figure 24-17. *(Host Profiles 17 of 30)*

Then, as shown in Figure 24-18, we have an ESXi host with a Host
Profile.

Figure 24-18. *(Host Profiles 18 of 30)*

To finish this discussion of attaching and applying Host Profiles to an
ESXi host or Cluster, I'll quickly show you how to add to a Cluster.

The only differences from attaching a Host Profile to an ESXi host
are that all ESXi hosts inside the Cluster will automatically be attached
to this Host Profile, and any new ESXi host you add to the Cluster will
automatically be attached to the Cluster Host Profile.

As shown in Figure 24-19, first right-click the ESXi host, select **Host
Properties**, click **Attach Host Profile**, and attach the Host Profile.
Click OK. Then, right-click the ESXi host, select **Host Properties**, and
click **Remediate**. It will start to Pre-Check and then Remediate all the
ESXi hosts.

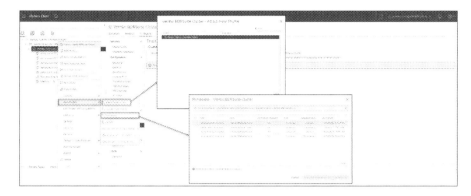

Figure 24-19. *(Host Profiles 19 of 30)*

24.5 Troubleshooting and Editing Host Profiles

Remediation failed: Mount failed**.**

In this case, we have an error. I will discuss this error here because it is essential to know how to troubleshoot and fix the Host Profile issues.

The first troubleshooting step upon encountering a Status of Remediation Failed is to click the **Details** option to get more information about the problem. As shown in Figure 24-20, in this case the error message is *Operation failed, diagnostics report: Mount failed: Unable to complete Sysinfo operation. Please see the VMkernel log file for more details.: Unable to connect to NFS server.*

479

Figure 24-20. *(Host Profiles 20 of 30)*

Not being able to connect to our NFS server means we cannot add the
ESXi host to the NFS server and mount the volumes shown in Figure 24-19.
We have two options here:

- Disable this option from the Host Profile and reapply
  it. The Host Profile will not mount any NFS volumes to
  this ESXi host. We needed to mount the NFS volumes
  manually afterward.

- Troubleshoot the problem, fixed on the source and
  then re-apply the remediation.

Before we proceed to the solutions, despite the failure of the
remediation, it does not imply that we accomplished nothing. Figure 24-21
shows that the vmkernels were created and the ESXi host was attached to
all vDS Switches.

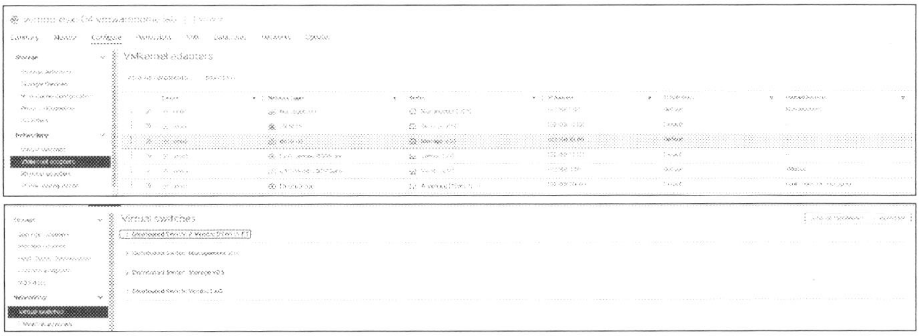

Figure 24-21. *(Host Profiles 21 of 30)*

It applied what it could and stopped when it encountered the error. The following sections explain both solutions to fix the problem.

24.5.1 Disable and Reapply

To disable the NFS storage configuration in the Host Profile, we need to edit the Host Profile, find the option, and deselect it.

Go to the Host Profiles section (using either option previously shown in Figure 24-1), right-click the Host Profile, and then click **Edit Host Profile**. In the *Edit host profile* window that opens, shown in Figure 24-22, click the **Settings** tab and click **All** to see all the configuration sections for the Host Profile. Expand **Storage configuration** to access the NFS storage configuration.

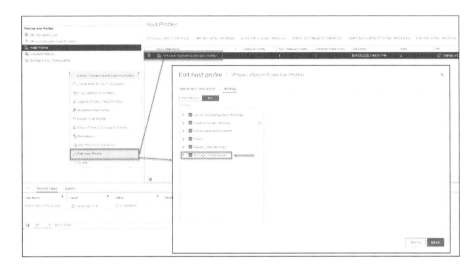

Figure 24-22. *(Host Profiles 22 of 30)*

Expand the **NFS storage configuration** section (because the error was about NFS volumes). As shown in Figure 24-23, there are two NFS entries because there are two NFS volumes to mount (Vembu-NFS-01 and Vembu-NFS-02).

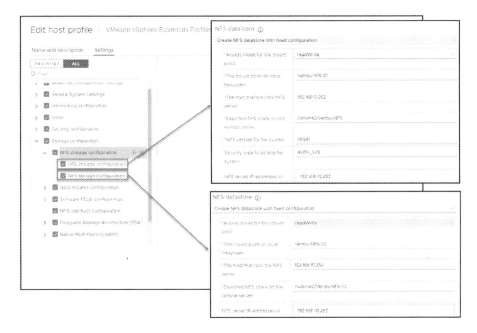

Figure 24-23. *(Host Profiles 23 of 30)*

Deselect (clear) the *NFS storage configuration* check boxes and *NFS user host configuration* check box to bypass the problem, as shown in Figure 24-24. Click **Save**.

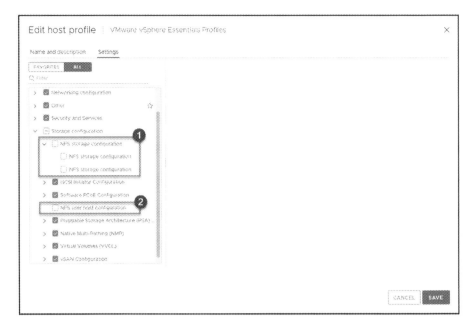

Figure 24-24. *(Host Profiles 24 of 30)*

After we go back to the ESXi host, reapply the ***Remediation.*** As Figure 24-25 shows, after the remediation, we have a Host Profile status of *Compliant.*

Figure 24-25. *(Host Profiles 25 of 30)*

24.5.2 If You Use iSCSI or Fibre Channel

These issues with iSCSI and Fibre Channel IDs and UUIDs when applying a Host Profile is never equal in all ESXi hosts, and I often encounter this type of issues. So it is best to disable Pluggable Storage Architecture (PSA) and Native Multi-Pathing (NMP) in the Host Profile before remediatione.

Note   It is possible to take some steps to fix the iSCSI/Fibre Channel issues, when applying a Host Profile, without disable PSA and NMP, but it takes an advanced understanding of Storage devices and PSA. So, it is best practice to disable PSA and NMP, doing so will not do any damage. When iSCSI LUNs are added to your environment, it re-creates all of all the IDs and UUDIS.

This is never equal in all ESXi hosts, and I often encounter issues. So it is best to disable this in the Host Profile before remediation.

Note   It is possible to take some steps to fix this without disabling it, but it takes an advanced understanding of Storage devices and PSA. So, it is best practice to disable it; doing so will not do any damage. When iSCSI LUNs are added to your environment, it re-creates all of this.

Figure 24-26. *(Host Profiles 26 of 30)*

Edit your Host Profile and deselect these two options, as shown in Figure 24-26.

24.5.3 Troubleshoot Why the NFS Server Is Unreachable

The second option is to troubleshoot why the NFS server is unreachable.

First, access the ESXi host SSH console. Then, look at the vmkernel.log file that the Host Profile logs referred to by using the command tail -20 /var/log/vmkernel.log.

The output in Figure 24-27 confirms that NFS server 192.168.10.252 is unreachable.

Figure 24-27. *(Host Profiles 27 of 30)*

Next, we will check our vmkernels and vmnics and try to reach the NFS server. The commands to do so are `esxcfg-vmknic -l` and `vmkping -I vmk1 192.168.10.252`. The output highlighted in Figure 24-28 shows that the ESXi host cannot reach the NFS server, meaning it cannot use the Storage network.

Figure 24-28. *(Host Profiles 28 of 30)*

I will have to double-check the connections and notice that the vmnics from 2 to 6 are not connected. I forgot to connect the network adapters when I created the nested ESXi host. After connecting the adapters for the Storage and VMs network, the ESXi host was able to connect to the NFS server.

In this case, the issue was easy to troubleshoot, and now we can reapply the Host Profile without the need to change or deselect any configuration options. After we fix the issues, we can reapply the Host Profile.

24.6 Importing and Exporting Host Profiles

Using Importing and exporting host profiles, we can export host profiles from one vSphere environment and import them into another. This allows easy sharing of configurations between different Clusters or vCenter Server instances. By exporting a Host Profile, we can save a particular configuration and then import it to apply the same settings elsewhere.

We can export and import the host profiles within the same environment for backup purposes or to apply the configuration to additional hosts.

24.7 Host Profiles Integration with Auto Deploy

Presenting all the features and advanced options we can use in vSphere and vCenter is beyond the scope of this book. vSphere and vCenter have so many features and advanced options that covering them all would create a huge book, so my goal is to discuss the most essential features of vSphere and vCenter. Although Auto Deploy is not considered one of those essential features, I find it sufficiently useful to merit a brief discussion of the advantages of integrating Host Profiles into Auto Deploy.

vSphere Auto Deploy is a feature provided by VMware that enables the setup of ESXi hosts. It simplifies the process by installing ESXi on fresh hardware, providing the flexibility to allocate and manage hosts from a central location. This feature proves to be beneficial in large deployments, eliminating the need for tedious manual configurations.

When you activate Auto Deploy on a vSphere Cluster, the Auto Deploy server will search for all hosts with PXE capability on the network. Subsequently, the server will download both the ESXi image and host profile to each host. Once the ESXi image and host profile have been downloaded, the host is booted and configured according to the host profile.

Auto Deploy enables the deployment of new ESXi hosts, the upgrade of existing ESXi hosts, and the reconfiguration of existing ESXi hosts. It can also deploy ESXi hosts in various environments, such as data centers, remote offices, and the cloud.

Auto Deploy provides advantages such as these:

- **Efficiency:** Auto Deploy enhances the deployment efficiency of ESXi hosts by automating their setup process. This capability is particularly valuable in large environments, where the manual configuration of numerous ESXi hosts would require a significant investment of time and resources.

- **Consistency:** Auto Deploy ensures that all ESXi hosts within a Cluster are configured consistently. This minimizes issues and enhances troubleshooting capabilities.

- **Reliability:** By guaranteeing the deployment and configuration of all ESXi hosts, Auto Deploy enhances the reliability of your vSphere environment.

Integration of host profiles with Auto Deploy enables the configuration of ESXi hosts with a set of settings during deployment. This feature enhances the efficiency and reliability of your vSphere environment.

Auto Deploy provides two modes for provisioning ESXi hosts:

- **Stateless Caching mode:** Allows ESXi to run directly from memory to a stateless Auto Deploy environment. However, it also caches the image to a disk. This means that even if there is no network connection or the Auto Deploy server is unavailable, the host can still boot using the cached image.

- **Stateful Install mode:** ESXi is installed onto the Storage of the server. This makes the host independent from the Auto Deploy server after its boot. Consequently, even if there is no network connection or the Auto Deploy server becomes unavailable, the host can still function without relying on a cached image.

As we see in the Figure 24-29 to use Auto Deploy and Host Profiles, create a customized image profile to utilize host profile integration with Auto Deploy. Then, associate the customized image profile with the Auto Deploy rule you wish to employ for deploying hosts.

Figure 24-29. *(Host Profiles 29 of 30)*

When a host is deployed using Auto Deploy, it downloads the customized image profile and applies the associated host profile. This ensures the host is configured correctly with settings before being added to the Cluster.

Now, we have an Auto Deploy rule with our Host Profile, as shown in Figure 24-30, and the new Auto Deploy ESXi hosts will be configured with the Host Profile configurations.

Figure 24-30. *(Host Profiles 30 of 30)*

Host profile integration with Auto Deploy configures Networking, Storage, Security, Firmware, and Software. We get the same advantages and options when using Host Profiles in an ESXi host or a Cluster. This reduces configuration efforts while ensuring configurations across all hosts in the Cluster.

Host profile integration with Auto Deploy enables compliance enforcement with policies and standards. This helps maintain security and adherence to established guidelines.

24.8 Summary

This chapter discusses Host Profiles in vSphere and how they can be used to automate and standardize the configuration of ESXi hosts. It covers the benefits of using Host Profiles, such as simplifying configuration management, improved performance, and reliability. The chapter also details how to create and apply Host Profiles, troubleshoot common issues, and integrate them with Auto Deploy for automated ESXi host deployment and configuration.

In Chapter 25, we turn our attention to two features that improve the flexibility and responsiveness of machines: VMware Hot Add and Hot Plug. We will dive into these features' capabilities and benefits, which include allowing for on-the-fly adjustments to resources like CPU and memory without disrupting VM operations.

CHAPTER 25

VMware Hot Add and Hot Plug

We will also discuss the limitations and considerations when utilizing Hot Add and Hot Plug to ensure you understand when and how to employ these features. Moreover, Chapter 25 offers guidance on enabling and configuring Hot Add/Hot Plug while addressing security concerns to guarantee an efficient implementation. This transition from Host Profiles to Hot Add and Hot Plug signifies a shift from optimizing host configurations to enhancing dynamic resource management capabilities for VMs within the VMware environment.

vSphere Hot Add and Hot Plug are functionalities in VMware vSphere that enable you to add or remove hardware resources from a virtual machine while it is running, without requiring a system reboot.

The following is a brief overview of these features:

- **vSphere Hot Add:** This functionality allows you to effortlessly increase the resources allocated to a VM, such as CPU and memory, while the VM is powered on. With Hot Add, you can dynamically adjust resource allocation without impacting running applications or services. This proves valuable when a VM requires additional resources to handle peak workload demands. For instance, if you have a VM hosting a

© Luciano Patrão 2024
L. Patrão, *VMware vSphere Essentials*, https://doi.org/10.1007/979-8-8688-0208-9_25

database server that experiences sudden user activity surge, you can utilize Hot Add to enhance performance by adding CPU cores or memory without disrupting the VM's operation.

- **vSphere Hot Plug:** This functionality seamlessly empowers you to add or remove hardware devices from a powered-on VM. These devices commonly include USB devices, network adapters, and storage controllers. By enabling Hot Plug, you can conveniently hot-swap these devices without causing any interruptions in the VM's functionality. For example, if you want to connect a USB drive to a machine already running or add a network interface card for load balancing, you can use Hot Plug. Likewise, if you no longer need a device, you can remove it without turning off the machine.

Both vSphere Hot Add and Hot Plug offer flexibility and convenience in managing and expanding your infrastructure. They eliminate the need for downtime when changing resources or hardware, making it easier to adapt to evolving workload demands.

25.1 Capabilities and Benefits of Hot Add and Hot Plug

The capabilities and benefits of the Hot Add and Hot Plug features extend to a wide range of tasks and scenarios within your VMware environment. These functionalities prove valuable in various contexts, allowing for dynamic adjustments and enhancements without interrupting virtual machine operations.

25.1.1 Capabilities of Hot Add and Hot Plug

The capabilities of Hot Add and Hot Plug are valuable for performing tasks such as the following:

- Increasing memory or CPU resources for a machine experiencing a heavy workload.

- Removing unnecessary devices.

- Conducting device maintenance without disrupting the machine.

Hot Add/Hot Plug support various types of devices, including

- Memory

- CPU

- Virtual disks

- USB devices

- Network adapters

25.1.2 Benefits of Hot Add and Hot Plug

The implementation of Hot Add/Hot Plug offers several benefits, including the following:

- **Enhanced uptime:** By allowing the addition or removal of resources without powering off the machine, Hot Add/Hot Plug significantly improves uptime. This aspect is particularly crucial for mission-critical applications.

- **Improved performance:** Hot Add/Hot Plug contributes to performance by enabling resource addition to meet workload demands. For instance, you can enhance memory capacity for a machine running memory applications.

495

- **Reducing downtime:** The features of Hot Add/Hot Plug can help minimize the amount of time spent on maintenance tasks, such as adding or removing hardware. For instance, it enables you to replace a disk in a running virtual machine with a new one without powering off the virtual machine.

25.2 How to Use Hot Plug with Your vCPU and vRAM

What's needed:

- Hot Add enabled on virtual machines that work with ESXi 5.0 or later and a minimum hardware version of 7

- Fault Tolerance vSphere Advanced, Enterprise, and Enterprise Plus doesn't work with Hot Add and Hot Plug

Hot Add must be enabled in the VM, but the Guest OS must support it. The table presented in Figure 25-1 outlines the Guest OS versions that support Hot Add and Hot Plug.

Guest OS Type	Guest OS Version
Windows	Since **Windows 7** and **Microsoft Windows Server 2008**
Linux	Since **CentOS 6.0**
	Since **Red Hat Enterprise Linux 6**
	Since **SUSE Linux Enterprise Server 11**
	Since **Ubuntu 10.04**
	Since **openSUSE 11**
	FreeBSD is not supported

Note: In some Guest OS versions, depends on the OS Edition

Figure 25-1. *(Hot Add-Hot Plug 1 of 6)*

The following are other points to consider:

- Not all devices support Hot Add/Hot Plug. It's essential to refer to the device documentation and check if it is compatible.

- The machine's performance may be affected when using Hot Add/Hot Plug. It is advisable to monitor its performance after adding or removing resources.

- Not all operating systems support Hot Add/Hot Plug. Consult the operating system documentation for compatibility details.

25.3 Restrictions When Using Hot Add/ Hot Plug

One of the most important restrictions and setbacks when using Hot Add or Hot Plug is CPU NUMA/vNUMA. Since this book does not have a chapter about NUMA/vNUMA, let's begin with a quick summary before discussing the restrictions. We'll then look at best practices for using Hot Add and Hot Plug with vNUMA.

25.3.1 What Is NUMA?

vSphere NUMA scheduling is a specific implementation of NUMA scheduling designed for the VMware vSphere virtualization platform. It optimizes the allocation of CPU resources and memory access for virtual machines (VMs) running on top of physical ESXi hosts with NUMA architecture.

Here's how vSphere NUMA scheduling works:

- **Home Node and Memory Locality:** Each VM is assigned a "home node" on the physical ESXi host. This node represents the preferred location for the VM's virtual CPUs (vCPUs) and memory. Ideally, the VM's memory will be allocated from the local memory of the home node to minimize memory access latency.

- **Balancing Workload and Memory:** vSphere NUMA scheduling aims to strike a balance between:

  - **Memory Locality:** Keeping VM memory and vCPUs on the same NUMA node for faster access.

  - **Overall Load Balancing:** Distributing VMs across available NUMA nodes to prevent overloading any single node with processing demands.

- **vNUMA for Guest OS Awareness:** vSphere can expose a virtual NUMA (vNUMA) topology to the guest OS running within the VM. This allows the guest OS to leverage its own NUMA-aware memory management for further optimization.

- **Dynamic VM Placement and Migration:** vSphere NUMA scheduling can dynamically adjust VM placement and memory allocation. It can migrate VMs to different NUMA nodes if doing so improves overall performance or memory locality for other VMs.

Benefits of vSphere NUMA Scheduling:

- Improved performance for memory-intensive workloads in VMs.

- Reduced memory access latency.

- More efficient utilization of available memory resources across the ESXi host.

Overall, vSphere NUMA scheduling helps ensure that VMs running on NUMA-based ESXi hosts have optimal access to memory resources, leading to better performance and resource utilization.

For NUMA scheduling to function properly in ESXi, there must be a minimum of four CPU cores and two CPU cores per NUMA node.

NUMA was created for multiprocessing memory where the memory affects memory access time.

Each CPU (NUMA node) has a dedicated amount of memory, while all the nodes share the I/O bus.

It is quicker to send data via an inter-processor bus than NUMA when the processor needs to access memory that is not local (i.e., its local memory).

For instance as we can see in Figure 25-2 shows an example of access between NUMA nodes 0 and 1.

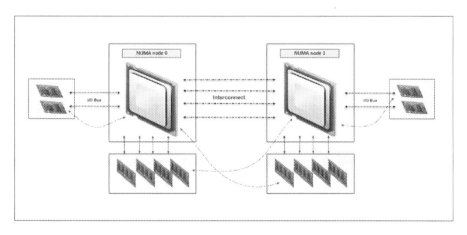

Figure 25-2. (Hot Add-Hot Plug 2 of 6)

25.3.2 Restrictions when using NUMA

Before implementing NUMA scheduling in your environment, it's important to consider some potential limitations:

Other type of limitations when implementing NUMA scheduling in your environment.

- **vNUMA:** Enabling CPU Hot Add for a VM automatically disables vNUMA (virtual NUMA). This means the virtual machine is unaware of which of its vCPUs are on the NUMA node. As a result, the guest operating system and applications lose the ability to optimize based on NUMA, potentially leading to decreased performance.

- **Increased remote memory access:** With vNUMA disabled, the VM may experience memory access. Remote memory access happens when a vCPU needs to access memory from a NUMA node, which can introduce latency and potentially impact performance. Evaluating the impact of increased remote memory access before considering enabling Hot Add/Hot Plug with CPU NUMA is essential.

- **Performance impact:** Disabling vNUMA and enabling CPU Hot Add can lead to reduced performance for the preceding reasons. It is recommended to assess the workload requirements and potential performance implications before deciding whether or not to enable Hot Add/Hot Plug with CPU NUMA.

- **Loss of NUMA optimization:** NUMA is designed to optimize memory access in socket systems. When vNUMA is turned off, the VM loses its ability to optimize performance using NUMA in-memory workloads.

Other limitations:

- VM Hot-Add memory maximum is 16 times the original memory size. Example: 4GB × 16 = 64GB.

- Linux VMs need to have a minimum of 4GB of memory to add 16 times Hot Add memory. If it is less (e.g., 3GB), it is only possible to Hot Add to a maximum of 32GB.

- Hot Add vRAM and vCPU work for Windows virtual machines when virtualization-based security (VBS) is enabled in the OS. To add vRAM or vCPU, you need to power off the VM.

  The primary issue when utilizing a VM with VBS enabled and Hot Add/Hot Plug is that the Hot Add/Hot Plug feature will not function for the VM. This is because VBS establishes an environment within the VM, isolating it from the rest of the system. As a result, accessing the VM's memory, which is necessary for Hot Add/Hot Plug, becomes unattainable when VBS is enabled.

  Even the Hot Add/Hot Plug is available in the VM, if you change the vCPU or vMemory, the Guest OS will not be aware of those changes.

For example in Figure 25-3 we see an example when creating a VM in VMware and can enable EBS.

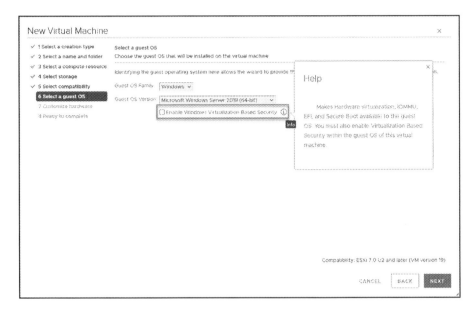

Figure 25-3. *(Hot Add-Hot Plug 3 of 6)*

25.3.3 Best Practices for Using Hot Add/Hot Plug with vNUMA

To mitigate any issues that may arise when utilizing Hot Add/Hot Plug in conjunction with vNUMA, it's crucial to adhere to the following recommended guidelines:

- Use Hot Add/Hot Plug only when necessary.

- Use a vNUMA configuration supported by Hot Add/ Hot Plug.

- Avoid using Hot Add/Hot Plug with CPU affinity software.

- Monitor the performance of the VMs after you make changes to their CPU resources, whether you're adding or removing them.

502

Before enabling Hot Add/Hot Plug, assessing workload requirements, performance implications, and limitations associated with Hot Add/ Hot Plug with CPU NUMA is crucial. Proper planning and benchmarking are recommended for performance and resource utilization in your environment.

Hot Add/Hot Plug is a powerful and helpful feature that can help improve VMs' uptime and management, performance, and reliability. However, knowing the restrictions and setbacks of using Hot Add/Hot Plug, mainly when using CPU NUMA, is crucial.

Following the preceding list of best practices can minimize the risk of problems.

25.4 Enabling and Configure Hot Add/ Hot Plug

To enable Hot Add for the vCPU and vMemory in your VM, click **Edit settings** on your VM to open the Edit Settings window. As shown in Figure 25-4, expand the **CPU** section and check the **Enable CPU Hot Add** check box for the *CPU Hot Plug* setting, and expand the **Memory** section and check the **Enable** check box for the *Memory Hot Plug* setting. Click **OK**.

Note   Options are only available to enable these options when the VM it is power off.. See Figure 25-4 with a power off VM and options available to enable.

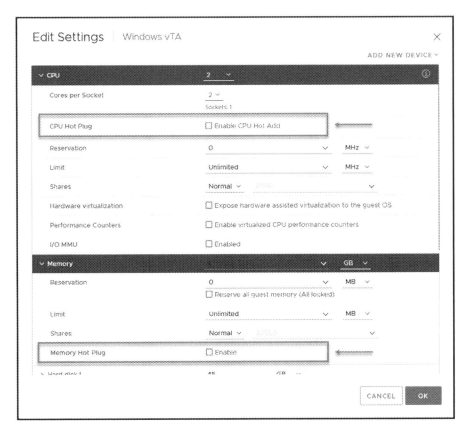

Figure 25-4. *(Hot Add-Hot Plug 4 of 6)*

Power on your VM and you can now add more vCPU cores and/or more vMemory to your VM and your Guest OS will recognized. Figure 25-5 shows an example of increasing a VM's CPUs from 4 to 12 and increasing its vMemory from 10GB to 18GB while the VM is power on.

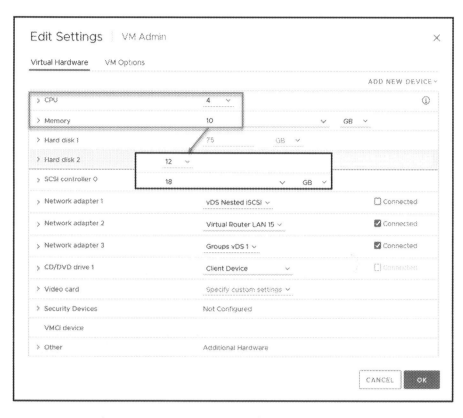

Figure 25-5. *(Hot Add-Hot Plug 5 of 6)*

Figure 25-6 shows the live changes take effect (in Windows Server 2019) in a matter of a few seconds. As shown on the right, the VM is now using the number of vCPUs and amount of vMemory set with Hot Add/Hot Plug enabled.

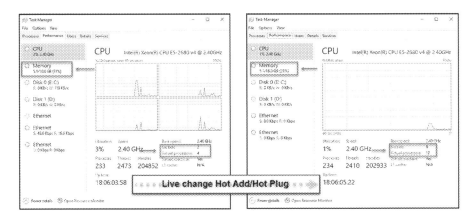

Figure 25-6. *(Hot Add-Hot Plug 6 of 6)*

To finalize the configuration of Hot Add/Hot Plug, when you add (hot plug) or remove (hot unplug) devices such as a virtual network adapter or a hard disk, the guest operating system immediately recognizes and makes these devices available for use. This functionality allows for seamless hardware adjustments without downtime.

25.5 Security Considerations for Hot Add/ Hot Plug

To fully understand the intricacies of Hot Add and Hot Plug functionalities, it is important to highlight their security aspects. In this section we will delve into the security considerations related to these features. Having an understanding of these implications will empower you to utilize Hot Add and Hot Plug while ensuring the security of your virtual infrastructure.

Although using Hot Add and Hot Plug is quite convenient, it's crucial to be mindful of the security implications involved. Here are some points worth considering:

- The Hot Add/Hot Plug feature has the potential to introduce a risk of devices being added to your environment. For instance, an attacker could utilize this feature to add a network interface card (NIC) to a machine and exploit it as an entry point into your network.

- The Hot Add/Hot Plug capability also poses a threat in terms of impacting the performance of your machines. An attacker could leverage this feature to repeatedly add and remove devices from a machine, leading to crashes or instability.

- Hot Add/Hot Plug is able to bypass security controls. A malicious actor could use this functionality to attach a storage device to a machine and install malware.

To minimize these risks, it is advisable to follow these security measures when utilizing the Hot Add/Hot Plug feature:

- Grant access to Hot Add/Hot Plug only to trusted users. This can be achieved by limiting the availability of the Hot Add/Hot Plug feature in the vSphere Client.

- Keep an eye on the usage of Hot Add/Hot Plug. Utilize the vSphere Client to monitor any additions or removals of devices to or from machines through Hot Add/Hot Plug.

- Implement security controls to safeguard your machines against potential attacks. For instance, firewalls and intrusion detection systems shield your machines from network traffic.

Following these precautions will assist in mitigating risks associated with using Hot Add/Hot Plug.

In addition to the preceding precautions, you should also implement the following security best practices:

- Keep your vSphere software and ESXi hosts up to date with the latest security patches.

- Use strong passwords and multifactor authentication for all vSphere accounts.

- Implement a least-privilege model for vSphere users.

- Regularly back up your virtual machines.

Following these security precautions can help protect your environment from the risks associated with Hot Add/Hot Plug. Additional tips for using Hot Add/Hot Plug securely:

- Only add or remove devices that are supported by Hot Add/Hot Plug.

- Avoid using Hot Add/Hot Plug with sensitive data devices.

- Use Hot Add/Hot Plug only when necessary.

- Be aware of the potential impact of Hot Add/Hot Plug on the performance of your virtual machines.

25.6 Summary

This chapter on vSphere Hot Add & Hot Plug covered the functionalities within vSphere that allowed for dynamic hardware adjustments to virtual machines without downtime. It detailed how Hot Add enhanced VM performance by enabling the addition of resources like CPU and memory during operation, and how Hot Plug allowed for the seamless integration or removal of devices like USBs and network adapters. The chapter also discussed security considerations, ensuring these features were used safely and efficiently, and included practical guidelines on using Hot Add/Hot Plug with vNUMA to optimize performance without compromising system integrity.

In Chapter 26, we'll explore Direct Path I/O Passthrough, which, like Hot Add/Hot Plug, offers direct access to physical hardware devices for enhanced performance. Chapter 26 provides an overview of Direct Path I/O Passthrough, thoroughly examines the prerequisites, and offers recommended practices for its implementation. Additionally, we will evaluate its impact on virtual machine performance and address security considerations. Lastly, I will guide you through the step-by-step process of enabling and configuring Direct Path I/O Passthrough, covering both passthrough and SR-IOV passthrough mechanisms.

CHAPTER 26

Direct Path I/O Passthrough

Direct Path I/O Passthrough is a complex feature and would require more than one chapter to review all the configurations, options, and use cases that are possible using Direct Path I/O Passthrough through several PCI devices. Such extensive coverage is beyond the scope of this book, so we will focus on this feature's main options and configurations.

This chapter explores the features of Direct Path I/O Passthrough in VMware vSphere versions 6.7 and 7.0. Over time, the capabilities of Direct Path I/O Passthrough have changed and improved in vSphere versions. Our main focus here will be understanding the configurations and options available in these releases.

This particular feature plays a role in achieving performance and minimal latency in specific scenarios by granting virtual machines direct access to physical hardware resources.

As we progress through this chapter, we will uncover the complexities of Direct Path I/O Passthrough. You will learn how to enable it, understand its advantages, explore its applications, and carefully consider its impact on performance, security measures, and recommended practices.

© Luciano Patrão 2024
L. Patrão, *VMware vSphere Essentials*, https://doi.org/10.1007/979-8-8688-0208-9_26

26.1 What Is Direct Path I/O Passthrough?

Direct Path I/O Passthrough is a feature that allows virtual machines to directly communicate with I/O devices without going through the virtualization layer. This enables the VM to interact with the hardware directly, minimizing overhead caused by the hypervisor. As a result, Direct Path I/O Passthrough enhances performance and reduces latency, which is especially beneficial for handling high-speed network interfaces or other devices requiring significant I/O operations.

Figure 26-1 shows the workflow and the ESXi host bypass to provide a Direct Path I/O Passthrough network to the VM.

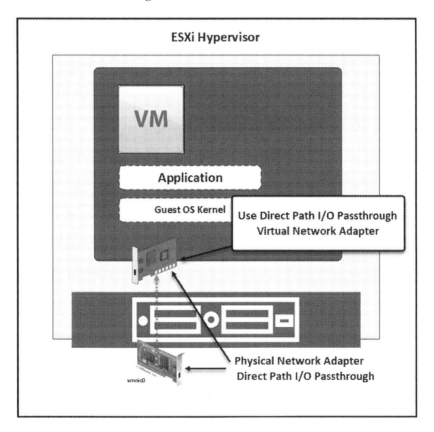

Figure 26-1. (*Direct Path I/O Passthrough 1 of 16*)

26.1.1 Understanding Direct Path I/O Passthrough

- **Bypassing the hypervisor:** Typically, a hypervisor sits between the VM and the physical hardware, managing the interactions between the two. However, Direct Path I/O Passthrough allows a VM to bypass this layer, communicating directly with the physical I/O devices.

- **Physical I/O devices:** Direct Path I/O Passthrough allows a VM to directly interact with physical I/O devices, such as network adapters, storage controllers, or graphics cards, bypassing the hypervisor layer. This can lead to better performance and lower latency for the VM.

The following types of devices can be utilized with Direct Path I/O Passthrough:

- **PCI and PCIe devices:** Direct Path I/O Passthrough primarily operates with PCI- and PCIe-based devices. Through this feature, a VM can directly access and interact with physical PCI and PCIe devices connected to the host, enhancing the performance of I/O operations.

- **Storage and network I/O devices:** Direct Path I/O Passthrough is supported for certain storage and network I/O devices, enabling more efficient data transfers and potentially boosting the performance of network-intensive applications.

- **Graphics processing units:** GPUs, especially those from Nvidia, can be accessed directly by VMs using Direct Path I/O Passthrough. This is beneficial in

513

scenarios requiring high-performance graphics processing or compute operations. It allows VMs to leverage the full capabilities of the physical GPU, providing a significant performance boost for graphics-intensive applications.

These device interactions enabled by Direct Path I/O Passthrough are crucial in environments where high performance and low latency are paramount, such as high-performance computing (HPC) setups, real-time processing applications, or any other scenario demanding rapid and efficient I/O operations.

- **Minimal interference:** Less interference from the hypervisor means reduced CPU overhead, leading to better performance and lower latency. This is particularly beneficial in I/O-intensive operations.

26.1.2 Importance of Direct Path I/O Passthrough in High-Speed Environments

- **Real-time processing:** In scenarios where real-time processing is crucial, the reduced latency offered by Direct Path I/O Passthrough can be a game-changer.

- **High-performance computing:** HPC environments often demand the kind of performance boost that Direct Path I/O Passthrough can provide.

- **Network-intensive applications:** Applications that require high-speed networking can significantly benefit from Direct Path I/O Passthrough, as it allows for faster data transfer and reduced network latency.

26.1.3 Direct Path I/O Passthrough Hardware Considerations

- **Compatibility:** Not all hardware is compatible with Direct Path I/O Passthrough. It requires support from both the physical hardware and the host system firmware.

- **Dedicated resources:** When a physical I/O device is passed through to a VM using Direct Path I/O, it is dedicated to that VM and cannot be shared with other VMs or the host system.

- **Device drivers:** The VM will need the appropriate device drivers installed to be able to communicate with the physical I/O device.

In summary, Direct Path I/O Passthrough is a specialized feature tailored for scenarios where high performance and low latency are critical. By enabling a more direct communication path between VMs and physical hardware, it facilitates a level of performance closer to operating on physical hardware directly, although with inevitable trade-offs and hardware considerations to keep in mind.

26.2 Requirements and Recommendations for Using Direct Path I/O Passthrough

Meeting technical configurations and compatibilities is crucial to ensure the secure functioning of Direct Path I/O Passthrough. These requirements play a role in enabling the functionality of this feature.

26.2.1 Requirements for Using Direct Path I/O Passthrough

The following are the requirements for using for using Direct Path I/O Passthrough:

- **Ensuring ESXi host and VM isolation:** For using Direct Path I/O Passthrough, it is crucial to maintain ESXi host and VM isolation. This is achieved by adhering to the PCIe 3.0 specification, specifically section 6.6.2. After a PCI device is reset, these standards help to establish a secure barrier between the ESXi host and the virtual machine, ensuring that the VM operations do not compromise the host's security or functionality.

- **Bus-level-granularity reset methods:** When using reset methods of bus-level granularity, ensure all PCI functions on the same bus are jointly designated to a single virtual machine.

- **PCI function eligibility under PCI Host Bridge:** PCI functions under a PCI host bridge should support either function-level reset (FLR) or D3Hot reset for Direct Path I/O Passthrough eligibility.

- **Multifunction PCI devices:** If dependencies exist between PCI functions of a multifunction PCI device, ensure that all dependent PCI functions are collectively designated for Direct Path I/O Passthrough to a single VM.

- **Peer-to-peer DMA transactions:** ESXi does not support peer-to-peer DMA transactions to/from a PCI passthrough device in a VM, ensuring all DMA transactions initiated by a passthrough PCI device only access the VM memory.

- **PCI functions behind legacy PCI bridges:** PCI functions destined for Direct Path I/O Passthrough should be placed behind PCI Express root ports or switch downstream ports.

- **PCI root-complex integrated endpoints:** PCI passthrough for root-complex integrated endpoints is supported for regular PCI functions but not for SR-IOV virtual functions as of this writing.

26.2.2 Recommendations for Using Direct Path I/O Passthrough

Although not mandatory, the following recommended practices can significantly improve the performance, security, and manageability of your Direct Path I/O Passthrough setup. These suggestions aim to maximize the benefits you can derive from this feature.

- **Configuration guidelines:**

  - Ensure that your ESXi host, guest OS, and PCI device are compatible, and confirm this by checking the VMware Compatibility Guide.

  - Ensure that the operating system version used in the VM is compatible with the ESXi version.

  - If your VM uses Legacy BIOS mode, you should adjust the .vmx file to allow for higher Base Address Register (BAR) allocation. This adjustment ensures that the VM can manage more extensive memory mapping requirements effectively.

  - Enable 64-bit Memory-Mapped I/O (MMIO) if your VM requires more than 32GB of total BAR allocation by modifying the `.vmx` file accordingly.

- **Hot-Add and Hot-Remove support:** Consider the support for hot-add and hot-remove of PCI devices, as it could be beneficial in certain use cases like adding or removing resources without shutting down the VM.

- **Network device passthrough:** On both cases Passthrough, applies ensure that the ESXi host is not currently using it for a network device. It is recommended to allocate the network device to a VM to set up passthrough configuration.

- **Consideration for NVMe devices:** If you Passthrough NVMe devices, ensure that the NVMe driver is loaded in the VM and the device is appropriately recognized. Be aware of the performance implications and ensure your setup meets the requirements.

- **Alternative perspectives:** Be open to exploring alternative configurations or setups like Single Root IO Virtualization (SR-IOV) if it suits your use case better.

  SR-IOV is a technology that allows a network adapter to present itself multiple times through the PCIe bus. SR-IOV can provide similar direct access to physical PCI resources while offering different features than Direct Path I/O Passthrough. SR-IOV is discussed further later in this chapter.

- **Endorsement of function-level reset (FLR):** VMware advocates for PCI Functions to support FLR for smooth operations.

- **Testing recommendations:** Conduct rigorous testing on specific platforms intended for use with Direct Path I/O Passthrough to ensure all the stipulated requirements are met, including common and corner-case scenarios.

26.3 Impact on a VM Performance and Security Risks

Utilizing Direct Path I/O Passthrough for PCI passthrough can significantly boost the performance of VMs by facilitating direct access to the hardware.

This is particularly beneficial in scenarios demanding high throughput and minimal latency, such as graphics rendering or real-time data processing. This direct route to the hardware bypasses the usual hypervisor layer, reducing the overhead of device emulation or virtualization.

Consequently, this might free up computational and memory resources for other VMs and applications. Besides, dedicating specific hardware resources to a VM can lead to more predictable performance, a critical feature for certain types of workloads.

- **Performance enhancement:** Direct hardware access can significantly improve VM performance, especially in high-throughput and low-latency scenarios.

- **Reduced overhead:** Bypassing the hypervisor reduces CPU and memory overhead, potentially freeing resources for other VMs.

- **Predictable performance:** Dedicating hardware to a VM provides more predictable performance, which is crucial for specific applications.

- **Positive:** Direct Path I/O Passthrough boosts a VM's performance by granting direct access to hardware resources. This is particularly advantageous for workloads requiring efficient communication with devices like GPUs and NICs.

- **Negative:** However, it is essential to note that configuring hardware resources or using Direct Path I/O Passthrough with workloads can reduce VM performance. Sometimes, using Direct Path I/O Passthrough may lead to decreased VM performance.

Security Risks:

Employing Direct Path I/O Passthrough can potentially expand the attack surface of the VMs. Direct access to physical hardware might expose the VM to vulnerabilities inherent in the hardware or its firmware. The usual hypervisor-mediated protection layer is bypassed in this setup, which might lead to a loss of some security protections.

Besides, the complexity of configuring and managing PCI passthrough necessitates a higher level of administrative control and understanding, which, if not handled meticulously, could lead to misconfigurations and thereby pose security risks.

To effectively address the security implications of using Direct Path I/O Passthrough in virtualized environments, it's crucial to consider several key aspects:

- **Device Driver Security:** The security posture of VMs is significantly influenced by the security of the device drivers used within the VMs.

- **Potential Risks Associated with Direct Hardware Access:** Granting VMs access to hardware resources through Direct Path I/O Passthrough can pose a security threat. If a VM is compromised, it could allow an attacker to exploit this access and gain control over the hardware.

- **Limited Control by the Hypervisor:** Utilizing Direct Path I/O Passthrough restricts the hypervisor's control over the allocated hardware resources, making it more challenging to monitor and safeguard the VM against potential attacks.

- **Compatibility challenges:** Not all devices are compatible with Direct Path I/O Passthrough functionality. Using incompatible devices can lead to stability issues and security vulnerabilities.

This overview underscores the need for careful implementation and monitoring when deploying Direct Path I/O Passthrough to ensure both performance and security are maintained.

One potential positive security aspect of Direct Path I/O Passthrough is that users being able to directly access hardware resources when they utilize Direct Path I/O Passthrough allows them to implement and enforce security controls based on the hardware, potentially improving the system's security.

Negative: However, it is important to note that irect Path I/O Passthrough allows users direct access to hardware resources, offering the potential to implement and enforce specific hardware-based security controls, which can enhance the system's security. However, it's crucial to recognize that this feature bypasses the traditional security layers provided by the hypervisor. If not carefully managed, this could expose the system to vulnerabilities or malicious activities, posing significant risks to the environment's overall security.

The following are extra suggestions to ensure that the usage of Direct Path I/O Passthrough is secure:

- Only assign devices to VMs that you trust.

- Implement security measures like firewalls and intrusion detection systems to monitor and protect your environment.

- Keep your hypervisor and guest operating systems updated with the latest security patches.

- Regularly back up your data and have a plan in place for recovering from disasters.

To clarify the closing remarks of this chapter, it's essential to note that using GPUs in virtual machines through technologies like vGPUs (virtual GPUs) is not equivalent to employing GPUs through methods like Direct Path I/O Passthrough. Each approach has distinct implications for performance, compatibility, and security within virtualized environments.

Passthrough GPUs (DirectPath I/O) and vGPUs fundamentally differ in managing and allocating GPU resources to virtual machines.

When using Passthrough GPUs (DirectPath I/O), a single VM can access a GPU directly, bypassing the ESXi hypervisor. However, it doesn't allow for sharing the GPU between VMs. Each VM requiring GPU resources would need its own GPU in this configuration.

By contrast, vGPU technology enables VMs to share a single GPU by dividing its resources among them. The ESXi hypervisor manages these resources to ensure each VM receives its share of the GPU. This approach is more flexible and efficient when not every VM requires the utilization of the GPU's power.

The table in Figure 26-2 summarizes the key differences between vGPUs and passthrough GPUs.

Feature	vGPUs	Passthrough GPUs
Virtualization technology	Yes	No
GPU sharing	Yes	No
Performance	Lower	Higher
Use cases	General-purpose workloads	High-performance workloads

Figure 26-2. *(Direct Path I/O Passthrough 2 of 16)*

To summarize, Passthrough GPUs (DirectPath I/O) do not allow sharing of GPU among VMs, whereas vGPU technology enables this core feature of sharing the GPU among multiple VMs.

Which technology is suitable for your environment and workload? The optimal choice of technology depends on your requirements. If you need to run GPU-accelerated workloads on an ESXi host, vGPUs can be a suitable option. On the other hand, if you require the performance for a single GPU, an accelerated workload using a passthrough GPU is recommended.

These are scenarios where vGPUs might be beneficial:

- When running desktop VMs that utilize graphics acceleration

- When running graphics rendering sessions

- When running VMs that rely on GPUs for tasks like machine learning or 3D rendering

And these are scenarios where passthrough GPUs could be advantageous:

- When running a VM that utilizes a GPU for machine learning or 3D rendering

- When running a VM that requires GPU power for HPC

- When running a VM that utilizes a GPU for video editing or other multimedia processing

26.4 Benefits, Use Cases, and Limitations of Direct Path I/O Passthrough

This section provides a brief overview of the benefits, use cases, and limitations of Direct Path I/O Passthrough.

26.4.1 Benefits

Using Direct Path I/O Passthrough offers the following benefits, among others:

- **Performance enhancement:** Direct Path I/O Passthrough enables direct access to physical PCI devices from within the VM, potentially improving performance, especially for high-throughput and low-latency workloads.

- **Device feature utilization:** Direct Path I/O Passthrough allows for utilizing specialized hardware features of the PCI device, which might not be available through virtualized drivers.

- **Resource dedication:** Direct Path I/O Passthrough allows dedicating specific PCI resources to particular VMs, ensuring predictable performance and isolation from other VMs.

26.4.2 Use Cases

To explore the diverse applications of Direct Path I/O Passthrough, let's consider its key use cases that enhance performance across different scenarios:

- **Graphics acceleration:** Direct Path I/O Passthrough is helpful for VMs requiring graphics acceleration, where a GPU can be passed directly to the VM.

- **High-performance computing:** In HPC environments, where maximum compute performance is crucial, Direct Path I/O Passthrough can be used to pass through high-performance networking or storage devices.

- **Low-latency applications:** Direct access to the hardware for applications sensitive to latency can provide the necessary performance improvements.

- **Real-time processing:** In scenarios requiring real-time processing, bypassing the virtualization layer for device access can be beneficial.

The following are examples of how and where Direct Path I/O Passthrough can be used in different industries:

- **Financial services:** Direct Path I/O Passthrough can be used to accelerate financial trading applications.

- **Media and entertainment:** Direct Path I/O Passthrough can be used to accelerate video editing and rendering applications.

- **Healthcare:** Direct Path I/O Passthrough can be used to accelerate medical imaging and drug discovery applications.

- **Scientific research:** Direct Path I/O Passthrough can be used to accelerate scientific computing and machine learning applications.

26.4.3 Limitations

VMDirectPath is the same as Direct Path I/O Passthrough. This feature in VMware environments enables virtual machines to access physical hardware directly, bypassing the hypervisor to enhance performance.

- **Some vSphere features:** Enabling Direct Path I/O Passthrough results in the loss of some core vSphere features such as the following:

  - VMotion

  - Cross ESXi HA

- Storage VMotion

- Fault Tolerance

- Device hot add

- Suspend and resume

- **Device compatibility:** Not all PCI devices or systems may support Direct Path I/O Passthrough, and compatibility should be verified.

- **Resource management:** Resources dedicated via Direct Path I/O Passthrough are not managed by the ESXi host, which may lead to suboptimal utilization.

- **Error handling:** Error handling might be less robust compared to using virtualized device drivers.

- **Complex configuration:** Configuration can be more complex and require more administrative effort to set up and maintain than standard virtualized setups.

26.5 Enabling and Configuring Direct Path I/O Passthrough

To enable and configure Direct Path I/O Passthrough, we must configure it per ESXi host.

As shown in Figure 26-3, select your ESXi host, click the **Configure** tab, expand the **Hardware** section, select **PCI Devices**, and click **All PCI Devices**. You will see then all the PCI devices in your ESXi host, and those listed as *Not Configurable* are not supported to use Direct Path I/O Passthrough. If you selected it, you should see a message stating *This device cannot be made available for VMs to use.*

The PCI devices that can be configured are those that are listed in a *Disabled* state. But be aware that some of those belonging to the ESXi host configuration (like storage and network adapters) are being used by the ESXi host. If you change them, you may lose your ESXi host configuration (you should get a warning when selecting those types of PCI devices).

So, if you plan to use Direct Path I/O Passthrough, make sure you use a suitable PCI device. The configuration of the device depends on the brand of your network card. Covering all the brands here is impossible, so I will demonstrate using a 10GB Mellanox network card on my system that is not being used by the ESXi host and shared into one VM directly. Check your network card documentation for the steps to enable it for Direct Path I/O Passthrough.

As step 4 in Figure 26-3 indicates, click the filter icon in the Vendor Name column head and search for the brand of your network adapter. I used the filter Mellanox, the result of which identified the PCI device I need (note the status is *Disabled*).

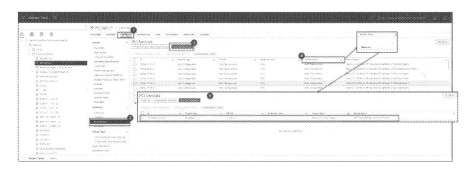

Figure 26-3. *(Direct Path I/O Passthrough 3 of 16)*

Figure 26-4 points out two different options that you can enable for your PCI device: Toggle Passthrough and Configure SR-IOV.

Figure 26-4. *(Direct Path I/O Passthrough 4 of 16)*

Passthrough and SR-IOV are two methods for configuring PCI devices in vSphere:

- **Passthrough:** Enables a VM to directly utilize a PCI device, granting it access to its capabilities without sharing with other VMs. Typically, Passthrough is preferred for demanding tasks like machine learning and 3D rendering.

- **SR-IOV:** Single Root I/O Virtualization is a technology that facilitates the sharing of a physical PCI device among multiple VMs. Each VM receives its virtual PCI device, which directly connects to the physical PCI device. This allows multiple workloads to be executed on an ESXi host.

The primary distinction between Passthrough and SR-IOV lies in the fact that Passthrough grants access to a PCI device for a virtual machine while SR-IOV permits multiple virtual machines to share one PCI device.

The adapter case that I am showing from my lab in Figure 26-3 and 23-4 the network adapter can be shared physically with several VMs.

Figure 26-5 provides a summary table outlining the variances between Passthrough and SR-IOV. While Passthrough traditionally offered the highest performance by allowing a VM to directly communicate with a device, SR-IOV technology has advanced significantly. Nowadays, SR-IOV can offer performance that is on par with Passthrough, while also providing the added benefit of device sharing among multiple VMs. This makes SR-IOV highly suitable for environments where device sharing is a requirement without a significant sacrifice in performance.

Feature	Passthrough	SR-IOV
Device sharing	No	Yes
Performance	Higher	Higher
Use cases	High-performance workloads	General-purpose workloads

Figure 26-5. *(Direct Path I/O Passthrough 5 of 16)*

I will demonstrate how to configure both options to explain how to work with both.

26.6 Enabling Direct Path I/O Passthrough

Select your PCI device and click the option **Toggle Passthrough** to enable Passthrough for the PCI device, as shown in Figure 26-6.

Figure 26-6. *(Direct Path I/O Passthrough 6 of 16)*

After enabling Passthrough, you must reboot the server and use the network card in one of your VMs. But before you reboot, I recommend creating a hardware label for your device to identify it better. As shown in Figure 26-7, I added the label "Network Card 20GB" for my Mellanox device.

Note   This step is not mandatory.

Figure 26-7. *(Direct Path I/O Passthrough 7 of 16)*

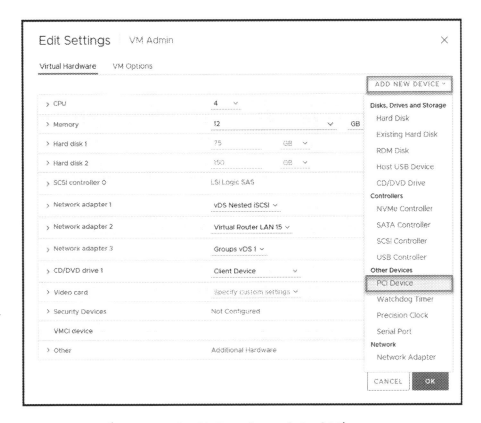

Figure 26-8. *(Direct Path I/O Passthrough 8 of 16)*

After you reboot the ESXi host, we select the VM that we want to use the PCI device and check the settings.

The network adapter then appears in the Edit Settings window as a new PCI device. As shown in Figure 26-9, after adding a PCI device, three types of Passthrough are available:

- **DirectPath I/O:** Enables direct access to a physical network adapter from a VM, bypassing the hypervisor for lower latency and higher performance.

- **Dynamic DirectPath I/O:** Allows more flexibility by dynamically turning DirectPath I/O on or off without rebooting the host.

- **NVIDIA GRID vGPU:** This option is irrelevant for network adapters because it is designed to share GPU resources among multiple VMs, not network resources.

For purposes of this example, I chose **DirectPath I/O**.

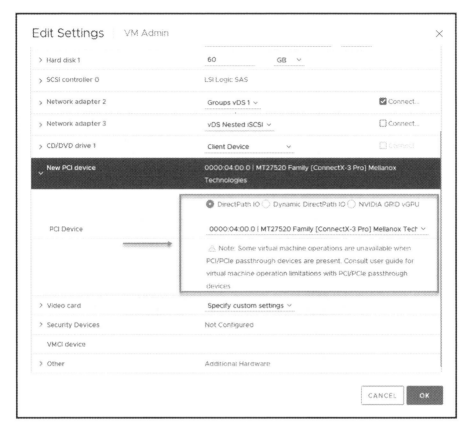

Figure 26-9. *(Direct Path I/O Passthrough 9 of 16)*

After configuring a PCI device in your VM, power it on, and the next step is to add the new network adapter to your Guest OS and configure it.

Figure 26-10 shows my new network adapter with two 10GB ports that were automatically added to my Windows Server without needing extra configurations.

Figure 26-10. *(Direct Path I/O Passthrough 10 of 16)*

26.7 Enabling and Configuring SR-IOV Passthrough

Using and enabling SR-IOV is a bit more complex and requires several steps and configurations for some network card brands before enabling SR-IOV. Again, the configurations depend on the brand of your network card, and since covering all the brands here is impossible, I will only discuss how to enable SR-IOV and add it to your VM as a network card. Check your network card documentation for the steps to enable your SR-IOV network card before you enable it.

I will demonstrate how to enable SR-IOV for the same Mellanox network adapter from the previous section and use five virtual functions (VFs) in SR-IOV.

Virtual functions in SR-IOV are lightweight PCI functions created by a physical PCI function (PF). Each VF has its own PCI configuration space and can be assigned to a virtual machine. This allows multiple virtual machines to share a single physical PCI device without having to share the full capabilities of the device.

Figure 26-11 shows the workflow and the ESXi host bypass to provide SR-IOV Passthrough VFs shared to three different VMs.

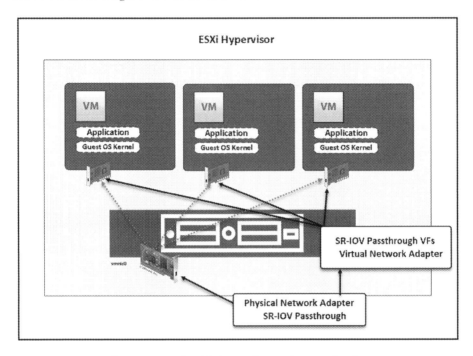

Figure 26-11. *(Direct Path I/O Passthrough 11 of 16)*

VFs are typically used for network interface cards (NICs) but can also be used for other types of PCI devices, such as graphics cards and storage controllers.

Here are some of the benefits of using VFs in SR-IOV:

- **Improved performance:** VFs can improve performance for network-intensive workloads, such as virtual firewalls and load balancers, because VFs have direct access to the physical PCI device without going through the ESXi host.

- **Increased efficiency:** VFs can help to improve resource utilization by allowing multiple virtual machines to share a single physical PCI device. This can help you to run more virtual machines on a single ESXi host.

- **Reduced complexity:** VFs can help to reduce the complexity of your virtualized environment by simplifying the configuration and management of PCI devices.

Here are some examples of when you might want to use VFs in SR-IOV:

- You must run multiple virtual firewalls or load balancers on a single ESXi host.

Note Consult the appliance provider documentation to ensure the appliance supports SR-IOV.

- You must run multiple virtual machines to access the network at high speeds.

- You must conserve resources and run as many virtual machines as possible on a single ESXi host.

This means that if you enable SR-IOV with five VFs, as shown in Figure 26-12 for my network adapter, you can use/share the network adapter with five VMs.

Figure 26-12. *(Direct Path I/O Passthrough 12 of 16)*

535

Note   You need to disable Direct Path I/O Passthrough to be able to enable and configure SR-IOV.

Again, you need to reboot the ESXi host so that changes are done.

After the reboot, my network adapter has SR-IOV enabled and five VFs available, as shown in Figure 26-13.

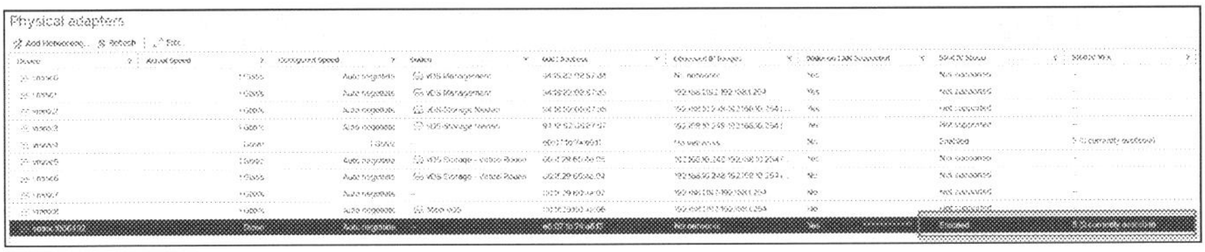

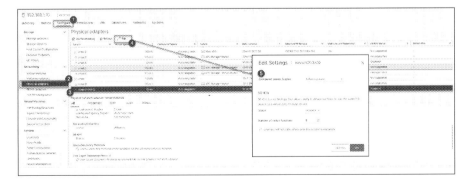

Figure 26-13. *(Direct Path I/O Passthrough 13 of 16)*

You can also enable SR-IOV directly on the network adapter. As shown in Figure 26-14, select the ESXi host, click the **Configure** tab, select **Physical adapters**, select the network adapter for which you want to enable SR-IOV, and click **Edit**. Then, change the *Status* to **Enabled** and add the number of VFs. Now, the network adapter has SR-IOV Passthrough enabled, like in the previous step.

Figure 26-14. *(Direct Path I/O Passthrough 14 of 16)*

Now, go to the VM and add the network adapter to use the SR-IOV.

Figure 26-15. *(Direct Path I/O Passthrough 15 of 16)*

After adding the network adapter to your VM, expand **New Network** in the Edit Settings window and select **SR-IOV passthrough** from the *Adapter Type* drop-down list, as shown in Figure 26-16. Click **OK** and then power on the VM.

Figure 26-16. *(Direct Path I/O Passthrough 16 of 16)*

26.8 Summary

In this chapter we examined the intricacies of Direct Path I/O Passthrough, encompassing its definition, prerequisites, and the potential implications it may have on the performance and security of machines. We have also delved into its advantages, practical applications, and limitations to equip you with the knowledge to effectively enable and configure this feature in your environment.

In Chapter 27 we turn our attention to another aspect of integrating hardware in environments: USB devices. Chapter 27 transitions from enhancing direct hardware access to exploring how USB devices can be integrated with your ESXi host. I will guide you through the process of enabling USB devices, ensuring that you can fully leverage the connectivity of your environment and expand its capabilities.

Add a USB Device to vSphere

In this chapter, we will explore the procedure of incorporating a USB device into a vSphere environment. This chapter covers the preparations, including an explanation of the concept of USB passthrough, and provides a step-by-step guide to configuring and handling USB devices in vSphere. By the end of this chapter, you will understand how to enhance your VM's capabilities by enabling USB connectivity, which guarantees a versatile and practical setup for different scenarios.

Adding a USB device to a vSphere and making it available to a VM is a similar the task of configuring DirectPath I/O passthrough discussed in Chapter 26.

Figure 27-1 shows the workflow and the ESXi host bypass to provide USB Device Passthrough, using an external USB disk to provide access directly to the VM virtual disk.

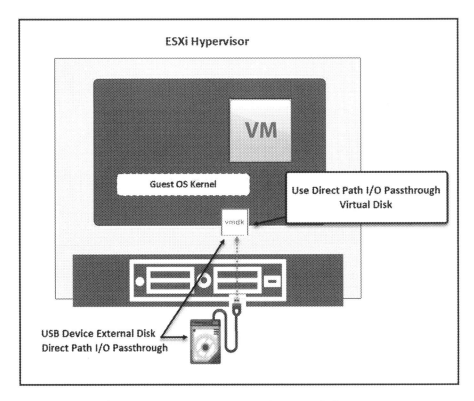

Figure 27-1. *(Add a USB device to vSphere 1 of 4)*

27.1 Enable USB Devices in the ESXi Host

First, you need to connect your USB device to a USB entry in your ESXi host and then reboot the ESXi host. Then, add a host USB device to the VM that you want to use this USB device. After you have a USB device, vSphere recognizes the USB device and shows it (in this example, I used an 4TB external disk).

The following types of USB devices are typically not supported for passthrough from an ESXi host to a virtual machine:

- USB devices with a bootable HID interface, such as mice and keyboards

- Real-time video cameras and audio devices that use isochronous data transfers

- Devices on which an ESXi host is installed

- USB CCID (chip/smart card interface) devices

- USB hubs

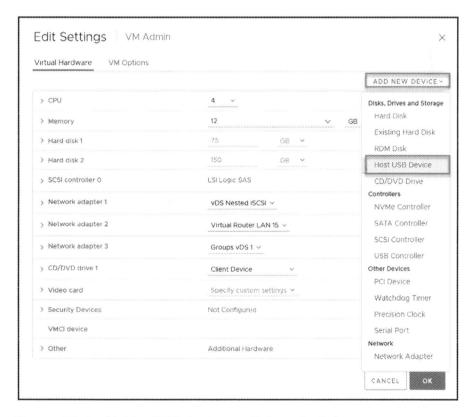

Figure 27-2. *(Add a USB device to vSphere 2 of 4)*

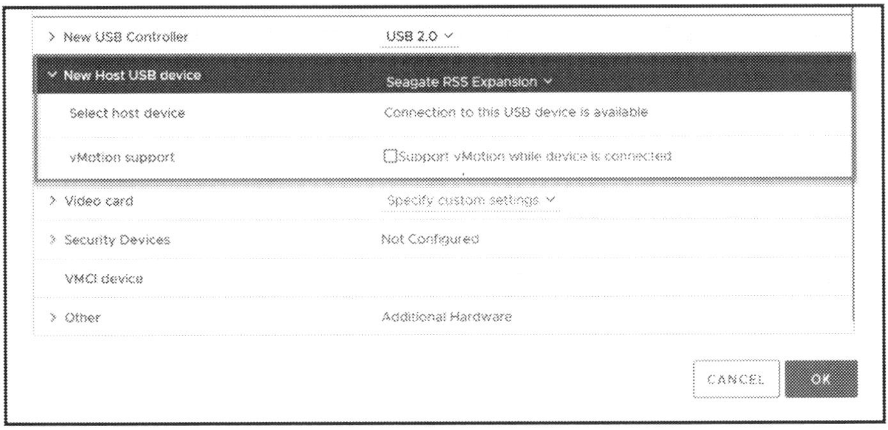

Figure 27-3. *(Add a USB device to vSphere 3 of 4)*

27.2 Adding a USB Device to vSphere with vMotion Support

In vSphere, when you add a USB device to a host, you can select the option to support vMotion while the device is connected. This means that even if a VM is migrated to another host using vMotion, the USB device remains connected to the VM, allowing for a seamless transition without interrupting the USB device's functionality.

The option *Support vMotion while device is connected* (see Figure 27-3) facilitates the movement of a VM with a connected USB device from one host to another without disruption. However, certain restrictions apply. For instance, all USB devices must be configured for vMotion, and the VM cannot be stopped or paused during the process. Additionally, the migration might fail if one or more devices are not enabled for vMotion.

> **Note**   If you do not plan to migrate a virtual machine with USB devices attached, deselect the *Support vMotion* option. This action reduces migration complexity, which results in better performance and stability.

We will not enable this option for our test lab since we don't need it.

After you add the USB device to your VM, power it on, and you can now use the external disk in your Guest OS. Figure 27-4 shows my 4TB external disk available to be used in a Windows Server VM.

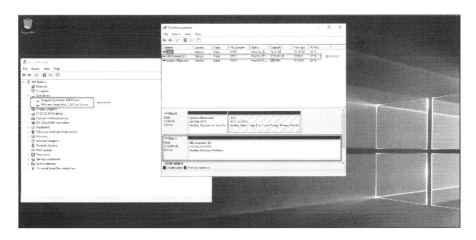

Figure 27-4. *(Add a USB device to vSphere 4 of 4)*

27.3 Summary

This brief chapter discussed integrating USB devices with ESXi hosts and improving the capabilities of your environment. In Chapter 28, we move on to an essential task in vSphere management: resetting and changing the vCenter root password. Chapter 28 will guide you through a step-by-step process to securely reset and modify the root password of your vCenter Server. This procedure is crucial for you to maintain access to the management hub of your vSphere environment.

CHAPTER 28

How to Reset the vCenter Root Password

Sometimes, dealing with credentials for infrastructure elements such as vCenter Server can be difficult when the root password is forgotten or personnel changes occur. Resetting the root password for vCenter when it is locked or forgotten is a step in gaining control, ensuring everything runs smoothly in a vSphere environment.

This chapter will guide you through the essential processes of resetting and changing the root password for vCenter. It is crucial to follow these steps carefully to ensure continuity of services and to maintain secure access within the vSphere environment. Proper execution of these processes helps prevent disruptions and access issues.

28.1 Reset the Root Password

To reset the password, we need to reboot the vCenter appliance and get access to the boot of Photon OS.

Connect to the vCenter console by launching the remote console and reboot vCenter.

© Luciano Patrão 2024
L. Patrão, *VMware vSphere Essentials*, https://doi.org/10.1007/979-8-8688-0208-9_28

To reset the root password for your vCenter Server Appliance, you'll start by rebooting the appliance and gaining access to the boot loader of Photon OS. This can be done by connecting to the vCenter's console, which is accessible via the vSphere Client. As shown in Figure 28-1, you'll launch the remote console. using option "Launch Web Console" or "Launch Remote Console" in the vCenter Server Appliance VM. During the reboot process, you'll need to quickly enter the vCenter bootloader to initiate the password reset procedure.

Figure 28-1. *(How to reset the vCenter root Password 1 of 4)*

Then, when the Photo OS is booting, press **e** on your keyboard to access the boot options. At the end of the Linux section, add the following command `rw init=/bin/bash`, as shown in Figure 28-2. To save and enter the boot bash, press **Ctrl-x** or the **F10** key.

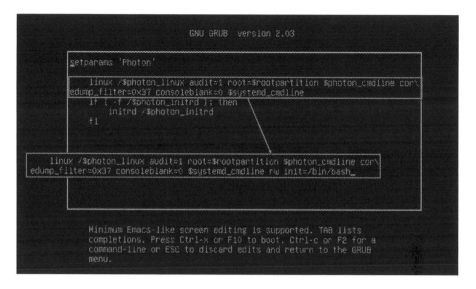

Figure 28-2. *(How to reset the vCenter root Password 2 of 4)*

Then, when you are inside the Photon OS console, type the following command: `mount -o remount,rw /`. Here, you have a couple of commands to have the root account lock information and reset the number of locks.

28.2 Reset the Root Password

If you know the root password and you just want to reset the root lock, this is the procedure.

To check how many failed attempts you have for the root password, type the following command: `/sbin/pam_tally2 -u root`. To reset this number to zero, type the command `/sbin/pam_tally2 -r -u root`. After this command resets the number to zero, you can umount and reboot.

Enter the command umount / followed by reboot -f. See Figure 28-3.

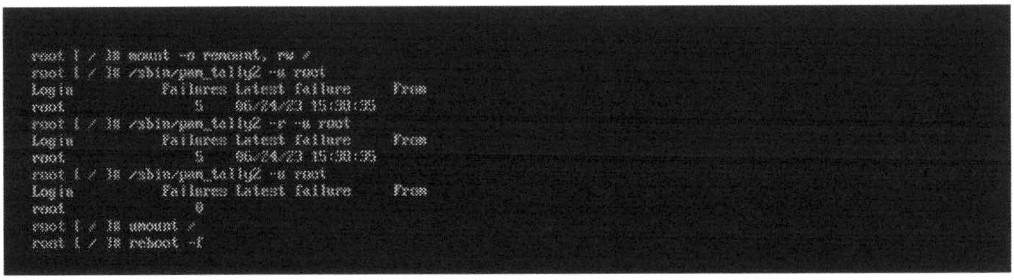

Figure 28-3. *(How to reset the vCenter root Password 3 of 4)*

Your root password is reset, and you can reuse the same password.

28.3 Change the Root Password

Besides the root account lock, you also lost the root password.

After you reset the root lock with the preceding procedure, type passd root. This will reset the root password, and you can type a new password, as shown in Figure 28-4.

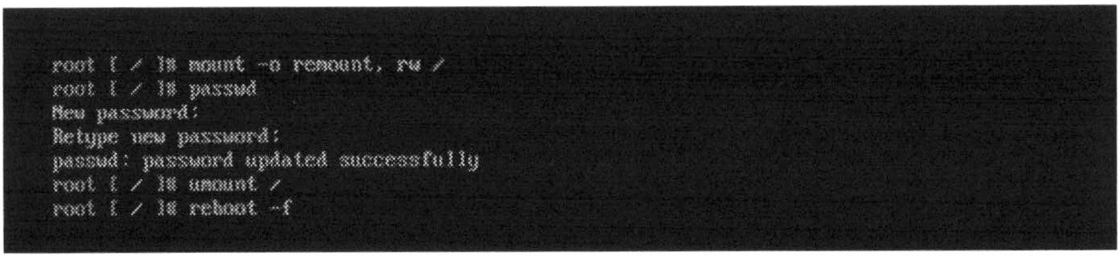

Figure 28-4. *(How to reset the vCenter root Password 4 of 4)*

With these steps, you can recover your root password from your vCenter Server.

28.4 Summary

This chapter provided a guide on how to secure your vSphere environment by resetting and updating the vCenter root password.

In Chapter 29 we move on to another important aspect of vSphere administration: maintaining the up-to-date status of your vCenter Server. Chapter 29 explores approaches for updating and upgrading vCenter, including both automated and manual methods, as well as online and offline scenarios. Performing these maintenance tasks ensures that your vCenter Server remains secure and efficient and incorporates the enhancements and features available.

CHAPTER 29

vCenter Update/Upgrade

Keeping your vCenter up to date is crucial to maintaining stability, security, and access to the features and improvements. In this chapter, I will provide you with step-by-step instructions on how to update or upgrade your vCenter, whether you are performing an update or transitioning to a new version.

Updating or upgrading your vCenter is a process that ensures the well-being and security of your environment. We will discuss the requirements, methods, and best practices to ensure a transition to the updated or upgraded version of vCenter Server.

Before you make any changes (updates or upgrades), you should always take a vCenter snapshot to be on the safe side. You already learned how to do this in Chapter 22, so create a snapshot of the vCenter now before making any changes.

Note   As I explain earlier vCenter, or vCenter server is the product, or the software that we can working(using vSphere Client) on that is installed in a appliance VM with the System Operation called PhotonOS and that VM Appliance is called VCSA.

And when we want to make changes in the appliance settings we need to use appliance software that is VAMI.

© Luciano Patrão 2024
L. Patrão, *VMware vSphere Essentials*, https://doi.org/10.1007/979-8-8688-0208-9_29

29.1 Automatic Online vCenter Update

To update your vCenter automatically, connect to vCenter VAMI (https://*IP- FQDN*:5480). In our example this is https://192.168.1.55:5480.

Note   VAMI stands for **v**Center Server **A**ppliance **M**anagement Interface for VCSA.

Log in to VAMI with your root password (the password that you created when you installed vCenter). See Figure 29-1.

Figure 29-1. *(vCenter Update 1 of 15)*

As shown in Figure 29-2, select the **Update** option, and vCenter should search for the latest updates and list them. If it does not, click **Check Updates** and select option **Check CD-ROM + URL** (this option means that vCenter will check if there is any ISO mounted on the VM virtual CD-ROM and check online on the VMware updates repository).

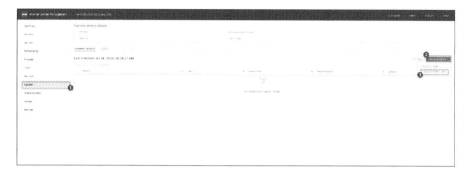

Figure 29-2. *(vCenter Update 2 of 15)*

Figure 29-3 shows all the updates that are available for my vCenter version. Since patches and updates are cumulative, you should select the latest one and release all the updates and patches after the actual version.

Figure 29-3. *(vCenter Update 3 of 15)*

After selecting the version you want to install, you can either choose **Stage Only** to copy files to vCenter and update later or choose **Stage and Install** after the stage is finished. For purposes of this example, select the **Stage and Install** option.

The Stage and Install Update wizard opens to the EULA page (see Figure 29-4). Review the VMware General Terms, check the **I accept the terms of the license agreement** check box (if you do), and click **Next**.

555

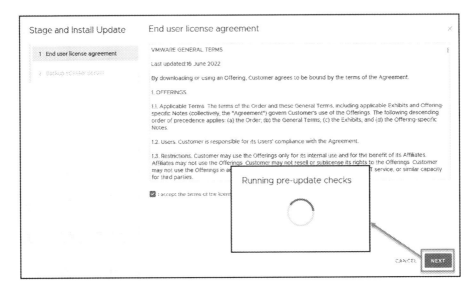

Figure 29-4. *(vCenter Update 4 of 15)*

Next, vCenter asks you to confirm that you did a vCenter backup before it will continue. Assuming you created a snapshot, check the box as shown in Figure 29-5 and click **Finish**. vCenter will start the installation process. Depending on your environment, this can take 20m, or 30/45m.

Figure 29-5. *(vCenter Update 5 of 15)*

You can see the browser has some intermittent refresh, and the % of the update is inaccurate. Just wait until you see the *Installation succeeded* message shown in Figure 29-6. If you don't see the message after a while, refresh your browser.

557

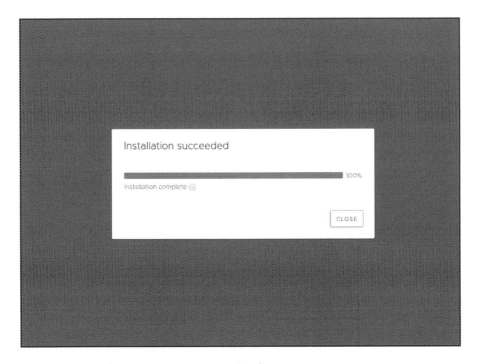

Figure 29-6. *(vCenter Update 6 of 15)*

After the installation is finished and you click **Close**, log in again to VAMI and reboot your vCenter as shown in Figure 29-7.

Figure 29-7. *(vCenter Update 7 of 15)*

After the reboot, your vCenter is not up to date, as shown in the example in Figure 29-8.

Figure 29-8. *(vCenter Update 8 of 15)*

29.2 Manual Offline vCenter Update

For security reasons, many environments do not have vCenter or even ESXi hosts connected to the Internet, in which case updating vCenter (or even vSphere) must be done offline and manually.

To download the patches in ISO, go to `https://customerconnect.` `vmware.com/patch#search` and download the patch ISO. Select your vCenter version and select the file to download.

Note   The preceding URL is only for downloading patches to your vCenter and is not for a full install. Any vCenter ISO downloaded from the main VMware Customer Connect portal is for a full install, not patches and download the patch ISO. As shown in Figure 29-9 you need to select VC (patches for vCenter) your vCenter version, in my case is 7.0.3, for this case the filter is "All Severities" since we want all updates for this patch, and select the file to download.

Figure 29-9. *(vCenter Update 9 of 15)*

After you have the ISO file, upload it to one of your vCenter Datastores (we have learned this in Chapter 4) and connect to your vCenter VM Appliance virtual CD-ROM as shown in Figure 29-10.

Note   All the steps are in the Chapter 4.

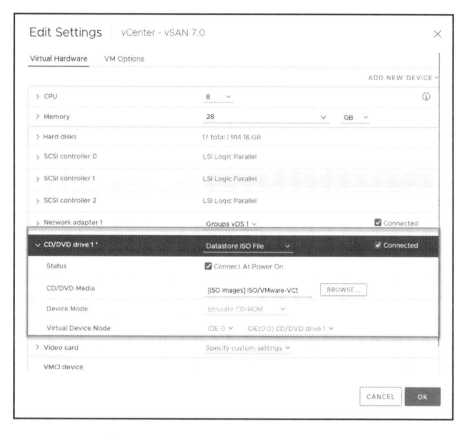

Figure 29-10. *(vCenter Update 10 of 15)*

Next, log in to your vCenter through the SSH console with a tool like PuTTY. If you find yourself in a bash shell (like shown in Figure 29-11), switch to the appliance shell with the command chsh -s /bin/ appliancesh root and restart your SSH session.

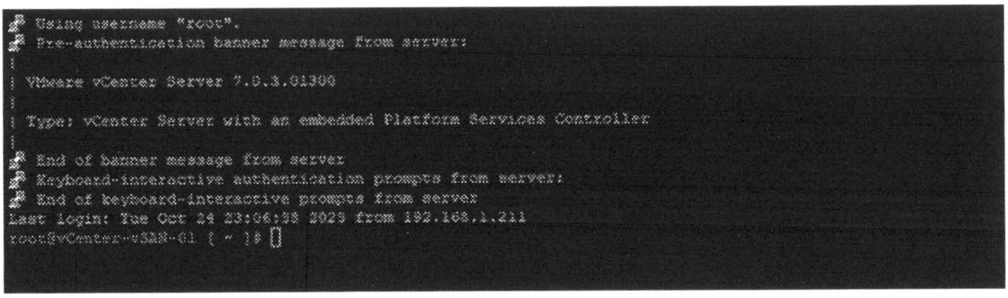

Figure 29-11. *(vCenter Update 11 of 15)*

After restarting the SSH console, you are now in the appliance shell and can run the appliance command to stage the ISO. You do so by running the commands indicated in the following three steps:

1. Run `software-packages stage --iso` to download patches to the appliance. After you run the command, you need to accept the VMware terms and conditions (see the bottom of Figure 29-12) to continue. Press **Y**. Then the staging starts.

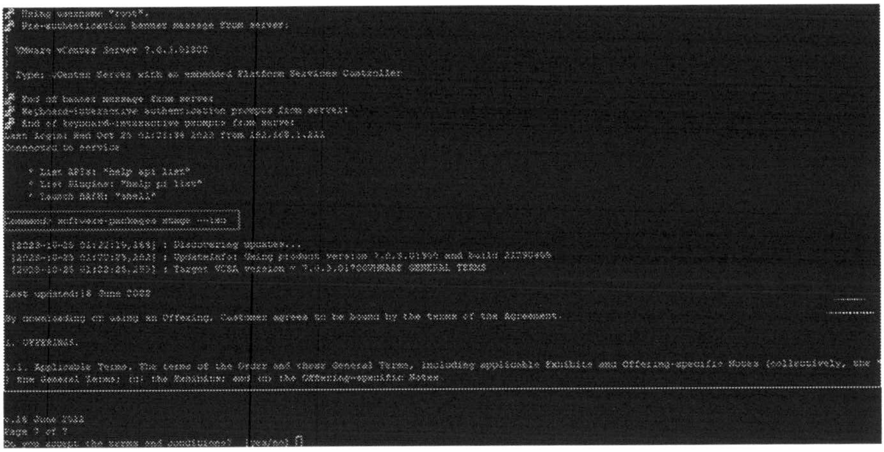

Figure 29-12. *(vCenter Update 12 of 15)*

2. After you get a *Staging process completed successfully* message, run `software-packages list --staged` (see Figure 29-13) to show the patches staged.

Figure 29-13. *(vCenter Update 13 of 15)*

3. After double-checking the patches that will be installed, run the `software-packages install --staged` command to start to install the patches in your vCenter. You should see the confirmation messages shown in Figure 29-14.

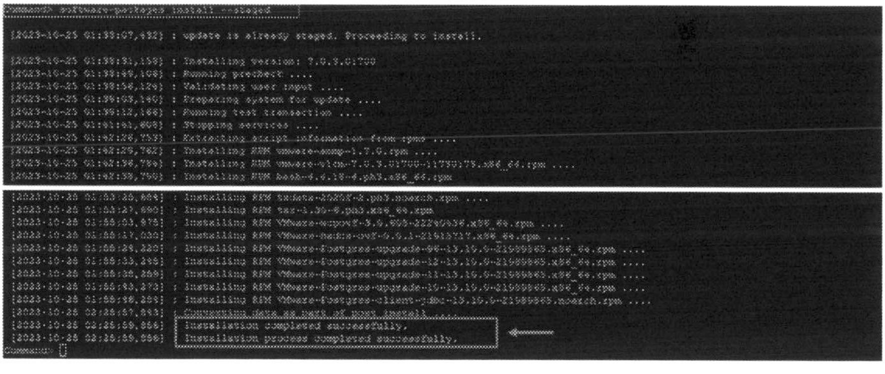

Figure 29-14. *(vCenter Update 14 of 15)*

After the installation is finished, vCenter will reboot automatically, and the patches are applied.

29.3 Automatic Offline vCenter Update

If you don't want to use the command line or SSH (some environments have SSH disabled for security reasons), you can also use VCSA VAMI to stage and install the ISO file that you connected to your VCSA VM.

With the ISO connected to your VM virtual CD-ROM, log in to the VAMI (https://*IP- FQDN*:5480), go to the **Update** option, and select the option **CDROM** as shown in Figure 29-15.

When the ISO you connected is displayed, you can do the same process we shown in the previous section for Automatic vCenter Update, by staging first, or do both automatically Stage and Install.

Figure 29-15. *(vCenter Update 15 of 15)*

Note   While using the command line or VAMI to read the ISO (Stage) connected to your VM and not receiving any updates listed, it could be due to the ISO being connected to your vCenter VM while it was powered on. To resolve this, you need to power down the vCenter, reconnect the ISO, and then power the vCenter back on before attempting again.

29.4 Automatic vCenter Upgrade

Upgrading your vCenter to a more recent version is a different process.

When a new version is available, you should see at the top of the vCenter window the message *New vCenter server updates are available* and an *Updates Available* message on the Summary tab, as shown in Figure 29-16. Click the **View Updates** option to see information about the new version and check if your version is supported to upgrade to the new version without any issues.

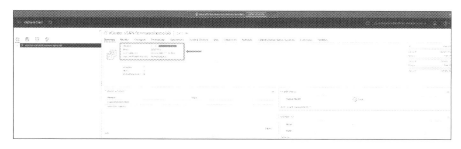

Figure 29-16. *(vCenter Upgrade 1 of 8)*

Figure 29-17 shows that a new version, vCenter 8.0, is available (at the time of writing). The next step is to use the Update Planner to double-check if your version has any issues to be upgraded to vCenter 8.0. Click the **Generate Reports** drop-down arrow and select the **Pre-Update Checks** option to get a report about the upgrade and see if there is any incompatibility to upgrade to vCenter 8.0.

Figure 29-17. *(vCenter Upgrade 2 of 8)*

Figure 29-18 shows the report I received, providing information about vCenter plug-ins from other VMware products that I have in this vCenter (like NSX, HCX, etc.). But in this case the warnings are not a showstopper; I can upgrade the vCenter and then upgrade the plug-ins after. However, before downloading the ISO, there is another preparation step.

Figure 29-18. *(vCenter Upgrade 3 of 8)*

Before upgrading your vCenter Server, it's important to assess compatibility with your current vSphere environment. Verify the interoperability of third-party products, earlier vSphere versions, and any plugins registered with vCenter, including solutions like NSX-T. The interoperability checks will highlight VMware products that might be affected and indicate whether third-party tools or plugins require updates to maintain compatibility with the new version of vCenter.

So, in the Update Planner, click the **Generate Report** drop-down arrow and select **Interoperability**. In my case, the Interoperability report shown in Figure 29-19 indicates that all versions are supported.

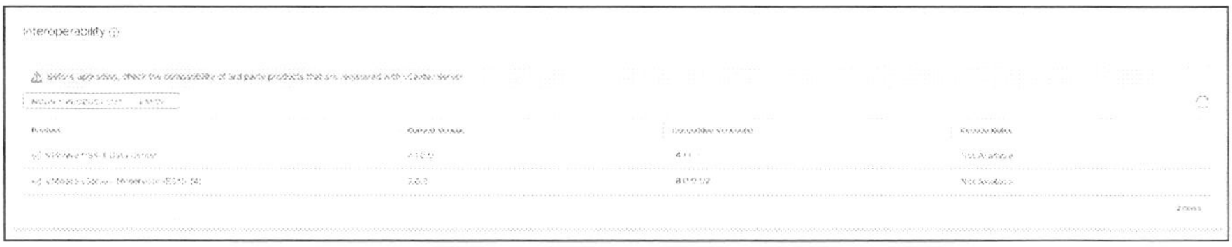

Figure 29-19. *(vCenter Upgrade 4 of 8)*

If everything is interoperable, return to **Pre-Update Checks** and click **Download ISO**.

After you download the vCenter ISO, launch it on your desktop (Windows or Mac) and run the setup/upgrade from there.

Once the pre-update checks confirm compatibility, proceed by downloading the vCenter ISO file. This file will be used to perform the upgrade. Launch the downloaded ISO on your desktop, whether Windows or Mac, and initiate the vCenter upgrade process through the setup. The upgrade itself is executed outside the vCenter's current environment using this setup program.

You need to mount the ISO into your computer and then run installer.exe. In the Windows OS, the file can be found in the following folder: \vcsa-ui-installer\win32.

The process to upgrade vCenter is almost the same as the process to install vCenter, explained in Chapter 8, so will not go through the full explanation. The only difference is that after you launch the Installer, use the **Upgrade** option, as shown in Figure 29-20, and need to connect to the vCenter you will upgrade.

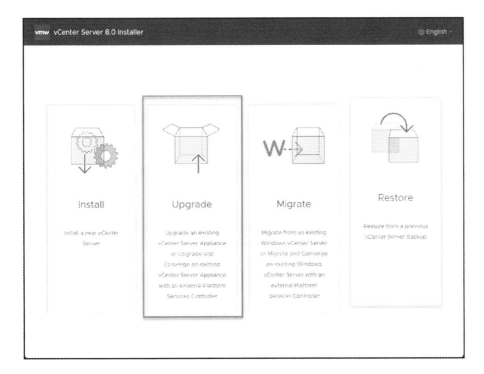

Figure 29-20. *(vCenter Upgrade 5 of 8)*

In the wizard screen shown in Figure 29-21, click **Next** to start the upgrade process. In step 2 of the wizard, accept the EULA and click **Next**.

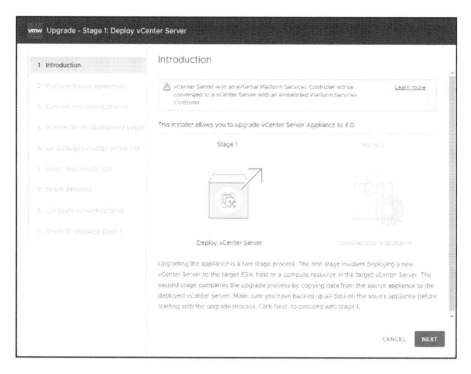

Figure 29-21. *(vCenter Upgrade 6 of 8)*

Then, you need to add the existing vCenter settings to upgrade into the upgrade setup.

In the upgrade process of the VCSA, step 3 of the wizard, as illustrated in Figure 29-22, involves entering the existing vCenter details such as IP or FQDN, SSO user and password, and the root password. This step is to connect to the source vCenter, which is the current vCenter Server instance you are upgrading from. The following step in the wizard will ask for details about the destination—the new environment where the upgraded VCSA VM will be deployed. This process essentially creates a new instance of VCSA and migrates your settings and data, after which the old instance can be decommissioned.

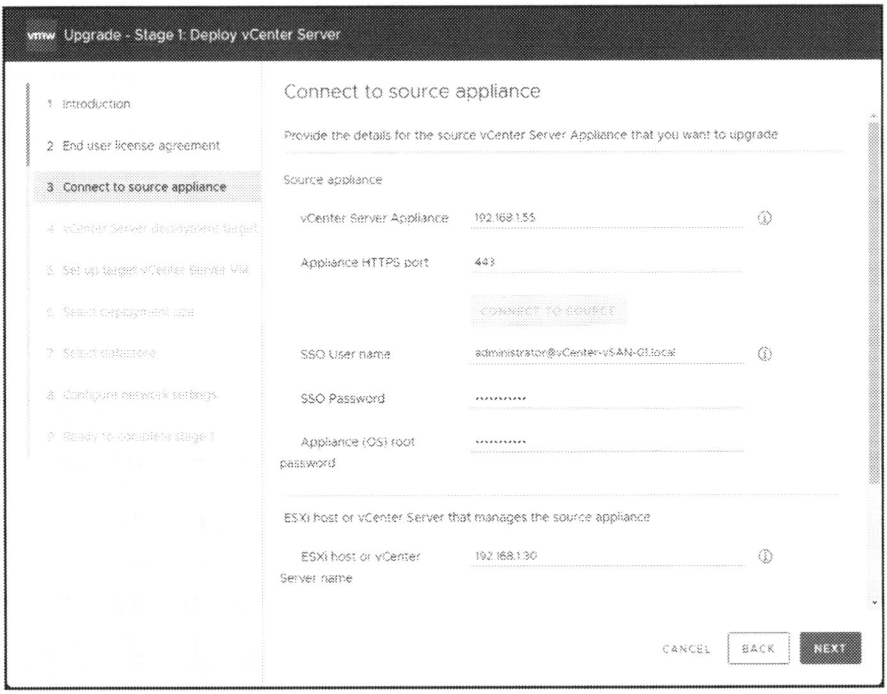

Figure 29-22. *(vCenter Upgrade 7 of 8)*

After step 3, the rest of the wizard steps are the same as the steps in Chapter 8 that you followed to install your vCenter. However, note that the step numbers differ by one. For example, Figure 29-23 shows step 4, in which you provide the vCenter/ESXi host where you will install vCenter v8.0 (the upgrade will create a new vCenter; after the setup is finished, it will power off the old vCenter). This is step 3 in Chapter 8 and is shown in Figure 8-5. Refer to Chapter 8 for a demonstration of the subsequent wizard steps.

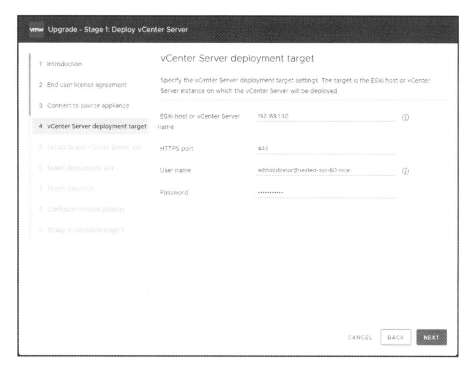

Figure 29-23. *(vCenter Upgrade 8 of 8)*

After you finish all the steps (don't forget that vCenter install and upgrade are done in two stages, as detailed in Chapter 8), your vCenter is upgraded and you can start upgrading your ESXi hosts.

29.5 Summary

This chapter covered updating and upgrading VCSA. It explained the importance of keeping vCenter up-to-date for stability, security, and features.

The chapter detailed two methods for updating vCenter: automatic online update and manual offline update. Automatic updates involve the VCSA checking for and installing updates directly from VMware repositories. Manual updates involve downloading an update ISO, uploading it to a datastore, and using the VAMI or command-line interface to stage and install the update.

Upgrading vCenter to a new major version involves a different process. The chapter explained how to use the vCenter Update Planner to check for compatibility issues before downloading an upgrade ISO. Upgrading involves running the downloaded ISO on a separate machine and providing details of the existing vCenter to migrate the configuration to a newly deployed VCSA.

Chapter 30 provides a detailed exploration of the processes involved in scanning for updates, remediating issues, upgrading VMware Tools, and updating ESXi hosts, all through the lens of VMware Lifecycle Manager (vLCM). The chapter equips you with practical insights into best practices and troubleshooting techniques specific to vLCM, aimed at ensuring the effective management and optimization of your vSphere environment.

CHAPTER 30

vSphere Lifecycle Manager

This chapter explores vSphere Lifecycle Manager (vLCM), previously known as vSphere Update Manager (VUM). We will focus on how this tool has evolved and its significance in managing your environment's life cycle of ESXi hosts. Using vLCM establishes, streamlines, and guarantees your system's reliability, updates, and security.

By the time you finish reading this chapter, you will have gained a grasp of vSphere Lifecycle Manager and its ability to improve the management of your ESXi hosts. Whether you are in charge of an environment or a sprawling data center, vLCM provides tools and features that streamline host management while guaranteeing the dependability and safety of your infrastructure.

vLCM encompasses a broad range of topics, and it is not feasible to cover every option and setting in detail in a single chapter, so we will discuss the most important tasks and settings to comprehensively understand key aspects of vLCM.

30.1 Introduction to vSphere Lifecycle Manager

To summarize, vSphere Lifecycle Manager is a tool seamlessly integrated into the vCenter Server. It offers a range of management features for

© Luciano Patrão 2024
L. Patrão, *VMware vSphere Essentials*, https://doi.org/10.1007/979-8-8688-0208-9_30

ESXi hosts, specifically focusing on software and firmware lifecycle tasks. Its integration into vSphere 7 adds capabilities to ensure enhanced consistency, up-to-date systems, and a simplified approach to managing clusters.

vSphere Lifecycle Manager is a significant tool in VMware's suite, offering several key features and capabilities:

- **Service integration:** vLCM is a feature embedded within the vCenter Server, eliminating the need for any installations. Once you deploy the vCenter Server appliance, the vLCM user interface is automatically enabled in the HTML5-based vSphere Client.

- **Unified software and firmware management:** Introduced in vSphere 7, vLCM brings together software and firmware lifecycle operations for vSAN clusters. This covers ESXi versions, drivers, VMware Tools, Virtual Hardware, and complete server stack firmware.

- **Lifecycle management innovations:** With the release of vSphere 7, new lifecycle management innovations were introduced to ensure up-to-date systems for customers. These include features like vCenter Server Profiles, vCenter Server Update Planner, and, of course, the functionality of vLCM itself.

- **Cluster-level management:** At a cluster level, you can efficiently manage hosts using the capabilities offered by vLCM. This feature is supported by services running on vCenter Server and ESXi hosts.

- **Centralized and simplified mechanism:** As a simplified VMware ESXi host management mechanism, vLCM allows you to handle ESXi hosts using images and baselines at a cluster level. Additionally, it facilitates a transition from baselines to utilizing vLCM images.

Select your vSphere Cluster and go to Update Tab and select option Baseline to go to vLCM, it is normal to get a warning similar to the following (see Figure 30-1) regarding an ESXi version that had issues and be informed that you should not use it in any of your ESXi implementations:

Do not use the non-critical baseline to update ESXi 7.0GA - 7.0U3b hosts. Use a baseline created with an ESXi 7.0 U3c or higher ISO image or Critical Host Paches baseline before applying any other patches to these hosts.

Always check this information, double-check if you use any of those versions, and follow the knowledge base process. In this case, *KB article #86447* is for ESXi hosts running 7.0 U3/U3a and ESXi hosts running 7.0 U2c/U2d (using an image-enabled cluster).

Figure 30-1. *(vLCM 1 of 1)*

If you are not using an image-enabled cluster, vLCM will also propose that you do so. We will discuss this in the next section.

30.2 Introduction to Image-Enabled Clusters

Before we create an image-enabled cluster, let's briefly explore this feature.

The vLCM image-enabled cluster is a feature that uses a model to manage ESXi hosts throughout a cluster effectively. It ensures that each host is set and maintained to a desired state, which includes the ESXi version, firmware, and drivers.

This approach guarantees consistency and reliability while simplifying upgrades and maintenance tasks. The cluster image comprises the ESXi base image and vendor addons for hardware integration and firmware updates. To utilize this feature, all hosts must be running ESXi 7.0 or a higher version from the same vendor and should not be stateless. Overall, this feature represents an advancement in enhancing the management of environments by making it more streamlined and efficient.

Here are the key aspects of this feature:

- **Declarative model:** Uses a declarative approach to ensure consistency across ESXi hosts within a cluster.

- **Desired state enforcement:** Sets and maintains a specific desired state for each host, including ESXi version, firmware, and drivers.

- **Cluster-wide management:** Allows uniform management of the entire cluster, aligning all hosts to the same configuration and version.

- **ESXi base image:** Includes a base image of VMware ESXi Server, necessary for the functioning of the cluster.

- **Firmware and driver integration:** Supports integration of firmware and drivers, ensuring that all hosts in the cluster are running compatible and up-to-date versions.

- **Vendor addons:** Optionally includes packages provided by hardware vendors, which can contain additional drivers and components for hardware compatibility.

- **Compatibility checks:** Automated checks ensure hardware and software compatibility within the cluster, helping to prevent conflicts or issues during updates.

- **Efficiency in upgrades and maintenance:** Simplifies upgrading and maintaining ESXi hosts, reducing the complexity and time required.

30.3 Create an Image-Enabled Cluster

To access image-enabled cluster to go the main vLCM dashboard, you can click directly in button "**Manage with a single image**" (not in the Figure 30-2) or select your vSphere Cluster, go to Tab **Updates** and option **Image** (see Figure 30-2).

Figure 30-2. *(Image-Base Cluster 2 of 11)*

Then you have two options: *Setup Image* and *Import Image*.

Note   Before we start this section, we cannot use any ISO vendor addons while using the nested environment. As it is normal, these are virtual ESXi hosts, not physical. So you can check and learn the options in your nested environment to learn, but create the image-enabled cluster, this work needs to be done in a physical environment.

So, our next steps are done in our physical environment, not the nested environment we have used in this book.

30.3.1 Cluster Image Setup

Clicking the **Setup Image** option shown in Figure 30-2 enables you to configure the cluster image in vLCM. The process involves selecting the components that will compose the cluster image. These components typically include the ESXi base image, vendor addons such as drivers or hardware providers, and firmware. You can choose versions of ESXi, firmware, and drivers for deployment across the cluster.

Once configured, this image becomes the template for all hosts in the cluster, ensuring consistency and uniformity. The cluster image setup process also includes compatibility checks to ensure the selected components work seamlessly with existing hardware.

This option is usually preferred when creating an image or modifying an existing one within the vLCM environment.

After you click **Setup Image**, you convert your ESXi into a customized image, as shown in Figure 30-3. In the *ESXi Version* drop-down list, select the ESXi version you want to use to create your image (as a best practice, you should use the latest version, but it is not mandatory).

Next, click Select in the Vendor Addon field You need to choose the addon image from your vendor. Since your vendor customize image is in here, you search for your vender name and select the approriate option from your vender as shown in Figure 30-3.

Note   In my initial configuration I selected the first option HPE Synergy Server Customization as explaining in the Figure 30-5, but then I need to change to the proper image that is HPE Customization for HPE Servers as shown in the Figure 30-3.

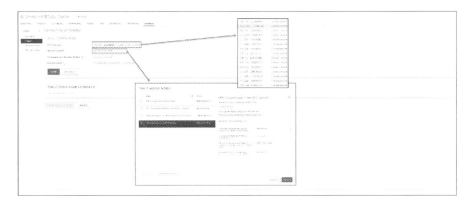

Figure 30-3.   *(Image-Base Cluster 3 of 11)*

Next, click **Select** in the *Firmware and Drivers Addon* field.

Note   You need to install a hardware security module (HSM) from your vendor to apply firmware into your ESXi or even use vLCM to upgrade your firmware.

In my case, the hardware support managers that HPE provides are part of its management tools, iLO Amplifier and OneView, which are deployed as appliances. These tools (HPE VIBs) must be installed to use this option. I don't have these VIBs installed, so the list shown in Figure 30-4 is empty. This type of tool is beyond the scope of this chapter anyway, so we will skip this option.

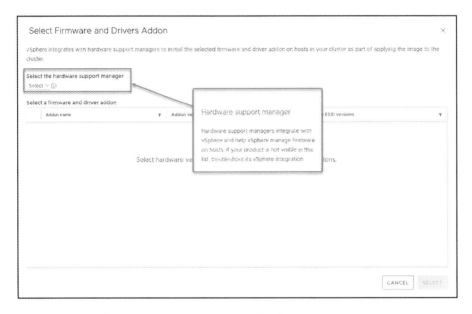

Figure 30-4. *(Image-Base Cluster 4 of 11)*

The *Components* option is used to add an extra driver to the image-enabled cluster image. Click **Show details**, change the *Show* drop-down option to **All components** (see Figure 30-5), select the drivers you want to add to your image, click **Add Components**, and click **Save** to save your options.

Figure 30-5. *(Image-Base Cluster 5 of 11)*

After you save your options, vLCM checks cluster compliance to make sure that all your options are compatible with your ESXi hosts that exist in the cluster. See Figure 30-6.

Figure 30-6. *(Image-Base Cluster 6 of 11)*

Figure 30-7 shows that four servers in my cluster are not compliant with the ISO image. I selected **HPE Synergy Server Customization** for the *Vendor Addon* setting, but this ESXi version is incompatible with an HPE DL360-G9 server. I need to select the ISO version **HPE Customization for HPE Servers**.

Figure 30-7. *(Image-Base Cluster 7 of 11)*

I close the Window and return to previous step, *Convert to an Image*, click **Edit**, change the *Vendor Addon* option to the proper ISO, and save it again.

But if you still have issues and the available images are incompatible with your ESXi host, run the option **Check for recommended images**, as shown in Figure 30-8. This option will search the VMware online repository and add the version that is compatible with your ESXi host.

Figure 30-8. *(Image-Base Cluster 8 of 11)*

Once you've selected a compatible image, the next step is to save it and then proceed with the pre-check by clicking **Run Pre-Check**. In my case, the pre-check flagged a few issues, as shown in Figure 30-9. It has warnings about driver inconsistencies between two ESXi hosts. Additionally, one host is the Fault Domain Manager (FDM). During the remediation process, discussed next, both of these discrepancies will be addressed, ensuring that both ESXi hosts are configured identically.

Figure 30-9. *(Image-Base Cluster 9 of 11)*

To continue to create **Image-Enable Cluster**, click "**Remediate All**," as shown in Figure 30-9. This provides details about what will occur during the remediation process of the ESXi hosts. See Figure 30-10. It's important to note that a reboot will be necessary as part of this process.

Figure 30-10. *(Image-Base Cluster 10 of 11)*

Check the box indicating that you accept the terms of the EULA and then click **Start Remediation** to start in Application remediation settings section, as shown in the Figure 30-11.

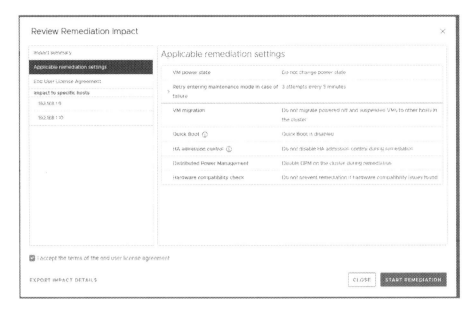

Figure 30-11. *(Image-Base Cluster 11 of 11)*

After you start remediation and the process is completed and all ESXi hosts are rebooted, It shows that all ESXi hosts in the cluster now share a consistent image, with a single unified image being deployed across all ESXi hosts. This consistency ensures streamlined management and uniform performance across the cluster.

30.3.2 Importing Images

Returning to the window shown in Figure 30-2, clicking the **Import Image** option allows you to import existing images into vLCM. This option is beneficial when organizations have predefined images previously configured and tested in environments or clusters that they now want to replicate in their cluster setup.

Importing an image can save time and effort, especially if it has already been optimized for hardware or operational requirements.

Once the imported image is implemented, it will ensure that the configuration of all ESXi hosts in the cluster aligns with the imported image. This choice is especially advantageous for organizations or service providers overseeing clusters, as it allows them to uphold a consistent setup across all clusters.

Both the Setup Image and Import Image options aim to make it easier to handle ESXi hosts in a cluster, ensuring that all hosts are running compatible with current software and firmware versions. This helps simplify the management process by reducing the complexity of managing host configurations.

30.4 Create and Manage Baselines

Maintaining consistency, security, and performance in virtualized environments across all ESXi hosts is extremely important. This is where the concept of *baselines* in vSphere Lifecycle Manager becomes crucial. A baseline in vLCM is a set of standards or specifications that includes updates, patches, or specific software versions meant to be applied to ESXi hosts. These baselines are the foundation for ensuring that all hosts within a cluster follow the configuration and software standards. This enables management and operational efficiency.

Creating and maintaining baselines is a process for managing virtual environments. It involves steps that ensure the environment stays up to date and well maintained. Initially, administrators need to identify the needs of their infrastructure, whether it is related to security updates or performance improvements. Based on these requirements, administrators can then create custom baselines, including a combination of patches, updates, and extensions tailored to the ESXi hosts' needs.

Once these baselines are established, they are applied to the hosts. Afterward, regular compliance checks conducted by vLCM help ensure that the hosts adhere to the defined baseline standards. If any hosts are non-compliant, they can be automatically or manually remediated to align with the baseline. This ensures consistency across all hosts and reduces the risks associated with vulnerable software.

30.4.1 Types of Baselines

The following are the type of baselines available in vLCM:

- **Patch baselines:** These apply patches or updates to the ESXi hosts. They can be critical patches, noncritical updates, or a combination.

- **Extension baselines:** These are used for adding or updating third-party software or addons on the ESXi hosts.

- **Upgrade baselines:** These are used to upgrade the ESXi hosts to a newer version of the ESXi software.

30.4.2 How to Create a Baseline

Select your cluster, click the Updates tab, expand Hosts, and select Baselines to see the default baselines configured during the initial setup of vCenter are available, each tailored to maintain the compliance and integrity of your ESXi hosts. These predefined baselines typically include critical security patches, updates, and upgrade packages, all aimed at keeping your environment secure, stable, and optimized according to VMware's best practices.

These default baselines are designed to simplify the management of updates and patches for ESXi hosts in a VMware environment. Here's an explanation of these default attached baselines, shown in Figure 30-12:

- **Critical Host Patches:**
  - This baseline includes critical patches released for ESXi hosts.

- Its primary focus is on security patches and critical bug fixes.

- It is automatically attached to ESXi hosts or clusters to ensure that critical vulnerabilities and issues are addressed promptly.

- **Non-Critical Host Patches:**

  - This baseline encompasses patches that are classified as noncritical.

  - These patches might include general updates, minor bug fixes, or enhancements that don't address critical security or stability issues.

  - While not as urgent as critical patches, they are important for maintaining the overall health and efficiency of the ESXi hosts.

- **Host Upgrade Baselines:**

  - These baselines are intended for upgrading the ESXi hosts to newer versions.

  - They include the full installation images of the newer ESXi versions.

  - Applying these baselines will upgrade the hosts to the latest or a specific version of ESXi, depending on the baseline settings.

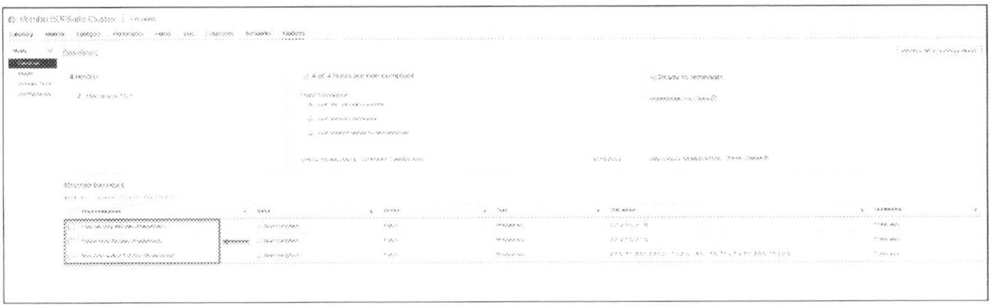

Figure 30-12. *(Baseline 1 of 13)*

The preceding baselines serve most environments, and usually you don't need to create more, but if you need a new and customized baseline, go to the vSphere Client Main Menu, select **Lifecycle Manager**, click the **Baselines** tab, click the **New** drop-down arrow, and select **Baseline**, as shown in Figure 30-13.

Figure 30-13. *(Baseline 2 of 13)*

Create an Extension Baseline

First, we will examine how to create an extension baseline, so select **Extension** in the first step of the Create Baseline wizard and click **Next**. As previously explained, extension baselines are for third-party software or addons, such as from hardware vendors (servers or devices).

For this example, I will demonstrate how I created a baseline with some drivers for my Mellanox network card. As shown in Figure 30-14, I have integrated only two extensions in my setup, but vLCM's flexibility allows adding as many as needed, tailored to diverse vendors and devices.

This adaptability is crucial for customizing the management of your environment.

Figure 30-14. *(Baseline 3 of 13)*

Typically, I recommend creating baselines specific to each type of ESXi host. For instance, you might have a standard server hardware setup. Still, if you enhance it with additional hardware like a new network card, video card, or other peripherals, I advise creating a specialized baseline for that particular configuration. This ensures that all ESXi hosts with similar hardware configurations receive the appropriate drivers, maintaining compliance with vendor standards and optimizing overall performance. By adopting this strategy, you ensure that each host is not only up to date but also fully aligned with the specific requirements of its hardware configuration.

After clicking **Next**, the Summary page of the wizard is displayed, as shown in Figure 30-15 for my baseline. You would then click **Finish** to create your baseline.

Figure 30-15. *(Baseline 4 of 13)*

Create a Patch Baseline

When creating a patch baseline, we have different options to add. The selection is for patches launched by VMware or any vendor.

Return to the Create Baseline wizard (as demonstrated in Figure 30-13) and select the **Patch** baseline type, as shown in Figure 30-16. Click **Next**.

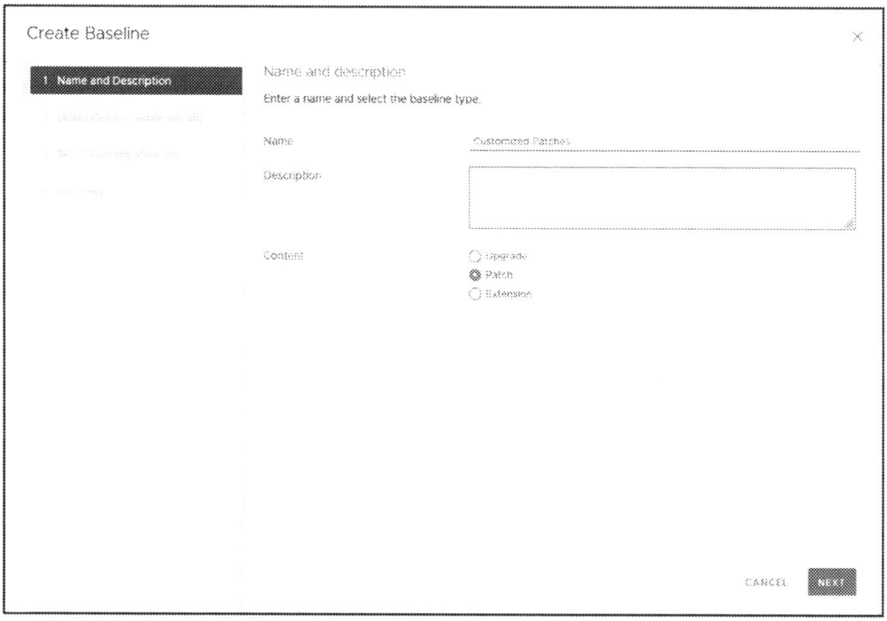

Figure 30-16. (Baseline 5 of 13)

In step 2 of the wizard, shown in Figure 30-17, you can choose the patches to include in this baseline. You can select patches based on various criteria. For instance, you might choose patches released within a specific timeframe, selecting all patches that fall within those dates. Alternatively, you can filter patches by their vendor, such as VMware or various hardware vendors. Additionally, you can select patches based on the product version, creating baselines specific to certain versions like 7.0x, exclusively 7.0.3, or even older versions like 6.7x. Further refinement can be done based on the severity and category of the patches, allowing for precise and targeted baseline configurations. For this example, I selected all patches launched for the Mellanox device. Click **Next** after you make your choices.

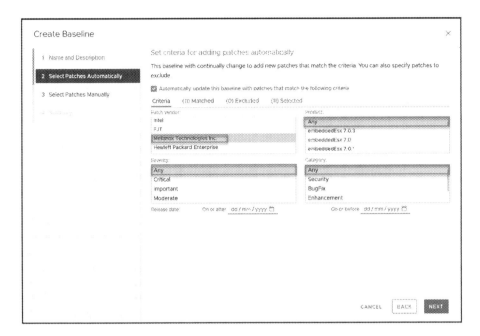

Figure 30-17. *(Baseline 6 of 13)*

Figure 30-18 shows that I have 11 patches that match my criteria. By default, all patches are selected to be added to your baseline, but you can use the check boxes to select the ones you want to add (I selected the first two) and deselect the ones you want to remove from this baseline.

Figure 30-18. *(Baseline 7 of 13)*

With my current selection, this baseline will automatically include all Mellanox patches. Whenever updates are released for these patches, they will be automatically incorporated into the baseline.

After clicking **Next**, step 3 of the wizard enables you to manually add any specific patch of your choosing. Regardless of whether there are updates for these particular patches, they will remain a constant part of your baseline.

We will bypass this section for now, so click **Next** to proceed to finalize your baseline. Figure 30-19 shows the summary of my choices.

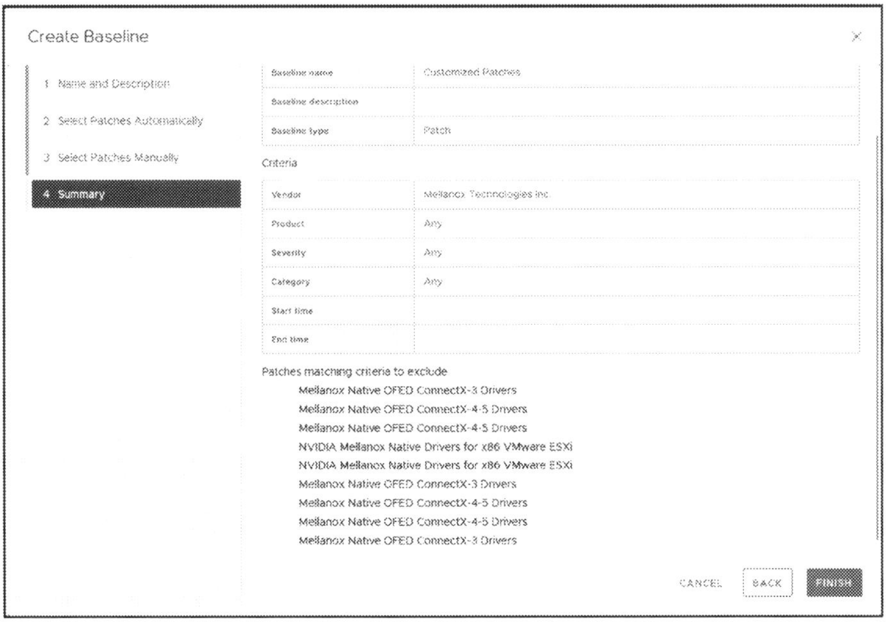

Figure 30-19. *(Baseline 8 of 13)*

Create an Upgrade Baseline

Finally, we will create a baseline to upgrade our ESXi hosts. Here, you must consider what type of vSphere version ISO you installed on your ESXi—for example, if you used a default vSphere ISO from VMware, a customized vendor like HPE, or another vendor.

For instance, upgrading from vSphere 7.0 U1 to 7.0 U3 or from 6.7 to 7.x or 8.x is feasible. However, it is crucial to note that upgrades can only be performed to versions supported by the VCSA in use. For example, a 6.5 host cannot be upgraded to 6.7 using a 7.0 VCSA ISO.

Before creating an upgrade baseline, upload the ISO you want to use into vLCM. To do this, in vLCM, download the ISO you need from the VMware Customer Connect portal (as explained in Chapter 3), and after you have the ISO downloaded to your desktop, you start importing the ISO, as shown in Figure 30-20, go to the **Imported ISOs** tab select your downloaded ISO, and click **Import ISO**.

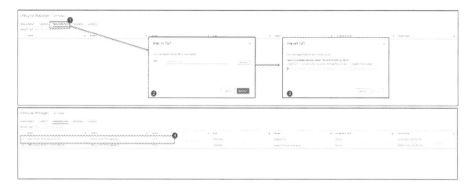

Figure 30-20. *(Baseline 9 of 13)*

Second image in Figure 30-20 shows that I uploaded the latest version of ISO VMware ESXi 7.0 Update 3n.

After you upload the ISO, you can launch the Create Baseline wizard to create your upgrade baseline. Click **Next**.

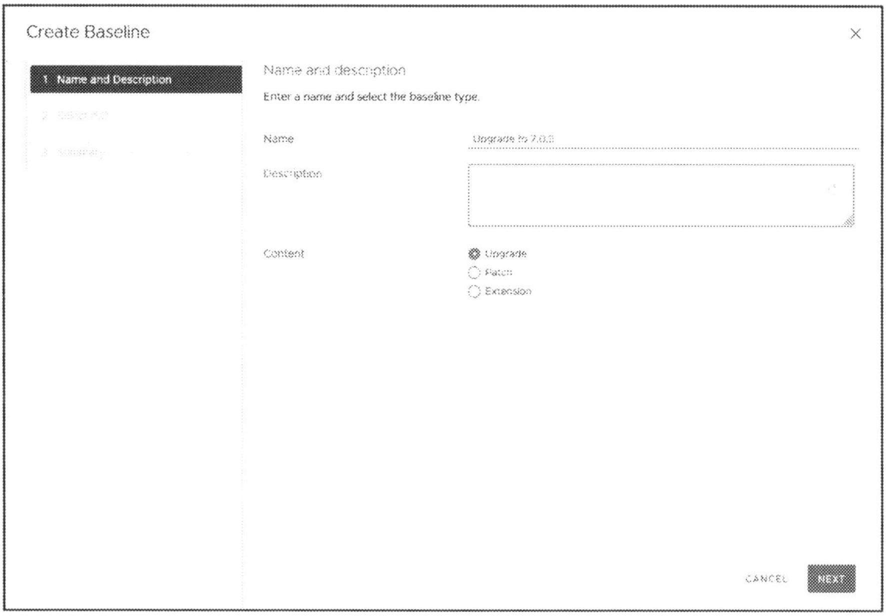

Figure 30-21. *(Baseline 10 of 13)*

In step 2 of the wizard, select the ISO and vSphere version you want to add to this upgrade baseline. As Figure 30-22 shows, I have two options: the default vSphere ISO from VMware and the customized vSphere ISO from HPE. Since this is a nested environment, we will select the default from VMware. For your case, if your ESXi host was installed with a vendor-customized vSphere ISO, then download and use it here. Click **Next** after you select an ISO.

Figure 30-22. *(Baseline 11 of 13)*

Click **Finish** on the Summary wizard page, shown in Figure 30-23, and you'll have a baseline for your upgrade tasks.

Figure 30-23. *(Baseline 12 of 13)*

As the three examples listed Figure 30-24 demonstrate, you can create a baseline based on many criteria. Which criteria you should choose all depends on the management of your environment and how you want to update your ESXi hosts.

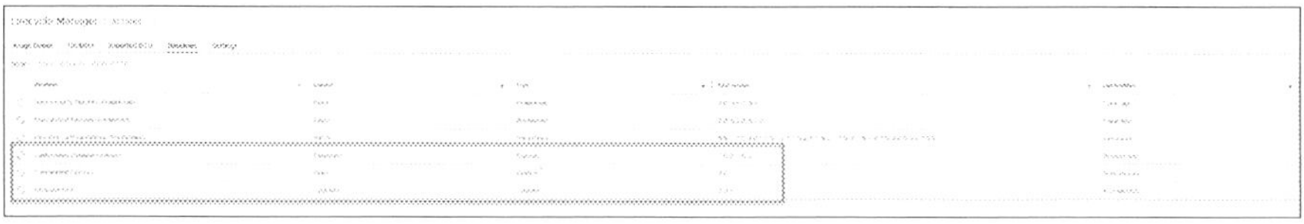

Figure 30-24. *(Baseline 13 of 13)*

30.5 Add and Remove Baselines to and from ESXi Hosts and Clusters

Now, you must add your baselines to your ESXi hosts or clusters.

As shown in Figure 30-25, return to your inventory view, select the cluster, go to the **Updates** tab, select the **Baselines** option, click the **Attach** drop-down arrow, and select **Attach Baseline or Baseline Group** to add the baseline.

Figure 30-25 shows the three baselines that I created. Assuming that you created three, you can add all three or just select one by using the check boxes. For purposes of demonstration in the following sections, I added all three.

Select all the baselines you want to add and click **Attach**.

Tip   As Figure 30-25 shows, the Attach drop-down list has a shortcut to create a baseline—no need to go to the vLCM administration.

Figure 30-25. *(Remove Baselines 1 of 3)*

Now the baselines you attached are available in your cluster.

The same process is used to add a specific baseline to a specific ESXi. Select the host and then add the baseline to that particular host, as demonstrated in Figure 30-26.

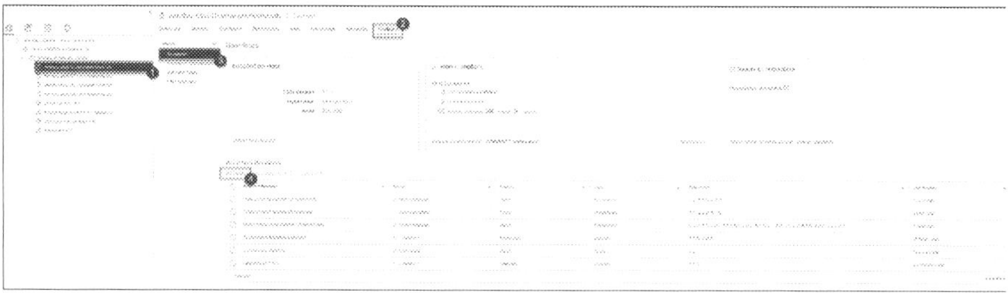

Figure 30-26. *(Remove Baselines 2 of 3)*

If you need to detach a specific baseline from a cluster or an ESXi host, simply select the baseline you wish to remove and then click the **Detach** button. See Figure 30-27.

Note   It's only possible to detach one baseline at a time. If multiple baselines are selected, the Detach option will become unavailable.

Figure 30-27. *(Remove Baselines 3 of 3)*

30.6 Scanning and Remediation

Having discussed the details of creating and managing baselines, we now progress to the vital stage of staging and remediating updates and upgrades. This step is essential in actualizing the strategies set out in your baseline configurations, ensuring that your ESXi hosts remain current and secure.

In vLCM, applying updates based on default or customized baselines involves the following three key steps (although the second step isn't always necessary, as discussed a bit later). These steps form a systematic process to ensure that ESXi hosts are updated effectively and efficiently.

1. **Check compliance:** This step involves assessing whether the ESXi hosts are in line with the specified baselines.

   - During the compliance check, vLCM compares the current state of the ESXi hosts against the standards set in the baselines (whether default or customized).

   - The outcome determines whether the hosts are compliant (matching the baseline) or non-compliant (deviating from the baseline).

   - Identifying non-compliant hosts is crucial, as it highlights which hosts need updates to align with the baseline requirements.

2. **Stage:** Staging is the process of downloading and temporarily storing the required updates on the ESXi hosts, but not yet applying them.

- This step allows hosts to prepare without causing immediate changes or potential downtime.

- Staging updates in advance can help manage network load, as the downloads are done before the actual update process.

- Staging also provides an opportunity to ensure that all necessary updates are ready and available on the hosts before proceeding with the remediation step.

3. **Remediate:** Remediation is the final step, where the staged updates are applied to the non-compliant hosts.

    - This step brings the hosts into compliance with the baselines, applying all necessary patches, updates, or upgrades.

    - Remediation can be scheduled to occur during maintenance windows to minimize impact on the environment.

    - Post-remediation, the hosts should comply with the baselines, reflecting the latest updates and configurations as defined.

Together, these three steps form a comprehensive approach to maintaining ESXi host updates in a vLCM environment, ensuring that the virtual infrastructure is secure, reliable, and performs optimally.

30.6.1 Check Compliance

Note   This procedure can be carried out at the cluster level or individually for each ESXi host. However, performing these actions at the cluster level is usually more convenient. There may be situations where a particular ESXi host is not up to date or has experienced problems during the update process. Sometimes, choosing and applying the update procedures for that affected ESXi host is important.

Since the compliance status is at the moment is Unknown to check compliance, select the cluster, click the **Updates** tab, expand **Hosts** and choose **Baselines**, Start by clicking on the **Check Compliance** option as shown in Figure 30-28.

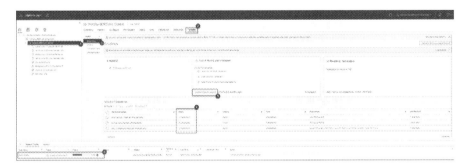

Figure 30-28. *(Scanning & Remediation 1 of 9)*

Depending on the scale of your environment, the time required to check compliance can vary. The progress bar shown in the bottom-left corner of Figure 30-28 gives you some indication of the progress. Smaller setups may take a few minutes, but larger environments could require more time to complete the process.

Figure 30-29 shows that some baselines are marked as non-compliant. Notably, this includes an upgrade baseline. This is expected since I have selected a higher version for the upgrade, leading to my current version being classified as non-compliant.

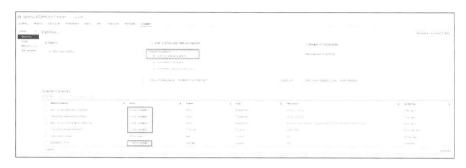

Figure 30-29. *(Scanning & Remediation 2 of 9)*

30.6.2 Stage

Now we will stage the updates to the ESXi hosts to prepare for the update process.

Note   Updates and upgrades cannot be remediated simultaneously and must be approached separately. While I demonstrate staging and completing updates first for clarity, it is often more practical in real-world scenarios to proceed directly with the upgrade baseline. This approach is generally preferred, as it streamlines the process without compromising the outcome. The staging of patch baselines, except in cases involving specific driver baselines, may not add significant value and can be skipped in favor of direct upgrades. The detailed steps for this will be covered in the following section.

As shown in Figure 30-30, select the baselines you want to stage and click the **Stage** option.

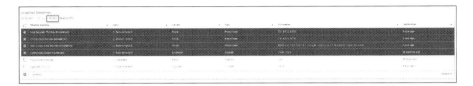

Figure 30-30. *(Scanning & Remediation 3 of 9)*

As Figure 30-31 shows, I have 63 patches to stage and 2 extensions. Normally, vLCM will download all the patches and install the ones necessary to fully update your ESXi hosts.

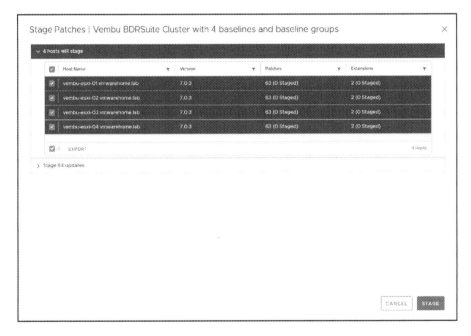

Figure 30-31. *(Scanning & Remediation 4 of 9)*

After successfully completing the staging process, which involves ensuring no failed stages by checking the recent tasks, we can move forward with the remediation step to apply the updates.

30.6.3 Remediate

During the remediation stage, it is essential to understand that rebooting each ESXi host is often required, typically one at a time. Contrary to common misconception, vSphere High Availability (HA) alone does not facilitate the migration of powered-on VMs to another host during this process. Instead, it is the Distributed Resource Scheduler (DRS) in fully automated mode that is required for this functionality.

DRS automatically balances workloads and migrates VMs to other hosts before the original host enters maintenance mode for the reboot. If you don't have DRS in fully automated mode, or need to manage the process manually for other reasons, you can select each ESXi host individually, put it into maintenance mode, and then apply the remediation.

Once the original host is empty and in maintenance mode, it will proceed with the reboot.

Before starting the remediation process, for automated handling, it's important to understand the existing baseline remediation settings of vSphere Lifecycle Manager.

Baseline Remediation Settings

To check or modify the baseline remediation settings, navigate to vLCM, click the **Settings** tab, expand the **Host Remediation** section, and select **Baselines** to review or adjust the configurations as needed. See Figure 30-32.

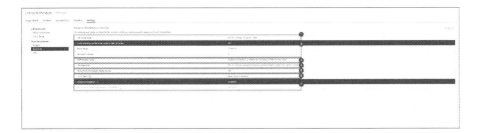

Figure 30-32. *(Scanning & Remediation 5 of 9)*

To provide a clear understanding of each setting in the Baselines Remediation Settings section, we'll go through them one by one (in the order shown in Figure 30-32).

VM Power State

When this setting is set to **Do not change VM power state**, as in Figure 30-32, VMs will remain in their current state (powered on, powered off, or suspended) regardless of the remediation activities on the host.

This option is important for environments where maintaining the current state of VMs is crucial, especially to avoid disruptions in services or applications running on these VMs.

Administrators need to be mindful when choosing this option, as it requires careful consideration of the potential impact on VMs if the host requires a reboot or other significant changes during remediation.

Selecting the appropriate VM Power State setting is essential based on operational requirements and the downtime or service disruption tolerance in the virtual environment.

Retry Entering Maintenance Mode in Case of Failure

This setting is crucial for ensuring successful remediation of ESXi hosts. When set to **On**, this feature enables vLCM to automatically attempt to put an ESXi host into maintenance mode again if the first attempt fails.

This is particularly useful in scenarios where the initial attempt to enter maintenance mode is unsuccessful due to transient issues or temporary conflicts on the host.

Retry Delay

This setting is set to **5 minutes** in Figure 30-32, which means that vLCM will wait for 5 minutes before retrying to put the host into maintenance mode after a failed attempt.

Number of Retries

Number of retries is set to **3** in Figure 30-32, which means that vLCM will make up to three attempts to put the host into maintenance mode. If all attempts fail, the remediation process for that host will not proceed, and manual intervention may be required.

This setting ensures that temporary issues don't permanently halt the remediation process. Automatically retrying increases the likelihood of successful host maintenance and, consequently, the successful application of updates or patches as specified in the baselines.

PXE Booted Hosts

This setting for PXE booted hosts plays a significant role in managing hosts that boot using PXE. The Preboot Execution Environment (PXE) is a network-based booting mechanism that allows ESXi hosts to boot using network interface firmware rather than from a local storage device. ESXi hosts booted via PXE often load their operating system and configurations from a central server, making them different regarding software management compared to hosts with traditional storage-based boot methods.

Figure 30-32 shows this setting set to **Disallow installation of additional software on PXE booted hosts**, which restricts the installation of any additional software on PXE booted ESXi hosts during the remediation process. The rationale behind this setting is that PXE booted hosts typically load their configuration from a server, and any additional software installed directly on these hosts could be lost upon reboot, as the host reloads its original configuration from the network. By disallowing the installation of additional software, this setting helps maintain the integrity and consistency of the PXE booted hosts, ensuring their configuration remains aligned with the central server's specifications.

This setting is crucial for environments where ESXi hosts are booted via PXE, as it helps maintain the consistency and predictability of the host configurations and avoids potential complications arising from software changes that might not persist after a host reboot.

VM Migration

The VM Migration setting is an important option in vSphere Lifecycle Manager's Baseline Remediation Settings. This setting dictates how virtual machines currently powered off or suspended are handled during the remediation of ESXi hosts.

In Figure 30-32, this setting is set to **Do not migrate powered off and suspended VMs to other hosts in the cluster**. When this option is selected, VMs in a powered-off state or suspended will not be migrated to other hosts in the cluster during the remediation process. This can be a strategic choice to reduce the operational overhead and complexity during remediation, especially if there is no need to move these inactive VMs.

This setting is particularly relevant in clusters where vMotion redistributes VMs for load balancing or vacates hosts for maintenance. Choosing not to migrate powered-off or suspended VMs may be preferable in scenarios where the migration of inactive VMs is deemed unnecessary or could potentially lead to resource contention.

It's important to assess the potential impacts on cluster resources and the time required for remediation when deciding on this setting. The decision to turn this VM Migration setting on or off should align with your specific maintenance strategies and operational requirements, considering the status of VMs in your cluster and the intended outcomes of the remediation process.

Disconnect Removable Media Devices

In vLCM, setting the option to 'No' ensures that during the remediation process, removable media devices connected to ESXi hosts, such as USB drives or external hard disks, will not be automatically disconnected even if they might interfere with the host's ability to enter maintenance mode. This choice instructs vLCM to leave all removable media devices connected throughout the remediation, regardless of their potential impact on transitioning the host into maintenance mode. This setting is critical as entering maintenance mode is often required for successful remediation.

This setting determines whether or not removable media devices (like USB drives or external hard disks) connected to ESXi hosts should be disconnected as part of the remediation process. The primary concern is whether these devices could interfere with the ESXi host's ability to enter maintenance mode, which is often required in the remediation process.

By choosing **No**, you instruct vLCM to leave all removable media devices connected during the remediation, regardless of their potential impact on the maintenance mode transition. This could be necessary if the connected devices are essential for the operation of the host or certain applications running on it.

Keeping these devices connected can be beneficial if they are crucial for the ESXi host functions. However, there is a risk that these devices might cause issues or delays in the remediation process, particularly if they prevent the host from successfully entering maintenance mode.

This setting requires careful consideration based on the specifics of your environment and the role of the removable media in your ESXi hosts' operations.

In essence, the choice to keep removable media devices connected should be made with an understanding of the potential benefits and drawbacks, especially regarding the ESXi host's ability to smoothly transition into and out of maintenance mode during remediation processes.

Quick Boot

This setting refers to the status of the Quick Boot feature in vSphere Lifecycle Manager's remediation process. When Quick Boot is disabled, the standard reboot process is used during host remediation.

- **Standard reboot process:** With Quick Boot disabled, hosts undergo a full reboot, including all hardware initializations and checks. This can be more time-consuming but ensures a comprehensive restart of the system. Disabling Quick Boot might be necessary on platforms that do not support this feature or in scenarios where a full hardware initialization is required for certain updates or configurations.

- **Quick Boot enabled:** Quick Boot significantly reduces the reboot time by skipping certain hardware initializations. This can be particularly beneficial during remediation processes, as it minimizes downtime.

It's important to note that Quick Boot is only supported on specific hardware platforms. Therefore, its usage is limited to compatible systems. If you have compatible hardware, enabling Quick Boot can streamline the remediation process by reducing each host's offline time. This can be crucial in environments where minimizing downtime is a priority.

In summary, the decision to enable or disable Quick Boot should be based on hardware compatibility and the specific requirements of your remediation processes. Enabling Quick Boot on supported systems can significantly improve efficiency, but ensuring that your environment meets the criteria for this feature is essential.

Parallel Remediation

The *Parallel remediation* setting in vSphere Lifecycle Manager is an important feature that influences the way ESXi hosts are remediated in a cluster. When you set *Parallel remediation* to **Enable**, it allows for the simultaneous remediation of multiple ESXi hosts within a cluster, but only those that are already in maintenance mode. This is particularly useful in speeding up the remediation process across a cluster, as multiple hosts can be updated or patched at the same time.

It is important to note that when parallel remediation is enabled, any hosts in the cluster that are not in maintenance mode will be skipped. This means that only the hosts that have been manually put into maintenance mode will be considered for parallel remediation.

Figure 30-32 also shows the *Parallel remediation* setting expanded to reveal the *Maximum number of concurrent remediations* setting, which allows you to specify the maximum number of hosts that can be remediated simultaneously. You can choose between automatic and manual settings for this:

- **Automatic:** The system will automatically determine the optimal number of hosts to remediate concurrently based on the cluster's capacity and other factors.

- **Manual:** You have the option to manually set a specific number of hosts that can be remediated at the same time. This gives you more control but requires understanding your cluster's capacity and tolerances.

611

Enabling parallel remediation can significantly reduce the time required to update or patch an entire cluster, especially in larger environments. However, it requires careful planning and consideration of the cluster capacity and the state of the individual hosts.

Editing Settings

After reviewing all the options in the settings, you can modify them by clicking **Edit**. Generally, most environments may not require alterations to these default settings. However, one of the settings frequently adjusted away from the default is the *Parallel remediation* option, which tends to be commonly modified based on specific environment needs. See Figure 30-33.

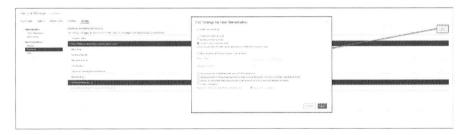

Figure 30-33. (*Scanning & Remediation 6 of 9*)

Having covered the last option in this section about vLCM settings, we can now turn to the remediation process.

Execute Remediation

To begin remediation, click the **Remediate** option on the Updates tab. Figure 30-34 shows the results of my staging process, indicating that 25 patches and 2 extensions were temporarily downloaded to the ESXi host. These will be applied once I confirm the remediation by clicking the **Remediate** button in the dialog box.

Figure 30-34. *(Scanning & Remediation 7 of 9)*

After you click Remediation, vLCM will then place this host into maintenance mode one ESXi at the time (except if you selected to do concurrent ESXi hosts), install the updates that we selected, and when is finish will perform a reboot of the ESXI host. As shown in the Figure 30-35 you can follow all these tasks in the task Tab.

Figure 30-35. *(Scanning & Remediation 8 of 9)*

Following the remediation process, as illustrated in Figure 30-36, all baselines are indicated as *Compliant* (along with a green check mark). This includes the patch and upgrade baselines previously set up. They are now marked as *Compliant* due to the updates I applied, which were part of those specific baselines.

In this instance, all the necessary updates have been successfully applied, meaning that no further updates or version upgrades are required to keep my ESXi hosts up to date.

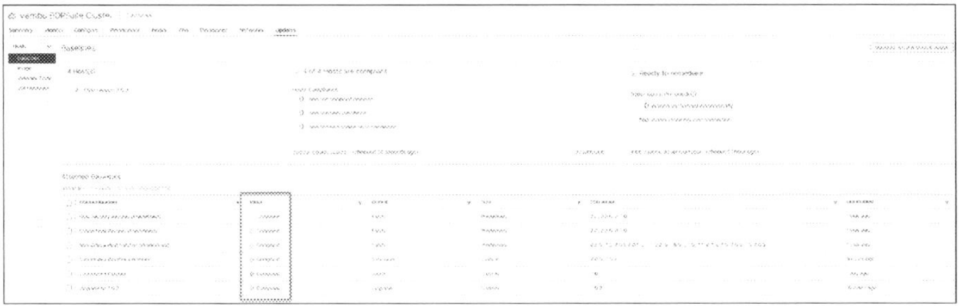

Figure 30-36. *(Scanning & Remediation 9 of 9)*

30.7 Upgrade VMware Tools with vLCM

In Figure 30-37 in VMware Tools option we can see all the VMs and their VMware Tools status and if the auto update is on or off. You can perform this upgrade immediately or opt for the Set Auto-Update' feature. This means that all VMs will be set to upgrade VMware Tools automatically whenever a new version is released.

The process of upgrading VMware Tools used to be manual and specific to each machine. However, after vSphere 7.0 using vLCM this task is significantly streamlines this task. VLCM automates the update process, making it easier to perform updates and ensuring that all virtual machines have a configuration.

Another advantage is that using vLCM guarantees compatibility between the VMware Tools version, the machine's guest operating system, and the ESXi host version. Overall, integrating VMware Tools with vLCM greatly enhances efficiency and establishes a unified standard across the virtual environment.

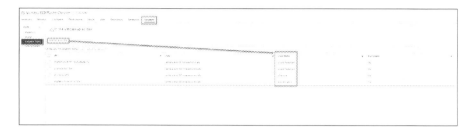

Figure 30-37. *(vLCM VMware Tools 1 of 4)*

The upgrade process for Virtual Hardware (vHardware) closely mirrors that of VMware Tools, as shown in Figure 30-38. Leveraging vLCM, this process can be fully automated, ensuring that all VMs are updated to the latest version of vHardware. This automation aligns the vHardware versions with the compatibility requirements of the current ESXi host version, seamlessly maintaining consistency and efficiency across the virtual environment.

Figure 30-38. *(vLCM VMware Tools 2 of 4)*

30.8 Upgrade ESXi Hosts

This section explains how to upgrade your ESXi hosts. Three distinct options are available for upgrading ESXi hosts:

- Use your predefined upgrade baseline

- Boot the ESXi host with an ISO to execute the upgrade during the boot process

- Perform the upgrade through the command line on the ESXi host

Each upgrade process for ESXi hosts is carried out individually, one host at a time.

Note   The second and third methods for upgrading an ESXi host are not performed using vLCM, but I cover them here so that you are aware of the alternatives to using vLCM.

30.8.1 Upgrade Using vLCM Upgrade Baseline

When upgrading your ESXi hosts by using your upgrade baseline, you use only the **Remediate** option, as shown in Figure 30-39, and do not use the **Stage** option. Since your baseline is already attached to the ESXi host, put the host in maintenance mode and click **Remediate** to launch the upgrade remediation.

Figure 30-39. *(Upgrading ESXi Hosts 1 of 6)*

Upgrading your ESXi host with vLCM is usually a simple process. As long as there are no compatibility problems with the hardware or drivers on your ESXi host, vLCM will handle the upgrade. It installs the new version and reboots the ESXi host, and that is it!

In the example shown in Figure 30-39, there was no compatibility issue, so the upgrade succeeded.

Note   To upgrade from vSphere 6.7 to vSphere 7 using vLCM, your vCenter needs to be at least version 7. Similarly, if upgrading from vSphere 7.x to 8.x, ensure your vCenter is compatible with the newer version.

Figure 30-40 shows that after I upgraded to the latest version and received a *Compliant* status for the upgrade, some patches and updates were still released after this version. These are indicated as *Non-compliant*. It is important to apply these updates to ensure that all ESXi hosts are consistent in their version and build. I used the previous step to update my ESXi host to the latest updates.

Figure 30-40. *(Upgrading ESXi Hosts 2 of 6)*

30.8.2 Upgrade Using Boot ISO

Upgrading your ESXi host with an ISO during boot is similar to the initial vSphere installation process described in Chapter 4. Simply attach the ISO to your server boot sequence (using tools like iLO, iDRAC, etc.) and then reboot the server.

As shown in Figure 30-41, the first step is familiar from when you initially installed vSphere: simply press **Enter** to continue.

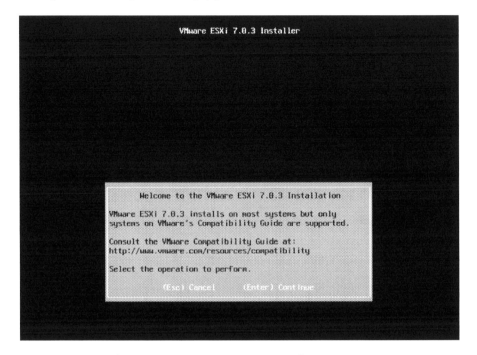

Figure 30-41. *(Upgrading ESXi Hosts 3 of 6)*

The next step, shown in Figure 30-42, is to determine the partition where your vSphere is installed. Press **F1** to view details about the selected partition. If vSphere is installed on that partition, you will see information regarding the vSphere installation. For purposes of this example, assume that vSphere is installed on the first partition. So, **Enter** to select it and continue with the process.

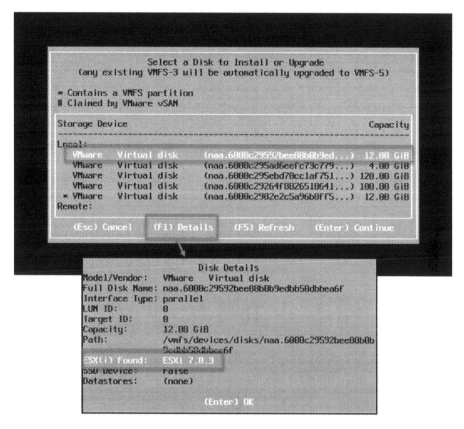

Figure 30-42. *(Upgrading ESXi Hosts 4 of 6)*

When you choose to install on the partition where your vSphere is
already installed, you get the two options shown in Figure 30-43:

- **Upgrade ESXi, preserve VMFS datastore:** Perform
  a clean install without deleting any VMs in your
  Datastores.

- **Install ESXi, overwrite VMFS datastore:** Perform
  a clean install while keeping the existing Datastores
  unformatted.

Note   If you have local Datastores with VMs or any data on the ESXi host, always ensure you are not formatting the VMFS Datastores. Although it is possible to recover data with the right tools and processes, it's challenging, and you would likely need VMware assistance to help you. But VMware support itself will not perform such recovery. You will always need a third-party tool/service to recover your volumes.

The focus of this section is upgrading ESXI hosts, so select the first option, **Upgrade ESXi, preserve VMFS datastore**, and continue with the upgrade by pressing **Enter**. Next, press **F11** to confirm your decision and start the vSphere upgrade process.

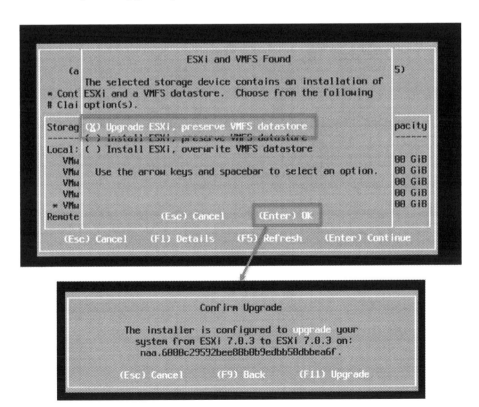

Figure 30-43. *(Upgrading ESXi Hosts 5 of 5)*

After the upgrade starts, vSphere is upgraded using the boot ISO.

30.8.3 Upgrade Using the Command Line

Upgrading vSphere via the command line offers a direct and efficient method for administrators to update their systems. I will show both methods to perform an upgrade, whether online or offline. Before you begin, it's essential to verify the current version of vSphere you are running to ensure compatibility with the upgrade path you intend to follow. Here's how to start the process by determining your current vSphere version.

To effectively upgrade vSphere using the command line, you first need to determine whether you'll perform an online or offline upgrade. This choice depends on your current environment and network capabilities. Before starting, it's crucial to verify your existing vSphere version to ensure compatibility and understand your baseline. You can do this by executing the following command in your system's console: vmware -v.

This command will display the current version of your vSphere installation, providing the necessary information to help you choose the appropriate upgrade method and version path.

Before upgrading, ensure that your ESXi host is in maintenance mode. If it is not already in maintenance mode, you can enable it directly from the console with this command:

```
esxcli system maintenanceMode set --enable true
```

Offline Upgrade

To manually upgrade vSphere using the command line, you must first log in and connect to your ESXi console via SSH. The initial step involves downloading the offline vSphere bundle, as shown in Figure 30-44. This file is available on the VMware Customer Portal in the same section where you originally downloaded your vSphere ISO.

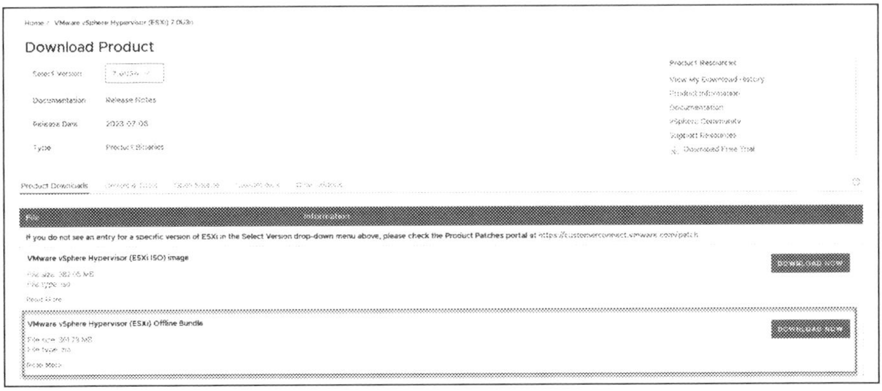

Figure 30-44. *(Upgrading ESXi Hosts 6 of 6)*

Next, you need to upload the image to an existing Datastore, and then you can run the upgrade from the ESXi console. For purposes of this demonstration, I uploaded the file VMware-ESXi-7.0U3n-21930508-depot. zip to the Datastore called Data.

When connected to your ESXi console, check the file path:

```
[root@localhost:~] cd /vmfs/volumes/Data/
[root@localhost:/vmfs/volumes/656f007d-d8b7e779-4f69-
005056969eb4] ls -la
-rw-r--r--    1 root     root      379368788 Dec  5 10:54
VMware-ESXi-7.0U3n-21930508-depot.zip
[root@localhost:/vmfs/volumes/656f007d-d8b7e779-4f69-00505
6969eb4]
```

After you have the file full path, you can run the upgrade command:

```
esxcli software profile update -p ESXi-7.0U3n-21930508-standard -d
/vmfs/volumes/Data/VMware-ESXi-7.0U3n-21930508-depot.zip
```

After the upgrade is finished, you will see a message like this:

```
Update Result
```

```
Message: The update completed successfully, but the system
needs to be rebooted for the changes to be effective.
Reboot Required: true
```

Now reboot your ESXi host, and the online upgrade is done.

Online Upgrade

Note   The steps outlined here are specifically for installing the standard version of vSphere from VMware, not a customized version provided by a vendor.

To upgrade your ESXi using the online method, first connect to your ESXi console. The next step is to list the available source files from the VMware online repository. You'll want to choose the latest version for the upgrade. To list the files, run the following command in the console:

```
esxcli software sources profile list -d https://hostupdate.
vmware.com/software/VUM/PRODUCTION/main/vmw-depot-index.xml |
grep ESXi-7.0U3
```

Remember, if your firewall blocks access, you will need to enable Internet access through the console. To do this, use this command:

```
esxcli network firewall ruleset set -e true -r httpClient.
```

Once done, you can list the vSphere files in the VMware online repository. Just rerun the command to see the list.

After you've got the list, choose the latest file for the upgrade. For instance, I used the ESXi-7.0U3so-22348808-standard image for the upgrade:

```
esxcli software profile update -d https://hostupdate.vmware.
com/software/VUM/PRODUCTION/main/vmw-depot-index.xml -p
ESXi-7.0U3so-22348808-standard
```

After the upgrade is finished, you will see the same type of message that you get using the offline upgrade:

```
Update Result
Message: The update completed successfully, but the system
needs to be rebooted for the changes to be effective.
Reboot Required: true
```

Now reboot your ESXi host, and the online upgrade is done.

30.8.4 Summary of ESXi Host Upgrade Options

To wrap up this section about upgrading vSphere, whether you opt for vLCM or manual methods, it is essential to remember the steps and considerations for each approach. When using vLCM, the process is more streamlined and seamlessly integrates with your existing VMware infrastructure, ensuring compatibility and ease of use. On the other hand, manual upgrades require hands-on involvement but offer greater flexibility and control over the upgrade process.

Regardless of which method you choose, always back up your data and configurations before proceeding and completing all compatibility checks. This will help maintain an efficient environment. With these upgrades, your vSphere environment will be kept up to date, secure, and ready to support your evolving virtualization needs.

30.9 vSphere Lifecycle Manager Best Practices

This chapter has already touched on several vLCM best practices, emphasizing the significance of a robust update process utilizing appropriate baselines and upgrades, which are crucial for maintaining an efficient vSphere environment.

This section delves deeper into best practices, breaking them down into specific sections. The following list provides a comprehensive summary of best practices, from baseline configuration to advanced feature utilization, to enhance your overall management experience in vSphere:

- **Establish a baseline for your environment:** To begin, set a foundation for your environment. Before utilizing vLCM, it is crucial to determine the hardware and software versions of your ESXi hosts' vCenter Server and other components. Understanding your environment will empower you to make informed choices regarding image creation and deployment strategies.

- **Create and maintain standardized image builds:** vLCM simplifies image creation and management by allowing you to define standardized image builds. These builds should include the base ESXi image, vendor customizations, and any additional software components required for your environment. By maintaining standardized images, you ensure consistency and simplify remediation processes.

- **Leverage image baselines and recommended images:** Image baselines provide a foundation for creating and managing standardized images. They define the minimum requirements for ESXi hosts, such as hardware compatibility, security patches, and software updates. vLCM automatically generates recommended images based on image baselines, ensuring your hosts run the latest recommended software versions.

- **Schedule regular remediation scans and remediations:** Schedule regular remediation scans to identify ESXi hosts that are out of compliance with your image baselines. Once scans identify non-compliant hosts, schedule remediations to update those hosts to the latest recommended images; automate these processes to minimize manual intervention and ensure consistent updates across your environment.

- **Implement a testing strategy for new images and updates:** Not all companies have a test environment to test the new updates/upgrades, but if possible, always use a test ESXi host before deploying new images or updates to production environments. It is crucial to test them in a staging or lab environment. This lets you identify and resolve potential issues before they impact your production workloads. Testing also helps to ensure that new images and updates are compatible with your existing infrastructure.

- **Monitor vSphere Lifecycle Manager logs and events:** Monitor vLCM logs and events to identify potential issues or errors. This proactive approach can help you troubleshoot problems early and prevent them from impacting your production environment.

In summary, when it comes to vSphere Lifecycle Manager, following best practices is crucial for managing your virtual environment. It involves establishing and regularly updating baselines using recommended images, conducting remediation scans, implementing testing strategies for new updates, and closely monitoring vLCM logs and events. Adhering to these practices can greatly improve your ESXi hosts' efficiency, security, and stability. These approaches focus on maintaining the state and proactive management to ensure that your infrastructure remains up to date and optimized for future demands and challenges.

30.10 Troubleshooting vSphere Lifecycle Manager

Troubleshooting vLCM often involves meticulously reviewing ESXi host events and log files. These resources are invaluable in identifying and resolving issues related to vLCM updates. It's important to regularly monitor these logs and events, as they can provide early indications of problems, allowing for prompt and effective resolution.

Sometimes, staging temporary updates or upgrades on an ESXi host might fail for various reasons. Listing them all here is impractical given the wide range of potential errors. To troubleshoot these errors, the first step is to check the events related to your vCenter/ESXi host in vCenter.

However, the update log is the best resource for a more detailed insight into any errors. You can find specific error messages and search online for solutions. The vLCM log, which records these details, is located at `/var/log/esxupdate.log` in your ESXi host.

30.11 Summary

In this lengthy chapter we thoroughly examined vSphere Lifecycle Manager (vLCM), including its significance as a part of VMware management. To ensure a grasp of this tool, let's revisit the main concepts we have carefully covered. The following list recaps the major sections:

- **Introduction to vSphere Lifecycle Manager:** This section introduced vLCM, a crucial tool for managing the life cycle of your VMware infrastructure.

- **Introduction to Image-Enabled Clusters:** This section introduced the key aspects of this vLCM feature.

- **Create an Image-Enabled Cluster:** This section discussed the steps to create an image-enabled cluster, enhancing the management of ESXi hosts.

- **Create and Manage Baselines:** This section guided you through creating and managing baselines for consistent configurations across your environment.

- **Add and Remove Baselines to and from ESXi Hosts and Clusters:** This section explored how to effectively apply baselines to your ESXi hosts and clusters and how to remove them.

- **Scanning and Remediation:** The process of scanning for compliance and remediating configurations was the key focus of this section.

- **Upgrade VMware Tools with vLCM:** This section demonstrated how using vLCM significantly streamlines the task of upgrading VMware Tools.

- **Upgrade ESXi Hosts:** This section delved into the methods for upgrading your ESXi hosts, ensuring they are up to date.

- **vSphere Lifecycle Manager Best Practices:** This section summarized the best practices for using vLCM efficiently.

- **Troubleshooting vSphere Lifecycle Manager:** This section briefly discussed how to troubleshoot common issues with vLCM.

Next, we will focus on the different types of backups for VMs, examine how these backups function, and review a list of the main third-party tools in the market for backing up VMware environments. Chapter 31 is essential for ensuring the safety and recovery of your virtual machines, an integral part of maintaining a resilient and secure virtual infrastructure.

CHAPTER 31

vSphere Backup and Disaster Recovery

In the changing world of information technology, the significance of having a backup and disaster recovery strategy cannot be overemphasized. This is particularly true for virtualized environments like those controlled by VMware vSphere, which store numerous essential applications and valuable data. This chapter explores how backup and disaster recovery play a role in maintaining business operations and safeguarding data integrity in virtualized environments.

Backup and disaster recovery is one of the most critical subjects in virtual environments (as in all environments). But in virtual environments, the risks began to significantly escalate in 2020, largely driven by the global shift to remote work due to the COVID-19 pandemic. This period saw a dramatic increase in ransomware attacks as cybercriminals took advantage of the new vulnerabilities exposed by widespread changes in business and personal behaviors.

Cybercrime and ransomware pose significant threats to organizations worldwide. In 2021, a ransomware attack occurred once every 11 seconds, targeting various organizations. This alarming frequency underscores the critical importance of having robust backup environments and comprehensive disaster recovery plans in place. Organizations must recognize that proactive measures are essential to safeguard their data and operations from such pervasive threats.

© Luciano Patrão 2024
L. Patrão, *VMware vSphere Essentials*, https://doi.org/10.1007/979-8-8688-0208-9_31

The goal of this chapter is to give you an understanding of the backup and recovery choices that are available for your virtual environment. This chapter is not intended to be a guide covering all aspects of backup and recovery. Instead, our main focus is on examining the tools and options available in the market, emphasizing their key features and how they apply to a vSphere context. That will provide you with a foundation to make decisions regarding which virtual environment backup solutions align with your specific requirements.

31.1 Importance of Backup and Disaster Recovery in Virtualized Environments

Numerous VMs share the same physical hardware resources in a virtualized environment. While this setup maximizes resource utilization and flexibility, it also introduces a single point of failure. A hardware malfunction or a catastrophic event could potentially render multiple VMs inoperative, bringing business operations to a halt.

The essence of backup in this setup is to create copies of data in your virtual environment, ensuring that it can be restored after data loss or corruption. On the other hand, disaster recovery extends beyond just data retrieval. It involves a range of policies, tools, and procedures to quickly restore system operations after a disaster. This includes recovering the data and system settings for running applications.

Furthermore, because virtualized environments are interconnected, it is essential to have a backup and disaster recovery plan that covers the data, settings, networks, and applications. This holistic approach ensures that recovery time is minimized during an event, thereby reducing the impact on business operations.

As we delve into the tools and methodologies offered in the vSphere suite for backup and disaster recovery, it's crucial to grasp and implement robust strategies. The 3-2-1-1-0 backup rule, an evolution of the traditional

3-2-1 strategy, provides a robust framework for data protection. The traditional strategy recommends maintaining three copies of your data: two on different local media and one offsite for disaster recovery. In the context of vSphere, this means maintaining backups of machines and data to ensure redundancy and minimize the risk of data loss caused by device failure or local disasters.

Building upon this concept, the 3-2-1-1-0 rule adapts to data protection requirements in cloud environments. Additionally, the 1-0 part of the rule suggests having one of these copies be immutable or unalterable to prevent data tampering, and ensuring there are zero errors during the backup process.

Additionally, the '1-0' part of the rule suggests having one of these copies be immutable or unalterable to prevent data tampering. The additional '1' refers to keeping an air-gapped copy physically disconnected from the network for security against cyber threats.

Lastly, the '0' emphasizes that there should be no errors during the backup process, underscoring the importance of testing and validating backups for their integrity and reliability. This comprehensive approach ensures that backups are not only secure from tampering and cyber threats but are also accurate and dependable when recovery is necessary.

When discussing incremental and full backups, it's also important to consider recommended retention times, which directly affect the recovery time objective (RTO) in case of a restore. Longer retention times can provide more recovery options but may increase RTO due to the larger volume of data to sift through during recovery. Conversely, shorter retention times can streamline the restoration process, potentially reducing the RTO. Balancing these factors is key to creating an effective disaster recovery strategy that aligns with your specific business continuity goals.

By implementing these principles within a vSphere environment, you can strengthen the reliability of your strategy. This will align with data protection practices, particularly as more organizations embrace cloud solutions.

By understanding the significance and implementation of disaster recovery plans, you will be better prepared to maintain integrity and ensure business continuity in your virtualized environment.

31.2 vSphere Data Protection Methods and Types

This section discusses the types of backups and options for safeguarding data in VMware vSphere. It is crucial to understand these methods to establish a backup and disaster recovery plan.

The vSphere environment presents both challenges and opportunities, making it crucial to select the right combination of data protection techniques to ensure the security and availability of your virtualized data. Within vSphere, various methods offer distinct advantages. For example, image-based backups capture a complete snapshot of a VM, which can be crucial for quick full-system restores, while incremental backups are efficient for frequent data protection, minimizing storage use and enhancing recovery speed. Each backup strategy is suitable for different scenarios within a vSphere setup, depending on the specific recovery needs and resources of the organization.

The core focus revolves around six pivotal data protection strategies:

- **Image-based backups:** Capture the entire state of a virtual machine at a specific juncture, encompassing the configuration, operating system, applications, and data.

- **File-level backups:** Selectively back up specific files and folders within a virtual machine, catering to protecting critical files and folders.

- **Application-consistent backups:** Ensure applications are backed up in a manner that retains their consistency, which is crucial for applications with distributed data.

- **Incremental backups:** Back up only the altered data since the last full backup, a method that optimizes both time and storage resources.

- **Synthetic full backups:** Merge multiple incremental backups to fabricate a full backup, reducing the resources required for full backups without hampering data restoration capabilities.

- **Offsite backups:** Replicate backups to a remote location, which is a practice pivotal for disaster recovery and ensuring data safety against local catastrophes.

These various backup approaches are designed to meet a variety of needs and situations, offering a system for safeguarding data and ensuring availability in vSphere environments. Depending on the organization's needs, the type of data, and the desired recovery goals, any of these methods can be utilized.

Backup tools are designed to automate and manage these processes, ensuring data protection and availability in your vSphere environment. They offer various features to streamline backups, manage snapshots, and execute replication efficiently, ensuring your data is always safe and recoverable.

31.3 Configuring and Managing vSphere VM Backup

In this section, we'll briefly touch on four popular backup tools, namely those from Vembu, Veeam, Hornetsecurity (formerly Altaro), and NAKIVO, known for their efficacy in virtualized environments, particularly when integrated with VMware vSphere.

Each of these backup tools has distinct characteristics. Some come with a more extensive feature set, making them suitable for varied purposes, while others are tailored for specific organizational sizes, such as enterprise or midsized entities. Notably, these tools' pricing and licensing models differ, significantly influencing an organization's choice based on budget and licensing preferences.

This is a quick feature overview for each tool.

31.3.1 BDRSuite by Vembu

- **Comprehensive backup:**

  Backup for VMware, Hyper-V, KVM, Windows, Linux, Mac, NAS, AWS EC2 Instances, Azure VMs, Microsoft 365, Google Workspace and Applications & Databases.

  Different editions tailored for small, medium, and enterprise businesses and managed service providers (MSPs).

- **Defend any ransomware threat:**

  Advanced security measures like Immutable Storage, Air-gap backups, Hardened Linux repository, Malware Scans before backup/recovery, 3-2-1 Backup, and more.

- **Instant recovery and granular recovery:**

  Instantly boot VMs and physical machines to ESXi, Hyper-V, KVM, Azure, AWS, etc.

  Granular File & Application-item recovery.

- **Flexible storage options:**

  Store backup data on local disk, NAS, SAN, or tape; on cloud storage such as AWS, Azure, Google, Wasabi, etc.; or in BDRCloud.

- **Automated backup verification:**

  Automated backup verification with screenshots to verify the data recoverability.

31.3.2 Veeam Data Platform (Veeam Backup & Replication)

- **Security and compliance:**

  - Guarantee survival by preventing accidental or malicious deletion or encryption of backups.

  - Verify security and compliance with automated scans using the Security & Compliance Analyzer.

  - Highlight threats, identify risks, and measure the security score of your environment in the Veeam Threat Center.

- **Cybersecurity and threat detection:**

  - Proactively detect threats with SIEM, YARA, and NIST cybersecurity best practices.

- AI-powered, built-in Malware Detection Engine for real-time data and file extension analysis during backup.

- Proactive Threat Hunting to report backup inconsistencies.

- Option for your cyber-threat tool to report infections directly into the Veeam Incident API.

- **Backup and storage efficiency:**

  - Direct-to-Object storage backups, trusted immutability, and advanced cyber resiliency.

  - Storage-Efficient Immutability with ease using native APIs on external dedupe storage.

  - Backup of Object Storage with powerful granular restore capabilities.

- **Cross-platform protection:**

  - Secure backup and fast, reliable recovery for Cloud, Virtual, Physical, SaaS, and Kubernetes applications across complex environments.

31.3.3 Hornetsecurity VM Backup

- **Tamper-proof backup:**

  - Backup data remains tamper-proof under the defined immutable policy, providing an extra layer of security against ransomware attacks.

- **Ease of use and setup:**

  - Get started quickly without the need for complex configurations.

  - Easy-to-use, intuitive UI for implementing a reliable backup strategy.

- **Storage efficiency and cost-savings:**

  - Massive storage savings with Augmented Inline Deduplication.

  - Efficient backup setup with minimal RPO and RTO.

- **Centralized management:**

  - Centralized management of backups and various accounts via one platform, the Control Panel.

- **Continuous data protection and WAN-optimized replication:**

  - Reduce downtime and data loss with Continuous Data Protection and WAN-Optimized Replication.

- **Ransomware protection:**

  - Ransomware Protection leveraging Immutable Cloud Storage.

31.3.4 NAKIVO Backup & Replication

- **Infrastructure scans:**

  - Regular scans to automatically protect VMs, physical machines, and Amazon EC2 instances.

- **Microsoft Office 365 data protection:**

  - Ensures the safety and integrity of Microsoft Office 365 data.

- **Complete data protection for servers and workstations:**

  - Provides data protection for Windows/Linux servers and workstations.

- **Backup features:**

  - Remote Backup, Deduplication, Data Encryption, Disaster Recovery, and more.

  - Fast and reliable backups with multiple recovery options to resume IT operations without downtime during any failure

31.4 Summary

Having a well-designed backup and disaster recovery plan is essential for safeguarding virtualized environments. vSphere offers a range of data protection methods, such as image-based offsite backups, which provide security measures tailored to different business requirements. Choosing tools like those from Vembu, Veeam, Hornetsecurity, or NAKIVO further enhances this resilience by offering reliable solutions.

However, maintaining a backup and disaster recovery strategy is an endeavor. It involves adapting to emerging technologies and threats to ensure data protection, business continuity, and operational resilience. As the landscape evolves, so must our backup and disaster recovery approaches. This underscores the dedication to protecting your data and preserving the integrity of your infrastructure.

This chapter introduces several key VMware products that are compatible with and integrate into the vSphere environment. We will explore VMware NSX, which offers capabilities for network virtualization, VMware vSAN for software-defined storage solutions, and VMware Site Recovery Manager (SRM), a tool that simplifies the planning and implementation of disaster recovery. Additionally, we'll touch upon VMware vSphere with Tanzu, which combines Kubernetes with the vSphere platform to enable application deployment and management. Each of these products plays a crucial role within the VMware ecosystem by providing specialized functionalities that expand the capabilities of your virtualized infrastructure.

The goal is to give you an overview of each product, explaining its features, use cases, and how it integrates with vSphere. This approach aims to provide you with a solid understanding of the VMware ecosystem and how these tools can be effectively utilized alongside vSphere, without delving into detailed technical information or step-by-step instructions.

CHAPTER 32

Other VMware Products

This chapter introduces several key VMware products that are compatible and integrate with vSphere. It doesn't dig into detailed technical information or provide step-by-step instructions. Instead, the goal is to give you an overview of each VMware product, explaining its features, use cases, and how it integrates with vSphere. By doing so, I hope to provide you with an understanding of the VMware ecosystem and how these tools can be effectively utilized alongside vSphere.

32.1 VMware NSX: Network Virtualization

VMware NSX enables developers to build cloud-native application settings with an agile software-defined infrastructure. As depicted in Figure 32-1, NSX is designed to make networking, security, automation, and operations accessible for new application frameworks and designs that use a variety of endpoint environments and technology stacks. NSX works with public clouds, bare-metal workloads, cloud-native apps, and various clouds.

Development organizations typically handle, run, and use NSX. IT and development teams can use NSX to choose the best tools for their projects.

© Luciano Patrão 2024
L. Patrão, *VMware vSphere Essentials*, https://doi.org/10.1007/979-8-8688-0208-9_32

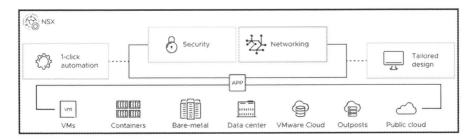

Figure 32-1. *Image source ©VMware*

VMware NSX is a network virtualization and security platform that encompasses everything from layer 2 to layer 7. It takes a software approach to extend networking and security across data centers, clouds, and application frameworks. By virtualizing network functions, NSX brings networking and security to the application's running environment, whether on virtual machines, physical servers, or other platforms.

32.1.1 What NSX Does

NSX isolates networks while providing software-based solutions for networking and security services. Its primary purpose is to manage and optimize network resources, ensuring a programmable infrastructure. The key components of VMware NSX consist of virtualized networking, security services, and a management plane. Each serves roles within the network infrastructure.

32.1.2 Challenges Addressed by NSX

How NSX Works:

An overview of the key components and mechanisms of VMware NSX, illustrating the core functionality that enables network virtualization.

NSX Use Cases:

Various scenarios where NSX proves invaluable, detailing how it addresses specific networking needs and challenges across different industries.

644

NSX addresses the following challenges:

- **Complex network configurations:** NSX simplifies complex network configurations, which makes managing and optimizing the network infrastructure easier.

- **Scalability issues:** NSX provides a scalable solution to growing network demands, especially in large enterprises with expanding data center operations.

- **Network security concerns:** Through its security services, NSX helps address network security concerns by providing micro-segmentation, firewalling, and other security features.

- **Multi-cloud networking challenges:** NSX extends networking and security across data centers, clouds, and various application frameworks, addressing the challenges of multi-cloud networking.

32.1.3 How NSX Works

- **Virtual switching:** NSX re-creates the entire network model in software, enabling virtual machines to communicate with one another in a logically abstracted layer independent of the underlying physical network.

- **Logical routing and switching:** NSX provides logical routing and switching, thus enabling connectivity among virtual machines across different networks and locations, all while keeping the traffic within the data center.

- **Security services:** NSX provides distributed firewalling VPN services and the tools to create security groups and policies for micro-segmentation to secure traffic at a granular level.

- **Network function virtualization:** NSX enables network services to be abstracted from the underlying hardware, turning them into software-based services, which are easier to manage and scale.

32.1.4 NSX Use Cases

- **Micro-segmentation:** NSX facilitates micro-segmentation of the network, enabling precise security policies to be applied at the individual workload level. This dramatically improves security within the data center by reducing the attack surface.

- **Automated network provisioning:** With NSX, network configurations such as switching, routing, and security policies can be programmatically provisioned. This automation speeds up deployment times, ensuring network services are available when and where needed.

- **Multi-cloud networking:** NSX provides consistent networking and security for applications running across multiple clouds. This is crucial for enterprises with a multi-cloud strategy, ensuring operational consistency and reducing complexity.

- **Disaster recovery:** NSX can enhance disaster recovery solutions by simplifying the network configurations required for a secondary recovery site, making the recovery process more efficient and less error-prone.

- **Load balancing and optimized performance:** NSX includes load-balancing capabilities to distribute network traffic evenly across several servers or network paths, ensuring that no single server becomes a bottleneck and improving overall application responsiveness and availability.

- **Visibility and troubleshooting:** Through its monitoring and analytics features, NSX provides insights into network performance and security, aiding in troubleshooting and ensuring the network operates as expected.

- **Remote access and VPN services:** NSX offers VPN services to connect remote users and sites to the corporate network securely. This is particularly useful for remote and branch office connectivity.

- **Container networking:** NSX provides networking and security services for containerized applications and Kubernetes environments, ensuring consistent operations across VMs and containers.

- **Secure access to applications:** By utilizing the security services in NSX, organizations can ensure secure access to applications, regardless of where they are located on-premises or in the cloud.

- **Compliance and regulatory adherence:** NSX aids in compliance with various regulatory standards by providing robust security features like micro-segmentation, firewalling, and encryption.

Each of these use cases demonstrates the versatility and capability of VMware NSX in addressing modern network and security challenges in various operational scenarios.

32.2 VMware vSAN: Software-Defined Storage

VMware vSAN is an enterprise-class software-defined storage area network (SAN) solution that operates within hyper-converged infrastructure (HCI) platforms. As a software layer that runs atop the ESXi hypervisor, vSAN is fully integrated with VMware vSphere, enhancing storage capabilities and management directly within the virtualized environment.

vSAN groups local or directly connected storage devices to make a single pool that all hosts in a vSAN cluster can use. In a hybrid vSAN system, magnetic drives are used for storage, and flash devices are used for cache. All-flash vSAN groups store data and add more space on flash drives. The vSAN Express Storage Architecture uses fast network ports and NVMe-based TLC flash drives. For the software-defined data center (SDDC), these designs offer a shared datastore that is resilient and optimized for flash.

With Storage Policy-Based Management (SPBM), vSAN gets rid of the need for external shared storage and makes setting up storage easier. With virtual machine storage rules, you can set the needs and limits of storage. In Figure 32-2 shows an example of vSAN architecture.

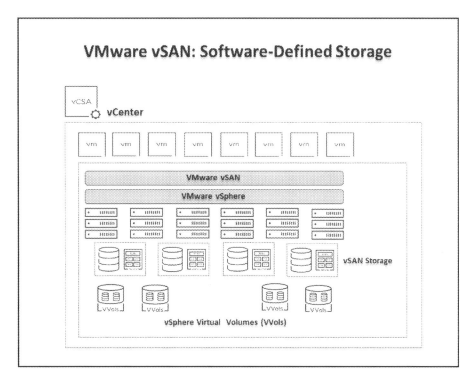

Figure 32-2. *VMware vSAN*

In a vSphere environment, VMware vSAN utilizes the cluster configuration to create a shared and distributed datastore. This datastore is managed directly by the ESXi hypervisor, enhancing user-friendliness. It allows users to easily specify their storage requirements, such as performance levels and availability needs. As a result, VMware vSAN significantly simplifies storage management within VMware environments.

32.2.1 What vSAN Does

VMware vSAN is a software-defined storage solution that consolidates storage resources across a vSphere cluster, creating a shared and distributed datastore. It combines directly attached data storage devices to provide a datastore suitable for virtual machines. Virtualizing the storage vSAN streamlines storage management, offers flexibility in resource allocation, and reduces ownership costs.

32.2.2 Key Functionalities of VMware vSAN

VMware vSAN offers the following key functionalities:

- **Hyperconverged infrastructure (HCI):** vSAN combines storage, computing, and networking into a single system to reduce data center complexity and increase scalability.

- **Storage policies:** vSAN enables the definition of storage requirements like performance and availability per application.

- **Data protection and disaster recovery:** vSAN provides native fault tolerance and supports features like replication and clustering services for data integrity and availability. vSAN does not include a native backup solution. Effective data protection within a vSAN environment typically requires integrating third-party backup tools, like the ones discussed in Chapter 31.

- **Storage efficiency:** vSAN Offers storage-saving features like deduplication, compression, and erasure coding to optimize storage utilization.

32.2.3 Challenges Addressed by VMware vSAN

VMware vSAN addresses the following challenges:

- **Storage complexity:** vSAN simplifies storage management in virtualized environments, reducing the need for traditional storage systems and expertise.

- **Costly storage infrastructure:** vSAN reduces capital and operational expenses by utilizing existing hardware or cost-effective, industry-standard servers.

- **Scalability limitations:** vSAN provides a scalable storage solution that grows with the needs of the business without requiring large upfront investments.

- **Performance bottlenecks:** vSAN helps overcome traditional storage performance bottlenecks through its performance optimization features.

32.2.4 How VMware vSAN Works

- **Datastore pooling:** vSAN aggregates local storage resources across ESXi hosts in a vSphere cluster to create a shared datastore.

- **Storage policy-based management (SPBM):** vSAN facilitates creating and applying storage policies to ensure the desired level of service.

- **Distributed RAID and erasure coding:** vSAN provides data protection at a lower storage cost by distributing data across multiple hosts in a cluster.

- **Data locality:** vSAN ensures data is kept close to the workload, improving performance by reducing the distance data travels.

32.2.5 Use Cases for VMware vSAN

- **Hyperconverged infrastructure (HCI):** Organizations can reduce the complexity of their data center by consolidating storage, computing, and networking into a single system with vSAN, aiding in more straightforward management and scalability.

- **Automated storage management:** vSAN Storage Policy-Based Management allows for automated control over storage resources, reducing the manual effort required to manage storage allocations and ensure compliance with storage policies.

- **Cost-effective storage solution:** Organizations can significantly reduce their storage infrastructure costs by utilizing existing or industry-standard hardware. vSAN's software-defined approach offers a more cost-effective solution compared to traditional storage systems.

- **Disaster recovery and business continuity:** vSAN supports native fault-tolerance, backup, and replication features, making it a suitable solution for organizations looking to improve their disaster recovery and business continuity strategies.

- **Dynamic scalability:** As organizational storage needs grow, vSAN allows for nondisruptive scaling, adding more storage resources to the cluster without downtime.

- **Optimized performance:** With features like an increased write buffer and efficient I/O handling, vSAN helps overcome traditional storage performance bottlenecks, ensuring optimal performance for critical applications.

- **Secure data at rest:** vSAN provides encryption for data at rest, ensuring that stored data is protected against unauthorized access.

- **Storage efficiency:** Organizations can optimize storage utilization by utilizing vSAN storage-saving features like deduplication, compression, and erasure coding, reducing the amount of physical storage required.

- **Support for containerized workloads:** vSAN supports Kubernetes and containerized workloads, allowing for consistent storage services across traditional and modern application architectures.

- **Remote office/branch office (ROBO) deployments:** vSAN is well-suited for ROBO deployments where simplified, cost-effective, and highly available storage solutions are crucial. Its ability to run on industry-standard servers makes it a practical choice for such scenarios.

- **VMware Cloud Foundation (VCF) deployments:** vSAN is a crucial component of VCF, providing the storage foundation for deploying the VMware SDDC (software-defined data center) stack.

The preceding use cases indicate how vSAN can tackle storage issues and provide an automated and effective solution in various operational scenarios.

Using a software-defined approach, vSAN meets the requirements of data centers by delivering scalable and optimized storage services. Its capabilities align perfectly with the challenges faced by data centers that need to provide a scalable and efficient storage solution.

32.3 VMware Site Recovery Manager

VMware Site Recovery Manager (SRM) is an add-on for VMware vCenter that enables organizations to recover from disasters, move sites, and test without interruption.

Several replication options, such as VMware vSphere Replication, work with Site Recovery Manager to make moving, recovering, testing, re-protecting, and failing back virtual machine workloads automatic, as depicted in Figure 32-3.

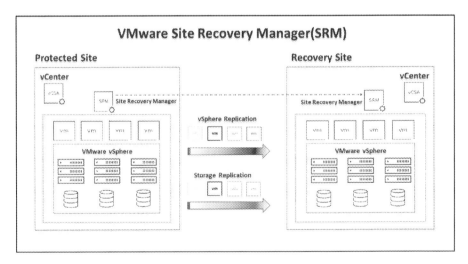

Figure 32-3. *VMware Site Recovery Manager*

Two sites, a protected site and a recovery site, use Site Recovery Manager servers to arrange how VMware vCenter Server works. This setup is configured so that when virtual machines at the protected site shut down, copies of them start up at the recovery site. The recovery site VMs take on the role of offering the same services as the protected site VMs by using data that has been copied from the protected site.

With SRM, you can automate the failover and failback process, reducing downtime and enhancing availability. This simplifies disaster recovery and ensures that your business continuity plans are robust and effective.

32.3.1 What VMware SRM Does

VMware Site Recovery Manager is a solution for disaster recovery and business continuity. It enables you to plan, test, and execute the recovery of VMs between a protected vCenter Server site and a recovery vCenter Server site. Seamlessly integrated with vCenter, SRM guarantees disaster recovery for environments by minimizing downtime and data loss during outages.

32.3.2 Key Functionalities of VMware SRM

- **Automated disaster recovery:** SRM automates the recovery process, ensuring rapid restoration of services post-disaster.

- **Nondisruptive testing:** SRM allows for testing recovery plans without affecting production environments.

- **Orchestrated recovery:** SRM coordinates the order of recovery to maintain application dependencies across multitier applications.

- **Failback and reprotection:** SRM simplifies the failback process to the original site and re-protects the virtual machines for future recovery needs.

32.3.3 Challenges Addressed by VMware SRM

- **Downtime minimization:** SRM significantly reduces downtime during unforeseen outages by automating and orchestrating disaster recovery.

- **Complex recovery processes:** SRM simplifies and automates complex recovery processes, ensuring accurate and timely recovery.

- **Business continuity assurance:** SRM provides the tools to test and validate recovery plans, ensuring business continuity regularly.

32.3.4 How VMware SRM Works

- **Protection groups:** SRM defines groups of virtual machines for protection and recovery.

- **Recovery plans:** SRM specifies the steps necessary for a coordinated recovery of applications.

- **Automated workflows:** SRM executes recovery steps in an automated, preplanned manner to ensure rapid recovery.

- **Failover and failback:** SRM automates the failover to the recovery site and failback to the original site, maintaining data integrity and availability.

32.3.5 Use Cases for VMware SRM

- **Disaster recovery automation:** Organizations with critical applications can leverage SRM to automate their disaster recovery processes, ensuring rapid recovery and minimal downtime.

- **Business continuity planning:** SRM provides the tools necessary for planning, testing, and executing recovery plans, ensuring business operations continue seamlessly during and after a disaster.

- **Compliance and reporting:** With its nondisruptive testing and detailed reporting, SRM helps organizations meet compliance requirements and provides evidence of recoverability.

- **Data center migration:** SRM can be used for planned migrations of workloads between data centers with minimal disruption.

- **Multisite workload mobility:** SRM facilitates workload mobility between sites, ensuring optimal performance and availability.

- **Enhanced cloud resilience:** In cloud environments like Azure VMware Solution, SRM enhances resilience by orchestrating and automating the recovery process.

These use cases portray how VMware SRM can ensure business continuity, reduce recovery times, and improve the overall resilience of virtualized and cloud environments.

32.4 VMware vSphere with VMware Tanzu

Running containerized apps in vSphere is possible with VMware vSphere with VMware Tanzu (often shortened to "vSphere with Tanzu"). On vSphere clusters, vSphere administrators set up Tanzu to make the platform developer-ready so that DevOps engineers and application developers can run Kubernetes apps independently.

Supervisors are vSphere groups that have been set up to work with Tanzu. vSphere managers can set up vSphere Namespaces on the Supervisor with a certain amount of memory, CPU, and storage. After setting up vSphere Pods, VMs, or upstream Kubernetes clusters through VMware Tanzu Kubernetes Grid, DevOps workers and application developers can run Kubernetes containers within the vSphere Namespaces. Your apps can then run inside these clusters.

vSphere with Tanzu is the next-gen vSphere designed for containerized applications, connecting the divide between IT operations and developers by offering a cohesive foundation for contemporary, cloud-native applications. It merges a Kubernetes control plane directly on the hypervisor level, empowering vSphere clusters for workload administration.

This fusion eases the execution of Kubernetes applications in a self-serve approach, streamlining the deployment and control of containerized applications on vSphere clusters.

32.4.1 What vSphere with Tanzu Does

vSphere with Tanzu bridges the gap between IT operations and developers by creating a developer-ready platform where Kubernetes applications can be run self-service. It modernizes the vSphere environment to accommodate containerized applications alongside traditional VM-based workloads, making it a single solution for both modern cloud-native applications and traditional applications, whether on-premises or in public clouds. See Figure 32-4.

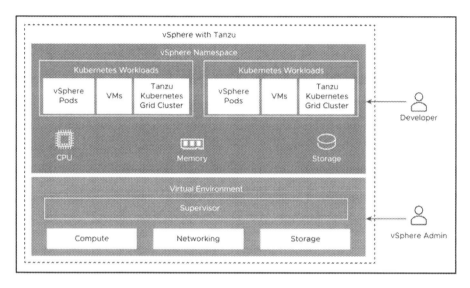

Figure 32-4.   *image source ©VMware*

32.4.2 Key Functionalities of vSphere with Tanzu

- **Kubernetes integration:** One of the trademark features of vSphere with Tanzu is the integration of Kubernetes, allowing organizations to run and support container-based modern applications on their existing infrastructure.

- **Self-service for developers:** vSphere with Tanzu provides a self-service platform for DevOps engineers and application developers to run Kubernetes applications.

- **Support for containerized and traditional workloads:** vSphere with Tanzu supports containerized applications and traditional VM-based workloads in a unified environment.

32.4.3 Challenges vSphere with Tanzu Addresses

- **Modern application deployment:** vSphere with Tanzu helps in deploying modern, cloud-native applications in a vSphere environment.

- **Developer and IT operations collaboration:** vSphere with Tanzu bridges the gap between developers and IT operations, providing a common platform to work on.

- **Infrastructure modernization:** vSphere with Tanzu aids in modernizing the existing infrastructure to support modern application architectures.

32.4.4 How vSphere with Tanzu Works

- **Enabling Tanzu on vSphere Clusters:** vSphere administrators enable vSphere with Tanzu on vSphere clusters to create a developer-ready platform.

- **Running Kubernetes applications:** vSphere with Tanzu allows for running Kubernetes applications in a self-service manner, with the necessary security, device, and networking configurations.

- **Management of VM images:** Through VM Image Service, vSphere with Tanzu enables VM images to be managed in a self-service manner using Kubernetes APIs.

32.4.5 Use Cases for vSphere with Tanzu

- **Application modernization:** vSphere with Tanzu supports modernizing existing applications and developing new cloud-native applications.

- **Infrastructure modernization:** vSphere with Tanzu enables data center infrastructure to be modernized to support both traditional and modern applications.

- **DevOps and Agile development:** vSphere with Tanzu accelerates DevOps and Agile development practices by providing developers with a self-service platform to deploy and manage applications.

- **Multi-cloud operations:** vSphere with Tanzu extends the vSphere environment to public clouds, enabling consistent operations across a hybrid cloud environment.

The integration of Kubernetes within vSphere, provided by Tanzu, allows organizations to extend their existing infrastructure to support modern application development and deployment practices, thereby aligning with DevOps.

32.5 Summary

This chapter focused on additional VMware products that complement vSphere functionality. It addressed challenges in areas like networking, storage, disaster recovery, and modern application development.

For networking, VMware NSX virtualizes network functions, simplifying management and enhancing security across data centers and clouds.

In storage, VMware vSAN utilizes a software-defined approach, pooling local storage to create shared storage for virtual machines.

Disaster recovery is aided by VMware Site Recovery Manager (SRM). SRM replicates VMs to a secondary site and automates the failover process.

Finally, VMware vSphere with Tanzu integrates a Kubernetes control plane within vSphere. This empowers developers to deploy and manage containerized applications independently.

CHAPTER 33

VMware Certification Overview

A VMware certification is about proving your skills and advancing your career by joining a respected and esteemed community of professionals.

After you finish reading this book, you will be prepared to embark on the journey to become VMware certified. That journey will help you open up possibilities, gain an advantage, and develop a deeper understanding of VMware technologies.

This chapter sheds light on the path to obtaining VMware certification. It describes several certifications offered by VMware, explains their benefits, and guides you on preparing to achieve and maintain these highly demanded credentials. Since this book is about vSphere, we will focus only on certifications related to vSphere and data center virtualization. Figure 33-1 depicts the official path for obtaining these certifications.

While the VCP-DCV (VMware Certified Professional - Data Center Virtualization) is a common starting point for those looking to get certified in VMware technologies, it's important to note that while obtaining the first certification is not mandatory to pursue higher certifications, completing the recommended training courses is typically required.

© Luciano Patrão 2024
L. Patrão, *VMware vSphere Essentials*, https://doi.org/10.1007/979-8-8688-0208-9_33

Note   For a detailed understanding of the prerequisites and recommended training for each certification exam, please visit the VMware Certification page `https://www.vmware.com/learning/certification.html` and select the Data Center Virtualization category. This resource provides comprehensive guidance on the qualifications needed and outlines the suggested learning paths for achieving each certification level.

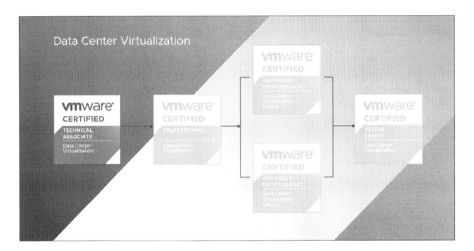

Figure 33-1.   *image source ©VMware*

Some of these certifications also include coverage of tools like vSAN and SRM, but the central core continues to be vSphere.

33.1 VMware Certification Importance, Tracks, and Benefits

VMware certifications hold a level of respect in the IT field because they confirm the proficiency and knowledge of professionals in VMware technologies and platforms. These certifications are available in tracks that cater to career paths within virtualization and cloud computing. Let's dig deeper into why VMware certifications are valuable and the different VMware data center–specific certifications that are available and their advantages.

The following are a few of the benefits of obtaining VMware certifications:

- **Recognition in the industry:** VMware certifications have a reputation for demonstrating a professional's expertise in managing, deploying, and designing VMware solutions. These certifications validate IT professionals' skill sets, helping them to stand out in the job market.

- **Employability:** Obtaining VMware certification can greatly enhance employment prospects because employers often prioritize candidates with recognized certifications. Certification showcases an individual's commitment and proficiency in the field, making them a valuable addition to any organization.

The following are the VMware certifications that focus on data center virtualization. They are presented in the order shown in Figure 33-1, which is the official VMware track for obtaining these certifications.

- **VMware Certified Technical Associate - Data Center Virtualization (VCTA-DCV):** This credential attests to a person's fundamental understanding and capabilities in data center virtualization utilizing VMware vSphere alongside associated technologies. It's tailored for newcomers to the field, eyeing a career intertwined with virtualization technologies. Professionals who earn this certification often step into the roles of entry-level virtualization administrators and technicians.

- **VMware Certified Professional - Data Center Virtualization (VCP-DCV):** This credential is designed for IT professionals who install, configure, manage, and optimize VMware solutions. It's the most common starting point for those looking to get certified in VMware technologies.

- **VMware Certified Advanced Professional - Data Center Virtualization (VCAP-DCV):** This credential is aimed at professionals who design and build VMware solutions (VCAP-DCV Design) or manage and optimize VMware solutions (VCAP-DCV Deploy).

- **VMware Certified Design Expert - Data Center Virtualization (VCDX-DCV):** This is the highest level of certification offered by VMware, designed for architects and solutions experts heavily involved in designing VMware solutions in a multidomain environment.

To pursue the VMware Certified Design Expert - Data Center Virtualization (VCDX-DCV) certification, candidates typically need to have advanced credentials; however, obtaining both the VCAP-DCV Design and VCAP-DCV Deploy certifications is not mandatory but highly recommended. The VCDX-DCV is geared towards those who have a deep understanding of VMware core components and their relation to the data center as well as the ability to design and implement VMware solutions in a multi-domain environment. Achieving VCAP certifications can significantly enhance a candidate's understanding and skills, making them better prepared for the VCDX-DCV certification process, which includes a rigorous evaluation of your design work through design defense.

For those aiming for the VCDX-DCV, it is advisable to achieve at least one VCAP certification (either Design or Deploy) that aligns with your specific career focus and expertise, as it provides a solid foundation and necessary skills for tackling the complex VCDX-DCV track.

The diversified certification tracks offered by VMware are meticulously crafted to cater to different career aspirations within the virtualization and cloud computing sectors, allowing professionals to choose a path that aligns well with their career objectives.

33.2 Preparing for VMware Certification Exams

Embarking on the journey to earn a VMware certification requires a strategic approach to ensure success. This section provides a roadmap for aspiring VMware professionals to prepare efficiently for their certification exams.

The following are, in general, the topics that the exam covers:

- **Administering Virtual Networks:** Configuring and ensuring seamless operation of virtual network settings

- **Virtual Machine Oversight:** Effective management and configuration of virtual machines

- **vSphere Deployment and Configuration:** Setting up vSphere and ensuring its proper installation

- **Handling Storage Resources:** Management and optimization of storage settings

- **Upholding Security Standards:** Ensuring compliance and bolstering security measures

- **Overseeing vCenter Server Operations:** Management and routine configuration of vCenter Server functionalities

---

Note   The following VMware exam preparation guide, will always provide you with the latest updates: `https://www.vmware.com/content/dam/digitalmarketing/vmware/en/pdf/certification/vmw-vcp-dcv-exam-preparation-guide.pdf`

To effectively prepare for a VMware certification exam, consider the following steps:

- **Familiarize yourself with the exam objectives:** The exam objectives outline the topics covered in the exam. You can find these objectives on the VMware website.

- **Refer to the VMware documentation:** The official VMware documentation is a resource for information on the VMware products and technologies. It is available on the VMware website.

- **Enroll in a VMware training course:** VMware Authorized Training Centers (VATCs) offer training courses tailored to help you prepare for VMware certification exams.

- **Utilize practice exams:** Practice exams are tools to evaluate your knowledge and identify improvement areas. You can access practice exams through the VMware website or from third-party vendors.

Here are some extra tips to help you prepare for a VMware certification exam:

- **Start your studies:** Avoid cramming everything into the last minute. Allow yourself time to study and review the exam objectives.

- **Create a study schedule:** Allocate time each day or week for exam preparation.

- **Find a study partner or group:** Studying with others can keep you motivated and focused.

- **Take breaks:** Avoid studying for hours without taking breaks. Stand up and move around every 20 to 30 minutes to prevent burnout.

- **Ensure you get sleep:** Being well-rested is crucial on the day of the exam.

- **Use VMware Hands-on Labs:** Use the free VMware Hands-on Labs for preparation for your exams: `https://labs.hol.vmware.com`. Filter the HOLs to vSphere topics by using the Filter By pane on the left.

33.3 Maintaining and Renewing VMware Certification

This section aims to provide a comprehensive overview of the current state of maintaining and renewing VMware certifications, emphasizing the importance of continuous learning and the flexibility offered by VMware in this process.

In today's rapidly evolving IT landscape, maintaining up-to-date professional certifications is essential. VMware, a leader in cloud infrastructure and digital workspace technology, recognizes the importance of staying current and has adopted a flexible approach to certification maintenance and renewal. The changes introduced in 2019 have simplified the process in several key ways:

- **No Mandatory Recertification Requirement:** As of February 5, 2019, VMware removed the mandatory recertification requirement for its certifications, including the VMware Certified Professional (VCP) and VMware Certified Advanced Professional (VCAP). This means that once a VMware certification is achieved, it remains valid indefinitely without the need for compulsory renewal.

- **The Value of Voluntary Recertification:** While recertification is no longer mandatory, VMware strongly recommends that professionals continue to update their certifications. The technology field is constantly advancing, and staying informed is crucial for maintaining expertise. Voluntary recertification demonstrates a commitment to professional growth, enhancing your credibility and value to employers and clients.

- **Upgrading Certifications:** VMware offers several paths for professionals looking to upgrade their certifications:

  - **For Recent Certifications:** Holders of recent certifications (e.g., VCP-DCV 2022) can upgrade to the current year's certification (e.g., VCP-DCV 2024) by completing a qualifying course or passing the relevant exam.

  - **For Older Certifications (2-3 versions back):** Upgrade to the current year's certification by passing the relevant exam.

- **For Certifications Four or More Versions Back:**
  Complete a qualifying course and pass the
  qualifying exam in the same track.

- **Certifications in Different Tracks:** If within three
  versions of the most current, passing the qualifying
  exam in the same track is required.

Note   Since policies and procedures around VMware certifications
can evolve, please refer to the official VMware certification site for
the most current and detailed information. This resource provides
up-to-date details on certification paths, prerequisites, and exams to
ensure your information is accurate.

Figure 33-2 provides an example of VCP paths.

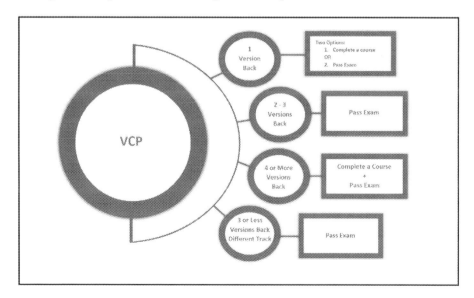

Figure 33-2. *image source ©VMware*

VMware recognizes the significance of staying up to date with industry trends and aligning development with career goals. By offering a flexible recertification approach, VMware empowers IT professionals to adapt to the changing needs of the industry.

Continuing to uphold and update VMware certifications after 2019 involves adaptability and a dedication to growth. While certifications have no expiration date, it is highly appreciated to stay up to date by pursuing paths of advancement. This strategy guarantees that VMware professionals stay ahead in terms of industry expertise and abilities, fully prepared to tackle the evolving landscape of IT challenges.

33.4 Summary

This chapter explored VMware certifications, their importance, pathways, and the dedication they demand. Next, Chapter 34 wraps up our extensive voyage into the realm of VMware vSphere by encouraging you to ponder everything you have assimilated and anticipate possibilities and advancements in virtualization.

CHAPTER 34

Embracing the Future of Virtualization with VMware vSphere

Now that you've completed your journey through the pages of *VMware vSphere Essentials: A Practical Approach to vSphere Deployment and Management*, it's time to reflect on the journey and look forward to the future possibilities in virtualization.

This book, inspired by a series of blog posts and fueled by my passion for VMware technology, has covered various virtualization topics to demystify and clarify the complexities of VMware vSphere for readers from diverse backgrounds.

From the chapters that laid down the foundations of virtualization concepts, benefits, and types to the chapters that explored vSphere's intricate components, I hope this guide has been an enlightening experience. We delved into aspects such as deploying and managing vSphere environments while addressing areas like networking, storage, and high availability. Whether you're new or experienced in this field, my goal has always been to illuminate the path toward mastering virtualization with simplicity and depth.

© Luciano Patrão 2024
L. Patrão, *VMware vSphere Essentials*, https://doi.org/10.1007/979-8-8688-0208-9_34

Your journey didn't stop at understanding how vSphere operates. You also explored features, resource optimization techniques, performance monitoring strategies, and automation. These topics serve as stepping stones toward gaining mastery over a fundamental technology in today's computing landscape.

This book was also intended to be a guide if you aspire to validate your expertise through VMware certifications. It will help you navigate the world of concepts and prepare you for certification exams. The knowledge shared in this book goes beyond theory; it provides tools to enhance your abilities in the IT field.

Whether you aspire to be an IT professional, a system administrator, a consultant, a trainer, or simply someone who is passionate about technology, your adventure with VMware vSphere is only getting started.

Stay curious, never stop learning, and be ready to adapt. The field of virtualization is constantly changing. Your ability to adapt and continuously learn will be the key to your success.

As we conclude, it is essential to acknowledge that the journey with VMware vSphere does not stop here. The IT landscape is constantly changing, with virtualization being at its core. VMware vSphere continues evolving, adapting, and leading in this changing environment, bringing forth challenges and opportunities. The knowledge gained from this book serves as a foundation, but the future demands continual learning, adaptability, and an insatiable thirst for knowledge.

In conclusion, this book is more than a guide; it is a trusted companion on your journey into the dynamic world of VMware vSphere. Your adventure in virtualization is only beginning. Embrace the future armed with the knowledge you have acquired and fueled by your curiosity.

I appreciate your decision to select this guide as your companion on this journey into virtualization and cloud computing. Here's to the many more virtualization adventures that lie ahead!

As I embarked on writing this book in mid-2023, VMware was on the verge of launching vSphere 8 in November of that year. Given the timing and the newness of vSphere 8, I decided to concentrate the content on vSphere 7. This decision was made to provide the most stable and comprehensive guidance based on well-established features and functionalities. However, it's important for readers to know that the principles and core features discussed are largely applicable to vSphere 8 as well, ensuring the relevance of this book beyond the version it primarily addresses.

Since the initial writing, there have been significant developments within VMware, including an acquisition by Broadcom. Despite these changes, the foundational aspects of vSphere have remained consistent, and I estimate that approximately 80% of the content in this book is still accurate for users of vSphere 8. The exceptions primarily include specific features that may have evolved and adjustments in maximum and minimum setting values.

I assure you that while this book focuses on vSphere 7, its applications and insights remain valuable and relevant, providing a solid foundation for understanding and working effectively with VMware's solutions, including the newer iterations.

Index

A

Active LACP mode, 308
Active snapshot, 429
All-Paths-Down (APD),
160, 369–371
Application virtualization, 4
Auto Deploy, 489–491
Automatic DRS, 342
Automatic offline vCenter
update, 564
Automatic online vCenter
update, 554–558
Automatic vCenter
upgrade, 565–571

B

Backup and disaster recovery
configuring and managing, 636
data protection methods and
types, 634, 635
Hornetsecurity VM Backup,
638, 639
NAKIVO backup & replication,
639, 640
strategy, 640
Veeam data platform, 637, 638
Vembu, 636

virtual environments, 631
virtualized environments,
632–634, 640
Back Up Key Provider, 243
Backup software, 433, 445
Backup tools, 635, 636
Baselines, vLCM
add/remove baselines to ESXi
hosts/clusters, 598, 599
administrators, 585
create and maintain, 585
critical host patches, 586, 587
extension baseline creation,
588, 589
hosts, 585
host upgrade, 587
non-critical host patches, 587
patch baseline
creation, 590–593
standards/specifications, 585
type, 586
upgrade baseline
creation, 594–597
BDRSuite by Vembu
automated backup
verification, 637
comprehensive backup, 636
flexible storage options, 637

© Luciano Patrão 2024
L. Patrão, *VMware vSphere Essentials*, https://doi.org/10.1007/979-8-8688-0208-9

M

X, Y, Z